D1452562

THE·FOUNDING
LEGEND·OF·WEST
ERN·CIVILIZATION

THE·FOUNDING LEGEND·OF·WEST ERN·CIVILIZATION

FROM VIRGIL TO VIETNAM

Richard Waswo

Wesleyan University Press

PUBLISHED BY UNIVERSITY PRESS OF NEW ENGLAND
HANOVER AND LONDON

Wesleyan University Press

Published by University Press of New England, Hanover, NH 03755

© 1997 by Richard Waswo

All rights reserved

Printed in the United States of America

5 4 3 2 1

CIP data appear at the end of the book

There is no story that is not true.

—UCHENDU

Contents

PART IV

From History to Social Theory

The Death and Rebirth of the Legend

PART V

The Legend Triumphant—and Protested

PART VI
The Legend in Our Time

Preface

This book attempts to tell the history of a story and to show how it is of central importance to western culture because it defines both what "culture" is and who possesses it (chapter 1). The very word comes from the Latin verb "to cultivate" (*colo, cultum*) and links all manifestations of "high" culture—from religion to art—to the act of tilling the soil. This definition is created by and for a settled agricultural community that sows, harvests, and builds cities; it qualifies as 'savage' (Lat. *silvestris*—"of the woods") all other relations that human beings may have with the earth, such as hunting, gathering, and nomadic pastoralism. The ancient icon of civilization that linked its cities with the surplus agricultural production that made them possible was that of Cybele, the Great Mother, who became the protectress of both agriculture and civic life, seated on a throne, wearing a crown of walls and towers. The modern tool that most efficiently accomplishes the material process necessary for this link to occur—clearing forested or "barren" land for planting—is a giant bulldozer blade called the Rome Plow. Its name is not accidental, but rather the result of the whole imperial history enacted and told by the ancient Romans, and subsequently appropriated and imitated by western Europeans. The founding hero of this history in Virgil's definitive version of the story is Aeneas, who, when Virgil inherited him, was already identified with the rituals and gods of agricultural production (chapter 2). Turning forests (or deserts) into gardens is at once the primary material process of western culture and a continuously recurring image that symbolically justifies it. It is the act that defines the founding hero.

The story of his deeds is that of the founding of an empire by escapees from the destroyed city of Troy: it is the plot of Virgil's *Aeneid* (chapters 3–4). The enormous prestige of Virgil as the voice of the greatest empire the west had ever known made the Trojans the ancestors of choice for medieval Europeans from Britain to Bohemia, from Iceland to Sicily. The legend of Trojan descent, continuously retold in many versions, became known in the Middle Ages as the *translatio imperii et studii* (chapters 5–7). It portrays domination and learning as parts of the same process of transmission and shows civilization to be that which comes from elsewhere. The story postulates the elsewhere as a single, long-ago-destroyed origin, which allows it to function as a claim, an entitlement, to civilization at its very source: a direct genealogical link to the Trojan characters in the legend, which makes whatever contemporary ruling class the fraternal equals of the ancient Romans. The story narrates the journeys and the successive settlements of frontiers by culture-bringers (sons of Troy Christianized as sons of Noah) who assimilate or destroy the indigenous people and ways of life they find there. For two thousand years this story was popularly regarded as actual history.

When it, gradually and painfully, ceased being so regarded (chapters 14–15), its plot had been reenacted often enough around the globe to permit its definitions and categories to be absorbed into other kinds of discourse: it had long been poetry, and in the seventeenth and eighteenth centuries, its structure, images, and arguments become parts of historiography, law, philosophy, social theory, and science (chapters 16–21). During this period, when the story is being recognized as a legend, its function alters. No longer concerned to establish a direct link with a Trojan ancestor, the story moves from identification with the characters in the legend to identification with its authors, the ancient Romans, now seen as the actual source of western civilization. Instead of claiming an entitlement to civilization on behalf of the tellers and founders, the story now justifies the disentitlement to civilization of those who must be assimilated to or destroyed by the new empire. The kind and extent of the empire, of course, had been greatly altered by the European discovery of the rest of the planet (chapters 8–13). The domination and learning that had been largely military and theological in the Middle Ages became economic and "scientific" in early modernity. Civilization, for example, did not mean commerce for Virgil, but it did for Camoens and Spenser and just about everybody afterwards. While the Trojan connection is ruled out as history, its plot of conquest and settlement becomes a universal historiography, a narrative of inevitable "progress" used to characterize all cultures. The tale, exploded as empirical fact, becomes the model by which facts are constructed. In myriad forms, the story continued, and continues, to be retold, from the nineteenth century to now—in novels, films, journalistic reports, political protests, military decisions, and recommendations of the World Bank (chapters 22–29).

So the history of this story is necessarily a mixture of fact and fiction; to tell it requires the recognition that this routine and obvious distinction is inadequate to describe the intricate relation between social practices in the real world and imaginative practices in discursive worlds. I shall be describing this relation as a kind of mutual reproduction—just like the chicken and the egg, where there is no answer to the question: which came first? The story that the Trojans founded Rome existed before the Roman state became an empire. At the moment when it did become one, Virgil portrayed its first emperor, Augustus, as a lineal descendant of Aeneas, now the imperial founder. Present events (and desires) continue to be read back into the retellings of the story—a process that accelerates during the dynastic conquests of the Middle Ages, the commercial ones of the Renaissance, and the formation of colonial empires afterwards. Yet fiction by no means merely follows fact: the story incorporates, and is changed by, events; but the events are pretty much exactly those that were in the story to begin with. I could also call this intricate process a kind of cybernetic feedback: a structure exists to perform an operation, and the results of the operation can change the structure, so that it adapts its next performance accordingly. Mutual reproduction and feedback are simple in outline, but complex in detail—as is this book.

These are but analogies for what is here attempted, for which I know of no clear precedent: the history of a story. It isn't the history of an idea, or an institution, or material circumstances, though it must include all these. It is the history of a plot that is continually enacted both in language and in the world. The story that contains the plot together with the later versions of the plot in ostensibly nonfictional discourses constitute one of the "grand narratives" that Jean-François Lyotard has assured us are dead in our postmodern age. I shall try to show that the report of this story's death is premature, that we are still, to some extent, *inside* this story, that we (members of occidental culture) have internalized it—or it us. Yet I could probably not even attempt to show this if Lyotard were not partly right, if the story were not partly dead, in the sense of having been sufficiently criticized and resisted to permit us to take some (necessarily) partial distance from it.

This distance is supplied by several converging lines of contemporary thought, which require acknowledgment. Michel Foucault (1970 and 1972) offers the powerful idea of "discursive practices," of the ways in which languages of investigation (theories) create their objects (facts). From critical theory as an offshoot of the sociology of knowledge (Habermas 1971) comes the principle that any form of intellectual inquiry or creation is fully comprehensible only as a part of a larger social nexus. This principle, descended from Weberian and other developments of Marxism, has in turn produced the useful and still warmly debated concept of "ideology" (Williams 1977) as structures of language serving at once to mask, perpetuate, reveal, and criticize the actuating motives of a given society or class. Finally, there is interpretive, or "poetic" anthropology (Geertz 1973 and 1983), which undertakes analyses of semantic fields over the widest possible range of discourses—from Balinese dancing to Moroccan law—in the effort to detect in the symbolic systems of a culture the modes of its material operation.

These lines of thinking, for which the works cited are but a kind of synecdoche, converge at a single point, which is the "foundation" of my investigation here. This point is the conviction that any form of language use—from the "highest" literature to the most banal advertisement—is not sufficiently to be understood apart from the social and historical practices that have formed it and that in turn it contributes to form (reproduction or feedback). The distance thus provided from the texts that our culture privileges as "art" also requires their analysis as (particularly influential) forms of language that give shape and direction to social, political, and economic aspirations and behavior.

The grand narrative of foundation and origin whose formation, development, ramifications, modifications, and effects constitute my subject is classified as a legend in the traditional taxonomy that scholars have made of such stories. This classification is made according to the nature of their agents, the presumed ontology of their events, and the kind of belief they are expected to command. It runs roughly like this: Myths tell about supernatural beings in a remote time and place, concern the sacred, and are regarded as fact. Legends tell about human heroes in a more recent time and more local place, concern the meeting of the sacred and the secular, and are regarded as fact. Folktales tell about any sort of agent—divine or human, animal or vegetable—in any time or place, are purely secular and are

regarded as fiction. Many contemporary oral cultures are found to possess only two
of these classes: "history" (myth and legend), which is "fact," and "fiction," which
isn't (see Bascom 1965).

This is the routine and reasonable distinction that my proposed history must
complicate. We think we know facts from fictions—as in everyday life we must;
our sanity depends upon it. We average neurotics can build castles in the air; but
only the psychotic, or the superstitious, or the "primitive" tries to live in them,
tries to *act out* what the stories say. And here is the complication: this classification
of discourses is made from *inside* the grand narrative of our founding legend; it
evolved to describe the kind of oral cultures that are by its definition more "primitive" than ours; it presumes and implies the entire chronology of "progress" from
that state to our own. Myths are designed to be acted out in sacred ceremonies (as
the sacrifice of Christ is reenacted in the Eucharist); legends offer heroes as models of prowess and achievement to be imitated. Folktales are merely amusing—
delicious fantasies not to be confused with real life, like cartoons (Don't try this at
home!). Omitted from the classification of stories, of course, is "Literature," which
is something else, even when narrative: explicitly self-conscious fictions (like folktales) that claim a subtle truth-value not that of "fact" and certainly not to be acted
out (unlike myths and legends). Centuries of technological sophistication and
bourgeois self-discipline have allowed us to imagine that we are both beyond the
culturally juvenile appeals of myth and exempt from the childish desire for legendary heroes. At the dawn of scientific modernity, in the early seventeenth century,
one of the greatest fictions ever written—*Don Quixote*—takes as its subject, and
makes a still puzzling problem of, our supposed emancipation from the childish
urge to act out stories. We have grown up and put away childish things; only
"primitive" cultures have myths today; *we* have Wallace Stevens.

The history of the founding legend, however, will reveal that our emancipation from, or growing out of, the appeals of myth is far from complete; that indeed
much of our greatest literature serves a mythic function in legitimizing current
practices; and that, in short, we still, like children, tend to do what we are told. The
history will also reveal the formation of our category of the "primitive," our placement backward in time of those present cultures that the legend defines as inferior to ours.

By "we" in this book, I mean we speakers of what B. L. Whorf (1956: 138)
called SAE—Standard Average European—languages, those which, related to
Greek and Latin, are spoken in the western European (and North American) culture whose domination of the planet constitutes its history since the early sixteenth
century. The forms that the legend of our own foundation acquired at the outset
of modernity have not ceased to enable its reproduction throughout the world.
The forms of domination have been succinctly chronicled by Eric Wolf in *Europe
and the People Without History*. His title aptly summarizes another consequence of
our modern invention of the "primitive," the "superstitious," and the childish. Rel-
egating myths and legends to cultures that are explicitly (as we shall see) regarded
as infantile, we deprive them of their indigenous history. Infants (Lat. *infans*—"in-

capable of speech") have little history and no language. Their history begins with us. Columbus "discovered" America in 1492, but only, of course, from our dominating perspective. Though Columbus did not find what he was looking for, what he found he also founded. He planted a flag and pronounced words of formal claiming; he took possession. What we find we tend to found, in this sense. Finders, keepers—losers, weepers. That bit of distinctly infantile doggerel is no bad summary of our relation to all the infantilized others in modern history.

For a foundation in our sense, which derives from the foundation of ancient Rome, has inevitably entailed the unfounding of somebody else. Our possession is their dispossession. The structuralist philosopher Michel Serres (1983) has meditated in fascinating ways on the implications of this process as it is narrated in the mélange of what we would call history, myth, and legend in the first book of Livy. Hercules slaying Cacus, Romulus Remus, the rape of the Sabines, the treachery of Tarpeia, the expulsion of the Tarquins—all these episodes in the founding of Rome, regardless of their basis in fantasy or fact, demonstrate the nature of the process, which is simply the price of foundation. The walls and towers of Rome rise over and upon the blood and bones of non-Romans. Its foundation is literally the death of its others, those who may not even be opposed, but who are or become alien to it.

The empire thus founded devised a public exhibition of the others that it went on to conquer: the parade in the metropolis of the spoils and captives, called the "triumph," of the victorious general. Octavius Caesar thus celebrated his total victory in the civil war with a triple triumph in 29 B.C. Images of this triumph, with its long procession of vanquished peoples from the Euphrates to the Rhine, conclude Virgil's description of the shield that Mulciber makes at Venus's request for her son Aeneas (*Aeneid* 8.722–28). The custom of the triumph is evoked by Walter Benjamin in his "Theses on the Philosophy of History,"[1] a lapidary essay that summarizes the kind of history and inspires the kind of distance that my subject requires. Benjamin is criticizing traditional positivist historicism for its empathic indolence—that is, granting automatic sympathy to the winners, and leaving the losers in oblivion. His metaphor for this historical procession is the triumph, in which the spoils are "cultural treasures," which must be viewed "with cautious detachment" because of how they were produced.

> They owe their existence not only to the efforts of the great minds and talents who have created them, but also to the anonymous toil of their contemporaries. There is no document of civilization which is not at the same time a document of barbarism. And just as such a document is not free of barbarism, barbarism taints also the manner in which it was transmitted from one owner to another. (1973: 258)

When I first read these words, years ago, I did not understand them. Not until I became interested, for quite accidental reasons, in the losers necessarily presumed

---

1. Written in 1940, but not published until 1950.

by the grand narrative of the transmission of dominion and culture did I realize that this book is an effort to understand Benjamin's apparent paradox: just how it could be that the most, and justly, admired achievements of civilization are also those of barbarism.

I offer this history of the story of the foundation of that (our) civilization as an exemplary case. In all the variety of its discourses, of presumed fact or acknowledged fiction, it creates what it has triumphed over, becomes what it subjugates. Whether in the "stateliest measure ever molded by the lips of man" (Tennyson's description of Virgil) or the dog Latin of the twelfth century, in the vernacular epics of the sixteenth or the racist propaganda and journalism of the nineteenth, the story never ceases to be told. And in the history of the west—which for the last five hundred years has become that of the globe—it never ceases to be enacted.

As the languages we speak determine how we know the world, so the stories those languages tell help to determine how we act in it. And the stories we tell about ourselves become the histories of other people. This is why "there is no story that is not true."

Acknowledgments

A book like this, one that poaches on large and very different terrains, would hardly have been possible without the bibliographical aid and advice of many friends and scholars. I have gratefully received suggestions from present and former colleagues Ivars Alksnis, John G. Blair, Mark Thornton Burnett, Guglielmo Gorni, Alan Howard, Bernard Schlurick, and Valeria Wagner. Others, encountered on various occasions over the years, have been no less generous: Richard Ohmann, John Pocock, François Rigolot, and Richard Symonds. Youssef Cassis and the late Sir Keith Sinclair graciously responded to inquiries, and Adam Piette did some admirable archival digging. I am indebted to all for providing me with maps to the territories; but none, of course, is in any way responsible for the detours I may have made or the infractions I may have committed once I got there.

Other colleagues have kindly responded to the additional imposition of reading parts of the manuscript. The efforts of Neil Forsyth, Michel Jeanneret, and Paul Beekman Taylor were always in the interests of accuracy and the reader's comfort; they may be praised and unblamed for such error and discomfort as remain. I am especially grateful for the kindness of Wlad Godzich, whose encouragement and advice brought the project to completion.

No such project could have been conceived or pursued without the resources of great libraries and the anonymous services of their trained personnel. Those of the British Library and the Library of Congress were particularly helpful and patient in responding to my pestiferous inquiries. I owe thanks to the Folger Institute in Washington and to the Warden and Fellows of Merton College, Oxford, for providing access to the collections in the Folger Shakespeare Library and the Bodleian.

Finally, I am grateful to the Librarian of Oriel College, Oxford, for permission to quote from the unpublished correspondence of Lancelot Ridley Phelps, and to the editors of the following journals for permission to reprint more or less different versions of chapters 1, 6, 7, and 15 that first appeared in their pages: *New Literary History, Exemplaria,* and *Intrecci e contaminazioni*; chapter 9 first appeared in *SPELL: Swiss Papers in English Language and Literature* 9 (1996): 53–63

Chapter 1

৯◗

THE STORY AND THE CULTURE

The Story

Once upon a time there was a great and prosperous city called Troy, built with the help of an unkept bargain with two gods. Since gods are not, in the long term, to be mocked, a consortium among them arranged for that city to be totally destroyed, by means of a stolen wife and a ten-year siege undertaken by an unprecedented alliance of Greek attackers. The noble Trojan, Aeneas (descended from an older ruling house than that which failed to keep the bargain), leads a band of escapees from the burning city, carrying his father and his household gods. Helped and hindered by two goddesses, after many vicissitudes, Aeneas and his band arrive in Latium, the western land foretold by Jupiter to be the seat of an empire without end. There, Aeneas takes to wife the daughter of the local king, subdues the local populations in a climactic battle, builds his walls, and establishes his household gods.

His descendants rule peaceably, founding more cities, until a prophecy foretells the birth of his great-grandson, Brutus, who will cause the death of his parents but will nonetheless after years of voyaging in exile be highly exalted. And so it occurs: his mother dies bearing him, and as a youth he accidentally kills his father while hunting. Sent into exile, Brutus liberates a band of Trojans enslaved in the Greek islands and there acquires a wife. He leads these through many adventures in France (founding Tours along the way) and finally arrives at the western land called Albion promised to him in a dream by the goddess Diana. Here he has only to drive away and exterminate a few giants before he can settle down for good, rename the country, and build the capital city of New Troy. Troynovant flourishes long ages before King Lud, having increased its walls and towers, calls it after himself, London—an act resented by his brother for eliminating the name of Troy.

This is the outline of the story as it appears in Roman epic of the first century B.C. (Virgil's *Aeneid*) and medieval history of the twelfth (Geoffrey of Monmouth's *History of the Kings of Britain*). It is known as the legend of Brut, the eponymous

founder of Brittany and Britain, or, in numerous other recensions in both the poetry and prose of the Middle Ages, as the descent from Troy. The story was popularly regarded as actual history from the earliest Roman historians in the third
century B.C. until the eighteenth century of our era. In all its versions its point is
to repeat, for whatever given locality or ruling house in western Europe, the
founding of Rome by Aeneas—making the subsequent founders his lineal descendants (or inventing other Trojan survivors) and putting them through the identical trajectory of wanderings from east to west until they come into possession of
the promised land. Such possession was indeed all that Aeneas himself accomplished; the founding of the city of Rome was left to later generations. In the
purely literary tradition, the story is exfoliated from a brief and unspecific prophecy made by one of the offended gods in Homer's story of Troy's fall. There,
Poseidon exempts Aeneas from the doom on Priam's house and destines him and
his progeny to be "lord over the Trojans" (*Iliad* 20.307). Taking this hint, the subsequent legends give various local habitations and other names to this dominion,
which includes (as we shall see) all of western Europe as far as Iceland.

What kind of a story is this, that selects a cultural origin that is always already
destroyed? For there is no doubt that what the homeless Trojans are bringing to
the west is nothing less than civilization itself. The "empire without end" (*Aeneid*
1.279) that Jupiter has given to the Roman heirs of the wandering Trojans includes
the transplantation of all arts and sciences, the bringing of a total culture. Celebrated in the Middle Ages as the *translatio imperii et studii*, this "transmission of empire and learning" is the central vision that the occident has of itself. The exercise
of domination and the production of high cultural artifacts travel together in this
description (and in our history); the term for their mutual journey is that of a
figure of speech—the Latin word for the Greek *metapherô* (to carry across, transfer). The implications of thus identifying the operations of literate eloquence—the
mastery of metaphor prescribed by classical rhetoric, linguistic translation—and
those of political subjugation have been well explored in a recent book, *The Poetics of Imperialism* (Cheyfitz 1991). The title is not metaphorical, but a literally exact
reminder that our civilization describes itself as doing in the world what it does in
words, linking its facts to its fables, transferring its own meanings as it translates all
into its own voice.

The voice that told the story of transmission spoke mainly in the Latin language, which was the primary medium of almost all formal education in the west
until this century. That voice and its story became our highest and most self-hon-
orific cultural tradition—the word itself means that which is "handed over." Rome
conquered Greece and assimilated its culture; the Christian Church found its center in Rome and declared Virgil's fictional prophecies to be literally true of the
kingdom of God, which it administered. Popes and emperors squabbled over their
respective jurisdictions in this administration for centuries. The supreme place that
such "transmission" occupies in all our culture, but especially the literary, was proclaimed with some poignancy by T. S. Eliot (see Kermode 1975: ch. 1), who mi-

grated from Missouri back to Europe in order to claim himself an heir to it. Eliot's need to be classical, Christian, and royalist is the desire to be civilized in western terms.

I wish to interrogate just what these terms are by examining the story as the etiology of our civilization, the founding myth that supplies our cultural identity, distinguishing it from others. Technically a legend, the story deals with the meeting of the sacred and the secular, a blend of historicized myth and mythified history typical of the genre and visible in other such stories as those in the Pentateuch and in the first book of Livy. It is a narrative about remote but human events, which explains them by means of other narratives about divine agency. It thus shares one of the important functions of myth in general, which is to explain an entire cultural system, to account for still-current practices and still-extant names.

Assigning the origin of our civilization to a nation and city that has been destroyed requires a narrative of displacement, exile, conquest, and reconstruction. The story is therefore structured as a journey, the search for a predestined and permanent home. The story thus presents civilization as that which comes from somewhere else. Specifically, it is borne by exiles from the east to the west. There, it is imposed by force on the indigenous population, who may or may not be given the opportunity to assimilate themselves to it. In any case, should they resist, they are wiped out. The image of civilization is the city, usually in the synecdochic form of walls and towers.

It is precisely its central process of *transmission* that makes this picture of civilization uniquely western—that is, Roman—and rather odd. Most civilizations—as well as most cultures that our tradition would classify as "primitive"—do not see themselves as having required transportation to their present location. The stories of cosmic and cultural origin that can be sampled in dictionaries of mythology typically confine themselves to the present space of the community: they are not about journeys. From Sumeria to Southeast Asia, from the plains of central North America to the deserts of Australia, from the jungles of the Amazon to those of the Congo, indigenous cultural communities tell stories about how local gods dealing with localized natural forces produced local people who brought knowledge, social organization, and identity to this group right here, distinguishing it often radically from that other group over there, across that river, behind the next ridge. Civilization, in short, is most commonly seen very much as a homegrown product. So it certainly was by the Greeks—for whom those who did not speak their language were simply "barbarians"—and the Chinese—whose word for their own nation means "middle" or "central" kingdom, the omphalos of the universe. We westerners, by contrast, are migratory and peripheral. We have not *produced* civilization; we have *been* civilized.

The oddity of this situation would appear reasonably enough to result from the actual history of our culture. It is after all the case that much of our culture—its alphabet, numerals, and religion, as well as many of its institutions and ideas—

originated in the near east and moved west by trade and by conquest. The direction of this migration is faithfully reproduced in the founding story, as is its nature, which is straightforwardly imperialistic. Similar circumstances can also account for similar founding stories current in the South Pacific islands, in which invaders bearing culture arrive from the sea, conquer the local folk, then intermarry with and rule them. These stories, as untypical as our own, have been illuminatingly compared (Sahlins 1985: ch. 3) with Virgil's and Livy's narratives of Aeneas and Romulus. Travel and transmission in the crucial encounter with the indigenes are the common features of these stories, and those which make our story uniquely Roman. Though the ancient Greeks founded colonies, they never ruled them from the metropolis and, above all, never told about them a story of travel and transmission. The stories the Greeks did tell—so fragmentarily that they did not constitute a literary genre—focus rather on the departure of the founder, the reasons for his exile or expulsion (see Dougherty 1993). The emplotment of the journey of the civilizer who comes from elsewhere records the Roman experience that will give a new shape to all the Greek materials incorporated into Rome's founding epic.

Among these materials is a major feature—both of our history and our founding story—that does not appear in the South Pacific analogues. This is the symbolic image of the transported empire: the city with its walls and towers. Cities are not just the hallmark of our civilization, they are part of its definition for archeologists and historians. Etymologically, both "civilization" and "civility" come from Latin and depend on belonging to a city (*civis, civilis*: citizen, polite; *civitas, civilitas*: city/citizenship, courtesy). Cities are literally what qualify us as civilized, and their prominence in the story suggests the precise nature of the civilization they embody. For the very existence of cities requires a particular kind and organization of food production. The standard historical scenario (McNeill 1963: chs. 1–3) may be summarized as follows: Civilization depends on the production of a large agricultural surplus of cereal grains, which permits the congregation of people in cities and their division into specialized occupations. It is the liberation of some from the labor of food production still enjoined upon the many that makes civilization happen. For this reason, it first happened where nature made it easy to produce a surplus: in the deltas and flood plains of the Nile, Tigris-Euphrates, and Indus rivers. Millennia were required to clear and bring under sufficient cultivation the forest-covered lands with capricious rainfalls of western Europe.

For the historian, this very gradual and lengthy development of the surplus production that gives rise to the building of cities literally requires the spread of civilization from elsewhere. Civilization, that is, in this particular form: massively producing agricultural communities settled in well-ordered and diversified cities. Nor was the link between this mode of social organization and this mode of food production lost on the ancient world. The near eastern goddesses of vegetation in general and grain in particular gradually become associated in ritual and art with the imperial metropolis. Greek Demeter was early identified with Roman Ceres (whence "cereal"), whose cult became under the Empire the exclusive prerogative of the imperial family (LIMC 4.1: 893). Phrygian Cybele, the even older Great Mother, became in the Hellenistic age the protectress of both agriculture and the city, typically depicted in art wearing a crown of walls and turrets, she is the sovereign of citizenship, the bestower of civility. Her temple on the Palatine was lavishly reconstructed by Augustus himself, and stood opposite his own house (Vermaseren 3: 3).

There is one more crucially important feature of both the fictional and historical plotting of the course of western civilization as the *translatio imperii et studii*. The founding myth is one way of explaining what historical circumstances are seen to have produced. All the retellings of the story of the descent from Troy had, by the sixteenth century, made it "possible to elaborate the Trojan origin of every European people, to account for the dispersion of the arts and sciences, and to provide an etymology of illustrious antiquity for every place name" (Hay 1967: 108). The crucial feature is that of "dispersion": the practices that constitute civilization as high culture—arts and sciences—are traced to a single source that is elsewhere than the area where they now flourish. The emplotment of "transmission" requires a (potentially infinite) regress back through successively destroyed, or renamed, cities to the one that disappeared long ago. The origin—and there's only one—infinitely recedes; but the story assures us that it's there. The subsequent power of this notion in western thinking is hard to overestimate. The myth's fictional explanation of the "dispersion" of cultural practices from a single source simply became the "diffusionist" theory of twentieth-century archeology. This theory was neatly summarized by V. Gordon Childe as "the irradiation of European barbarism by Oriental civilization" (quoted in Renfrew 1973: 17). And that is the meaning, in a nutshell, of the fiction's plot: if it's "civilized," it can't have originated *here*—and vice versa.

The strictly diffusionist theory has only in the last generation been invalidated by the technology of radiocarbon dating, which shows Stonehenge to be as old as some of the Pyramids. Oriental "irradiation" no longer suffices to explain the remains of megalithic cultures around the globe; nor are their producers to be regarded as "uncouth yokels" (Renfrew 1973: 16–17). Yet, even as this theoretical form of the fiction's meaning was being discredited, another was springing up to take its place. This is the occasional vogue for speculating that the culture of the whole planet is due to extraterrestrial intervention. Such speculation can take radically opposed forms, from relatively learned and rational argument (von Daniken 1969) to narratives of encountering creatures from flying saucers (Vorilhon 1978). This latter form has produced, as our millennium approaches, a sect in Europe and Canada called the "Raëliens," named after the extraterrestrial messenger of the beings who created humanity. But whether as scholarship or as pop cult, thus to extrapolate the plot of the myth into outer space suggests the stranglehold that the story still exercises over the western mind. We appear unable to imagine any other conceptualization of our history than the one it gives us, and because our cultural values came from elsewhere, so must those of the entire earth. Without interstellar "irradiation," we remain "yokels."

The ethnocentricity of such projections needs no emphasis; and the particular form of civilization—ours—that is reflected in, defined by, and propagated through the founding legend will reproduce itself throughout our history and our literature at the expense of other kinds of civilization, which, in our terms, are not recognizable as such.

The Culture

The plot of displacement—the destroyed origin that demands successive destructions for foundation to occur—and the symbolic image of the city—the settled, ordered, and diversified agglomeration that requires massive surplus production of cereal grains—together constitute civilization in the SAE languages we speak. From one material basis to one mode of social organization, via the destruction of that mode in one location to its violent transplantation to another—this process is what the modern west has imposed on the globe in the name of progress. As we shall see, the invaders of the west in this story, whether divine or human, are themselves the bringers of *culture* in all its senses: agricultural techniques as well as arts and sciences.

The very word belongs to an etymological triad in SAE that encapsulates the relations and processes privileged as civilization: cult/cultivate/culture (Fr.: *culte/ cultiver/culture*; It.: *culto/coltivare/coltura*; Ger.: *Kult/kultivieren/Kultur*). All are derived from Latin *colo* (p.p. *cultum*), which means to dwell and to worship as well as to till the soil. Permanent settlements on cleared land reaping regular harvests, building their walls and towers skyward, creating institutions of religion, law, craftsmanship, and art, all of which finally get recorded in writing—such is civilized society. Exported from a metropolis, the units of this society are "colonies." Its forms of worship, derived from cults of fertility gods, and all its forms of knowledge and refinement—intellectual, aesthetic, moral—depend on tillage in a fixed location, on the controlled nurture and growth of vegetation, animals, and human tastes. This is what "cultivation" means.

Opposed to cultivation, which is civilized, is savagery, which isn't. And what is savage (*silvestris, silva*) is literally "of the woods." It is land and people that remain uncultivated. To be *incultus* is to be savage, rude, and dumb. Our languages thus encode the forms of fear and contempt felt by a settled agricultural community for other modes of material and social organization. They determine our awareness of what is "cultured," and they deny the honorific title of civilization even to quite remarkable achievements by societies otherwise organized. For example, even the contemporary archeologist illuminated by radiocarbon dating must withhold the title from megalithic cultures. Whatever feats of engineering, transport, solar observation, personnel management, and piety were necessary to erect Stonehenge do not qualify. With no surviving evidence of cities or writing among megalithic peoples, the fair-minded archeologist can only describe them as "before" civilization (Renfrew 1973).

The exclusion of societies long shrouded in the mists of "pre"history from the honorific designation of civilization would matter less if it stopped there. Even there, some students of native American cultures have reason to complain that our notion of prehistory may be simply another form of denying history to the cultures that we have displaced or destroyed. With respect to the requirement of writing, one form of such a denial has been the failure to acknowledge that the pictographs of several Mesoamerican cultures even constitute writing at all (Brotherston 1986). But the exclusions implied by the picture of civilization in our founding story have not stopped anywhere yet. The polar opposite of that picture, in language and in life, is the supposed savagery of forest-dwellers. Hunters and gatherers are as far beyond the pale of civilization as it is possible to be. More ambiguous and complex is the marginality of the other major mode of life long practiced in the west—that of nomadic and seminomadic pastoralism.

The most privileged picture of this way of life is presented to the west, of course, in the book of Genesis. The contrast between it and what has become our view of civilization testifies to the power of the basically Roman myth over even our official religion. But the Bible is, as usual, ambivalent on the matter. One stratum of the interwoven stories of origin in Genesis—that concerning Jahweh—seems clearly the myth of a nomadic, herding culture. To this culture, the *enemy* is the settled, city-building, agricultural society of the coastal folk, the Canaanites, who worship the usual multiplicity of fertility gods. Against these, Jahweh declares himself as the unique lord of the historical destiny of the roving, often enslaved, Israelites. The good brother, Abel, is a herdsman; the bad one, Cain, is a farmer. Jahweh likes the former's offering of burnt flesh and is unhappy with the latter's of grain. And in this story, the fratricidal brother is himself the founder of cities.

So much for the contrast. The mixture of history, myth, legend, and law that characterizes the Old Testament in its widely differing temporal layers of composition goes on to record the settlement of the Israelites themselves. God gives Moses instructions to dwell in the promised land, dispossessing its inhabitants and dividing its cities among the tribes (Numbers 33–35). By the time of Solomon, Israel is capable of paying for the cedar to build the temple in Jerusalem with grain exports (I Kings 5:11). The urban monarchy of the Israelites is a far cry from their nomadic wanderings. Though traces of ritual values from their nomadic way of life persist, that way of life is largely superseded by the settled, agricultural one that it originally opposed. This historical trajectory neatly coincided with the one that would later be developed from the founding story. In sum, though nomadic pastoralism was initially a source of positive cultural values in the west's sacred book, it is even there marginalized by being a thing of the past. And in Virgil, the west's secular epic of foundation, it is marginalized in the same way (as we shall see) as a kind of mythic nostalgia.

What we have learned from Freud about the return of the repressed in the dreams of an individual will be seen also to characterize the dreams of a collectivity, as recorded in the many retellings of our founding legend. What it excludes, those other ways of life against which it defines itself, will return, in the fullness of time, to be recuperated in another way—as guilt, as sport, as game, as entertainment. This, of course, does not make the exclusion any less real, or any less disastrous, for those who are excluded.

In the actual history of the western domination of the globe since about 1530, the exclusions have sometimes amounted to extinction. As far as I know, no one has yet compiled a list of the cultures, and their languages, that have disappeared, casualties of our appropriation of the planet. Such calculations as have been attempted barely suggest the enormity: in Brazil alone, of over 230 tribes whose names were recorded from 1500 on, over 130 are now extinct (Hemming 1978: 492–501). The earliest and best-known examples of cultural elimination—the Incas and the Aztecs—were inadvertent, the results largely of disease (see McNeill 1976). The conquistadors did not wish to exterminate these sedentary, recognizably sophisticated empires, but merely to enslave them. Other peoples, organized differently, more mobile and hostile to interference, like the Caribs and the Pequots, were deliberately wiped out. Still others—hundreds (thousands? tens of thousands?) of native American tribes in both hemispheres—simply faded away. Deprived of the forests that sustained their (by our definition) savage ways, they declined and died.

One of the most affecting and best documented such disappearances was that of the Tasmanians (see Bonwick 1870 and Robinson 1966). Their random slaughter by settlers was followed by governmental efforts to preserve them by removal to another island. There, they simply failed to reproduce. The way of life thus destroyed has been subsequently estimated to be from 10,000 to 30,000 years old. That is, the Tasmanians dwelled continuously in their island forests for somewhere around twenty millennia—a "tradition" and a history four or five times as old as any that survives today, including our own, which put an end to theirs.

But the Tasmanians, of course, cleared no fields and built no cities. Though their language had several dialects, they apparently used no writing system (the incuriosity and stupidity of reports on their language make it impossible to know: see Milligan 1859, Bridges 1971, Ryan 1972). They roved from place to place. Just how in fact they lived, and as a community, for so long, how their culture evolved, what stories they told, what ambitions they cherished, what gods they worshipped, what songs they sang, what foods they relished, we shall never know. They died before ethnography was born. Not much fuss was made about their death; it was not a major event in world history—just another in a very long series of what the nineteenth century got rather used to. How easily this occurred, how smoothly such disappearances were ignored, or justified, or regarded as simply inevitable—this, I submit, was the comforting effect of the definition of civilization we inherit from the founding legend. The Tasmanians, and countless others both like and unlike them, were not civilized. That is, we did not have to perceive them as such; they were excluded, savage. That was the comfort. And that comfort may well be one of the reasons that our founding story was sufficiently reiterated to become our legend, and that this legend first acquired its force in a canonical literary tradition, and that this tradition came to constitute a large part of our high culture, and that we wish, perhaps as desperately as Eliot did, to acquire this culture so that we too will be civilized and not uncultivated, *inculte*. For if we so remain, who will stop anyone from dispossessing or exterminating us? We would then deserve it, being savage.

Who has stopped anyone yet? As I write, in the rain forests and desert places of the earth, the dispossession of those who, like the Tasmanians, merely live on and with the land, can be measured by the hectare, the barrel, the ton, and the customarily alcoholic despair of the dispossessed. And, just as a century ago, there isn't much fuss. There are a few organizations, as there were then, too ludicrously underfunded to make much difference, to protest to governments, and now to the IMF and the World Bank, and convene sessions of United Nations Committees. There are books and articles where information is available for those who care to seek it out. And for those who care, now as then, the response is often one of sentimental indignation. This was the usual tone of what little fuss was made in the later nineteenth century; it could rise occasionally to real eloquence and genuine paradox. Today, it is more likely to be cooler in its expression; good investigative reporting on the deliberate ethnocide practiced by the New Tribes Mission and the Summer Institute of Linguistics in South America has been published in the British press. There is some fuss.

But it is inadequate in two ways: quantitative and qualitative. Both kinds of inadequate response result, I believe, from the power of our founding legend still to control our responses to the ever-ongoing destruction of "traditional societies" or "tribal peoples"—designations that today avoid the word but still often carry the condescending sense of "primitive." To us, people who roam forests and build no walls are not *quite* people; our legend, mediated through all kinds of discourses in all our languages, thus defines them as some sub-, pre-, or proto-humanity not *quite* entitled to whatever full measure of compassion we are presumably obliged to bestow on others more like ourselves. So there is too little fuss, and what there is is likely (this, too, is built into the legend) to be nostalgically romanticized. To find the savage "noble" is merely to use that category and that presumed way of life as a corrective mirror to whatever evils are perceived in whatever urbanized civilization we belong to—from Virgil's Rome through Rousseau's Paris to Lévi-Strauss's. Our category of the savage as the uncultivated, whether sub- or superhuman, whether degraded or idealized, remains as it was created to be, always and irrevocably *other* than us. Other, that is, not just descriptively, but normatively—not just *different*, but better or worse than, inferior or superior to, us. It would appear to be the most difficult thing in the world to acknowledge difference without placing it on some scale of value where we ourselves are the standard, whether deficient or preeminent, of measure. To see the other in an otherness that is genuinely other than the image of what we detest or desire would be the beginning of a more adequate response.

Such a response has been offered imaginatively by a few contemporary novelists. Most recently, Mario Vargas Llosa has dramatized, in *The Storyteller*, the oral performances of an indigenous and nomadic culture in Amazonian Peru and juxtaposed them with his own career of storytelling in other media and other worlds. Ursula Le Guin's *The Word for World is Forest*, written during the war in Indochina, remains the most sustained effort I know to imagine what a wilderness-ranging culture would look and feel like. The members of her invented society live in trees and maintain spiritual relationships with and by means of them. Her book is an explicit and politically motivated countermyth to the picture of forest-roaming savagery that is the opposite of civilization in our founding story. And my ensuing account of that story aims to be a more adequate response in another direction. By examining the formation, development, and deployment of our categories of the civilized and the savage, I hope to offer an understanding of this process that will reveal it as the result of historical circumstance and cultural choice—not as divinely or naturally ordained. What people have produced, people can change—but only if they understand that they, the culture and the language they inherit and transmit, did indeed produce it. And only if the people in question can see themselves less as the dominators of the planet and more as fellow travelers on it. For to see the other merely as other requires the acknowledgment that for others we are merely other, too.

A contemporary anthropologist finds this the harder task:

> To see others as sharing a nature with ourselves is the merest decency. But it is from the far more difficult achievement of seeing ourselves amongst others, as a local example of the forms human life has locally taken, a case among cases, a world among worlds, that the largeness of mind, without which objectivity is self-congratulation and tolerance a sham, comes. (Geertz 1983: 16)

Our form of life and its cultural—in all senses—heritage is one local example (unexampled only in its immense power); the Tasmanians were, and the Yanomami are, other local examples. The former are, as a cultural community, extinct; the latter are gravely threatened. The agent and accessory of their destruction was and is our culture and its notion of civilized progress.

For the memory of the human race to lose a single human language and the form of life coextensive with it is a tragedy, even if it occurs without active intervention from elsewhere. When such intervention is sanctioned and glorified, as it is in our legend of the *translatio imperii et studii*, the tragedy becomes peculiarly monstrous, moves into realms of horror that baffle and benumb. I want to register that horror here, because I shall not be discussing it; I don't know how. Some contemporary novelists—mostly from the third world, like Achebe, Naipaul, Ngugi—have discussed it; the most recent form of cultural displacement, theirs by ours, is their terrain. But displacement, as in the founding story, is what our culture is all about. It took western Europe, after all, about 1500 years even to begin decolonizing itself from the Latin language, to legitimize as "culture" and "art" the forms of life that occurred in vernacular languages, and to make them objects of serious study. Ironically, at the very moment when this was happening, Europe was also expanding around the world in ways that would make other vernaculars unavailable for study.

The rationale for this expansion lay ready to hand in the ancient link between settled agriculture and cities as constituting civilization. The presence of this link in the history and literature of Rome bequeathed to the west a myth of civilization that ruled hunters, gatherers, and nomads out, and found any human way of relating to the earth other than by clearing and planting it to be simply primitive. To the formation of that myth I now turn.

Part I

❧

THE FORMATION OF THE LEGEND

IN ROMAN ANTIQUITY

Chapter 2

AENEAS AND AGRICULTURE

Roman Archeology

Why Troy? Why did the Trojans in general and Aeneas in particular get chosen as the founders and cultural ancestors of Rome? The earlier answers given to these questions by the few classical scholars who asked them focused on two particular and mature moments in Rome's imperial career. The first was the simple prestige accruing to Virgil's portrayal of Aeneas's piety and patriotism (Bömer 1951: 44–47). The second was the political utility, for the earliest Roman historians, of claiming a venerable lineage for the state that had defeated Carthage and taken over the eastern Mediterranean (Hanell 1956: 161–63; Alföldi 1964: 143). Though both answers identify conditions propitious to the growth of the legend in their respective periods, the materials and practices out of which the legend was formed were present much earlier. Aeneas as hero and as god was associated with locations in southern Etruria and Latium for two or three centuries before the second Punic War (third century B.C.). Such presence is attested by archeological remains whose precise purpose, origin, and significance is still being debated by the excavators and the experts.

This evidence consists of the following: 58 terracotta statuettes portraying Aeneas carrying Anchises, his father, on his back and holding the container of his household gods, the *penates*. The statuettes were concentrated in two ancient Etruscan cities, and all date from the last quarter of the sixth century B.C. (Schauenburg 1960). At the site of Lavinium, the ancient capital of Latium, were discovered as recently as 1959 thirteen enormous stone altars dating from the sixth to the fourth centuries B.C. The gods worshiped here were Venus, Ceres, Castor and Pollux, and the *penates* (Castagnoli 1975). After the treaty that established Roman hegemony over the Latins in 338 B.C., Aeneas was worshiped in Lavinium under the name of *Aeneas Indiges* (Galinsky 1969: 159). Near this site is the legendary tomb of Aeneas, a sixth-century structure enlarged in the fourth, which bore an inscription recorded by Dionysius of Halicarnassus in the third century to "the father of the local gods" (*patros theou chthoniou*) identified by Livy with Aeneas under the name of *Iuppiter indiges* (Sommella 1974). Also in the general area of Lavinium is a disputed tombstone inscription (ca. 300 B.C.) apparently identifying Aeneas as a *lar*—which might be either a deified ancestor or a god/demon of field and fertility (Galinsky 1969: 155–58; Cornell 1977: 79).

Before touching on the problems of interpreting this evidence, we must note that Aeneas was not the only wandering hero from the eastern Mediterranean to be commemorated in the remains of the Italic peoples, the Etruscans and the Latins, whom Rome eventually dominated. Odysseus and Hercules are attested even earlier, also in figurines and vase paintings. Both more famous for adventures than Aeneas, their presence clearly indicates that Rome as she later became had a choice of exiled, semidivine personages who might function as the prestigious ancestor sought by her earliest historians. These provide the earliest written references to the choice of the Trojans as the ultimate founders of Rome.

The first surviving mention of Aeneas in this role is by Hellicanos of Lesbos, an historian of the fifth century B.C., as quoted by Dionysius (Cornell 1975: 5; Dury-Moyaers 1981: 53). The legend appears to have been fully formed by the close of the third century, in the work of the Sicilian Greek historian Timaeus and the Roman Fabius Pictor. Timaeus, celebrating Rome's victory in the first Punic War, recounts the kind of marvelous events that will appear in Virgil: the appearance of the white sow and thirty piglets to mark the site of Alba Longa, and the prophecy that the wandering Trojans' hardships will be such that they will be reduced to eating the tables on which their food is served (Alföldi 1964: 251ff.). The prophecy (*Aeneid* 3.255–57) comes true when the Trojans' first meal in Latium consists of meat on flat, consumable pieces of bread (7.112–17). The serving of such proto-pizzas was a feature of the Lavinian cult of the *penates*, identified by Timaeus as those brought from Troy by Aeneas (Dury-Moyaers 1981: 67). For Fabius Pictor, who may have written in the second century to justify Roman colonization of Greece instead of, like Timaeus, in the third (see Mattingly 1976), the Trojan connection was fully exploited to endow the rising Romans with a glorious lineage and a noble past (Hanell 1956).

For Rome's political purposes, the very ambiguity of the Trojans' relation to the Greeks constituted their attraction and utility. Although the Homeric "enemy," the Trojans were yet regarded as descending from Greeks, sharing their past and their language; they "could be viewed as both Greeks and non-Greeks" (Galinsky 1969: 95). They were ideally placed, in other words, to furnish Rome with a cultural identity that both assimilated it to and distinguished it from that of Greece, providing both the prestige of association and the pride of independence. During this period of the Roman rise to dominance in the Mediterranean (third to second centuries), there were clearly compelling reasons to select the Trojan connection as the founding story.

The connection, however, had been long available for such selection. Particular historical circumstances and purposes can explain the selection; but the availability has other and deeper grounds that made the descent from Troy uniquely appropriate as the founding legend of the west. One kind of suitability, though, it shared equally with its potential competitors: either Trojan or Greek would have served faithfully to reflect the direction of cultural migration from east to west. The Greek colonies on the Italian peninsula and in Sicily, the possible origins in Asia minor of the Etruscans themselves, are instances of the westward flow of near-eastern culture that becomes conceptualized as the diffusionist theory of occidental history.

The exact pathways and extent of this motion are the main subjects in the disputes of the experts over the archeological evidence. The discovery of the altars in Lavinium sufficiently establishes for some that contact between Greece and Latium was direct and did not require mediation from either Etruria or Sicily. Whether the statuettes were votive offerings, whether they demonstrate an actual Aeneas cult, whether they were produced for the tastes of a local market, why their appearance is confined to a relatively brief period of time—are all matters of debate. Just what those monumental altars were *for* is uncertain, as is the precise meaning of such terms as *indiges* and *lares*. Just when Aeneas became a cult figure in Lavinium, just how and why he and the Trojan connection were transferred from there to Rome, just when that connection became generalized from a few patrician families to the Roman people, just what the relation is between his story and that of Romulus and Remus—all are subjects of argument.[1]

There is, however, virtually no argument among all the specialists on the key point that gives Aeneas the edge over other potential eastern candidates for the role of founding ancestor. This was simply his, and the Trojans', absorption into and identification with "ancient Italic rites of fecundity" (Dury-Moyaers 1981: 206) by roughly the middle of the first millennium B.C. Aeneas himself was superimposed on and acquired the attributes of the ancient *Sol Indiges*, who, whatever his name means, was the solar/earth god who provides water (Dury-Moyaers 1981: 211–15). Aeneas and Troy became our ancestors because they were associated, certainly in Latium and perhaps in Etruria, with the gods who presided over the kind of settled, surplus-producing agriculture that gives rise to cities and our kind of civilization. The associations are multiple and unmistakable. Before reviewing them, it is tempting to speculate that they may go back much farther in time, to whatever conception the ancient world had of Troy itself that made its famous fall the numinous and elegiac event it became in Homeric and subsequent epics.

Since Schliemann's great discovery of Troy a little over a century ago, the excavators of the multilayered, repeatedly destroyed and rebuilt, site have fixed on level VIIA as the material remains of the city Homer sang. This city was burned in about 1260 B.C., roughly the midpoint in ancient estimates of the date of Troy's destruction (from 1334 to 1135). The plausibility of such a date is enhanced for scholars by the fact that all the centers of Mycenaean culture on the Greek main-

---

1. The main contentions are reviewed and principal positions defended by Galinsky, Cornell, and Dury-Moyaers.

land were shattered by 1200. "The great centres that are recorded in the Catalogue of ships as having contributed the chief contingents to the expedition to Troy under Agamemnon, lay deserted or dilapidated, the remaining inhabitants facing a harsh struggle for survival" (Blegen 1963: 163). It would thus seem that Troy became numinous as the memory of a whole civilization lost.

And the kind of civilization it was may be inferred from one of the distinguishing features of level VIIA: this is the presence of very large *pithoi*, storage urns with stone lids sunk in the floors of the houses. Archeologists read in this feature efforts to maximize storage space in an overcrowded place, and suggestions of the needs of an emergency (Blegen 1963: 154–55). Equally important is what the urns stored, presumably like their rather smaller counterparts, earlier and later, all around the Mediterranean: wine, olive oil, and grain. Troy was also celebrated in song, story, and Homeric epithet for its breeding and raising of horses. The winter maintenance of herds of large domestic animals requires, of course, enough surplus of grain and its by-products to feed them as well as the human population. So here is Troy as the perfect image of our kind of civilization: its topless towers surrounded by waving fields of grain, rows of neatly tended vineyards and olive trees, herds of grazing cattle. It was destroyed; but it will not cease to be recreated in the west.

It is more than appropriate that Aeneas should bring out of the burning city for transplantation in Latium and Etruria those "household gods" that the Romans called *penates*. This word is derived from *penus*, which meant storehouse of food, or granary (Bömer 1951: 54). Apparently these gods moved from storehouse to hearth by means of food-storage chests in the home to become identified with familial ancestors (Bailey 1932: 49). Their worship was especially prominent in Lavinium, where the power of their connection with harvest and grain storage continued long after Roman domination of the area. After the treaty of 338, priests from Rome came annually to Lavinium to conduct sacrifices to the *penates*. They were identified there from much earlier times with Castor and Pollux, who, along with Venus, Ceres, and Liber, were all parts of local cults that were agrarian, fecund, chthonian (Dury-Moyaers 1981: 211, 223–24). Aeneas himself was worshipped in Lavinium until the second century A.D. (Dury-Moyaers 1981: 249).

All of the gods named at the site of the thirteen massive altars were those of agricultural production. In central Italy Venus had long been associated with Ceres in rites designed to ensure "vegetal fecundity" (Schilling 1954: 19–20). The Greek Aphrodite in her numerous Italic forms had generally traded her function of promoting joyous seduction (the Etruscans had another goddess for this purpose) for one of promoting the growth of seeds. Venus, of course, was Aeneas's mother; and one of her later Roman names was *Venus Frutis*. Pliny and Servius record an ancient claim that Aeneas brought this goddess to Laurentum from Sicily (Galinsky 1969: 115–16). However she got there, the Venus Erycina (of Eryx in Sicily, which Thucydides said was a Trojan settlement), later known as Aphrodite Aineias, appeared on coins with ears of grain (Galinsky 1969: 69–70). In the later empire, Sicily supplied the grain that fed both the Roman populace and its legions, without, however, diminishing wheat production in all of Italy (White 1970: 66). In Latium, at any rate, were gathered the federated Latin cults of Venus and other deities, including her son Aeneas, whose business it was to promote such production, as well as that of gardens and vineyards. The size of the altars where their sacrifices were performed, as well as the drainage ditches around some of them, suggest that cattle were used for the purpose.

Though the extent of Etruscan influence on these cults in Latium—which had been colonized by Etruscan traders by 650 B.C.—is debatable, the agricultural basis of the Etruscans' quite remarkable civilization is unambiguous. Their place in the development of the story, however, is scarcely ascertainable, for their past is buried—some scholars would say was consciously occulted—in Rome's legend of itself (see Alföldi 1964 and Keller 1975). Their language, which seems neither Indoeuropean nor Semitic, has been largely deciphered, though the experts continue to argue about how to read it (Woudhuizen 1992). In any case, before the Romans overcame them, the Etruscans had created in central and northern Italy precisely the landscape of civilization implicit in the image of Troy and in the founding story. Centered in what is now Tuscany, the Etruscans drained the lower Po valley and built in the fourth century a great port at Spina (north of Ravenna). Such hydraulic skills, used for the first recorded time in western Europe, produced enormously fertile fields of grain and vineyards (Keller 1975: 175–78). The Po valley later joined Sicily as the two great breadbaskets of the Roman empire. The central territory of the Etruscans, between the Arno and the Tiber, the sea and the Apennines, underwent dramatic transformation around 700 B.C.: "fields, groves, and gardens replaced impenetrable thickets of bushes and trees"; woods were cleared and swamps reclaimed for the plow; mining, shipping, transalpine commerce, and, above all, the building of cities—that "precondition of any higher civilization"—allowed them easily to dominate the "indigenous semi-barbarians," who were herdsmen (Keller 1975: 39, 101).

This depiction of the Etruscans is by a contemporary historian wishing to retrieve them from Roman obfuscation and neglect; but it of course recapitulates in detail just the kind of culture-bringing that the Romans, via the Trojans, will either claim for themselves, or displace, as Virgil does, into a mythic past. According to the same scholar, the ritual for founding and all details of the layout of a city were simply taken over by the Romans from the Etruscans (Keller 1975: 85). Whatever the extent of their debt to the Etruscans or their unwillingness to advertise it, the Romans certainly assimilated the practices and concepts of reducing a wilderness to cultivation as their notion of civilization and found its source in Troy.

Though the exact cultic status of Aeneas in Etruria, as evidenced by the statuettes, remains doubtful, it is generally accepted that he was popular and significant there by the end of the sixth century (see Galinsky 1969 and Scullard 1967). In addition to the depictions of Aeneas carrying his father and the *penates*, there are others showing him in his role of heroic warrior (Galinsky 1969: 125–28). The fusion of these two images—the skilled fighter, the son dutiful in service to and as fertility god—will be of crucial importance to the development of the legend. For they will eventually coalesce into the hero who is both invader and cultivator, imperialist and culture-bringer, military leader and civil architect. For the Etruscans, Aeneas was a hero; for the Latins, a god of agricultural fecundity. Rome inherited both traditions and firmly attached the latter to its invention of Trojan ancestry. Heroes alone were plentiful; but only Aeneas, son of a Venus who had herself become the twin of Ceres, patroness of grain, was the hero who linked military enterprise with the mode of food production and the mode of social organization that constituted the civilization that passed from east to west. When his legend became consciously and officially promoted, beginning with the emperor Augustus, coins minted in the colony of Asia minor called Ilium made all the connections explicit. Heads of Augustus have on their obverse Aeneas carrying Anchises; Troy and Rome herself as personified females appear, like the Great Mother Cybele, with turreted crowns (Wroth 1894: 61–63). The image of the divine patroness has become that of her ultimate product: The cleared field and the regular harvest make possible the city. The supreme city, transplanted by the Trojans, effaces their name and takes (or invents) that of a local eponym, Romulus. But the feminine noun used by the Greeks for the name of Rome (*rhômê*) meant "force."

Other, less important, cultic practices and etymological coincidences also served to link Troy with the pre-Roman Italic peoples. Depicted on a number of figurines and vase paintings found with those of Aeneas in Etruria is a sort of military exercise involving riders on horseback with round shields and a kind of labyrinth. The Etruscan word inscribed on the latter is *truia*; the exercise was known as *lusus Troia*, the "Trojan game" (Alföldi 1964: 278–87; Dury-Moyaers 1981: 146–47). *Troia* was the name of the beach at the mouth of the Numicus, the river over which Aeneas's supposed tomb was built. The Indoeuropean word *troia* meant (as it still does in Italian and in French—*la truie*) sow. This animal was associated with fertility by the Latins and was, as noted earlier, incorporated into the founding story as early as Timaeus.

So Aeneas, predestined in Greek myth to rule over the remnant of the Trojans, brings his *penates* to Italy where he, the son of a Venus already devoted to agricultural production, becomes identified in worship with other local sun and water divinities and is celebrated as a warrior. The famous piety of Aeneas thus results, for the Romans, from the form of worship characteristic of a settled agricultural community, in which the production of grain and the maintenance of cattle are of supreme importance. This Aeneas, inherited by the early historians and by Virgil, is in all respects the founding father of an empire that comes from elsewhere, clears fields, and builds walls. For the later west, of course, he takes his definitive character from Virgil's epic of foundation.

Chapter 3

ॐ

THE EPIC OF HISTORY

Virgil's *Aeneid*

The *Aeneid* is virtually unique among ancient epics in the straightforward-
ness of its direct, commissioned, political purpose: to glorify the creation
of the Roman Empire by Octavian. Neither a tragedy—like the *Iliad* and
the *Beowulf*, an elegy to something great that comes to an end; nor a comedy—
like the adventures and triumphant homecoming of Odysseus; nor yet a massive
compilation of all sorts of narratives—like the *Mahabharata* or the Old Testament,
the structure of Virgil's poem is that of a journey toward an historical destiny that
is already fulfilled. It is a linear teleology that is paradigmatic, in the recent and brilliant analysis of David Quint (1993), for an entire subsequent poetic tradition of
"winners' epics." From the beginning, Virgil places himself and his readers with
the gods—as superior to all the characters in the foreknowledge of the future that
they cannot know—hardly ever relinquishing the perspective of the present from
which everything has already happened.

What makes it happen are the competing wills of the gods, "the high power of
those above" (*alto vi superum*), which, from the first sentence, exile the hero and
make him suffer much,

> until he founds a city
> And brings his gods to Latium: whence the race
> Of Latins, Alban lords, and walls of lofty Rome.
>
> $(1.5-7)^1$

Aeneas knows only that Troy will rise again in Latium (1.205–206), and for him
this is but a hope used to encourage his followers after their shipwreck, while he

---

1. dum conderet urbem
   inferretque deos Latio; genus unde Latinum
   Albanique patres atque altae moenia Romae.

I quote the Loeb text; translations are mine.

himself feels only anxiety. The anxiety is shared by his mother, who requests clarification of Jupiter. He in response summarizes in advance the plot of the poem and recapitulates the historical outcome that it will not narrate: the legendary history of Rome down to the actual history of Augustus's victory in the civil wars (1.257–96). Aeneas, promises Jupiter,

> In Italy shall wage great war and crush
> Ferocious peoples, then for his own folk
> Establish codes of custom, laws, and walls.
>
> (1.263–64)[2]

Generations pass until Romulus founds the walls of Rome and calls its people Romans, on whom, says Jupiter, "I place no bound of time or space; / Empire without end have I given" (1.278–79: *ego nec metas rerum nec tempora pono*; / *imperium sine fine dedi*). Throughout the passage, and the poem, the long chain of historical causation and transmission is kept in view, always to offer an etiology for Rome now, a lengthy pedigree for the names of places and persons. Jupiter here explains, for example, that Ascanius, Aeneas's son, will in the new land become known as Iulus—from Ilus, his name when Ilium flourished—the progenitor of the Julian house and hence of glorious Augustus, who has finally closed the gates of Janus, the temple of war.

Rather more is involved in all this than flattery of the current regime. Though Virgil was made well-off by gifts of property, presumably from Maecenas and Augustus himself, to whom he read a few books of the poem as it was being composed, he designed his epic to focus on larger issues. What these are may be inferred from the poem's retrospective structure and the paramount place of the gods in its action. Both features are uniquely Virgilian, and both produce the text's most notorious problem: the passivity of its hero and the general apparent lack of any human agency in its events. Any founding story, of course, is concerned to provide etiologies for present practices and illustrious descents for present rulers. It is the particular way that Virgil performs this that I call "retrospective"—obliging the reader (or hearer) to share the Olympian perspective from the beginning, and making that perspective all-determinant. The characters in the poem, for all their vicissitudes, play roles we know to be already fixed. Jupiter has both the first and last words on the main outcome; though Venus and Juno struggle throughout the poem to influence this in opposite ways, it all happens—because it all has happened—as Jupiter declares.

Virgil's gods, of course, are very different from Homer's: though they disagree, they never grumble and quarrel as Homer's do; they are never comic, but always dignified. They are separated from humanity not merely by being immortal and capable of assuming whatever shape they like for whatever purpose, like Homer's, but also by governing every aspect of the main action in ways that Homer's never

---

2. bellum ingens geret Italia populosque feroces
   contundet moresque viris et moenia ponet.

do. The plot of the *Iliad* is attributed to the will of Zeus (*dios boulê*, 1.5), but only as a "narrative convention" of oral storytelling (Nagy 1979: 113, 263). Though Zeus is said to apportion both victory and grief (*kratos* and *achos*) to both sides in the conflict, its episodes are always and equally motivated by the actions and reactions of its characters. The motive for the whole plot is Achilles' reaction to an act of Agamemnon's. The divine will in Homer is always mediated through, and is a figure for, human desires. And this will is far from omnipotent: Zeus cannot save his own son, Sarpedon, from his destined death (16.432–34). And the climactic event of the poem, the slaying of Hector, is something that Zeus would prevent if he could; but even he must give way to the scales of fate. The plot of the *Iliad*, in short, is more consented to than decreed by Zeus.

In the *Aeneid*, by contrast, Jupiter has decided everything in advance; all Juno can do is make it tougher for the human actors; she cannot alter the outcome. Though the gods' wills are often mediated through human desires, they remain as often wholly independent of them. The structure of the plot and all the obstacles to its fulfillment are announced and provided by the gods. If it is "so great a task to found the Roman nation" (1.33: *tantae molis erat Romanam condere gentem*), that is directly because of Juno's wrath. The gods arrogate all causality to themselves; they incarnate it. This principle is read back into the retold mythic source of the whole action. Aeneas learns it from his mother, who appears to him in burning Troy as he is about to slay Helen, blaming her for the city's destruction. Not Helen, not Paris are culpable, Venus tells him, but rather "the unkindness of the gods" (2.602: *divum inclementia*), and then she shows him in a vision Neptune, Juno, and Athena busy at their work. The gods in the *Aeneid* are in their structural role not figures of desire at all, but figures of history (see Williams 1983: 35–36). And the poem will demonstrate that history—what has happened and what will happen in the world—is not controlled by will or desire.

The part that the pious hero plays in the great task of foundation is quite remarkably negligible. Aeneas initiates, of his own volition, no course of sustained action in the poem. He reacts to others; he worries, he hesitates; he never, by himself, quite knows what to do. Often under great pressure, his mind wavers, in one famous simile (8.21–25), as a flickering light, reflected from a basin of agitated water, plays over the walls and ceiling of a room. Throughout the poem, he seeks and receives constant encouragement and instruction from gods, furies, prophets, and shades. Generally, he does as they tell him to do, so long as their advice is sufficiently specific. Mere knowledge of the ultimate outcome doesn't help him much. The ghost of his first wife, Creusa, first informs him as he vainly seeks her in crumbling Troy, that he must endure long exile and plow many seas before arriving in Hesperia, "where Lydian Tiber / Flows with gentle motion through rich, well-tended fields" (2.781–82: *ubi Lydius arva / inter opima virum leni fluit agmine Thybris*). But Aeneas has no idea where Tiber is. Having sailed to Delos, he prays to Apollo, who tells him to seek the land of his forefathers (3.94–96). (Dardanus, the founder of Aeneas's house, was, according to Virgil, born in Italy.) Aeneas and his band misinterpret this as Crete, where they duly go. There, the *penates* themselves tell him in a dream that not Crete but Hesperia, lately called Italy, "as mighty in arms as in rich soil" (*potens armis atque ubere glaebae*), is the ancestral place (3.161–66). They sail off and are blown by a storm to an island in the Ionian sea where the eldest of the furies finally confirms that Italy is indeed their goal (3.253). The knowledge that we the readers share with the gods is never available to the characters. For them, destiny is hard to figure. Their and Aeneas's perplexity is understandable. But the imperative to do something is relentless. The formulaic command that Aeneas hears from the fury (3.169) and from old Tiberinus (8.59) is the leitmotif of the dilemma: "arise and act, goddess-born!" (*surge age, nata dea*)

The problem is to know just what to do—and where to do it. The one thing Aeneas knows and repeatedly does is to build walls. About this action there is no dubiety, no need for planning, no debate; he does it, as it were, instinctively. Having built the ships that take them forever from where Troy once was, Aeneas and his people first land in Thrace:

> Here am I brought, and on the curving shore
> First ramparts raise, opposing hostile fates,
> And name it from my name Aeneadae.
>
> > (3.16–18)[3]

Warned by the spirit of Polydorus, a Trojan who was here betrayed by a local king, to leave this place, Aeneas packs off to Delos, receives from Apollo the oracle, which he misreads, and is blown by a favorable wind to Crete. Encouraged by these omens, he sets everyone busily to work:

> Thus eagerly do I erect the chosen
> City's walls and call it Pergamum.
> I urge my people, gladdened by the name,
> To love their hearths and raise their fortress high.
> On the dry shore the ships were all aligned,
> Our youths engaged in weddings and new tillage,
> While I dispensed just laws and civil peace.
>
> > (3.132–37)[4]

This idyll is immediately broken by a pestilence of drought that withers the grass and ruins the crops. In his resulting distress, Aeneas has his instructive dream of the

---

3. feror huc et litore curvo
   moenia prima loco, fatis ingressus iniquis,
   Aeneadasque meo nomen de nomine fingo.

4. ergo avidus muros optatae molior urbis
   Pergameamque voco, et laetam cognomine gentem
   hortor amare focos arcemque attollere tectis.
   iamque fere sicco subductae litore puppes;
   conubiis arvisque novis operata iuventus;
   iura domosque dabam.

penates, which is then confirmed by the fury and is later reinforced in lengthy detail by the prophet Helenus (3.374–462), who tells him exactly how to get to Italy and whom to consult on arrival for further information. Aeneas must be told the stages of his temporal progress (and that of Rome after him); but he has no need to be told his function. He has that down pat: he is a founder; he founds automatically and obsessively. And what he founds is that agrarian, city-building society over which he presided as Italic fertility god. He builds, names, plants, and rules. He is architect, general, cultivator, and judge. He is the bearer of that civilization that came from Troy.

In the poem Aeneas does the one thing he is sure of doing only on these two aborted occasions: foundations not in the destined western land. The foundation for which these are but rehearsals does not take place in the poem; what we might expect to be the logical climax of the plot is not dramatized. Instead, it is subsumed in the sweeping temporal prospects of Rome's whole history that unfold in a variety of ways and circumstances—especially in the visit to the unborn dead of the underworld (bk. 6) and in the pictures on the shield that Venus has Vulcan construct for her son (bk. 8). Withholding the climax by subsuming it in the retrospective structure, like the Olympian point of view, the attribution of all causality to the gods, and the consequent perplexity and passivity of the hero—all are features of a design to focus on the nature of the historical process itself, the problematic place of human beings as historical agents. The epic is not only praise of the newly created empire, though it is that; it is also an account of the cost of that empire and an enactment, in its own structure, of how its own subject—history—gets made.

Troy was, and will remain, destroyed; Rome is (and, Jupiter promises, will remain) the mistress of the known world. In giving definitive literary form to the legend that links these two facts, Virgil retains his inherited hero's symbolic function, as founder, but places him in a kind of narration where he must remain unaware of it. The gods, and we the readers, are aware of it; for us it has all already happened; it is our past. For Aeneas as a character in the poem, it is the unknowable future. Aeneas is twice made to *see* this future, but he cannot understand it; it provides him with no knowledge on the basis of which he can act. The first occasion is the parade of the unborn Roman dead that Anchises shows to him in Hades. After Romulus, Anchises exhibits a female personification of Rome, her seven hills surrounded by a single wall, as Cybele, "the Berecyntian Mother / Borne in her chariot, turret-crowned, through / Phrygian cities" (6.784–85).[5] Anchises goes on to evoke at length the horrors of civil war, but responds to Aeneas's questions by telling him not to ask about such "vast sorrow" (6.868: *ingentem luctum*). The episode concludes with a description of the two gates of sleep: those of horn, through which pass the shadows of truth, and those of ivory, through which "The shades send up false dreams to those above" (6.896: *falsa ad caelum mittunt insomnia Manes*). Anchises dismisses Aeneas and the Sibyl through the ivory gates.

5. qualis Berecyntia mater
   invehitur curru Phrygias turrita per urbes.

Interpreters have long puzzled over this curious and resonant detail: in what sense is the history that Aeneas has been shown "false"? One sense is surely to cast an ironic light on the Augustan triumph the poem celebrates; another may simply be to suggest the illusory status of such underworld visions (see Williams 1983: 47). Yet another, with respect to the place of the hero (for whose sake the spectacle is performed) in the poem, is to suggest that the history might as well be false for all the good it will do him. Like the initial information that his destiny will be found in "Hesperia," it provdes him with no basis for decision or action. His greatest trials and perplexities in war are yet to come, and he will need and get other instructions on how to endure and manage them.

The second view Aeneas gets of the future is the depiction of Rome's wars on the shield of Vulcan (8.626–728), which concludes with the triple triumph of Augustus in 29 B.C. and its long procession of conquered nations from the Nile to the Rhine. Here is Aeneas's reaction:

> All these on Vulcan's shield, his parent's gift,
> He wonders at, and, knowing not the deeds,
> Rejoices in the image, lifting up
> Onto his shoulder all his descendants'
> Fate and fame.
>
> (8.729–31)[6]

Aeneas does not, cannot, know what his own acts will determine. In the gap between his ignorance and our knowledge lies no small part of Virgil's irony: If Aeneas knew, really knew, all that "vast sorrow" his dead father bids him not inquire about, would he act at all? If he knew the history that he will, by founding, determine, could he found it? Is the price of empire, in suffering and mutual slaughter, worth it? Is ignorance of the consequences a necessary precondition for human action in history? Not only does the poem's retrospective structure pose these questions in that gap between its characters and us, who share the knowledge of the gods, but one of its characters who bridges this gap, by dying, makes such questions explicit in an extraordinary plea. Anchises addresses the yet unborn spirits of Julius Caesar and Pompey as sons of his own blood and begs them not to let their country devour herself in civil war (6.832–35). He is asking history not to happen. But it is too late—for him and for us, who know that it's already happened. For Aeneas, it is too soon; he sees and hears but does not know, cannot grasp. Better so: let him not ask; dismiss him through the ivory gate. The ultimate founding, the one that counts, cannot be dramatized in the poem; for then Aeneas would have to know, would have to be as dubiously gifted with foresight as we, the gods, and the dead Anchises are with hindsight, to know the full temporal con-

---

6. Talia per clipeum Volcani, dona parentis,
    miratur rerumque ignarus imagine gaudet,
    attollens umero famamque et fata nepotum.

sequences of what he does. Let him rather shoulder the burden of historical agency unaware—for with awareness, who would bear such a burden, such a fate?

The burden, appropriately, is a weapon of war, radically altered in its iconography from that of its ultimate source in Homer, the shield of Achilles. That shield contains images of all in human life that is *not* war, all that must be left out of that hero's fiercely concentrated excellence: his honor as a warrior. And even Achilles, his wrath satisfied, is touchable at the end by compassion. The shield, and the trajectory, of Aeneas are the opposite. For Aeneas is not just one utterly superlative individual; he is a culture, a whole civilization and its empire. He is the means of transplanting, securing, and extending it; that means is war. Pious Aeneas, the ever-uncertain worrier, the caring general, always compassionate of others' sufferings, even those he is made to cause, like Dido's: this figure so unlike Achilles becomes, at the very end of the poem, as wrathful as he. The echo is of course deliberate: Aeneas, enraged by the sight of his enemy, Turnus, wearing the arms of his fallen comrade, Pallas—just as Achilles saw Hector wearing those of Patroklos—ignores Turnus's dignified surrender and furiously kills him. War fills even pious Aeneas with its fury; even he, at last, succumbs to Juno's furies who have incited the passions of everyone.

The poem ends, or breaks off, suddenly at this point, with the spirit of Turnus winging its way to join the shadows below (12.952), that numberless array of the victims, and perpetrators, of empire. Is the poem really unfinished, as may be inferred from Virgil's instructions for his executors to burn it? Or did he indeed finish it, the instructions referring merely to his fanatical care for polishing and completing the few truncated lines that remain? Whatever the poet's intent, his text seems perfect as it stands. There can be no triumphant, ceremonial conclusion in which Aeneas participates for the same reason that there is no triumphant, climactic scene of the founding. The poem is about history as the *consequences* of actions, which are necessarily unknown to the actors. This is its brilliance and its point. Aeneas is the human actor in history as famously described by Karl Marx (1934: 10): "Men make their own history, but they do not make it just as they please; they do not make it under circumstances chosen by themselves, but under circumstances directly encountered, given, and transmitted, from the past." The circumstances under which Aeneas unknowingly makes history are directly encountered, given, and transmitted, from the gods. The poem has, in fact, already ended—just as it began—with Jupiter obliging Juno to accept the empire he decreed in book 1 (12.818–40). In a final concession to her wrath, which has caused all the wars in Italy, Jupiter agrees that the name of Troy shall disappear, that the new nation, united by a single language, will keep its indigenous name of Latins. Satisfied, Juno quits the field, and with her goes any cause or motivation for further narrative. The story has been told. Jove has only one detail to mop up—withdrawing Juturna's aid from her brother Turnus—to ensure the victory of Aeneas and his allies over the Rutulians. Turnus resigns Lavinia—whose possession was the immediate occasion of the war—to Aeneas in his gracious speech; the dynasty has begun. And the actual end of the poem

is the single act of passion that Aeneas commits in it—a killing that is almost irrelevant, now that all has been decided; a final ironic coda to Jove's symphony; the last,
and noblest, victim of its composition.

Jove has stated the theme of his symphony at the outset, and has clashed the
cymbals at its close. In between, he has left many details of its orchestration to his
subordinates, mainly Juno and Venus, intervening himself only when their temporary collusion threatens to halt its majestic progress in Carthage. The gods, in
the poem, cause history. They and their messengers provide for its human actors
the necessary instruction, in the case of the hero, and the necessary motivation to
oppose him, in the case of his opponents. Virgil, it is usually and reasonably presumed, as a neoteric and an admirer of Lucretius, highly educated in the rhetoric
and philosophy of his age, did not believe in the literal existence of the gods. Why,
then, are they all-determinant in the poem? The critics of the European enlightenment, delighting in Newton's demonstration of a mechanistically perfect universe, called the supernatural creatures of ancient epic the "machinery." They
meant this usually in the somewhat slighting and condescending sense of cogs and
gears and wheels—mere instruments, easily replaceable by others, to transmit force
elsewhere generated. But Virgil's gods are in fact machines in our present sense—
not available either to Romans or Londoners of Pope's time: they are engines; they
generate the action of the poem; they make it go. Like Pope and us, Virgil lived
in an age whose intellectual avant-garde preened itself on being emancipated from
myth, having matured into more sophisticated and self-conscious fictions, even,
like us, into "realism." But Virgil saw farther, and so designed his poem to demonstrate the still constitutive power of myth, of fiction itself, to determine perception and therefore to make history.

The gods—and all their subordinate messengers, their oracles and spokesper-
sons—in the *Aeneid* are history as what has already happened. They are the past,
seen with hindsight, as organized into causal and explanatory narrative. They are
what we know and how we know it only after the fact. They are, literally, fictions: the kind of stories we tell ourselves to order the past. They tell Aeneas what
to do, and he does it, thus determining a future that he cannot know. Though in
the poem we are made to share the knowledge of the gods, in life we are Aeneas,
necessarily unable to share it, perplexed and hesitant. Yet he, and we, must act—
so we do what we are told; we enact the stories of our past, and so reproduce the
version of it that the stories give us. One foundation follows another. This is the
historical process that Virgil's great poem presents. History gets made by people
enacting stories. We in the west will make ours in large part by enacting this one,
the very story that Virgil himself is (re)telling, our founding legend.

Chapter 4

༄

THE CENTER OF THE *AENEID*

The Arrival of the Culture-Bringers

The structural climax of the founding story is the arrival of the invading cultivators from the east in the western promised land. This scene is the moment of fulfillment in the narrative when the long-delayed end of the journey is reached, when the prophecies come true. Though many complications follow, as many have preceded, this moment, it is the raison d'être of the story: to bring the eastern exiles to the seat of future empire. The moment is as crucial to the story's meaning as to its structure, for it introduces the problem of what the relationship is to be between the heroic invaders—the predestined rulers—of this place and its local population—those already there, the aboriginal inhabitants. In Aeneas's two misplaced foundations—of Aeneadae and Pergamum—this problem did not arise; these sites were either uninhabited or deserted. The problem is reserved, appropriately, for the site that counts, the ultimate, predestined one.

In the *Aeneid*, the moment of arrival is complex and diffuse, occurring in two stages: the landing in Latium and the embassy to Latinus's palace (bk. 7), and the final penetration up the Tiber to the actual site of Rome (bk. 8). The importance of the moment is signaled in part by its very diffusion, but more obviously by its central placement in the poem and the reinvocation of the muse (7.37–44) to aid the poet in his now larger task and greater subject. This greater subject is the "terrible wars" (7.41: *horrida bella*), the battle narratives that occupy most of the poem's second half. For the initial relationship to the indigenes, occasioned by alliance with one royal house, will be war against the rest.

The end of their journey is made clear to the travelers by the comic fulfillment of the prophecy that they will be reduced to eating their tables. Camping on the coast, they are inspired by Jupiter to place their scanty meat and vegetables on thin, flat cakes (Virgil never uses the ordinary word for "bread"; here as elsewhere the staff of life in any form is *Cereale* or *Cererem*—the capitalized gifts of Ceres), which they then also consume. Iulus jests that they're even eating their tables, whereupon Aeneas recalls the prophecy and rejoices that they have discovered their home and

29

fatherland (7.110–34). Aeneas prays, in order, to Tellus—the earth (female), "first of gods,"—then to Jove, the "Phrygian Mother" (Cybele), and his parents (135–40). The discovery is confirmed by Jove thundering from a blazing cloud, and the Trojans excitedly conclude that "The day had come to found their promised walls" (145: *advenisse diem, quo debita moenia condant*).

There follows the embassy to King Latinus, who, already enlightened by prophecy, will welcome the Trojans and promise Aeneas his daughter Lavinia. The Latins, we learn, are a "nation of Saturn" (7.203) and live in a city where Latinus's lofty palace of a hundred columns is redolent of their history and contains images of their gods: Italus and his father Sabinus, planter of vines, shown with a pruning-hook (178–79). Aeneas is thus confronted on his arrival in the western promised land not with a race of savage boors but with a society of settled hierarchy and ancient agrarian traditions like his own. And it is destined, of course, to become united to his own. Virgil pays tribute, throughout the second half of the poem, to all the presumed ancestral strains of the contemporary Roman nobility: Etruscan and Latin as well as Trojan. History, as Jove decrees it in the poem, had decided which of the local populations would be assimilated to, and which extirpated by, the new order.

The extirpation gets underway with Juno unleashing the forces of hell (7.312) to plunge the entire region into war. The fury she summons fills Turnus's mother with rage at the breaking of his betrothal to Lavinia, inspires him to organize resistance to the Trojan invaders, and provides the triggering event in the slaughter of Silvia's stag by Ascanius. One of the victims of the resultant skirmish is an old farmer (who tries to make peace), the richest and most respected in Ausonia, who had five flocks of goats, five herds of cattle, and fields worked by a hundred plows (7.538–39). Juno dismisses the fury, well knowing that since blood will have blood (554) this skirmish will suffice to inflame the whole region. So it does; the Latins demand a declaration of war.

Virgil takes the opportunity to explain the Ausonian origin of the custom, now followed by great Rome herself, of opening the gates of the Temple of Janus (7.601–15)—gates within which, we recall, *Furor* still rages though shut up by Augustus (1.290). The poet narrates the whole ceremony as performed against a wide range of Rome's enemies between then and now. Such etiologies are not only part of the very purpose of a legend, but are used consistently by Virgil to keep the present before our eyes as a consequence of the past. With respect to this particular ritual, and to the whole situation of war in Italy among its own peoples, the retrospective strategy powerfully recalls the preceding two centuries during which the gates of Janus never closed, as well as the civil wars won by Octavian, those wars that Anchises begged his sons not to start. The telescoping of time—narrating an "origin" that, though past, is continually reenacted right up to "now"—occurs in the very grammar of the narration. "There was a custom" (601: *mos erat*), it begins; and after the custom is described, Latinus "was ordered" (617: *iubebatur*) to perform it. These verbs in the past tense, those of the story of origin, literally enclose the account of the ceremony of declaring war, all of which is told in the present tense.

Virgil's habitual telescoping of time gives particular significance to what is ordinarily called, as a tense, the "historical present": not only is the present a consequence of the past; not only does the past bound the present, setting its limits; not only is the past thus always present—but both together, merged in continual reenactment, are only too likely to constitute the future. This implication is here the more powerful for remaining unstated: *Furor* is still, is always, present in this empire, just waiting to get out.

In the resumption of the story of origin, the enlightened Latinus, wishing the Trojan alliance, refuses to let him out. So Juno does it, with her own hand smashing open the gates of war (7.621–22). And so five mighty cities begin forging weapons. Virgil describes this in a typical and resonant lament for the worst effect of war in general and civil war in particular: the destruction of agriculture (prefigured by the most considerable victim of the skirmish), the turning of plowshares into swords.

> They hollow out safe coverings for the head,
> Bend willow frames for shields; breastplates of bronze
> Or smooth and glinting greaves they hammer out
> From ductile silver: for this, all honor
> Ceased to coulter and to scythe; for this,
> All passion ended for the plow.
>
> (7.632–36)[1]

The poet's own experience, of course, had alerted him to this central paradox in the picture of civilization and its transmission that he himself is handing down to the modern west. "Culture"—of grain and grapes, of poems and philosophies—requires peace; but the means of transplanting both kinds is most often war. Virgil was dispossessed of his patrimonial farm near Mantua in a general seizure of lands on which to resettle the veterans of Philippi. He had fictionalized the pathos of such dispossession in his first published work (*Eclogues* 1 and 9). Later, at the request of Maecenas, he spent seven years producing the most elegantly versified set of farming instructions ever written, the *Georgics*, in order to lend high cultural prestige to the cultivation of the earth, to encourage precisely the agricultural labor devastated or neglected during the civil wars. The first *Georgic* itself (which teaches the tillage of grain; the other three treat, in order, vines and fruits, herds, and bees) ends with a similar lament for the failure to honor the plow, for melting pruninghooks into swords. Virgil is indeed central to European civilization, as T. S. Eliot proclaimed, not least because he responded so powerfully to its basis in agricultural production.

1. tegmina tuta cavant capitum flectuntque salignas
   umbonum cratis; alii thoracas aenos
   aut levis ocreas lento ducunt argento;
   vomeris huc et falcis honos, huc omnis aratri
   cessit amor.

Here, that basis, and the lament for its destruction, are read back through the centuries into the arrival scene of the founding story. The arrival has precipitated war; and the rest of book 7 gives the muster, collectively and individually, of the warriors. All flock to their general, Turnus, "and leave the wide fields bare of husbandmen" (8.8: *et latos vastant cultoribus agros*). Aeneas witnesses these preparations with mounting dismay, the Trojans being obviously and greatly outnumbered. In his perplexity he gets, as usual, specific instructions and consoling prophecy from a god, this time from the river-spirit, Tiberinus (8.36–65). The prophecy is that he shall directly find the white sow with her thirty piglets, who will indicate the place where Ascanius, in thirty years, will found Alba Longa. The instructions are to sail up the Tiber and seek alliance with King Evander and his Arcadians, who live in a city on the hills. Aeneas obeys with alacrity, equipping his galleys, finding the sow and sacrificing her to Juno, rowing night and day up the river.

As the Trojans finally glimpse Evander's settlement, the tenses of Virgil's verbs perform in a single sentence the telescoping of time that will, throughout the episode, evoke Rome as she now is at the moment when Aeneas is seeing her as she is not, but was. Careful reading here becomes vertiginous, as the language attributes to the characters what not they, but only we, can see. From afar, the Trojans "see" (*vident*—present) walls, a fortress, and the scattered roofs of houses, which "now" the power of Rome "has lifted" (*aequavit*—perfect) to the sky, but which poor domain Evander "was then ruling" (*habebat*—imperfect: 7.98–100).[2] The perfect tense is used for the reader's present and for the future of the characters; the present tense is used for the characters' present (which it cannot be), and the reader's past; the continuous past, more conventionally, returns us to the characters' present. Our present is both our past and their future; their present and their future is our past. The grammar is yet clear, kept so by temporal adverbs and strict subordination; we can figure it out. The dizziness lies in the rapid transition from one temporal perspective to another; all are virtually conflated at this moment when the Trojans first see the site of Rome and those sky-reaching walls which, though they aren't there yet, are there for us. They have arrived, and the great edifices of Rome now will continue to spring up, in the poet's language, by the magic of his temporal prestidigitation. There is no need to dramatize the formal founding; the consequence is present at the arrival.

The Trojans land at the site of the cattle market in Augustan Rome, are recognized and warmly welcomed by Evander, and participate in his celebratory feast to Hercules. A temple to Hercules and one to Ceres flanked the great altars of the marketplace in Virgil's day. Evander then takes them on a tour of the not yet extant but constantly evoked city.[3] The glory and wealth of Rome now—its golden

2. cum muros arcemque procul ac rara domorum
   tecta vident, quae nunc Romana potentia caelo
   aequavit, tum res inopes Euandrus habebat.

3. The exact locations and itinerary are worked out in the commentaries: see Conington and Nettleship 1883, Gransden 1976, Eden 1975, Fordyce 1977. The most telling detail appears to be that Evander's hut is located on the Palatine just where Augustus's famously modest house then stood.

towers and temples—are continually juxtaposed to the poverty and rusticity of Rome then—the low dwellings, bristling thickets, and mooing cows. It is typical of Virgil that he should at this moment of structural and geographical fulfillment in the narrative evoke the splendor of the city in a context that implies a moral criticism of it: the dignity and simplicity of Evander and his community (who appear to be herdsmen) and his caution to Aeneas to become worthy of a god by daring to scorn riches (8.364). As usual, the temporal perspective of the present, from which this advice is derived and to which it is directed, makes it superfluous for the hero. Aeneas reacts to the sightseeing tour much as he does to the pictures on his shield: he admires without knowing.

The temporal telescoping, however, that extends this narrative moment forward—the tour of Rome's present that Aeneas cannot know—also extends it backward, to encompass the legendary history of this place on the seven hills— stories about Rome's past that he can know and delights to hear (8.312). Evander tells these to him: in one extended and one brief story, the Arcadian King recounts one episode in and then the original moment of the bringing of culture to the seven hills of Rome. Again, the diffusion of the moment is remarkable: the climax of the founding story that withholds the actual founding is pushed forward through our past to our present and at the same time is shoved backward through a more remote past to a myth. Such is Virgil's brilliant grasp of history unfolding as the enactment of stories.

Evander is well placed to tell these stories, since he is the current representative of the hero they all incarnate: a culture-bringer, social organizer, and ruler from the east now settled in the promised land of the story that Virgil is telling. He is one in a chain of such heroes, whose chronological succession is as follows: Saturn—Hercules—Evander—Aeneas—Augustus. He is the central one, the pivot, and it is through him that Aeneas, and we, learn about the earlier two. In the longer story, told first, Evander, explaining why his community worships Hercules, narrates how that hero slew in this place the cave-dwelling, semihuman monster Cacus, who had stolen some cattle (8.185–275). Cacus, a son of Vulcan, is otherwise indigenous; he lived, breathing fire, in a cavern reeking of blood under the cliff by the Tiber where Evander tells the story, which commemorates his people's deliverance from their terror of this chthonic monster. Hercules lifts away a huge rock, almost a mountain, exposing his den, and braves the smoke pouring from his throat to enter and strangle him. The cattle are liberated, and the people marvel at the features of the brutish corpse, "the rough bristles / on the chest of the half-man, half-beast" (8.265–67: *villosaque saetis / pectora semiferi*).

This is of course but one of Hercules' numerous exploits (others of which are mentioned in the worship service), but it is a resonant one in the context of the arrival. Cacus is already there, a native inhabitant, and is a cattle thief and murderer with superhuman powers; the Arcadians consequently require superhuman assistance to get rid of him. He lives in the earth, which conceals him from ordinary perception; cliff-removing technology—in the form of Hercules' strength—is necessary to uproot him. He is one figure of the indigene, identified with the land in this place where those golden towers will one day appear. That they may appear, he must be displaced. So the earth-dwelling, fire-breathing monster is killed and dragged into the light of day, where his now harmless but horrifying body (in a passage that later poets will remember) becomes an object of wonder. And the place becomes fit for human habitation and the unmolested pasturage of cattle. It seems possible that the story records some ancient memory of a volcano that extinguished itself in a final, cataclysmic, eruption. It is also tempting to read it as a sort of Lucretian allegory for those natural forces that are so terrifying when we do not know their causes—here the cause, mastered by being destroyed, is exposed and known, extinguished and dead. No longer a threat, it can be closely inspected, can become an object of knowledge. But in the context of its telling, the most striking feature of the story is what must be done to the land and its native indwellers before it can become the site of empire, the locus of civilization.

It is precisely this feature of the story that is the main point of the next, briefer, story that Evander tells Aeneas when, the worship of Hercules concluded, they set off on their tour. This story is the final backward shove of history into myth, the very beginning, the ultimate founding, the original moment of culture-bringing to the seven hills of Rome. And the teller of the first foundation is himself a founder:

> Then King Evander speaks,
> The founder of the citadel of Rome:
> "These groves belonged to native Fauns and Nymphs
> And men from tree trunks born, from hardy oak,
> Who had no code of custom and no culture,
> And knew not how to yoke the ox, collect
> Or store the yield, but fed on branches' fruits
> And victuals of toilsome hunting."

The culture-bringer to these aborigines was the god Saturn, who

> Gathered in one place this ignorant race,
> Scattered through mountain heights, and gave them laws.

(8.313–22)[4]

There are three linked features in this description of the indigenous folk that will determine western perceptions of them forever after:

---

4. tum rex Euandrus, Romanae conditor arcis:
   "haec nemora indigenae Fauni Nymphaeque tenebant
   gensque virum truncis et duro robore nata,
   quis neque mos neque cultus erat, nec iungere tauros
   aut componere opes norant aut parcere parto,
   sed rami atque asper victu venatus alebat. . . .
   is genus indocile ac dispersum montibus altis
   composuit legesque dedit."

1. They are identified with the landscape they inhabit; here the identification takes its strongest, most archaic form: they are autochthonous, literally "sprung from the land itself."
2. They are totally uncivilized, have no fixed abode, no social conventions nor arts *because* they do not plow, plant, harvest, and store, but instead:
3. They live by gathering and hunting.

All these features of course derive from various, and competing, global theories of human origins and progress toward civilization that were current in classical myth and philosophy. As the commentaries inform us, Virgil has plundered texts from Hesiod to Lucretius (see Lovejoy and Boas 1935 for relevant excerpts) to present this picture of the indigenes as the autochthonous siblings of forest-dwelling spirits, who do not know how to constitute a human society because they do not cultivate the earth in a settled way. Evander's discourse, however, does not offer this depiction as a global theory, but as local (mythic, of course) history: this is what the inhabitants of this place once were, the indigenes of these groves, their original possessors (*tenebant*).

They were savages, and they were civilized by Saturn, the Roman god of agriculture, which brings with it socioculture. He fixes them in one place, this god of the plow and ancestor of Latinus, present king of "Saturn's nation," and thus supplies their total lack of *mos, cultus*, and legal order. His intervention is benevolent, and ushers in a very brief golden age, which is then dissipated by greed and warfare into the usual chaos of history (8.324–27), in the course of which the place often changed its original name, *Saturnia tellus* (329). The slide from peaceable cultivation to the violence of war is quick and easy. Its cause is repeatedly named, throughout the bellicose preparations in the narrative present of books 7 and 8, by the same name as the civilized ideal it destroys. Saturnia is Juno herself, early identified with the Greek Hera, consort of Zeus/Jupiter, queen of the gods, and daughter of Cronos, later identified by the Romans with their culture-bringing Saturn. Juno, a daughter of Time, unleashes the furies of war. A little time is all it takes to dismantle the golden age; the Saturnia that is settled agricultural civilization is doomed by another Saturnia. The identity of the name suggests that the activities are inseparable: our civilization is self-doomed; our clearing and planting and wall-building entails, somehow necessitates, violence, war, destruction.

Civilized life, as we value it, as Virgil's language here implies, *is* war. The original moment of civilizing, by means of agri- and socioculture-bringing, is displaced into Rome's mythic past, whence it immediately degenerates into Rome's historical past. Hence the need for the repeated foundings, the chain of heroes, and the diffusion of both through time when the site of empire is reached. For Virgil, civilization is fragile and constantly menaced (self-menaced, by another Saturnia), always needing to be reachieved. Most of book 8 narrates its successive reachievements in this place by those heroes who come from elsewhere: in the mythic past, Saturn and Hercules; in the narrative present, Evander and Aeneas; in the unremittingly implied (and actual) future, Augustus. It is reachieved by the establishment of peace (lawgiving), but such peace as necessarily follows war.

Those against whom Aeneas must war are not, indeed, savage indigenes, but people who have already received the kind of civilization that he bears and Rome inherits—therein lies much of the pathos of the second half of the poem. But the Latins, along with the Etruscans and Rutulians, have perhaps not received quite enough of it, or have degenerated from it. For there are clear indications that they are on a lower cultural level than the cosmopolitan Trojans. Few Latin warriors are properly equipped: most throw lead pellets, wear wolfskin caps, and go half-barefoot (7.685–90). In battle, these "rustic" (*agrestis*) ranks are but an hors d'oeuvre for Aeneas (10.310–11). One commentator can thus infer that the association between the Trojans and Evander's Greeks shows "the need for alliance between the cultivated nations to bring civilization to the rude Italians" (Fordyce 1977: xxvi). In the ever-evoked future, the Italians may get civilized; but in the narrative present, most of them get dead. Virgil is more aware than some of his commentators of the cost of achieving our particular form of civilization. And his presentation of rusticity, in the form it takes among those very Greeks—the humble frugality and dignity of Evander and his Arcadians—has positive values that rebuke those of the achieved empire. The inference, however, is typical and is authorized not by the way Virgil tells the story but simply by the story he tells: the cultivated bring civilization to the rude. Virgil questions and problematizes these categories; he investigates their meaning and operation; the myth doesn't. The power of the myth, its centrality to western culture, is, I suggest, partly responsible for Virgil's immense prestige; it is also responsible for a general subsequent blindness to the brilliant skills that deserve the prestige by modifying the myth.

In sum, it would be hard to overestimate either the intelligence or the complexity and ambivalence of Virgil's founding epic. But it would be hardly possible to overestimate its influence on the subsequent literature and history of the occident. The influence, of course, is exercised a great deal more by the story than by the way he tells it. For example, of the many more or less direct imitations of the *Aeneid* that will both extend the story to and regard it for about a millennium as the history of most of Europe, none will reproduce those features of its structure and language that focus on the problematic role of the human actor in the historical process. None will present, as Virgil does, history getting made by the enacting of stories. None will consequently depict the arrival of the culture-bringers with anything like Virgil's techniques of diffusion, telescoping, and displacement. All, on the contrary, will simply narrate it as a single event—bang, it happens once and the empire marches on. But what will happen that once will be what Virgil located in the mythic past. The hero will encounter indigenes who are either monsters or savages (or sometimes a combination of the two). The intervention of the human culture-bringers, since they are not gods, like Saturn, will never be benevolent for the indigenes who are either to be assimilated to the invaders or crushed by them. Historical actors, as well as writers of history and poets, will prove to be more like Aeneas than Virgil. They will enact only as much of the story as they can understand. They will make history under circumstances transmitted from the past, which include this legend of the transmission of empire and culture. Virgil's great poem itself demonstrates and investigates the process by which it will be interpreted, imitated, and (re)enacted. All its nuances and subtleties will be lost as westward the course of empire takes its way.

Part II

THE LEGEND AS HISTORY

IN THE MIDDLE AGES

Chapter 5

THE LEGEND AND THE LANDSCAPE

Agri- and Other Cultures

The founding legend as Virgil told it became for the remaining few centuries of late classical antiquity the supreme poem of the supreme poet. The *Aeneid* was the model of Latin eloquence in schoolrooms and was enshrined in temples for consultation by priests. Different philosophical schools vied with each other in reading out of the poem allegories of their own particular doctrines. Virgil himself was regarded as a divine oracle and became an object of cultic worship. Thus did the destiny of the writer reenact that of his hero, both becoming exemplary of, even a synecdoche for, the entire culture that Rome inherited from Troy.

This immense cultural prestige could not rest unclaimed by either party in the ensuing struggles between paganism and emergent Christianity. Each side continued to the end of the fourth century to mine the Virgilian oeuvre and ape the Virgilian style in defense of its own position. But the assimilation of the poet to the new religion, and consequently the survival of his texts in the medieval west, had been secured early in the fourth century by no less a personage than the emperor Constantine. To the first Christian Roman emperor, desirous of maintaining the unity of the empire even as he moved its capital to Constantinople, the writings of Virgil could not be consigned to the old dispensation, but had to be claimed to be perfectly consistent with, because prophetic of, the new. Since they had long been regarded as the sum of all wisdom, practical, theological, and prophetic, it remained only for Constantine to maintain that what they prophesied was in fact the comings (both first and second) of Christ.

In an oration made to the Council of Nicaea in 325 and preserved by Eusebius, Constantine gives the detailed explication of Virgil's fourth *Eclogue* that resulted in its being known to subsequent tradition as the "Messianic" eclogue. The poem, which rather playfully predicts the coming of the Golden Age as the result of a son to be born to some noble Roman (never convincingly identified), is presented as the crowning testimony of the ancient world to the divinity of Christ.

In it, says Constantine, the "prince of Latin poets" divined the sacred truth and occulted it in allegory. The birth it celebrates is that of Jesus; the Golden Age looked
forward to is that of his Second Coming; the child's glorious career adumbrates
the massive conversions to Christ and the founding of his church; the poem's conclusion addresses "the divine spirit" in gratitude for its "sure promise of immortality" (Zimmermann 1822: 1099–1103). The habits of prophetically allegorical reading were well established in both Hellenistic and biblical interpretation, and
Constantine exploited them to naturalize the singer of Rome's political empire as
a proleptic citizen of her new spiritual one. The Holy Roman Empire could possess Virgil not only as the finest user of the language of its church, but also as the
diviner of the truth it preached.

This assimilation was, and would remain, sufficiently complete to make Virgil
Dante's natural choice as a guide through the Roman Catholic underworld of
much later development. Nor did the *Aeneid* ever lose its position as the model of
Latin perfection in the schoolrooms of the western world. Between the fourth and
the fourteenth centuries, however, schoolrooms were few and far between in the
Europe of the "barbarian" invasions, the collapse of the old empire, and the gradual development of feudal society. That society, one of its historians reminds us,
was during most of its formation necessarily rural in character; the growth of
towns to the extent that would create the differentiated occupations and activities
of an urban world did not occur until the end of the twelfth century (Duby 1973:
370–72). Throughout this period, with the exception of a few centers of monastic learning, Virgil and his epic were names rather than books. From such manuscript fragments as survive—mainly those of commentaries on the *Aeneid* by
Servius and T. C. Donatus—scholars infer the continued reproduction of Virgil's
text and explain the absence of contemporary copies of it by postulating its simple demise from wear and tear (Holtz 1985).[1] Whatever the case, the founding
story was generally known rather by résumé and reputation than by detailed study.
Virgil's version was conflated with others, and with myriad oral traditions that we
can only guess at concerning the migrations and conquests of the various tribes
that the Romans called barbarians, and against whom they fortified their borders—
on the Danube, the Rhine, the Tweed, and the Welsh marches.

With respect to the survival of Virgil's texts in the Middle Ages, there is another
fact, another absence, that suggests the intricate relation between legends and life,
between literary tradition and social formation. This is simply the complete neglect,
or ignorance, of the *Georgics*. One scholar, having observed this, finds it easy to
understand because the relation of people to the earth has changed entirely: in feudal society there were no gentleman-farmers; serfs, the actual cultivators, couldn't
read, and their lords saw land only as prey for conquest. Virgil's profound feelings

---

1. The eight surviving fourth- and fifth-century manuscripts that are the basis of Virgil's text today
do not appear to have been employed before the Renaissance. Fragments of commentaries exist from
the seventh century, nearly all made in the British Isles, though the earliest surviving medieval texts (in
cursive script) date from the early ninth century.

for the cultivation of the land and the continuity of its maintenance and possession were wholly lacking in Germanic tribes (Grimal 1985: 414–16). No doubt they were, and the more so when we consider that the feudal lords temporal were themselves mostly illiterate. A rural military (or even clerical) aristocracy, centered on the self-sufficient manor (or abbey) and its village, is not the kind of social organization—the urban agglomeration dependent upon a surplus-producing agriculture—that generated the legend in the ancient world, and will eventually regenerate it in the modern. One form of intensive cultivation—of land—generates another—of letters. Small wonder, therefore, that these ages seem scarcely civilized to later observers, especially to the Renaissance humanists who defined them as a historical period of terrible degradation ("dark" ages) between ("middle" ages) the grandeur of classical Rome and the present moment of desire for its recovery. The idea of civilization that thus condemns the period is precisely that of the legend, the founding story that the period itself transmitted and elaborated. What it did not elaborate was, of course, just that aspect of the legend used to condemn it: the links between the cultivation of crops and tastes, between high towers and high literacy.

These links begin to be restored to the legend only when the landscape of Europe begins to permit their comprehension. And the legend in all its aspects will receive its fullest elaboration (in England and France) only after the massive improvements in agricultural productivity that will result (particularly in England and France) in the greatly increased population and the town-centered life of the twelfth century. Until then, it is hardly surprising that the legend remained largely undeveloped, serving merely to connect the contemporary world with an ancient lineage whose prestige is obvious but amorphous, a vague notion of glory whose cultural import is scarcely grasped. For the form of civilization that the legend defines and celebrates did not exist in Europe for about eight centuries. It took that long for whatever combination of planting, herding, hunting, gathering, trading, and marauding that constituted the subsistence of "barbarian" life to give way to intensive, surplus-producing agriculture. It took that long for the forests that sustained the variety of "barbarian" occupations to be cleared for massive and permanent planting. And *why* this even occurred at all no one really knows.

Until recently, no one ever bothered to ask the question. Only lately have some anthropologists begun to criticize the assumption that to cultivate was simply "inherent in human nature," the inevitable teleology of the race (Harris 1977: 181). It didn't require explanation. Recent researches, as well as common sense, suggest that it does. Observation of present-day hunting and gathering social groups reveals that mode of life to be more efficient than exclusive cultivation: it secures a more varied, reliable, and all-seasonal diet for less work (Cohen 1977: 141). In total opposition to the unexamined cliché (which will arise in early modernity) that forest-ranging savages—i.e. hunting and gathering societies—lead arduous and precarious lives, present observations find that the members of such societies work only from two to five hours a day to secure their food (Harris 1977: 179). By contrast, agriculture is hard, unending, and, in capricious climates like those of transalpine Europe, often unrewarding work. Why do it? Why abandon multiple, and easier, sources of subsistence for principal reliance on one that, when it failed, as it often had to, being at the mercy of the weather, brought catastrophic famines? Above all, why clear those millions of hectares of forest in the first place? According to one estimate, France by 1300 contained one million *more* hectares of arable land than it does now (Gimpel 1975: 80). Imagine how many man-hours of labor, felling trees and pulling stumps with hand tools and oxen, filled those eight centuries to produce the landscape that Shakespeare would have one of his fifteenth-century noblemen call "this best garden of the world" (*Henry V* 5.2.36). Why all this occurred is not self-evident.

It seems reasonable to doubt that this age-long transformation of the western European landscape from forest to garden would have occurred at all were it not for the picture of civilization transmitted to those less salubrious climes by the ancient Mediterranean world. And the remaking of the northern landscape to conform to that honorific southern model—another way of describing the abandonment of roving "barbarism" for settled "civilization"—certainly required the coercion of an enormous labor force, and consequently a social system that could coerce it. What typical Visigoth, what average Burgundian, what normal Frank—and it took over a score of their generations—would *choose* to give up a life of casual labor and energetic plunder for one of unremitting and backbreaking work? Seen from the perspective of the individual barbarian, the transition to our form of "civilization" appears most unlikely. That it was in fact unlikely is suggested by how long it took, as well as by the nature and demise of the first so-called "empire" it produced—that of Charlemagne.

Centered in the upper Rhineland in the fifth century, the territory nominally controlled by the Franks extended by 814 from the Channel to the Oder and the Danube (excepting Brittany), from Flensburg to Rome and the Pyrenees. Though famous for importing the British monks who stimulated the "Carolingian Renaissance," the Frankish empire did little but exact tribute from conquered territories. Its warriors were neither settlers, cultivators, nor city-builders. Charlemagne himself, despite his achievements both military and administrative, and despite his being crowned emperor by the pope in 800, did not much resemble the Augustus to whom he was frequently compared. Indeed, the plan he drew up in 806 for dividing his realm among his three sons—a typically Germanic custom—implies that he regarded it not at all in the Roman way, but simply as the traditional spoils, if rather larger than most, of a Saxon ring-giver's enterprise. (The plan, of course, was frustrated by the deaths of two of the sons before his own, and the third inherited the empire alone, only to preside over its dissolution.) Even more remarkable is the absence of any claim to Trojan/Roman ancestry for Charlemagne in Einhard's hagiographical panegyric on his life. Although some of its passages are simply copied from Suetonius's life of Augustus, there is no mention of the already standard lineal derivation of the Franks from the Trojans; instead, Einhard plunges right into Charlemagne's immediate Merovingian forebears, ignoring any genealogy of either the tribe or the royal house (Halphen 1967). The Roman legacy, the idea of the Roman *imperium*, is there in the model of Augustus; but it is given no direct connection with either its legendary past in Troy or the actual career and practices of Charlemagne.

That the Trojan connection was already available (as we shall soon see) but remained unused by Charlemagne's "official" biographer clearly indicates that the legend had not yet acquired the ubiquitous force and presence that it soon would. (For in other texts written both during and after his lifetime, Charlemagne is solemnly proclaimed a son of Priam: see Tanner 1993: 70–71, and Goez 1958: 77). I think it had not yet acquired force precisely because its full cultural meaning remained obscure and, indeed, irrelevant in an "empire" based not on an urban center, dependent on intensive agriculture, but rather on a kind of seminomadic militarism, dependent on what local resources force could extort. Of course Charlemagne had himself built a throne and a palace—but he was very seldom in it. And the landscape through which he tirelessly traveled was not yet the garden that English kings so coveted in the fourteenth and fifteenth centuries.

The achievement of that garden raises again the question of the labor that created it—as well as its models in the ancient world. For the kind of intensive, massively producing agriculture that feeds the city and underwrites our notion of civilization seems always to have required some form of coerced labor. Though the size of agricultural estates in the ancient Greek and Roman worlds appears to have fluctuated considerably, their workers, the people who actually tilled the soil, were outright slaves, prisoners of war, or serfs. Free day labor might be hired to help with harvests, but the vast bulk of the labor force, then and throughout the Middle Ages, worked not by choice but by compulsion. Though local arrangements of serfdom—rights, services, tributes—varied greatly in both periods, the principle did not: the laborer was bound to labor, and one of the primary functions of the municipal, national, imperial state or the feudal baron was to keep him at it. As a legal institution, serfdom ended in England a little before it was introduced in eastern Europe; it lasted in parts of the Habsburg monarchy until 1848 and in Russia until 1861. The very gradual and uneven emergence of a freeholding peasant class, tilling the soil mainly in its own interests, first in England and later in parts of continental Europe, would finally produce the sturdy, independent, "yeoman" farmer of much extolled virtue, who, with the addition of some education, would become the model citizen of Thomas Jefferson's infant Republic. The attractiveness of this image, itself a downward social scaling of the gentleman-farmer of Athens and of Rome, has often served to obscure the fact that through most of our recorded history the people who own the land and the people who intensively cultivate it are usually not the same people.

The paradox that our kind of urban refinement has always rested economically on the coerced agricultural labor of an underclass has produced a variety of contradictory cultural and social attitudes. That profound feeling for agriculture expressed in the *Georgics*, so powerfully revived and indeed practiced by the likes of Jefferson in America, was in both eras the instrument of state propaganda, a deliberate effort to inculcate the values appropriate to the settlement and intensive cultivation of rural or wilderness areas. And against the idealized image thus produced of the gentleman or independent yeoman farmer has always existed the amused contempt of city-dwellers for the rustics who actually till the soil. From the poems of Theocritus (third century B.C.) to the standard repertoire of today's jokes about hicks and yokels there is ample evidence of metropolitan scorn for precisely those people who make the metropolis possible. The opposed stereotypes—Cybele, city-goddess of grain, against the clownish rustic; the gentleman-farmer, worthy peasant, against the mindless hayseed—have always been with us. They are eloquent testimony to the ambivalence of the material facts of our civilization, acknowledging its basis in the kind of agricultural production that requires an enormous labor force to clear and cultivate the earth, whose members cannot share in the other forms of cultivation thus made available.

In the early Middle Ages, peasants are scarcely noticed in the literature that is forming the ideology of Christian feudalism—except to be regarded as pagans, paupers, and rustics who are sinful, dangerous, and illiterate, more beasts than men (Le Goff 1966). Such attitudes are crystallized in the semantic history of the word that originally denoted the laborer who is legally bound to the land he tills: the "villain." In the later Middle Ages, such stereotypes are played with in the genre of Troubadour lyric called the *pastorella*: an encounter between a knight errant and a dairymaid or country lass, who, like the rustics in the standard jokes, was not always victimized or seduced by the city slicker. Folk humor, even when imported into "higher" literary forms, like the intricate poems of the medieval courtly entertainers, ordinarily finds ways to revenge itself on the "official" culture.

That culture, at any rate, kept the founding legend alive during the "dark" ages—between the collapse of the western Roman empire in the fifth century and the explosion of agricultural productivity in the tenth and eleventh—by incorporating it into kinds of discourse then recognized as history: the chronicle and the genealogy.

Chapter 6

৯✦

THE UNFINISHED CITY

Chronicle Histories

Hi story, for the early Middle Ages, was constituted mainly by the universal chronologies, derived from the Bible, of Eusebius, St. Jerome, Isidore of Seville, and Gregory of Tours, brought up to date by a local compiler. That of St. Jerome included a summary of the *Aeneid*, presented as part of the actual history of Rome. The compilers were monks, usually unidentified, whose texts could deal with events in both church and state and which varied considerably in narrative coherence, from a mere list of happenings year by year to real prose compositions, with accounts of psychological motivation and moral criticism of behavior. Such compilations typically had more than one author, each extending the chronicle of events, and were often at the same time summaries of their great Christian predecessors.

In two such compilations, one from the mid-seventh and one from the early eighth century, are found the earliest surviving attributions of Trojan ancestry to a northern European people. Each of these chronicles presents a rather different account of the Trojan origins of the Franks.

The first, known as the chronicle of Fredegar, interrupts its virtual repetition of Jerome to tell the following story: Priam raped Helen, and from the Trojan diaspora occasioned by the consequent destruction of the city arose the Franks. Priam was their first king, Friga the next. The group split into two parts, one going to Macedonia, to become the invincible race of Philip and Alexander; the other, led by Friga, wandered long across Europe. They elected Francio—whence their name—as their king, who finally established them between the Rhine and Danube and the sea. There, they too remained invincible, dominating others and never being conquered, like their relations the Turks. At this point, the chronicle takes up Jerome's summary of the *Aeneid*, adding to its account of Aeneas settling in Latium the information that while he was doing this, his brother, Friga, was ruling in Frigia and Saul was king in Palestine (Krusch 1888: 45–47).

47

In the next book of the same chronicle, a résumé of the same story—now credited to Jerome and Virgil—is inserted into a recapitulation of Gregory of Tours' description of the Franks and Turks as sister peoples. The Trojans divide into Macedonians and Europeans, as before; then there is a second division of the latter: those under Francio go to the Rhine and become Franks; others remain on the Danube, electing Torcoth as their king, and become Turks. One additional detail is also provided: Francio's people started to build a city on the Rhine "in the image of Troy," but left it unfinished (Krusch 1888: 93; Monod 1885: 86–87). In the following book of the same chronicle, further variants to the story are added in the course of recapitulating Dares Phrygius's account of the Trojan War (the version, better known to the Middle Ages than Homer's, in which Aeneas betrays the city to Ulysses). Here, Pherecides is said to be the father of Frigio, who is the father of Franco. The location of his people is unclear, but they are contemporary with the house of Iulus in Rome (Krusch 1888: 198–200).

The second chronicle, called the *Liber Historiae Francorum*, is much less concerned with recapitulating universal chronologies and simply begins with the following story of origin: Aeneas ruled over Ilium, and the Trojans were a potent people who fought the Greeks for ten years. After the fall of the city, Aeneas led some to Italy, while Priam and Antenor led twelve thousand more to Pannonia, where they built the city of Sicambria[1] and grew into a great nation. They gave the Roman emperor Valentinian essential aid against the Alans, upon which he named them Francos—which means "fierce, of hard and bold heart." Later, the Romans demanded tribute of them, which they refused. So Priam led them to the Rhine, where his son and Antenor's co-ruled for many years. Finally, they elected Priam's grandson Pharamond as their single king. And from here, as in Fredegar, the genealogy continues down to Meroveo and the actual Merovingian monarchs (Krusch 1888: 241–44).

The first thing one might notice about these earliest medieval efforts to transpose the plot of the *Aeneid* to northern Europe is, despite their brevity, the variety and discrepancy of their details. Indeed, these are such as to have mightily exasperated the nineteenth-century scholars who exhumed and edited the texts in search of hard historical "facts" in the positivist mode. They merely dismissed such stuff as pedantic chaos and absurd fabling. Though not "true" in their sense, the discrepant fables nonetheless testify to something quite real in the formation of the self-consciousness of Europe. That very discrepancy—so great between the versions in both texts as to lead one modern scholar to the conclusion that they are wholly independent from each other (Wallace-Hadrill 1960: xii)—is itself the sign of a lively and continuous oral tradition. As we all know, and as studies of folklore amply confirm, stories that pass from mouth to ear scarcely survive one re-

1. Pannonia was the Roman province consisting mainly of the Hungarian plain. The Sicambri were an ancient Frankish tribe annihilated by Drusus; a Roman legion was named after them. The name of the city, in the form "Schambry," survived until the sixteenth century as a peasant appellation for old Buda (Eckhardt 1943: 19).

telling intact, let alone generations of retellings. Just from its relatively wide variance within these brief written recordings, we may infer that the tale of Trojan
origins was pretty constantly *told* in that area of northern Europe from which the
Franks were rapidly expanding their hegemony. Further evidence of frequent oral
transmission is the very repetition of the story, with differing details, in the single
chronicle of Fredegar. The compilers of this text (there appear to have been at
least two), like oral poets, are reluctant to leave out any version of a tale they happen to know. A good story is always worth adding to as well as repeating. And its
distribution is further assured by being written down. Fredegar's chronicle survives
in thirty-four manuscripts, making it, according to the plausible criteria of one
scholar (Guenée 1980: 255), if not the age's equivalent of a best-seller, at least a
moderate success.

The second thing one might notice about both versions of the story is that, despite their variations, they each accomplish the same three purposes. First, they
provide a noble etiology for the military prowess and the rugged independence of
the Franks. Second, they are very careful to assert a chronology that shows the
Frankish nation to have developed, not *from* ancient Rome, but rather parallel to
it or even in competition with it—its sibling rather than its child. Third, they are
at pains to explain the renaming of the Franks—exactly how, though once Trojans, they came to be called otherwise. These common objectives are the more impressive for being realized in such varied ways, in terms of such discrepant details.
Whether they had a patronymic king or received an honorific sobriquet; whether
they refused Roman tribute or were as indomitable as Alexander the Great;
whether Friga is Aeneas's brother or Frigio is Iulus's contemporary—all the differences serve the same ends. And these ends are those of the formation of an embryonic national myth, the assertion of a prestigious lineage and an imperial destiny. These claims are quite remarkably Virgilian, though made at a vastly lower
level of sophistication. Virgil too had to explain how the Trojans became Latins
and how the Romans, while assimilating so much from the Greeks, had neverthe-
less their own independent origins and development.

Indeed, there is a remarkable parallel in the utility of the Trojan connection for
the Romans with respect to Greece and for these northern Europeans with respect
to Rome. In both cases, the Trojan ancestry offers a relation between their descendants and the historical centers of cultural prestige—Greece and the Roman empire—that is both close and adversarial; it offers association with a memory of
glory while maintaining freedom from subjection to the power, cultural or military, that went with it. The story is a perfect myth of collective self-creation, which
recasts paternity as fraternity: we don't really come from those potent folks whose
language we must laboriously acquire (Greek for the literate Roman; Latin for the
Germanic monk) and whose privileged texts (Homer then, Virgil now) we must
imitate—not at all. They're just our brothers, our equals, our associates, our competitors (Valentinian), our allies (Evander). Our fathers are way back, in that long
ago destroyed city, forever dead, forever inaccessible. Cultural paternity is displaced
into myth, so that we can become our own fathers—just as sons must struggle,

physically or psychically, to displace their fathers so that they may become fathers in their turn. It is no wonder that a story as satisfying as this should cease to present itself as myth or as literature in order to command literal belief as history.

For history it had been since the third century B.C. for the expanding Romans, history it now was in 700 for the expanding Franks, and, despite many later assaults on its authenticity as such, would so remain for just about exactly a millennium. The terminus of the widespread acceptance of the legend as history, the last occasion on which the literal truth of Trojan ancestry appears to have been a matter of serious dispute, was the jailing of a French scholar in 1714 for having claimed (correctly, of course) that the ancestors of the French were not Trojans but Germans.[2] There were, naturally, political reasons for treating him so harshly, as there have always been immediate political motives and meanings in the writing of any history. It has never escaped the attention of scholars that the legend of Trojan descent—from Fabius Pictor through Geoffrey and his poetic translators to Spenser—gets recorded, retold, and applied to new places and peoples during precisely their periods of military expansion or imperial ambition. It was especially useful to crusaders as well as to later efforts to assert the ethnic unity of rising nations (Beaune 1985). The function of the legend, in whatever local circumstances, to justify and legitimize the acquisition of or desire for some kind of political hegemony is obvious.

So it certainly is in the chronicle of Fredegar and the *Liber Historiae Francorum*, both compiled as the Franks are taking over ever more territory in western Europe. The insistence in both texts on the ancient independence of the Franks, and in one version specifically on their refusal of tribute to ancient Rome, is patently designed to curb and forestall the claims and protestations of the papacy—the present Rome. The insistence on the ferocity of this people is even a kind of threat, as well as a typical kind of Germanic boasting. But these manifestly present motives and meanings are smuggled into the past and offered in the discourse that was then history, the sober, clumsy prose (in execrable Latin that was the despair of its nineteenth-century editors) recounting of the succession of rulers and their exploits. The legitimizing function of the legend is here only in its crudest form: "We've always been powerful, so watch out." The compilers took from the oral traditions of the founding story only what they could use and understand, and their circumstances limited this use primarily to assertions of military prestige.

But the rest of the story was there, too, though not exploitable in the landscape and in the kind of empire inhabited by the Franks. It was not even exploited by Charlemagne himself. Still, the structure of the story was intact, even if its full meaning was not grasped. The Virgilian geographical trajectory was there, interestingly transferred from sea to land. The westward migration of the Trojans from Thrace to Hungary to the Rhine was quite easy to picture, given what northern Europe looked like on an eighth-century map (see Eckhardt 1943). And Aeneas, after all, had made his first aborted foundation in Thrace. The whole crucial matter of foundation, of course, receives no emphasis whatever in the chronicles; yet

2. This little episode is recounted in chapter 14.

it is there: uncomprehended now, but still available. In one version, Priam and Antenor build Sicambria; in the other, the patronymic Francio starts to build a new Troy on the Rhine but doesn't finish it. That unfinished city is the perfect image of the state of the legend and of transalpine Europe at this period. The city won't get finished and the legend won't be developed until more intensive agricultural production permits the first to occur in fact, so that the second can occur in fiction. Fiction, of course, called history. But which is which? Without the legend, would there have been the remaking of the landscape on its model?

Before reviewing what little is known about that remaking, it remains to consider the next earliest chronicle that will link the Trojans to what will become Britain as the earliest linked them to what will become France. This is another, even more chaotic and various than usual, compilation made in the early ninth century called the *Historia Brittonum*—traditionally attributed to Nennius, the name by which it was often known. Like Fredegar, if he ever existed, he didn't write it (see Dumville 1975). And like that earlier chronicle, this one aims to attach the exploits of a succession of tribal rulers to the universal chronologies of Eusebius, Jerome, Isidore and Orosius—all cited, summarized, and copied as usual. Also like the earlier chronicle, this one records multiple versions of the descent from Troy, not only as presumed variants of a living oral tradition, but also in a conscious effort to bring them into some relation with the biblical genealogies of the written sources. This emphasis on lineal succession, to the exclusion of any direct claims or threats of ferocity or independence as made in the Frankish chronicles, appears to be a subtler, more scholarly kind of legitimation—as it might well be for a people, the Britons, already dispersed, invaded, no longer holding much of their former territory. The legitimation, even the identity, of the Britons is, in short, more cultural than political. The assertion of Trojan origins could serve one kind of purpose for a dominant group and another for one in process of dispossession. There is perhaps one still political implication in the mere fact that the "history" of the Britons got thus written down when it did. The island (England and Wales) that produced most of the thirty-five manuscripts in which the text (in various different stages) survives, had in fact remained, along with Brittany, independent of Charlemagne's empire. To endow the island and its "original" inhabitants with a noble genealogy exactly parallel to that claimed by the Franks, was ipso facto to assert a form of equality with them—not military, but cultural and historical.

Such appears to be the case from the way, or ways, in which the founding story is here told. Its most detailed version, the one that Geoffrey of Monmouth will repeat, elaborate, and make famous three hundred years later, is as follows: Brut was the son of Silvius, the son of Ascanius. He fulfills the prophecy made at his birth that he will be the death of his parents and is sent from Latium into exile. Because his great-grandfather, Aeneas, killed Turnus, Brut is also expelled by Greeks from an island in the Tyrhennian sea. "And he came to Gaul where he founded the city he called Turnis. And then he came to that island which took its name from his name, i.e. Brittania, and filled it with his people and lived there. From that day to this Britain is inhabited." The next chapter of the text gives another name and genealogy to the hero: here Britto is Aeneas's brother, who ruled Britain while Post-humous, Aeneas's grandson by Silvius, ruled the Latins (Lot 1934: 154–55).[3]

In a later chapter, the text recounts the standard derivation of the known world's population from the sons of Noah: The people of Asia come from Shem, those of Africa from Ham, and those of Europe from Japheth. Japheth's grandson, Hessitio, had four sons: Francus, Romanus, Alamannus, and Britto, who gave their names to the four nations of "Franci, Latini, Alamanni et Britti." From Hessitio's brothers descend, as eponymously, the rest of European peoples—all lineally traced back to Adam and God. The following chapter, in an obvious effort to link the Trojan and Noah lineages, merely produces a longer list, placing Bruto at the end of a chain that goes back to Japheth through Histion, a couple of early Roman kings, Aeneas, his son and father as they appear in the *Aeneid*, and a couple of his Trojan ancestors as they do not (Lot 1934: 161–62).

The confusion of such a farrago of oral memories and often copied texts is apparent; but the impulse that produced it is worth pondering. Its obsession is to de-rive nations from names, to claim legitimacy for a collectivity in just the same way as for individuals: by inheriting the name of a father. The model is of course bibli-cal, and the task as seen by these compilers simply to generate, by means of rather fertile etymological invention, for all known secular societies, a straight patrilineal descent from God the father. This of necessity involved Noah; now, and hencefor-ward, it involves the Trojans too. And it identifies them as proto-Europeans—not by where they came from, but by where they ended up. The thinking is locked into a backward extrapolation from the present through a secular origin (irrecoverably destroyed) to the ultimate divine origin. It is etiological thinking, typical of myths and legends. If there are Britons, there must have been a Brut, or a Britto, or a Bruto; if Franks, a Francus, or a Francio, or a Franco. The story does what myths and legends do, and in the terms peculiar to the local circumstances of developing Christian feudal society. These patrilineal terms also, of course, assert the most di-rect kind of continuity, the most obvious form of temporal order. From father to son, from generation to generation: this seems valued so highly, in and for itself, this imaginative proliferation of lists of "begats," as to suggest the intensity of the desire for what it celebrates. Continuity—of any sort of public order—was scarcely a fea-ture of life in the Europe of the "dark" ages, and especially in Britain, where the col-lapse of Roman rule, the settlements of Angles and Saxons warring with the Celts, the Viking raids and occupation, made the duration of all enterprise as chancy and elegiac as the forms of heroism recorded in Anglo-Saxon poetry. The repeated and discrepant genealogies, the filling-up more or less anyhow of those patrilineal lists, furnishes as the discourse of the past what is missing from the present. That dis-course dreams the desire of duration.

And so the *Historia Brittonum* is more sensitive than its Frankish siblings to the cultural themes of the legend: to foundation and continuous habitation. Like Ae-

3. One manuscript presents Brutus as the son of Silvius and the brother of Romulus and Remus (Lot 1934: 228).

neas, Brut is a multiple founder; Tours is just a warm-up—as well as, presumably, an expiation for his great-grandfather's slaughter of Turnus—for his settlement of the island that, along with his people, bears his name. Once again the chronology, confused enough in most respects, is clear on the crucial point of contemporaneity with ancient Rome. The Britons' foundation, like the Franks' pedigree, makes them the fraternal coevals (in one version literally, where Britto is Aeneas's brother) of the greatness that would become Rome.

In these earliest surviving records of the legend as applied to transalpine Europe, there is of course no mention of the "culture" that the Trojan descendants bring north: for the good reason that it isn't there yet. What will produce it—the move from agricultural self-sufficiency to the marketing of surplus production in a network of towns—remains a matter of inference and argument among historians. That it was produced, however, by roughly the middle of the twelfth century, seems generally agreed. A major result of such production was the astronomical and unique increase in the foundation of towns in central Europe during the thirteenth century (Braudel 1985: 90–96). The explosion in agricultural productivity that provided such development seems to have occurred from the tenth to twelfth centuries. From such few statistics as were recorded (these from the abbey of Cluny), yields of grain increased during this period from 100 to 200 percent (Duby 1973: 250–52). Since the records mention no change in agricultural methods—of planting, fallowing, or fertilizing—their historian must deduce an enormous improvement in plowing. Another historian attributes this improvement to the invention of the horse collar, which permitted the use of an animal twice as fast as the ox; and to the widespread use, by the eleventh century, of the wheeled plow with two blades (one for penetrating and one for breaking heavy soils) and a plate or moldboard, which turned the furrow as it was made, thus aereating the soil. With the addition of a toothed cultivator for mixing decayed vegetable matter with the soil, this new technology not only allowed the cultivation of land not previously arable, but accomplished in one operation what had taken two or three before (Gimpel 1975: 54–62). Besides such gains in mechanical efficiency, there was also the increasing practice of three-field, triennial, crop rotation, which reduced nonproductive fallow time from a half to a third. Of equal importance, perhaps, was the warming trend in the climate of Europe, which reached a peak between 1000 and 1200 (see Higounet 1966). Taken together, all these developments seem sufficient to account for a general reversal in the proportions of the European landscape between the ninth and twelfth centuries: from forests interspersed with cleared fields and villages, to cultivated lands surrounding towns interspersed with forests.

Nowhere, perhaps, was this transformation more apparent than in northern France, the home of the next people whose appetite for conquest would give the founding legend its most elaborate and influential form. The Normans, of course, had settled Normandy as invaders, abandoned their Scandinavian languages for French, and were enjoying by the eleventh century the prosperity and population increase made possible by the improvements in agriculture. By the end of that century, their warlords had invaded and settled in England, Apulia, Calabria, and Sicily, creating in the process "a myth of themselves as world conquerors" (Davis 1978: 257). The most famous and long-lasting of their victories—the battle of Hastings—was celebrated in a Latin mini-epic poem of the twelfth century, which "assimilates more or less explicitly the conquest of England by the Normans to that of Italy by the Trojans" (Tilliette 1985: 123). Norman historians as well as poets knew enough of the stories of antiquity to find flattering comparisons for their patrons. Guillaume de Poitiers, the contemporary biographer of William the Conqueror, compares his combat with Harold to those of Achilles with Hector and Aeneas with Turnus; he goes on to brag that William did in a single day what took Agamemnon ten years and Rome even longer (Foreville 1952: 198, 209).

Such comparisons, moreover, had been made possible by the discourse of the history that dreamed the desire for duration of the Franks and the Britons, the history that sought patrilineal continuity through the etymology of present place-names, the history that preserved the founding legend in a landscape that obscured its cultural significance.

Chapter 7

§✎

THE CITY FOUNDED

Geoffrey of Monmouth

By the early twelfth century, the landscape had evolved sufficiently to permit the recovery of its cultural significance in Geoffrey of Monmouth's *History of the Kings of Britain*. Here the city—London as Troynovant—is not only finished, but embarks on its own imperial career. And Geoffrey's text enjoyed a similar career: extant in over two hundred manuscripts, it qualifies as a best-seller all by itself, without even counting its copious progeny, all the subsequent retellings in vernacular prose and verse of the histories of Brut and King Arthur (see Faral 1929 and Tatlock 1950). Though hardly a great literary stylist, Geoffrey was a deft storyteller, a genius at the kind of compilation that composed what his age knew as history. From all his sources, acknowledged or invented (the identification of the one he claimed is still a matter of scholarly dispute), written and oral, Geoffrey created a swift and coherent narrative that achieved enormous popularity and commanded literal belief in the face of hostile criticism both contemporary and later. The first book of his *History* contains the story of Brutus, modeled on the *Aeneid* and expanded from the principal version in the *Historia Brittonum*. The crucial difference from its medieval predecessors is that it is now emphatically, and once again, a story of foundation.

And what is founded is no less than the entire landscape of the island, with whose description the book begins:

> Britain, the best of islands, is situated in the Western Ocean, between France and Ireland. . . . It provides in unfailing plenty everything that is suited to the use of human beings. It abounds in every kind of mineral. It has broad fields and hillsides which are suitable for the most intensive farming and in which, because of the richness of the soil, all kinds of crops are grown in their seasons. It also has open woodlands which are filled with every kind of game. Through its forest glades stretch pasturelands which provide the various feeding-stuffs needed by cattle, and there too grow flowers of every hue which offer their honey to the flitting bees. At the foot of its

windswept mountains it has meadows green with grass, beauty-spots where clear
springs flow into shining streams which ripple gently and murmur an assurance of
deep sleep to those lying on their banks. (53)

Although earlier texts about Britain had also begun with its geography, they did
little but enumerate its dimensions and list its cities and rivers. Geoffrey, however,
presents it as a garden of considerable Virgilian resonance, whose soporific pastoral beauties appear last in order, as a kind of reward for the labor implied (but un-
mentioned) in the previous items of praise. For Britain is not a garden yet, at the
outset of the story; it simply has the potential to become one, a potential that is
realized only after it is founded.

The story Geoffrey tells of Brutus is a mini-version of the seaborne wanderings of Aeneas, whose great-grandson he is, exiled from Latium by being the
(accidental, though prophesied) cause of the deaths of his parents. He and his followers do battle with Greeks on a Mediterranean island, where he finally acquires
as a wife the daughter of the king he defeats. Re-equipped with ships and supplies, he sails to another island, where he receives from the goddess Diana in a
dream a prophecy of the sort of empire familiar from the *Aeneid*:

> "Brutus, beyond the setting of the sun, past the realms of Gaul, there lies an island
> in the sea, once occupied by giants. Now it is empty and ready for your folk. Down
> the years this will prove an abode suited to you and to your people; and for your de-
> scendants it will be a second Troy. A race of kings will be born there from your stock
> and the round circle of the whole earth will be subject to them." (65)

Despite the relative clarity of the directions, Brutus and his band make erratic
progress westward, having adventures in North Africa and Mauritania before passing the pillars of Hercules and entering the estuary of the Loire in order to repro-
vision. Here they do lengthy battle with the Gauls and found the city of Tours.
Despite these victories, Brutus finds his people outnumbered by the Gauls, and so
chooses to reembark and "seek out the island which divine prophecy had promised would be his." Impelled by favorable winds, the Trojans "sought the promised
island, and came ashore at Totnes" (71).

This is the structural climax of the founding myth: the arrival of the culture-
bringers, the moment diffused by Virgil through time and space in the central
books of his poem, the moment virtually ignored in the earlier medieval accounts.
Geoffrey's version of it is terse, but it is both complete and climactic; it ends the
first chapter of his book. Its very opening performs a miniature telescoping of time
that leaves no doubt about its significance:

> At this time the island of Britain was called Albion. It was uninhabited except for
> a few giants. It was, however, most attractive, because of the delightful situation of
> its various regions, its forests and the great number of its rivers, which teemed with
> fish; and it filled Brutus and his companions with a great desire to live there. When

they had explored the different districts, they drove the giants whom they had discovered into the caves in the mountains. With the approval of their leader they divided the land among themselves. They began to cultivate the fields and to build
houses, so that in a short time you would have thought that the land had always been
inhabited.

Brutus then called the island Britain from his own name, and his companions he
called Britons. His intention was that his memory should be perpetuated by the derivation of the name. A little later the language of the people, which had up to then been
known as Trojan or Crooked Greek, was called British, for the same reason. (72)

The story goes on to deal with the problem presented by the indigenes (Diana's
prophecy having proved somewhat premature). A particularly "repulsive" giant
named Gogmagog, who uprooted oak trees to use them as clubs, led an attack on
the Trojans while they were worshipping their gods. All the giants were then slain,
except Gogmagog, who was saved for a wrestling match with Corineus, Brutus's
most faithful companion and strongest warrior, who finally tossed Gogmagog off
a cliff into the sea. Brutus inspected his whole kingdom, looking for a suitable site
to place his capital, and found it on the Thames, where "he built his city and called
it Troia Nova. It was known by this name for long ages after, but finally by a corruption of the word it came to be called Trinovantum." Still later, when Lud became king, "he surrounded the capital with lofty walls and with towers built with
extraordinary skill, and he ordered it to be called . . . Lud's City, from his own
name." This caused a quarrel with his brother, "who was annoyed that he should
want to do away with the name of Troy in his own country." At any rate, when
Brutus built the city, "he presented it to the citizens by right of inheritance, and
gave them a code of laws by which they might live peacefully together." This occurred while Brutus's uncle, Aeneas Silvius (a son of Aeneas), was ruling in Italy
(73–74).

It is apparent that Geoffrey's Virgilian pastiche has been superimposed on the
historical vision and purposes of the earlier chronicles and genealogies. The three
functions of the orally transmitted legend—the assertion of military glory, of siblinghood with ancient Rome, and the explanation of lost Trojan names—are all
fulfilled here, but are now subordinated to the crucially recovered themes of
founding. The status of the invaders as cultivators, city builders, religion- and lawgivers is clear. Ostensibly historical Trojans here play the role of Saturn, bringing
cultivation and justice where neither existed before. Brutus and his band like the
richly stocked rivers and forests; but they neither fish nor hunt. They till the land
and put buildings on it. Not much emphasis is placed on the divine prophecy
(which is not quite correct) and its fulfillment; Geoffrey is a long way from achieving the Virgilian perspective on how history is made. For him, it suffices at this
moment that the Trojans simply *want* the land. So they take it. The indigenes they
take it from aren't quite people, of course, but monsters. The giants aren't
identified with the land at the outset; they are literally driven inside it, scattered
into its nonarable parts by the invaders. There is no information given on the

giants' mode of living, no stress on their lack of *mos* and *cultus*, since they're off the scale even of savagery, being subhuman. One can be briefly preserved for sport. There need be no sympathy for their extermination. The new order cultivates the land, builds its capital city, and marches toward empire. The foundation has occurred.

And only after its occurrence, after the land is cultivated, after the tribe has altered its face, does Brutus name it. The backward extrapolation of history from present names of places, people, and languages is here continued, of course, but in a way that suggests a subtler meaning (which will be fully appreciated by Spenser). Naming—or renaming—becomes coterminous with civilizing in our sense: the invaders mark their possession by their speech; the patronymic origin memorializes itself by giving its name to both land and speech; the land becomes simultaneously an object of exploitation and a subject of writing. And in one further development, pregnant of future writing, the promised land—traditionally the object of speech, the recipient of grammatical, divine, or human agency—is itself personified. It "filled Brutus and his companions with . . . desire"[1]—thus completing its identification by language with its identification *with* language. For the land does what the theory of Jacques Lacan attributes to language: it creates desire. Described in more usual terms, Geoffrey's locution displaces the agency of desire from the people to the land. The object of their wish to possess becomes the willing subject, the initiator, of that wish. The locution, of course, is common in Troubadour love lyrics; the land here plays the role of the lady. Few subsequent colonial landscapes will offer themselves quite so cooperatively (as, in the poetry, did few ladies); but the satisfactions of so imagining the transaction are exactly analogous to those of the whole myth of the already destroyed origin. The patriarchal collectivity creates itself, constitutes its own origin, and so must reproduce itself on an implicitly feminized landscape. It is no accident that Geoffrey begins his second chapter (75) with the statement that Brutus had, "in the meantime," consummated his marriage and produced three sons, who will become the patronyms of the regions of Britain.

Foundations—and bestowing names—are, as in Virgil, successive. Brutus begins with Tours, which he names after a fallen nephew called Turnus (not, as in "Nennius," after the hero slain by his great-grandfather). Lud, having furnished the city with lofty walls and towers, can give it its modern name regardless of his brother's dismay. As the Trojans became Latins in Latium, Franks on the Rhine, so they became Britons in Britain. Geoffrey's purpose in endowing this already displaced people with the Trojan title to civilization, like his very identity, is still matter for scholarly argument. But whether or not Geoffrey was really born a Welshman, and whether or not his glorification of the Britons was designed as subtle flattery of his Norman masters, he had inherited a story already ambiguous in its portrayal as imperial culture-bringers of those who had already in fact played the opposite role

---

1. The Latin is: "Ameno tamen situ locorum et copia piscosorum fluminum nemoribusque pre-electa affectum habitandi Bruto sociisque inferebat." Wright 1984: 13.

of indigenes in the successive invasions of the island by Angles, Saxons, Vikings, and Normans. So in order to give the story of foundation its full dimensions, to supply the role of the indigenes, Geoffrey borrows from folklore the giants, just as Virgil borrowed from myth the nymphs and tree-born men who were the original inhabitants of Rome. And in order to complete the imperial dominion of the Britons, Geoffrey presents their greatest hero, King Arthur, as a conqueror of most of Europe, a figure of distinctly Norman ambitions. To transform the indigenous/displaced into the invading/displacers certainly tempts speculation about Geoffrey's personal loyalties. But the terms of that transformation, the terms of the myth and its entitlement to civilization, have wider significance in the history of the twelfth century as a whole.

For it is apparent that, for whatever particular reason, Geoffrey was adroitly using these terms to present as civilized a particular group of people who had not been so regarded. His elevation of the Britons to this eminence was especially resented by two younger historians, William of Newburgh and Gerald of Wales. They were the first in a long line of dissenters to accuse Geoffrey of making it all up—not because they had any more rational or critical notions of what history was, but simply because they felt the traditional contempt for the very people that Geoffrey was praising.

> Normans and Anglo-Normans universally spoke of British descendants in Wales and Brittany in language derived from Bede. They were perfidious, belligerent but unsteady, uncivilized, and suspicious. Although the word *Britones* referred, in the twelfth century, specifically to the Continental Bretons, the same attitudes and adjectives seem to have been applied to all Celtic peoples, including the Scots and Irish.

William of Newburgh included also the Welsh and thought that the lot were "outright barbarians" (Partner 1977: 64). Aside from their religious recalcitrance or unorthodoxy, which is what of course irritated Bede (the author of the great ecclesiastical history of England, which narrated the triumphant conversion of the island), the Celts were, and would remain, the seminomadic indigenous opponents of the invading, city- and castle-building cultivators. Other historians contemporary with Geoffrey, William of Malmesbury and Henry of Huntingdon, justified the Norman Conquest by denigrating both the Anglo-Saxons and the Celts; Richard of Hexham, about 1150, regarded the Picts as "bestial" (Gransden 1974: 205–206, 217).

The Normans were but the most spectacular example of the most recent kind of invader: a society impelled to expand by the prosperity and surplus population resulting from increased agricultural productivity. Such conditions made most of northern France by the mid-twelfth century a rival of the heretofore more cultivated south (Aquitaine); the north became a "mainstay for the crusading movement, filled the cathedral schools with scholars eager for self-advancement, promoted . . . urban artisans . . . and mercenaries" (Warren 1973: 5). Geoffrey, writing in the service of the Normans in the 1130s, follows his known source ("Nennius") in locating Brutus's first foundation on the banks of the Loire, thus crediting him with the most fully "cultured" region to date in French-speaking Europe. Other expanding societies were also in the eleventh and twelfth centuries moving out into the fringes of their largely pastoral and poorer neighbors. Another recent historian has described how, as they did so, they came to regard these neighbors as wandering, unreliable barbarians, creating "a hostile stereotype to salve their consciences and justify their conquests" (Bartlett 1982: 177). The stereotype, however, didn't require creation, but merely deployment; it lay ready to hand in the founding legend's characterization of the indigenes and in the very meaning of the word that everybody agreed did not describe them: civilized.

So Geoffrey, in retelling the legend at a time when the settled cultivator had again become the culture-bringing imperialist, was telling the story that many wanted to hear; only he was telling it about people who, until then, had been its victims, not its perpetrators. Small wonder that his text should therefore have aroused astonished indignation and at the same time received the ultimate accolade of continuous reproduction, in one form or another. For the story could be appealing and useful to almost any faction in the Anglo-French feudal domains, providing entitlement to culture for a subject people and linking them more closely to their present rulers. For these rulers, the epically quarrelsome and ablest monarchs of the century, Henry II and Eleanor of Aquitaine, the story offered the usual legitimation of political ambitions (Kelly 1952: 100). Wace turned Geoffrey into French verse as the *Roman de Brut*, and dedicated it to Eleanor in 1155, just after she had become Queen of England. Fifty years later appeared Layamon's Middle English poetic version, called *Brut*. By now, the turn of the thirteenth century, the utility of the legend for just about everybody was clear. Layamon, for example, does not at all share Geoffrey's partisanship for the Britons at the expense of the Saxons. Geoffrey had, after all, to explain why the Britons finally lost dominion of the island (see Leckie 1981), and he did so by invoking their fatal disunity and preaching a very Virgilian sermon on the horrors of civil war, which left vineyards and homesteads devastated (264–65). Layamon merely sees the Britons as having been conquered by the superior Saxons, one passage of dominion among many (1.87–88). But the local or ethnic loyalties of one writer or another do not much matter; the story's appeal is the force of the legend itself, and anyone can use it—anyone, that is, who finds a foundation by invading culture-bringers to be the essence of civilization.

That just about all literate Europeans did so find it is shown by the explosive rush of ruling houses and cities to claim Trojan ancestry, to invent genealogies linking the ruler's family or the place to the sons of Priam or of Dardanus. What seems to have begun as a claim to buttress the dignity of the lesser nobility in the late eleventh century became by the thirteenth a myth of "collective ennoblement" (Beaune 1985: 335). French kings could use the claim to forestall domination by either emperor or pope, as well as to denigrate the English as mere Saxon upstarts. The English could embrace their Brutish heritage and claim precedence over the Franks by virtue of their more direct descent from the nonpareil Aeneas.

Trojan connections were established before the thirteenth century for the counts of Boulogne, of Flanders, and the dukes of Orléans, for the cities of Paris, Rheims, Tours, and Metz. During that century were added Nîmes, Narbonne, Troyes, Toulouse, and Clermont (Beaune 1985). In about 1200, the Icelandic statesman Snorri Sturluson began his compendium of Norse mythology (evidently influenced by Geoffrey or his imitators) by identifying the gods themselves as exiles from Troy (Young 1964: 25–26). By the end of the next century, Trojan ancestors had been found for Wenceslaus IV, King of Bohemia (Graus 1975: 87). The official chronicles of France ritually began with with some version of the Trojan migrations and, by the thirteenth century, left no doubt that the Trojan connection had fully recovered the cultural dimension that was obscured in the earliest versions. Here the Trojan hero, whatever his name, is clearly a *civilisateur*, having three functions: he founds cities, gives laws, and brings language by planting his towers and castles in a *pays gastine*, or "barren land" (Beaune 1985: 351–52). Barren, however, only in the sense of uncultivated: the archaic word *gaste* (cognate with Eng. *waste*) was applied to any agriculturally unexploited territory, forest as well as desert (Le Goff 1988: 47–59). The hero founds, in short, the kind of agriculture on which the rest of our culture is based.

This role is equally clear from the way in which the medieval French rewrote the story of Aeneas himself. The *Roman d'Eneas*, produced in northwestern France in the later twelfth century, is divided into two major episodes: the tragic sojourn with Dido and the (lengthier and freely invented) courtship and winning of Lavinia. At first glance, it seems to be merely a fanciful reduction of the epic to the amorous themes of chivalry. But, as one scholar has pointed out, the bipartite structure seems firmly based on the central notion of foundation: the first fails; the second succeeds (Marchello-Nizia 1985). In both, possession of the woman is possession and rule of the land. To be a successful founder requires (1) coming from outside; (2) having broken some interdiction or taboo; (3) retaking the land of one's ancestors; (4) installing oneself in a *terre gaste*, or "barren territory" (Marchello-Nizia 1985: 257–59).

What is interesting about these conditions is that they are more or less exactly those that a contemporary anthropologist finds in the founding tales of both ancient myth—Zeus, Aeneas, Romulus, Oedipus—and modern cultures in East Africa, Hawaii, and Polynesia (Sahlins 1985: ch. 3). The "more or less" is crucial, and in this case well illustrates Sahlins' point that a mythic structure is not usefully seen "as a static set of symbolic oppositions and correspondences" (77). It varies, in short, according to the historical experience of the tellers of the tale. The tellers may yet, however, be eager to conform to an inherited pattern. We recall, for example, that Virgil reached far back into mythology to fulfill conditions three (Dardanus was born in Italy) and four (the picture of Rome in bk. 8 as formerly *gaste*). Condition two may have been satisfied in the epic merely by Aeneas's tarrying in Carthage; but in the medieval poem it is emphasized by (otherwise bizarre) accusations of cowardice and homosexuality leveled at the hero. Brut and the rest of the eponymous Trojan migrants usually satisfy all the conditions except

the third—naturally enough, given the circumstances of intra-European colonization. By contrast, the third condition was heavily stressed as a justification of the
crusades. Pope Urban II, launching the first crusade at Clermont in 1095, is made
by his historian to utter the largest possible extension of this claim: "For the Christian, the whole world is an exile and the whole world a fatherland; thus exile is fatherland, and fatherland exile" (Hay 1967: 32). The symbolic equation of woman
and land is also capable of interesting variation. Geoffrey's Brutus must do battle
to gain his wife in the usual way; but it's not her territory that is his promised land.
That land, however, as we noticed, acts in the story's language just as ladies do in
the period's poetry. As another scholar said of the millennium during which the
story of Trojan origins was history: "A non-elastic myth is a dead myth" (Beaune
1985: 331).

And our founding myth was very much alive throughout this period: first only
as a vague memory in an oral tradition, and second, after the landscape of transalpine Europe began to be more garden than forest, and its life to be more centered
on the towns that were springing up everywhere, as a precise evocation (in a much
simpler form) of the Virgilian model. Layamon's version of Wace's version of
Geoffrey's account of what Brutus and his band do in the promised land goes like
this: "They made towns, they tilled the earth; corn they sowed, meadows they
mowed . . . for it was all their own that they looked over" (1.82). "For the Middle
Ages," writes Marchello-Nizia, "the founder is also a colonizer and producer of
wealth" (260)—as indeed he was before and ever shall remain.

With respect to the wealth he produces, and the importance of this activity in
the western colonization of the rest of the globe, it is worth noticing the general
coincidence of the rise of agricultural productivity, the growth of towns, the colonizing activities of conquerors and crusaders, the proliferation and popularity of
versions of the founding legend and of claims to Trojan ancestry, with the increasing use of money. Reimported into Europe from the Islamic world in the ninth
and tenth centuries, "by 1100 money was established in the main centres, and had
begun the long process by which it penetrated every part of the economy"; at the
same time the words *pecunia* and *feoh* (which both originally designated *cattle*) lose
their associations with property and come to mean exclusively cash (Murray 1978:
57–58). The use of money, of course, was both cause and consequence of the function of towns as markets—the number of which also astronomically increased in
the twelfth and thirteenth centuries. In the more traditionally cultural sphere, there
were the cathedral and monastic schools that fed the "twelfth-century renaissance"
and would soon become the first universities (Bologna, Paris, Oxford); and there
were the churches themselves, constituting the first great age of Gothic architec-
ture. Europe was getting rich; a new middle class of town-dwelling merchants and
artisans was in the process of formation. As our world thus moved toward what
we know as its early modern (i.e. preindustrial) condition, it found its own history
in the legend that it was both reproducing and reenacting.

There is one particularly crucial consequence to the qualification of the legend
as history, its incorporation in the discourse of supposed fact: What is thus qualified

as actually past becomes usable as precedent for present actions and desires. History makes law. Geoffrey's account of Brut dividing the island of Britain among his three sons is alleged in legal negotiations by two late medieval English kings to justify England's claim to feudal sovereignty over the Scots. Edward I thus cited Geoffrey in a letter to Pope Boniface in 1301 (Stones 1965: 96–98). A century later, Henry IV demanded fealty from the Scottish king, sending a team of canon lawyers to cite the whole genealogy from Brut the Trojan and to urge that "old chronicles" have full weight as law (Nicholson 1974: 220). Such deployment of the founding story is explicit and obvious compared to its later and subtler uses once it is discredited as genuinely historical discourse. By then, however, its plot will have been sufficiently reenacted to constitute the actual facts of recent history, and in this form will pass into the prescriptions of a whole new branch of the legal profession called into being by that reenactment: international law.

What happens in the world (events), the selection, recording, and interpretation of those happenings (history), and what we think should happen in the world (law), are not finally divisible domains. They are all linked, mediated, and in part constituted by fictions, the stories we tell that dream our desires for duration, dominion, and identity. The particular story our founding legend tells realizes our desires for these things, but only by denying them to others. The sons of Troy and of Japheth have constructed out of Roman and Judaeo-Christian fictions their mandate to subjugate the globe.

Part III

❧

OLD FRONTIERS IN NEW WORLDS

The Legend in the Renaissance

Chapter 8

ϑ☙

COMMERCE AND CULTURE

Patterns of Trade and Art

Before Europe's "discovery" of new worlds in both east and west, her richest empire and most powerful metropolis was that of Venice. This mercantile oligarchy was but the most successful of the northern Italian city-states that came to dominate the European economy in the late Middle Ages, owing to its maritime trade linking the Mediterranean to the Black Sea and finally to the Atlantic (see McNeill 1974 and Wallerstein 1974). Based on the kind of high agricultural productivity first exploited in the Po valley by the Etruscans, the prosperity of northern Italy generated industry, trade, the development of reliable currencies, the invention of credit mechanisms and merchant banking—and the cultural movement we know as the Renaissance. At the height of this prosperity, the fall of Constantinople to the Ottoman Turks in 1453 closed off one of its main sources, the Asian trade in spices and luxuries. The ascendancy of Venice passed into very gradual decline, and her maritime rivals, especially Genoa, sought to recapture this trade in other directions. Such was the situation and motivation that led the Genoese seafarer, Christopher Columbus, shipwrecked on the coast of Portugal, to take service in that nation's efforts to find profits in the islands of the South Atlantic and along the coast of West Africa. Finally, as we all know, he managed to persuade the Spanish monarchs to fund an expedition to reach the Indies by sailing west.

The agriculturally based prosperity that fueled commercial expansion, and all the technological and financial mechanisms of its operation, produced at the same time and in the same place the self-congratulatory "rebirth" of classical languages and learning in which the ancient usage of Latin was fetishized as the hallmark of the educated, and the idea of ancient Rome became the measure of human greatness. The cultural prestige that Roman antiquity had never lost became, with the increased availability of more, and more complete, versions of its texts, enormous. The weight of this prestige, its status as model, especially for literary production, was as much a burden as a stimulus. The resulting ambivalence in the artistic theory and

67

practice of imitation from the fourteenth to seventeenth centuries has been finely described by Thomas Greene's *The Light in Troy*.

The title of the book (taken from a poem by Yeats) has no direct reference to the legend of Trojan descent, but evokes in the largest sense the ambition and anxiety, the desire and despair, of the attempt to become what one admires, to create oneself and one's world in the image of a glorious past. The pathos and nostalgia in the central effort of European literature at this period is well symbolized by the always already destroyed origin, the story of whose destruction—told in the *Iliad* and recapitulated by Aeneas in the *Aeneid*—was itself the link between the two greatest poets in what the Renaissance decided was the greatest of all literary genres, the epic. The pathos and the nostalgia are inherent in the notion of civilization as transmission, as requiring transportation from elsewhere, as incapable of being homegrown, as necessitating repeated exile, invasion, reachievement, and refoundation. However poignant the pathos of these efforts for imaginative writers—a small and privileged minority indeed—the definition of civilization that imposed it also supplied rather more actual suffering for those about to be integrated into the global system of western European commerce.

In the ancient world, of course, southern Italy and Sicily had been the site of actual Greek colonies; and the legend of Aeneas's foundation, following Evander's and Saturn's, reflected the fact. Italy, in short, had the clearest and most direct title of all to the Trojan ancestry so tortuously asserted by the medieval Frankish and British narratives. Nor did this claim go unexercised: over a hundred Italian cities supposedly had their own legend of Trojan foundation (Buck 1963: 68).[1] What is interesting is that none of these legends appears to have been recorded as early as those of Fredegar and Nennius. That of Venice seems typical: The usual compilation of divergent stories, begun in the late eleventh century, attributes the foundation to Antenor; later redactions replace him with Aeneas (from whose mother's name "Venetian" is derived), presumably in the effort to gain priority over both Rome and Padua, which also claimed Antenor. Earlier accounts of the city's origins make no mention of the Trojans, who become increasingly stressed in the thirteenth century as a way of asserting the city's ancient independence (Carile 1976: 147–51).

With respect to northern Europe, this later and narrower use of the legend in contexts of local rivalry suggests that Italy, unlike the literally less cultivated transalpine regions and peoples, had no need, as they did, to emphasize the entitlement to civilization that the Trojan connection guaranteed. Italians could take for granted that they were the direct heirs of the empire that came from Troy, no matter how degenerate they appeared to the likes of Dante and Petrarch. Their landscape, with occasional depredations, had been a garden since Roman times and before.

---

1. Buck cites this ostensible fact, repeated in later scholarship, from Graf 1882: 1.25. But I have not been able to verify it, since Graf claims it on the basis of a fifteenth-century poetic résumé of Virgil and other versions of the Trojan story, which is no evidence at all.

It was those who had to create the garden where none existed to whom the legend spoke most powerfully, and it was there that its meaning received the fullest elaboration—both earlier and later. Referring to this agricultural transformation, an historian writes: "The marvelous tenth to thirteenth century development of northwestern Europe had been a frontier phenomenon, based on replication in what started as waste forest lands of locally almost self-sufficient communities" (McNeill 1974: 110). And it was precisely on that "frontier," which replicated and relocated itself from the Rhine to the Thames and the Tweed, where the legend of the migratory transmission of civilization was being performed, that the legend itself had been, and would continue to be, most completely retold as history. And now, at the end of the fifteenth century, the frontier was about to cross the seas, and the legend to find a global theater for its performance. The historian (who is American) does not need to tell us what constitutes the "frontier"; he writes from within the legend that defined it, the assumptions of which we all share: it is the border between the civilized and the savage, namely, between cultivated and uncultivated land. In the definition enforced by the very plot of the legend, and blandly assumed in the historian's grammar, "forest" is the simple equivalent of "waste."

The reasons why, in our culture, it is so are obvious enough, but they throw into relief one part of the legend's meaning that is undergoing a subtle alteration and will soon acquire primary significance as the frontier expands to take in virtually the rest of the world. This is, quite banally, the part played by the profit motive—always present in some sense but now assuming not merely centrality but a new sense, which, in the fifteenth century, is altering the meaning of an old word: commodity. The *terre gaste* that the legendary *civilisateurs* conquered, cleared, planted, and peopled became a commodity in the older sense, which was implicit in Geoffrey's description: it became useful, serviceable, agreeable—productive of the goods that could sustain a large and sedentary population, goods to be consumed on the spot. The *OED* records the first English use of "commodities" as goods for *sale* in 1436; similarly, in the fifteenth century the word is first used in French to mean the "profit" accruing from such sale. And from here it is but a short step to Shakespeare's ironic praise of "Commodity, the bias of the world" (*King John* 2.1.574), as the motive to secure such profit: expediency, the desire for gain as explicitly opposed to "honor." From goods for use, to goods for sale, to the results of selling, to the desire to obtain these (at whatever sacrifice of principle): the very history of the word encapsulates the formation of the social practices that will determine the subsequent use of the legend that helped to produce them. These practices are thus described by our historian: "the real novelty of the economic pattern woven through all the waterways of Europe by Italian seamen and merchants in the fourteenth to fifteenth centuries was the increased importance of cheap bulk commodities" (McNeill 1974: 110). As the circulation of such things as grain, timber, coal, wool, textiles, and metals—goods for sale—gained momentum and volume, it altered the meaning of another key word in just the same direction as that of "commodity."

   This was the word for that formerly regulated space where goods were sold: the "market," the physical and semantic motion of which has been brilliantly analyzed in Jean-Christophe Agnew's *Worlds Apart*. As a name for the specific place, or time, or congregation of people at which goods were offered for sale, the word entered English (from the Romance languages) probably in the twelfth century; by the sixteenth it is wholly unsituated, and has come to mean the general activity of sale, purchase, or valuation, wherever and whenever occurring. "As a matter of customary usage, the process of commodity exchange had spilled over the boundaries that had once defined it" (1986: 41). The market became placeless, diffused; and the word moved in its designations from place to process to principle to power. The direction of this motion is parallel to that of "commodity"—from object of use to desire for profit—and Agnew describes it as a "gradual displacement of concreteness. . . . The attributes of materiality, reality, and agency ordinarily assigned to the sphere of social relations (or to God) were implicitly reassigned to the sphere of commodity relations, as supply and demand took on a putative life of their own" (1986: 56). Though "putative" at the period of its formation, the life of the commodity market—the dominance of exchange values over intrinsic ones—will soon absorb the founding legend in its self-reproduction around the world.

   Producing goods expressly for sale; storing them or transporting them in order to use time or space to maximize profits; devising currencies and credit instruments to facilitate such transactions—there is nothing new about these activities per se. But, as the semantic history of these key terms in our languages shows, they were new to late medieval and early modern Europe. And the European expansion that they stimulated will result in a dimension of their exercise that is unprecedented, a "market of global magnitude" (Wolf 1982: 352). This is the "world-economy" whose formation and consolidation from 1450 to 1750 is narrated by Immanuel Wallerstein (1974 and 1980), and whose consequences for non-Europeans have been traced by Eric Wolf (1982). It has indeed a life of its own, in the propagation of which our founding legend, mediated by a great variety of cultural discourses, will play a crucial role—as it has already done in the remaking of the northern European landscape on the ancient, southern, Mediterranean model, helping to create the kind of prosperity in the kind of system that Europeans will transplant overseas.

   Forests, in this system, are "waste" in more ways than as the simple binary opposite to civilized cultivation inscribed in our founding myth. The power of that opposition, however, has never diminished, so it becomes important to observe how it prevailed over, elided and obscured, the actual uses of the forest even in the Europe that was clearing them. Forests were never wholly waste: they were always exploited for game and hides, honey and beeswax, fuel and timber, and as forage grounds for pigs; the surface area, hence the value, of a forest was often measured by the number of pigs it could feed (Higounet 1966: 387–92). But none of these casual exploitations ever modified the mythic identification of the forest as waste. And the exploitations were far too casual to count for much in the burgeoning new commerce of commodities markets. Timber counted—but only once, since regrowth took far too long to make replanting a steady source of profit. Much better, once cut over, to make the land produce at least an annually harvestable commodity. In the system of regular commodity production for the placeless market, forests are a liability—"waste" in the new sense of being simply unprofitable. So they are doubly doomed: an unproductive resource (except by being destroyed) in the new commerce, as well as the site of savagery in the old but ongoing myth; the abode of thieves, elves, and witches; the refuge of pagan heretics, madmen, and the odd hermit. To the terror of the forest in folklore and the marginality of its inhabitants in actual life is added the insuperable defect of low productivity.

High productivity, on the other hand, in grain fields, vineyards, and orchards from Piedmont to Tuscany generated the commercial enterprise and the wealth that gave such cities as Venice, Florence, Genoa, and Milan (all of which had histories of Trojan foundation by the thirteenth century) economic dominance in Europe on the eve of its overseas discoveries. And this dominance coincided, of course, with the cultural. For the historian, this coincidence explains the time-lag in the exportation of the Renaissance northward, as well as that between the exercise of each form of dominance:

> Yet as the scope of Italian economic management decreased, Italian leadership in Europe shifted onto a different plane. For reception of what we know as Italian renaissance culture in trans-Alpine Europe became a really live possibility precisely in proportion as local economic life began to achieve an Italian level of complexity and sophistication. Hence, for a century or more after Italian cities ceased to exercise economic primacy in Europe (roughly after 1500) Italian cultural influence upon the trans-Alpine hinterland continued and indeed increased in importance. (McNeill 1974: 116)

One of the most prominent and extended examples of such a simultaneously economic and artistic time-lag is that between the creation of the Palladian villa in Italy and its fashion in England. Palladio designed his classical Roman villas as country houses for the merchant princes of the Veneto in the mid-sixteenth century. Although his treatises and his style influenced a number of churches and royal buildings (like the Banqueting House in Whitehall) in seventeenth-century England, the villas themselves did not begin springing up there until the early eighteenth. It took about a century and a half, until England was well on the way to achieving the (global) economic primacy that Venice had earlier (regionally) enjoyed, for the Palladian villas on the Brenta to be reproduced on the Thames. Similar conditions produced a similar class with similar tastes. As the Gothic cathedrals of the Middle Ages followed the development of urban and town markets, so the artistic monuments of the Renaissance followed with some exactitude the shifts in economic dominance occasioned by control over commerce on a larger scale. As this moved from its fourteenth- and fifteenth-century focus in northern Italy, Madrid had its (brief) moment, southern Germany had a share (thanks to its mines), France tended to import Italians, and the Netherlands enjoyed in the earlier seventeenth century an artistic flowering that matched its hegemony in world trade. The apparent exception—Rome itself—was but the recipient of the wealth generated everywhere else and dispensed on all kinds of artistic production by the notorious line of Borgia, Medici, and della Rovere popes.

In other words, the "frontier phenomenon" of the reclamation of forests for agriculture also replicates itself in the geographical motion of cultural influence and production. But in the latter, the frontier becomes a threshold of commercial activity instead of a physical or political boundary. The fact of our civilization as *transmitted* from someplace else created these frontiers, which are reproduced in the founding story as the site of its climax (where the culture-bringers meet the indigenes), the logical necessity of its plot. The legend will continue to dramatize this in physical terms as the direct transplanting of empire and culture, domination and learning—what the medieval world called the *translatio imperii et studii*. But the motive and agency of this transfer in the Renaissance is commerce, which will of course become, and become synonymous with, empire: a *translatio commercii et studii*. We shall see how this agency is incorporated into the legend by the greatest poet who retold it in the period, Edmund Spenser.

Despite the vast increase in both economic and artistic complexity and sophistication during the period, despite the growth of specialized occupations and administrative bureaucracies in cities that were approaching modern levels of opulence, chaos, and crime, it is necessary to recall that all of this was made possible by the form of labor that was still everywhere predominant. Of the occident in about 1500 an historian writes: "Work was overwhelmingly a matter of tilling the soil, and the population of Europe was overwhelmingly a population of peasants," the basis of whose social values and organization, from the Atlantic to the Urals, "was tillage for grain" (Hale 1977: 199–200). Perhaps one should also recall that agricultural production today, exponentially increased by chemicals and machines, still remains the basis of our way of life. This massive productivity, of course, no longer engages the labor of most of the population, so most of us no longer inhabit a "peasant" culture. Agriculture in the west today, in a transformation completed by postindustrial technology but begun about 1450 (in what economic historians call the "long" sixteenth century), is a highly capital-intensive enterprise. With the largest portion of today's labor in the west located in the tertiary sector (producing services rather than goods), it is easy to forget that this could not be so if agricultural productivity were less immense.

We are likely to be surprised by the fact that California—which is itself an economy equal to that of Italy or Canada, the home of high-tech and the media image of the society of the future, hardly a "rural" kind of place—leads and has led the United States for forty years in agricultural production (Clements 1989: 5–6). No state in the Great Plains or in the semitropical South produces nearly as much annual revenue as the grain fields, orchards, and vineyards from the slopes of the northern Sierras to the Mexican border. It seems no coincidence that California is also the historical center of the film industry and its extension into television and video. Since these media are the twentieth-century vehicles for our culture's legends of itself, it is appropriate that they should be created where the most ancient basis of that culture has been most highly developed.

Chapter 9

EVERYBODY'S GENEALOGY

Forgers and Popularizers

That portion of our culture's *studii* which consisted in the historical discourse of the descent of Europeans from Noah and the Trojans achieved its most remarkable exfoliation during the Renaissance through the agency of a singular, because fraudulent, book. Called usually the *Antiquitates*, it was first published in Rome in 1498 and written by Annius (Giovanni Nanni) of Viterbo, a Dominican who was the papal theologian to Alexander VI. It consists of seventeen fragmentary texts—interspersed with elaborate commentaries—supposedly by various ancient authors, like Fabius Pictor and Berosus the Chaldean. (An edition of the texts alone, without the commentaries, also appeared in Venice in 1498.) Annius claimed to have received these fragments from two Armenian monks in Genoa in 1471. Just as was the case with Geoffrey of Monmouth, the scholarly debate over the authenticity of these texts was immediate, and lasted for about two centuries (see Jung 1966: ch. 2). But unlike the case of Geoffrey, whose putative British "source" is still disputed, the very Latin used by Annius's ostensibly ancient authors was enough to suggest to scholars both then and now that the texts are forgeries. This was apparent even to the Dominican last-ditch defenders of Annius in the eighteenth century, who were obliged to argue that he wasn't a knave, but just a fool to have been imposed upon by those Armenians. Later scholars, however, have convincingly shown that Annius was himself the forger and identified his motives for that labor (Joly 1870: 543–44; Danielsson 1932; Tigerstedt 1964).

The very fact of forgery, however, shows an interesting change in the material circumstances of the transmission of the legend about transmission. With the advent of printing, the traditional reliance on the authority of authors acquires a new form and gives a new scope to fraudulence. Geoffrey claimed to have seen a "book" in the indigenous language which he was merely rendering into Latin, the language of universal civilization as he knew it. Thus claiming to follow a source was a typical move in most medieval discourse, which placed supreme value on authority as opposed to originality. But in a manuscript culture, texts were laborious to reproduce; Geoffrey felt no need to provide even a sample of his claimed source, since he was (supposedly) making it available in Latin. But the humanism of the Renaissance had as a primary aim the recovery of complete and accurate classical texts, an aim that fetishized the written word in general, and Ciceronian style in particular, still in the age of script. Print, the revolution in the technology of communication in the late fifteenth century, made reproduction easy, and so imposed a further criterion of authorial authenticity: his very words, his text itself.

Forgeries, of course, were not unknown in script cultures—the most famous one in the west being that of the "Donation of Constantine," which was definitively unmasked by Lorenzo Valla about 1440 (see Coleman 1922). But the pressure to produce them increased in response to both the new philological insistence on textual purity and the new physical means of reproducing texts. The desire to have the authority's exact words, banal as it seems to us, is a Renaissance desire; the Middle Ages were largely content with his name and a paraphrase of his words. This is one reason why Virgil himself was for so long rather a name than a book, and why the Renaissance so copiously produced, and argued about, translations. The *Aeneid*, for example, was not entirely *translated* into any European vernacular until the last quarter of the fifteenth century. Medieval French versions of the poem are merely summaries of its content, taken as history and enriched by interpolated accounts of the whole later legend from Friga (Aeneas's brother) through Francion to Pharamond (Moufrin 1985).

So Annius, to lay any claim to scholarly credit in the high Renaissance, evidently felt obliged to provide the texts, to follow the typical humanist model of the edition and commentary. But what went into this new bottle was very old wine indeed. For the words that Annius puts in the mouths of his miscellaneous authorities are simply designed to produce a genealogy and chronology to end all genealogies and chronologies: to show, as his own commentaries explicitly insist, that the peoples and rulers of western Europe all descend directly from Noah, that their civilization is not just coeval but prior to that of Greece and Troy and Rome. Both the impulse and the materials to demonstrate the siblinghood of present Europe to past antiquity had existed for centuries, in the medieval chronicles we have examined. Annius pushes both to their farthest extension, exaggerating the impulse by replacing parallel with prior development, and inventing new materials. The demonstration proceeds by unmasking virtually the whole body of Mediterranean myth to reveal that the stories about the pagan gods, especially those who were *civilisateurs*, like Saturn and Hercules, are but garbled and mendacious versions of the actual deeds, the true history, of Noah and his progeny. True history is biblical— necessarily, because of the Flood, more ancient than the coopted, occluded versions of it reflected in heathen mythology.

The key text, and by far the longest, in the demonstration is attributed to (the real historian of Babylon) Berosus (under whose name many subsequent versions of Annius's text are known), who lived in the third century B.C. But Annius predates his existence by a century or two and makes him the reporter of an immeasurably antique tradition concerning the doings of Noah and his incredibly various progeny (1512: fol. 104). Berosus was a not unskillful choice, since he was known to the learned world by fragments quoted in Eusebius, was thought to have instructed the Greeks in astronomy, and was located in Babylon—the site of the presumably first civilization to have descended from Mount Ararat (not far to the north), where the Ark landed (Gen. 8:4). This geography was also cannily considered by Annius in the tale he told of the provenance of his sources: Ararat is in what used to be Armenia, and where more logically should such texts have been preserved than in the oldest Christian country in the world? Annius is doing his best to be convincing in the disciplinary manner of humanist philology; but he apes its new techniques in order to fake a text that basically opposes its aims and tastes.

The story that Berosus is made to tell is well described by the title of its English paraphrase, which radically reduces all the cumbersome scholarly apparatus of Annius to brisk narrative: *An Historical Treatise of the Travels of Noah into Europe* (Lynche 1601). Even in this streamlined form, the narrative is too confused and contradictory to summarize; but its main thrust can be sampled easily enough. Noah, quite simply, is the ur-civilizer, the single source from which our entire culture is diffused by his "travels." He and his whole biblical family are simply identified with all the known, plus a few unknown, gods and demigods in all previous mythology. He is literally the "key to all mythologies" that Mr. Casaubon (in George Eliot's *Middlemarch*) was laboring to discover. Annius beat him to it.

After the Flood, Noah taught plowing, viticulture, mathematics, astronomy (and all else) to the Scythians (the ancient inhabitants of the lower Caucasus). He is literally the beginning of everything; hence what the Romans feigned of their god Janus is true of him. The marriage of Janus and Vesta (heaven and earth) is a figure for that of Noah and Tytea; their first offspring were forty-five giants called, after their mother, Titans (1512: fol. 110ᵛ). Noah then begat the three sons—Shem, Ham, and Japheth—whom he installed as rulers of their respective continents— Asia, Africa, and Europe. Japheth begat a line of nine kings of Gaul, beginning with Sabatius (in some recensions called a "nephew" of Noah, which is hardly possible), whose just rule was transmuted into the pagan Greek stories of Saturn. The fictions of Saturn were also told about Noah himself and Ham, who is similarly the real original of Zoroaster, Pan, and Sylvanus. Ham married Rhea and begat Osiris, the original of Jupiter in all his avatars, and Isis, the similar equivalent of Juno and Ceres. They brought tillage to Egypt and in turn produced (incestuously, but this is overlooked) Hercules of Libya. And it is, of course, this character's wanderings and adventures that the ancient Greeks erroneously attributed to their own Hercules, who was nothing more than a pirate. The Libyan (later known as the Gallic) Hercules was the king of Gaul, Italy, and Spain. At some earlier point, however, Noah himself, along with his grandson (or nephew) Saturn, had to take over Italy personally when Ham, not content with Africa, invaded it; Noah founded Rome, and his rule there is what Virgil mentions as the golden age in *Aeneid* 8. This testimony is corroborated (Annius's usual method) by the text attributed to

Cato, where the same Virgilian passage is also cited (1512: fol. 66). The Libyan Hercules had three wives, from whom descend long lines of kings of Franks, Etruscans, and Gauls. The second of these lines produces Dardanus, called the founder of Troy, and so on down to Priam's cousin, Bavo, king of the Belgic Gauls, and Hector's son Francus, king of the Celtic ones.[1]

Needless to say, the names of these dozens of western European kings between the Flood and the fall of Troy are carefully chosen for the most part to be patronymic of peoples and places (a few have the names of Greek deities, just to show where the Greeks stole them). So, in the line of Gauls descending from Japheth, there is, for example, a Paris, a Lugdus (the Roman name of Lyon was Lugdunum), and a Lemannus (probably intended for the Germanic people the Romans called Alemanni), to whom later embroiderers upon Annius would credit (via Lake Léman) the foundation of both Lausanne and Geneva (Deonna 1929). For such enthusiastic readers of Annius, and they were many, literally any European location or person could (with some imagination) be fit into or derived from his riot of toponymous patronyms.

Annius performs on a grand scale, with the alleged support of the latest "discovery" made by scholarly research, the chronological linking between the genealogies of Noah, the Trojans, and the Europeans that had been attempted only in outline by the medieval chronicles. He filled the gaps, all right, and what he filled them with was designed almost to reverse one of the main meanings of our founding legend. For Annius wants to show that our civilization did not originate in antiquity, that it first happened here, where we now are, that it was exported from here to the near east and then reimported later. Noah created it himself here in the west, and his descendant the Libyan Hercules was the pivotal common ancestor of Spaniards, Italians, Gauls, and Trojans alike—with the Greeks and the Romans as but Johnnies-come-lately. The kind of anxiety and tension inherent in the legend's obsession with cultural paternity finds in Annius its clearest and most extreme expression. The Trojan connection by itself had always served as a way to recast cultural paternity as fraternity. It allowed the Romans to see themselves as the coevals, not the heirs and imitators, of the Greeks; it allowed the Franks and Britons to see themselves as the siblings, not the diminished offspring, of the Romans. The Noah connection as fabricated by Annius allows all Europeans, at the moment when modern nation-states are beginning to form, to see themselves no longer even as the siblings of either dominant ancient culture, but as ancestral to both. The patrilineal obsession is thus revealed as supremely paradoxical: it is desperate to invent a line of fathers that will supersede or come before or cancel out another line. Our myths invent fathers in order to assure us that we have none, that we are self-created. We want to be our own origin.

But in the terms of our own culture, of course—with cities, dependent on surplus-producing agriculture, and writing as the criteria—we cannot be. And nobody

---

1. Annius's incoherent genealogical table of all this—fols. 110ᵛ-112ᵛ—is abridged to a handy chart by Jung 1966: 51.

thought, then or now, of changing the terms, of altering the criteria of civilization that came to western Europe from the ancient Mediterranean world. No one
suggested that the forest-dwelling hunters and gatherers or the pastoral nomads of
Europe's real past and part of its present were anything but savages and barbarians.
Our landscape was tilled; our market towns and noble courts had become the sites
of universities, printing houses, and academies both formal and informal for the
instruction, dissemination, and discussion of Greek and Roman texts whose "rebirth" was what the Renaissance meant. And it is precisely against this whole
accelerated privileging and prestige of classical antiquity that Annius is reacting,
"against the exaggerated worship of the Graeco-Latin tradition" (Joly 1870: 543).
Annius fakes the new learning in order to oppose its reverence for just those forms
of classical writing—mythography, history, philosophy, and epic—that transmit
and define our civilization. So, having displaced the real text-producers as cultural
fathers in favor of the Scythians and Babylonians, he was yet obliged to come up
with some texts by them: mainly Berosus, whom he uses to validate, by elaborating on, the origin of civilization as sketchily described in the west's supreme text,
the Bible.

The attempt at displacement failed, of course, as it had to. In fact, the result was
pretty much the opposite: far from displacing the ever-ambivalent cultural paternity of classical antiquity, the popularity of Annius more thoroughly reconciled it
with the authority of the Bible. The priority on which he insisted was happily
taken over for the purpose of flattering the nascent nationalisms of the continent,
but wholly without effacing or displacing the Trojans and their legend from the
great chain of transmission. Annius made it possible for Europeans to have it both
ways: the Trojans are our ancestors, but their ancestors were ours, too; we're just
one big family. We Europeans, that is: Annius is consciously seeking to form the
conception of Europe as western Christendom by excluding Byzantium, now in
the hands of the infidel Turks (Tigerstedt 1964: 302–305), who are now excluded
from the Trojan descent (since that came from Europe) that they had shared in the
earliest chronicles. But the identity of Europe thus formed remained, like its landscape and its new architectural style, despite Annius, quite as classical as Christian.
The Renaissance response to Annius was not, as he might have hoped, to produce
epic poems about Noah's civilizing mission throughout Europe or histories showing how we are related to the Babylonians, but rather to go right on with new
vigor, perhaps even with a better Christian conscience, repeating as epic and as history the founding legend as the descent from Troy. As Virgil had long been Christianized, so Noah was now classicized: he did not replace the culture-bringing
heroes and deities of ancient myth; he just became another of them, the happily
syncretic functional equivalent of Saturn, Hercules, and all the emigrants from
Troy.

The vogue for Annius lasted throughout the sixteenth century and was concentrated in the transalpine region—that former "frontier"—where the founding
legend had already received its fullest medieval development. Although two translations into Italian of his text were published during the century in Venice, no re-

printings of it seem to have been made in Italy after its first appearances in Rome and Venice. But his text, sometimes abridged of its lengthy commentary, went through six editions in Paris, three in Lyon, two in Antwerp, and one each in Basel, Heidelberg, and possibly Strasbourg, before its final reprinting in Wittenberg in 1612. Paraphrases into other vernaculars than English also appeared. In addition to arousing the indignation of many serious scholars, Annius was accepted by some, and his work stimulated a great deal of philological debate as well as historical imagination (see Grafton 1990).

The most potent agent of his popularity, especially in France, was Jean Lemaire de Belges, who reproduces, embellishes, and extends Annius's enterprise in a way that perfectly illustrates the impulse to syncretic reconciliation that utterly defeated Annius's wish to bypass the Greeks and Romans altogether. Lemaire's large tomes, published between 1509 and 1512, refocus on the Trojans with a vengeance, as his title indicates: *Les Illustrations de Gaule et singularitez de Troye*. What the book does is to recount virtually all the extant lore about the Trojans, uniting the romances about the fall of Troy with the legends of the descent from Troy as amplified by Annius and with particular emphasis, of course, on the Gauls as the glorious progenitors of the French. But Lemaire, whose father was German and whose mother was a daughter of the last Duke of Burgundy, is not narrowly nationalistic; he is equally interested in providing entitlements to civilization for Germans, Austrians, and Habsburgs (Joly 1870: 559). He dedicated his first volume to Margaret of Austria, Regent in the Netherlands for the nephew she was raising there, the future Holy Roman Emperor Charles V, who was the last to have truly imperial pretensions. Lemaire shares Annius's aim to create an ideal conception (at a time when Europe is riven by rival monarchical ambitions) of a Christian Europe unified and united against the Turk by means of a noble ancestry that owes nothing to ancient Greece and Rome.

One scholar describes this effort as one of "cultural decolonization" (Dubois 1972: 38). So it certainly was for Annius, and Lemaire dutifully repeats the chronology that makes Noah's wanderings and the list of Gallic kings ancestral to Troy. But Lemaire never stresses the falsehood of the Greeks as Annius constantly does, and goes on blithely to recapitulate all the stories of Trojan foundation that he knew. That of Brutus and Albion is summarized, with no credit to Geoffrey (1882: 2.296). Lemaire delights in furnishing, by repetition or invention, Trojan ancestors for a long list of locations from southern France to Holland and upper Franconia, not forgetting the "Sicambrians." And this activity constituted his enormous influence on subsequent regional historians (Joly 1870: 582–89).

Lemaire made specifically Trojan origins more popular than ever. He thus reinforced what Annius had labored to make superfluous. He was able to do so simply because the myth had already been enacted as history. The Trojan ancestors may have been fictions; but the colonizing, planting, city building, and lawgiving had in fact occurred, and the attachment of this form of civilization by Virgil to Rome and to Troy was too old and too strong to be resisted. It was not, finally, by its picture of civilization that Renaissance Europe would begin to decolonize itself from the Greco-Roman antiquity it so ambivalently admired. It was rather by the use of vernacular languages, the conscious cultivation of spoken mother tongues and their legitimation as objects of serious study. And even this was secured only at the price of assimilating vernaculars to the canons of grammatical and rhetorical description devised for and taken over from Latin and Greek (see Waswo 1987: ch. 4). Even here remains some form of colonization—as how could it not, since, as every version of the legend (including that of Annius) and every episode of its enactment demonstrates, we get civilized only by being colonized. Someone must transmit "culture" to us in all its forms—who does so and when are irrelevant to this unchanging dynamic. Our civilization is not a spontaneous production; it always comes from elsewhere, and it does so repeatedly. No matter if Noah brought it here first; others must bring it later. One foundation follows another.

Thus at the height of the Renaissance, in the decade between 1498 and 1509, appeared two texts that were seminal for the continuation of the legend as historical discourse. Annius gave the luster (however much tarnished by dissenters) of the new scholarship to the oldest form of that discourse, the patrilineal chronology. And Lemaire extended it with cheerful abandon, fusing the romance of Troy with its legend, enrolling Noah in the ranks of classical culture-bringers, popularizing just that (later) foundation that Annius had attempted to elide and subsume, and inspiring a host of writers to do likewise (for examples, see Jung 1966: 52–68).

The Trojan foundation was also reinforced by one other writer who emulated both his predecessors, using the techniques of Annius to counter the Gallic patriotism of Lemaire with his own exclusively German variety. This was Joannes Trithemius (Johann Tritheim), Abbot of Sponheim, who invented two ancient Frankish sources, Hunibald and Wasthald. These he alternately quotes and summarizes (just as Annius had done with his), in order to produce an unbroken patrilineal chronology from Marcomirus (here, a son of Antenor; in medieval French romance, a brother of Aeneas) down through Charlemagne to the early German (Holy Roman) Emperors. His text, first published in 1515, was popular for a century. Though much less ambitious in its fraudulence than Annius's, and even less convincing, since he offered no story at all about the provenance of the manuscripts he claimed were now lost (see Joly 1870: 551–52), it had much the same purpose: to justify by faked scholarship the inherited medieval legend of Trojan lineage with all its etymological fantasizing of patronyms and toponyms. And just as in the Middle Ages, the legend could be pressed into service for different political occasions or groups. What Annius used to dignify present Europe as opposed to ancient Greece and Rome, Lemaire focused on France and the Rhineland; Trithemius simply appropriates the entire (legendary) history of the Franks for the Germans. They are the real heirs of Troy, subject to no one, and hence the true inheritors of the present Empire.

The freedom and dominion of the Franks is asserted from the beginning of Trithemius's text (a prefatory letter to his Bishop) to the end of it. Noah is wholly ignored; Trithemius is concerned more with legitimizing power than with making a cultural claim, and for this the Trojans serve exactly as they served in the eighth-century *Liber Historiae Francorum*, which is the basis for Trithemius's embellishments. Marcomirus leads his people from the Danube to the Rhine, in the course of which their name alters from Trojans to Scythians to Sicambrians to Franks. Doing so, he but follows a prophecy of Jove, which informs him that his brothers are Brutus, the ancestor of the Angles, and Romphaea, that of the Saxons. So he makes a treaty with the Britons and must subdue the Gauls (Trithemius 1601: 2–4). The Franks take their name from their seventeenth king, Francus (13); the old story of their refusing tribute to Valentinian is repeated, along with the Roman praise of their toughness and ferocity in the cause of liberty (31–32). Thus does Trithemius, like Lemaire, only more narrowly partisan, return to the Trojans what Annius had tried to displace onto their mythical forebears: their status as imperial founders.

Together with Geoffrey of Monmouth, these three texts and their imitators, diffused by the new technology of print, indeed made it "possible to elaborate the Trojan origin of every European people, to account for the dispersion of the arts and sciences, and to provide an etymology of illustrious antiquity for every place name" (Hay 1967: 108).

It does not seem accidental that these texts should have been produced just when Europe is first becoming aware that the planet contains another hemisphere. At the moment when this unimaginably wider frontier is beckoning the commercial energies and imperial ambitions of the maritime nations, their inhabitants are being made more intensely aware of the numerous, smaller frontiers in their own past: all of those borders between cultivation and the *inculte* where civilization, carried by Noah, Saturn, Hercules, and the sons of Troy, first encountered us. The repeated settling of frontiers by colonists constitutes the foundations in the legend; the defining character of our civilization is precisely the "transmission" that equates it with colonization. And Europe is just on the verge of repeating its own experience of foundation, just as it is now repeating the legend of that experience, around the globe.

Annius, in fact, dedicated the *Antiquitates* to Ferdinand and Isabella of Spain, probably intending no more by it than flattery of the Aragonese origins of his pope. But it is more than a pleasant coincidence that his fake "discovery" of ancient sources should be presented to the very patrons of Columbus's real discovery of a future part of the world (a future part, that is, of the European world: another frontier that would get civilized as the site of commodity production). For the two dimensions of these two different discoveries—temporal and spatial—will themselves coincide in the European perception of the indigenes in the new world. What explorers and colonizers will see in those distant places is their own past, as pictured in the founding legend; and what they will do is what the culture-bringers in the legend did to them. As they do it, they will modify the legend accordingly; and when the legend ceases, at length, to be credited as history, it will diffuse itself through poetry into the discourses of philosophy, law, and science.

Chapter 10

EPIC VOYAGES

Poets and Colonizers in the Sixteenth Century

The first examples of the literary stage of the legend's diffusion, inspired initially by both the prestige of Virgil and the new relevance of his imperial theme, are the complete epic of Luis de Camoens and the unfinished one of Pierre de Ronsard. Both published in 1572, each is a hymn to nationalism that attempts a Virgilian treatment of one dimension in the coinciding "discoveries" of Columbus and Annius. Camoens, a Portuguese aristocrat who was for some time a civil servant in India, narrates the triumphant voyage of Vasco da Gama to and from the Malabar Coast.

In the first canto, Jove addresses the gods and promises to the sons of Portugal (the meaning of the poem's title, *Os Lusiados*) many years of rule over the oceans of the east. Venus aids this project, but Bacchus takes the Virgilian role of Juno, who opposes it and thus generates all the usual vicissitudes. Escaping from one of these to the island of Madagascar, Gama bends the ear of its friendly monarch to a lengthy account of the glorious history of Portugal. Arrived in Calicut, Gama learns all about the caste system and local customs from a friendly Moor (i.e. Arab), and imparts in his turn to the local prince how noble the Portuguese are. On the way home, there is an (Odyssean) interlude on a paradisical island where Gama hears a long prophecy from a Siren about the Portuguese governors of India. Since the (actual) trajectory is from west to east, and since the (actual) situation is not yet one of colonization, but merely exploration or "discovery," the issue of the poem is not culture-bringing, but rather the opening of seagoing access to the foreclosed overland trade routes. The prominent nineteenth-century English translator of the poem, Sir Richard Burton, quite appropriately called it "the Epos of Commerce" (Camoens 1880: xii). But this subject quite suffices for Camoens to invest it with Virgilian dignity, insisting that the truth of such a voyage is superior to Ariosto's fictions and that his hero, Gama, "claims all Aeneas' fame" (1.11–12). Opening up a trade is the equivalent of founding an empire.

The immediate precedent Camoens (invidiously) cites, and whose stanzaic form (ottava rima) he uses, prompts the observation that the great Italian epics of the Renaissance did not indeed find their subjects in the contemporary world. The chivalric tales of the court of Charlemagne and the crusades were what engaged the imaginations of Boiardo (sometimes reluctantly), Ariosto (often ironically), Tasso (piously), and their patrons, three generations of the Este family in Ferrara. The choice of the old *chansons de geste* about Roland (Boiardo's *Orlando Innamorato*, 1506; Ariosto's *Orlando Furioso*, 1532) and Godfrey of Boulogne (Tasso's *Gerusalemme Liberata*, 1575) as subjects for episodic, often called "romantic," epic treatment no doubt resulted in part from the Estensi association with French interests and courts throughout this period (Gundersheimer 1973: 276–77). The choice also reflected highly aristocratic tastes far removed from any concern with empires of trade and commerce. The appeals of these stories, greatly sophisticated by the attitude of their narrators, remained those of medieval romance: military and amorous exploits offering wide scope for the exhibition of noble personal behavior, plus the delights of supernatural enchantment.

Yet even here there is still room for the legend of Troy, if possibly for no other purpose than to provide the usual flattery of the Este princes. In the *Innamorato*, Ruggiero relates his lineage to Bradamante, beginning with the fall of Troy (3.5.19) and explaining that Astyanax—Hector's infant son—was saved, escaped to Sicily, and began the line that eventuates in Pippin and Charlemagne, thence to an Italian branch and himself: "my race is from Troy" (*da Troia è la mia gesta*, 3.5.37). In the *Furioso*, Ariosto has Ruggiero summarize the same descent from Hector (36.70–72) and adds the detail of his "Trojan" heraldic device (26.99), which is of course that of the Este. Camoens's Italian predecessors thus continue, as many others will do, to make standard use of the Trojan legends in a dynastic context, whereas Camoens adapts the structure of the *Aeneid* to a national one.

What Camoens adapted to his nation's venture in space Ronsard seeks to apply rather to the temporal history of his nation, the legend as found in the pages of Lemaire de Belges. *La Franciade* is designed as the exact parallel to Virgil's epic: the founding story of a nation that will secure immortality for its author. The hero, Francion (also called Francus), was in his childhood (in this version) Astyanax himself. Saved from the flames of Troy by a ruse, he escapes to Epirus; grown up, he is told by Mercury how to sail to the mouth of the Danube. On the way he is shipwrecked by Neptune and Juno onto Crete, where there are amorous intrigues and a descent to the underworld, and where he stays—since the poem goes no further than this, the fourth book of a projected twenty-four. But the Virgilian design is clear enough, its ambition reinforced, even burdened, by numerous verbal echoes amounting sometimes to a kind of pastiche.

Though the story remains untold, Jupiter has, as in Virgil, predicted its outcome and specified its significance in the first book. Francus, we learn, will marry a German princess on the Danube, but will lose her before reaching the banks of the Seine. There he will found in honor of his uncle Paris a city that is now only grass;

but he will furnish it with marble edifices rising to the stars. Francus will die un-
vanquished; but his people will lose the name of Trojans and the city be deserted
after him until Pharamond revives it. From him will descend Merovée and all the
French kings down to Charles IX, of whom Jupiter says, "I've not limited the empire" (1.191–265). The first scene of the poem's action finds Francion and his Trojans worshipping Cybele, who plays the role of Venus to the hero, and who is
shown here with "her head adorned by cities" (*le chef de citez atourné*, 1.419). In the
later parade of French monarchs in the underworld, we see Marcomire in Sicambria (4.778) and learn that Merovée will change the name of the nation from Gaul
to France in memory of our hero (4.1063).

Ronsard's project well illustrates the power of the Virgilian model to reabsorb,
for the classicizing Renaissance poet, the legends popularized by Lemaire that Annius sought to attach directly to Noah. The power comes not merely from the new
pertinence of the imperial theme of the supreme Latin poet, but also from the very
fact that the story he told is, and remains, our founding legend. The links that story
forges from the ancient history of our culture—between agriculture and cities, emigration and conquest—are perfectly understood by Ronsard even though he
never gets to the climactic scene in their plot. His replacement of Virgil's Venus
by Cybele, the turreted Phrygian goddess of grain, foregrounds the associations
that Venus in Latium had for the Romans but that had been largely overshadowed
by her other attributes in the Renaissance. The contrast between a Paris of grass
and one of marble is taken straight from Aeneas's tour of the site of Rome. And
the promise of unlimited empire to Charles IX, king of France and patron of the
Pléiade (to whom the poem is dedicated), is the mutually flattering reassertion of
the symbiotic relation between Augustus and Virgil, prince and poet. The death of
this young king two years after the publication of the first four books supplied
Ronsard with his public excuse for not finishing the poem—though few of its critics much regret this, regarding the excuse as a convenient way out of a subject that
proved uncongenial in the performance. One can well imagine that so strict an imitation of the model became too tedious a task.

There was also, for the humanistically educated poet, the nagging question of
the historicity of the subject, its status as authentic truth in a newly critical age.
Aware of the scholarly controversies over such as Annius and Lemaire, poets like
Ronsard and Spenser were torn between the attraction of the legend and their understanding of what an epic poem ought to be. For it was supposed to be historical, based at least (with permissible embellishments) on the great deeds of great
men that actually happened. Hence Camoens's boast of superiority to Ariosto. The
epics of Homer and Virgil were regarded as in general true accounts of real
events—a conviction that long endured. Virgil was corroborated in part by the first
book of Livy, and so unassailable. Homer and the very existence of Troy were also
unquestioned then. But two more centuries of skeptical philology and the opening of the near east to tourism in the late eighteenth century would produce a
scholarly consensus that Homer was but a fable. Troy could not be found. This
consensus, however, did not prevent several generations of antiquarian tourists

from looking for it, as Lord Byron did (*Don Juan* 4.77), and insisting on its existence in the absence of physical evidence.

Such wishful nostalgia, itself a testimony to the power of the ancient conviction that epics were true, was finally, of course, vindicated as fact by Heinrich Schliemann, who (as an amateur defying the expert consensus of his day) dug up the physical evidence of Troy in the early 1870s. Or so we now, at any rate, believe; we know what constitutes evidence; we have chemistry and carbon dating, and these have made the fable fact. But perhaps all fables were, or will be, fact; perhaps all facts are first, or once were, fables. Certainly our founding legend was and is both at once: the history of our desire and our desire for that history; it both fictionalizes the real and realizes the fiction—continually. Uchendu (a character in Chinua Achebe's *Things Fall Apart*) was right: "There is no story that is not true."

By Renaissance criteria, Homer and Virgil were true. To harness them, by imitation, to a contemporary imperial nationalism therefore demanded some adherence to facts. Ronsard is enchanted with Lemaire's version of Gallic history, but cannot be sure that it is fact. He expresses ascending degrees of unease with this situation in the original and the later expanded prefaces to *La Franciade*. In the first, he implicitly admits that the tale of Trojan Francus may be dubious as history, but defends it as being at least "probable," thus preserving some factual claim for his material. In the second, the claim is just about abandoned: Ronsard divorces the poet from the historian (as Aristotle did) and says that the former does not care about the latter's kind of truth; the poet's domain is merely the "possible."

The general question of what could be said to be true in any fictional composition had, of course, been debated since antiquity, and was a particular issue in the arguments about the Italian epics of the sixteenth century. Ronsard's solution, later eloquently expressed by Sir Philip Sidney, typifies the conclusion reached by the Renaissance to the ancient debate "by which Europe became conscious of fiction as an activity distinct from history on the one hand and from lying on the other" (Lewis 1954: 319). Literature, that is, was not merely falsehood—as it was for perennial strains of Platonism and Christianity—but was seen to possess a kind of truth-value (usually moral) different from that of the "facts" of history. However satisfactory, then and later, as an answer to the general question, it did not entirely remove either the ancient distrust of fiction itself or the special obligation of the epic to be at least partly "historical."

Camoens could vaunt this obligation, hailing Gama as the equal of Aeneas; Ronsard found it necessary to deny that it was an obligation. Other aspirants to epic composition would also have to deal with the same problem. Probably the most successful solution was found by the writer of the most successful modern epic of all, John Milton. He managed to maximize the truth-claims of *Paradise Lost* in both literal and moral senses: his story, as he frequently announces, of the commission of original sin is the determining historical fact, as it is the determining moral truth, of the human condition. But Milton's epic is unique in more ways than one, and his maximal truth-claim is secured by the abandonment of the specifically nationalistic purposes of other poets. In his youth, however, he shared these purposes: King

Arthur was first on his list of possible epic subjects when he was an undergraduate (Hughes 1957: 130). To have chosen this subject in the mid-seventeenth century, when the historical veracity of its main source, Geoffrey of Monmouth, was pretty thoroughly eroded among the learned, would have required Milton to adopt the solution of Ronsard. Thus to sever the (figurative, moral, symbolic) truth of his epic from any notion of the literal truth of empirical accuracy would surely not have been congenial to Milton's radical Protestantism. Since Luther, its battle cry had been for the one *literal* sense of saving Scripture under which all possible kinds of truth were subsumed. For Milton (in *Aereopagitica*), truth may present herself to mortals only as dismembered fragments difficult of access; but there is no doubt that she is finally one and indivisible. No doubt, too, the idea of glorifying British history lost its lustre after what was to Milton the catastrophic failure of the revolution in whose service he had sacrificed his sight. For whatever reason, he finessed the problem, relinquishing mere national destiny to focus on that of humankind. The problem remained for Spenser, who adapts the Arthurian material to specifically Elizabethan purposes, and who expected from his Queen the same kind of reward as Augustus gave to Virgil. He didn't quite receive it; the project was, like Ronsard's, unfinished; and Spenser's text confronts the problem of historical truth in a variety of ways, as we shall observe.

Before doing so, it is necessary to look briefly at those expanded horizons whose "discovery" gave new impetus to the imitation of Virgil. Ronsard's attempt was to retell the Trojan founding legend of his own nation; the Portuguese Camoens ignored the legend to tell the story of a commercial foundation in Virgilian terms. Spenser will incorporate the latter motive in the former story, with variations dependent on the way in which those horizons were in fact being perceived by sixteenth-century Englishmen.

While the poets of transalpine Europe were busy during the sixteenth century trying to catch up culturally with Italy, other Europeans were busy creating, by conquest and colonization, the global economy of the modern world. Hitherto undreamed-of wealth in gold and silver was pouring into and out of Spain, producing equally undreamed-of rates of inflation (the "price revolution" of the long sixteenth century), along with unprecedented opportunities for investing the resultant capital in myriad forms of commercial exploitation. And in the long term, of course, it was these forms of commerce, and not the mere extraction of precious metals, which created the global market and provided the basis and motive for the most extensive and powerful empire the planet has known, the British.

Not yet the ruler of the waves that she would later become, nor even yet a serious competitor for the possession of the globe that Pope Alexander VI had divided between Spain and Portugal in 1493, Britain was not at all the likeliest candidate to achieve the hegemony that she later enjoyed. How she did achieve it, through a centuries-long combination of sometimes related, sometimes haphazard, developments agricultural, sociological, religious, industrial, and military, is far too complex and contested a story to summarize here (a good summary is Lloyd 1984). But, even at England's entrance as a minor player in the global sweepstakes at a time when Spain seemed overwhelming and Portugal monopolized the spice trade, one can observe the presence of both attitudes and methods that would prove lasting and determinant and were partly shared by her strongest later rivals, France and Holland.

The attitudes were simply those of bourgeois mercantilism, and the methods those of the modern corporation, born in the sixteenth century as the chartered joint-stock company for the precise purpose of carrying on trade and planting colonies in distant quarters of the globe. Neither was wholly new, but both together, supported by a friendly government (which could be monarchical or republican), constituted an efficient means to exploit in various ways, as sites of commodity production, both the peripheral (north and east) parts of Europe itself and the rest of the world. The piratical exploits of Sir Francis Drake and the flamboyantly self-destructive searches for El Dorado by Sir Walter Raleigh are the famous exceptions that can obscure the much less romantic rule that the expansion of European hegemony in general, and of English in particular, was not achieved by daring acts of theft (however profitable) or by desperate hopes to strike it rich (however unlucky).

Hegemony was achieved rather by the formation of a system designed to produce steady, continuous profits by marketing commodities that either old or new territories could be made to produce. The system of trading in what McNeill called "cheap bulk commodities" was already in place, dominated by northern Italy, within western Europe by the late fifteenth century. It remained only to fit the rest of the world into it, using the newly found territories as sources of profit-making products, most of which (except timber and grain) did not grow in Europe. Tobacco, sugar, cotton, beaver pelts, cocoa, pepper, and later, tea and coffee were the new bulk commodities that Europe used other parts of the world to provide. Their provision required different kinds and degrees of skill and labor; the latter requirement of two of them, sugar and cotton, created another market for another commodity: slaves. The utterly unquestioned aim was just to produce commodities, to make any part of the earth yield whatever could profit Europe. This aim, this use, wholly altered the ways of life of countless local populations from Hudson's Bay to Lake Victoria: the names follow the use and are given by the users.

Far more typical, therefore, and more important than the escapades of such as Drake and Raleigh, are the routine responses of more ordinary Englishmen to the new horizons of the Americas: they see there terrain to be commercially exploited. Ample testimonies to this aim were conveniently collected, with the help of the principals and of government officials, by Richard Hakluyt in 1589, precisely to encourage such activity. The enthusiasm of these men for the immense prospects of the task is well conveyed by Sir John Hawkins's description of Florida in 1564: "The commodities of this land are more then are yet knowne to any man: for besides the land it selfe, whereof there is more then any king Christian is able to inhabit, it flourisheth with meadow, pasture ground, with woods of Cedar and Cypres, and other sorts, as better can not be in the world" (Hakluyt 1589: 541).

Hawkins goes on, as almost all the explorers did, to give a list of the local flora and fauna. The latter include unicorns, and so, he deduces, lions. (One assumes he didn't actually see a unicorn; forms of wildcat exist in the interior woods, but he could hardly have gone far enough from the coast to see any, and they are in any case not lions.) Hawkins was not a fanciful fellow, but a hardheaded sea captain, pioneer English slavetrader, and later treasurer of the navy.

The juxtaposition of his observations and deductions is more than merely quaint. It is precisely analogous to the maps and sea charts of the period—those whose purpose is to make practical navigation possible, with compass lines and latitudes copiously indicated, along with, in the empty spaces of land and water, meticulous drawings of wonderful and bizarre monsters of a vaguely reptilian kind. The map, an actual guide to new places, contains the old dragons of immemorial European imagination. In just the same way, Hawkins looks at new space and reasons that it must contain old time. He sees the land straightforwardly as an object of exploitation, an enormous source of commodities, and he blandly animates it with creatures from the European past (one fictitious and one real), the logic of whose linkage is purely imaginary and symbolic. Where there are unicorns, there must be lions, for that is what the old stories say. The symbolic linkage is of course that of the lion and unicorn on the royal arms of England, and Hawkins might be suspected of making a subtle claim for possession (or maybe a joke) by finding these beasts in Florida. But neither his prose nor his career suggests much subtlety: that is the point. He articulates the European aim to produce commodities from a new landscape in which he finds forms of life from a legendary European past. He sees what he desires, and finds what he has been told in stories. It is a miniature blueprint of the way in which the story of our founding legend will operate in the consciousness of commodity-seeking Europeans to determine their perception of both the landscape and its human inhabitants.

Creating commodities so far away, however, required capital investments on an unprecedented scale. In the system of intra-European coastal trading in "bulk commodities," from the Black Sea to the Baltic, individual merchants could, like Shakespeare's Antonio, finance by themselves four or five "argosies" at once (though gossip in the play also credits Antonio with "ventures" to Mexico and the Indies: *The Merchant of Venice* 1.3.18). But longer and more hazardous voyages required equipment and victualing for the open sea; and the production of commodities in those vast American spaces required even more—whole colonizing populations of management and labor. And so the former casual consortium of multiple investors became the formal and legal structure of the corporation: the joint-stock company whose shares were saleable, thus becoming another form of commodity. To make investment in them attractive, these companies received a charter from the crown, that is, a monopoly on trade with, or plantation of a colony in, a given area. Such grants of monopoly privileges, like tax-farming, had long been used by monarchs as a way of rewarding individuals. When such grants were extended to companies engaged in overseas operations, they were usually accompanied by wide-ranging, if not absolute, judicial and military powers over the area concerned. *De facto* teeth were required to protect the *de jure* monopoly from both foreign and domestic encroachment. For unexplored territories (North America as opposed to India), enormous grants of land were also made, based on what the monarch could claim by "right of discovery." So it was that in the course of time the Hudson's Bay Company literally owned most of Canada, and the East India Company gradually became the government of India.

It is intriguing to observe that the model of the joint-stock company framed by the English, and soon imitated by their rivals, for the commercial exploitation of the globe was immediately applied to the organization of the modern world's first mass entertainment industry: the public theaters of Elizabethan London. Although the acting companies received no royal charters, their legal status was secured as liveried servants to some aristocrat, and two of the companies—the Chamberlain's (after 1603 the King's) Men and the Admiral's—enjoyed a monopoly in London decreed by the Privy Council in 1598 (Gurr 1980: 42). And the economic principle, of colonization and of dramatization, was identical: investors shared in the profits proportionally to the amount of capital they invested—in a voyage, an acting company, or its playhouse. Shares were transferable by purchase or inheritance. The Globe, in which Shakespeare became a shareholder at its construction in 1599, was thus aptly named in terms that reverse the ancient metaphor—"all the world's a stage"—since the stage of a joint-stock company venture was in fact the world. On the stage of the Globe were enacted, as fictions, some of the dreams of dominion that were being enacted, as facts, on the farther-flung stage of the larger globe.[1] And both kinds of enactment were financially organized in the same way.

One such organizer on that larger stage was Sir George Peckham, the "chief adventurer"—that is, principal investor—in Sir Humphrey Gilbert's voyages to colonize Newfoundland in the 1580s. Peckham wrote what amounts to a prospectus for the enterprise, praising its prospects and justifying its every aspect by precedents, Roman and biblical, that reproduce the old frontiers in the new world. He aims "to proove that the voyage, late enterprised for trade, trafficke, and planting in America, is an action tending to the lawfull enlargement of her Majesties Dominions, commodious to the whole Realme in general, profitable to the adventurers in particular, beneficiall to the Savages, and a matter to be attained without any great . . . difficultie" (Hakluyt 1589: 704). The initial justifications concern the most troublesome aspect of planting a colony: how to deal with the people who are already there. Peckham asserts that Christians have the right, by "Law of Nations," to trade and dwell among savages. The formation in contemporary terms of what would become international law (which will be examined later) was in fact barely underway when Peckham was writing. The ancient tradition out of which it developed is what Peckham here invokes: the various senses and applica-

---

1. There were several plays (now lost) on the European conquest of the new world as well as on various episodes from Geoffrey's version of the legend, of which the most compendious appears to have been Day and Chettle's *The Conquest of Brute* (Schelling 1908: 2.548), which was acted by the Admiral's Men in 1601 (Harrison 1933: 219).

tions of *ius gentium*, a branch of Roman law that regulated commerce and contracts, dealt with relations between states and was often a synonym for the vaguely
philosophical *ius naturale*—normative precepts of "natural reason" valid for all peoples and places.

The assumption of such moral universals had long been an integral part of
Christian philosophy, and would receive powerful contemporary restatement from
a more famous Englishman than Peckham. Richard Hooker, the great Anglican
theologian, explains that "the Law of Nature" is that "which human Nature know-
eth itself in reason universally bound unto, which also for that cause may be termed
most fitly the Law of Reason." This law is composed of what is self-evident to
human understanding, and may therefore be known as a consensus of all previous
thought, which is equated with God: "The general and perpetual voice of men is
as the sentence of God himself. For that which all men have at all times learned,
Nature herself must needs have taught; and God being the author of Nature, her
voice is but his instrument" (Hooker 1593: 506–11). Such universalism is about to
be sorely tested by the European experience of savages—who do not seem to have
learned what Nature and God have taught us. But it will not ever be relinquished,
this ancient habit of attributing to the timeless, natural (and divine) constitution of
the world the moral principles and cultural arrangements that are constructed in
history by human societies.

Peckham invokes this attribution to claim our Christian "right" to colonize the
territory of savages; there's no argument for it nor need there be; it's a given. Along
with the right goes the Christian obligation to convert the savages to the saving
faith. He distinguishes two forms that our Christian encounter with the savages
may take: one where we "are admitted . . . to quiet possession" and one where we
are "unjustly repulsed" (Hakluyt 1589: 705). "Unjustly," of course, because it's our
"right" to be there; and the assertion of that right turns out to be strategically crucial. Without it, we might be compelled to see ourselves as doing what in fact we
are doing—intruding (to put it mildly) on someone else, in which case to be "repulsed" would seem both logical and just. But our "right" forecloses this possibility. So where the savages assent to this, there's no problem. We woo them with
cordiality and trinkets, and soon "enjoy such competent quantity of Lande" as we
may desire, "considering the great aboundance that they have of Lande, and howe
small account they make thereof, taking no other fruites thereby then such as the
ground of it selfe dooth naturally yeelde." And where the savages don't assent to
it, there's no problem either, since we simply beat them into submission. That this
is lawful, says Peckham, is demonstrated by all of history, both before and after
Christ: "puissant Emperours and Kings have performed the like, I say to plant, pos-
sesse, and subdue" (706). Thus Joshua dispossessed the Canaanites; thus Constantine enlarged his empire by subduing barbarous heathens (707–708).

Peckham's list of legitimizing conquests, along with the names of the historians
where he's found them, extends over two full folio pages. Even he is conscious of
the overkill of justification here, declaring it necessary because he has heard that
some who are not "meanely learned" think it "scarce lawfull" to take over territo-

ries and plant the Christian faith by violence (709). By now, though, what is lawful has slid the whole way down the usual ambiguity of the term, from the prescriptive ideal to the descriptive practice. Just as the divine principle is for Hooker what men have always thought, conquest is justified for Peckham because it's what men have always done. It's justified by the stories of our own past; it needs those stories for that purpose. And as conquest proceeds in magnitude and intensity, the stories get retold in a kind of increasing volume, with a new edge of urgency to their legitimizing function.

Peckham doesn't mention the Trojan story (though others will); but he doesn't have to. For it's already there, in the very category of the "savage" as, specifically, the failure to exploit the land agriculturally as we do. The ancient gap between savage gatherers and civilized cultivators is even further widened by the newly sharpened motive to produce commodities for a world market. All this becomes amply clear as Peckham swings into his real subject, which is how very profitable—in social and political as well as economic terms—our "trade, traffic and planting" will be. With ports on the coast, it will be easier to fish the great banks. Since savages love garments, "what vent for our English clothes will thereby ensue" (710). This will restore prosperity to now depleted villages at home and stimulate the enlargement of the navy; the idle who now "annoy" the state may be set to work. Noblemen can there found vast estates, and merchants will there find a long list of commodities easy of access because of deep rivers. The savages, finally, will "blesse the houre" of our arrival, being "more then fully recompensed" by Christianity for "all the commodities they can yeeld us" (711–13). The language neatly absorbs our religion into the whole process of commodity exchange, making it a nice bargain for us: we give the spirit (which has no cash value) and get the flesh (which does). Peckham is wholly silent on how conversion is to be accomplished. He hardly cares, since, even if it isn't, the savages will have from us purely material benefits that exceed those we have from them. For they're now so ignorant as not even to know how to manure and develop their land, the tenth part of which "may yeeld more commodities to the necessary use of mans life, then the whole now doth: What cause of complaint may they have? . . . I doe verily thinke that God did create land, to the end that it should by culture and husbandry, yeeld things necessary for mans life." Besides the knowledge of how to till the soil, the savages will receive "honest manners," good government, "mechanical occupations, arts and liberall sciences," protection from cannibals, and an end to human sacrifices (714).

And there it is, the old *translatio imperii et studii*, the blueprint for European colonization, whole and intact, justified by God and history, legitimized by mutual profit-taking, poised on the threshold of its enactment as a self-fulfilling prophecy of our expansion around the world. Every argument, motive, and rationalization adduced by Peckham will be incessantly repeated for the next three hundred years, as the scenario of the prophecy is performed on the great stage of the real globe. "Thus shall her Majesties dominions be enlarged," Peckham triumphantly concludes, "all odious idlenes from this our realme utterly banished, divers decaied townes repaired, and many poore and needie persons relieved, and estates of such as now live in want shall be embettered, the ignorant and barbarous idolaters taught to know Christ" (717). The premise of the program, the very keystone of its justificat-ion, is just that supposed ignorance. The savage in his forest (or the giant in his cave) lacks all *mos* and *cultus*. This is why, even if conversion fails, he can't help being bet-ter off by getting just the material improvements of our civilization. His presumed ignorance, which is his very definition in the founding legend, is the enabling fiction of the scenario as well as its moral justification. He must be seen to be ignor-ant and immoral as the legend prescribes; hence we can save him from himself. And so he is, must be, alleged to practice cannibalism and human sacrifice.

Longer books than this one have attempted to trace the history of these obses-sive terrors to the western imagination. From Greek myth through ancient Med-iterranean practice and Christian ritual to medieval accusations (of Jews and witches) and finally to the extremely problematic reports by European explorers of the Caribbean and the South Pacific, the specter of cannibalism has occupied a permanently nebulous place in our psyche, and has hence assumed a powerful place in our fantasies about others. Peter Hulme (1986: 80–87), reviewing some of this literature, and especially the derivation of the modern term in SAE from un-confirmed accusations of the Caribs—"Canibales" to the Spaniards—suggests that ferocious people-eating was less a practice of theirs than a projection of ours. Con-temporary anthropologists now sift the archives with great care, and find the prac-tice in specific funerary and ritual contexts (Brown and Tuzin 1983). Whatever the contested history of the practice, it seems clear that the legend, which tells us what savagery is, is determining our perception of what these people do—whether they do it or not. The explorers' assumptions were quite sufficient to imbue the whole population of the Americas (and later, of Africa) with a taste for human flesh. It appears in this discourse as the ultimate enormity, the essential evidence for the utter absence of *mos*. Lesser enormities also appear with regularity. What is inter-esting is that other perceptions of the savages also appear, quite contradictorily, jux-taposed with these in the accounts by some of Hakluyt's humbler witnesses.

These more naive observers reveal what the legend conceals, and will conceal more effectively in later forms of colonial discourse. A sailor, David Ingram, offers this pleasant contradiction as a summary description of the natives on the north coast of the Gulf of Mexico in 1568: they are, he says, "brutish and beastly," and "naturally very courteous" (Hakluyt 1589: 558). A merchant, Henry Hawkes, mar-vels at the kind of contradiction he sees in the Mexican Indians around 1572: they are "given to much beastliness, and void of all goodness," since they commit sod-omy and incest when drunk. Yet, he goes on, "they are very artificiall [i.e. skillful] in making of Images, with feathers. . . . The finenes and excellencie of this is won-derfull, that a barbarous people as they are, should give themselves to so fine an art as this is" (548). Here are witnesses whose eyes are violating their minds, and they simply record the fact. They can afford to do so, since they are not concerned, as Peckham was, to justify the operation. For if the savages are courteous and skilled in artistic craft, the justification evaporates.

An even larger contradiction appears in the context of another kind of justification. Ralph Lane, reporting to Raleigh about his settlement on Roanoke Island in 1586, finds its prospects grim. The soil is thin and unpromising, so that nothing else but "a good mine," he thinks, "or a passage to the Southsea" can attract colonists (742). Thomas Heriot, another of Raleigh's agents, wishes to scotch just such false rumors that Roanoke is unprofitable. He does so first by listing all the "merchantable" commodities the land itself affords. He then describes the native agriculture: they neither fertilize nor plow, but rake up mulch and stubble and burn it. Their yields, he claims, of corn, beans, and peas, are about 200 bushels per English acre, whereas a yield of 40 bushels of wheat per acre in England "is thought to be much" (752–54). Their agriculture requires less labor, and they get two harvests a year. Heriot's defense of the potential of the place continues by vaguely describing the Indians' way of life, in order to demonstrate that they are not threatening or hostile. He finds them intelligent enough to appreciate the superiority of our equipment, for, "although they have no such tooles or any such craftes, Sciences and artes as wee, yet in those thinges they doe, they showe excellencie of wit." And by this they may be "brought to civilitie" (759–60).

The very fact that the savages do indeed cultivate and plant (if without benefit of plow), and do so more efficiently than the English (taking Heriot's point even while doubting his figures), fundamentally contradicts the legendary picture of them. That they do not know how, in any way, to till the soil is the sine qua non of what their name means. They merely "gather," as Peckham said, what the earth "naturally yields"; they do not, as we do, control and dominate that production. If they did, they'd be civilized. Almost as if he sensed this dangerous inference from his observations, Heriot is careful to deny that they actually have "civility"; they've only the potential for it. And of course they can't reach it by themselves, but must be "brought" to it by us. We are the culture-bringers in two senses: we bring it to them (in the Americas as it was brought to us, from east to west), and once we're installed where they are, we bring them to it.

Thus the legendary meanings of what it is to be, and to become, civilized or savage remain intact, untouched by observations that would contradict them. Here, at least, the observations are nonetheless made; many like them will continue to be made. But none will be allowed to question the legendary categories or to halt their diffusion into other discourses. This is one form of the determining power of fiction over perception. The savage is actually seen to have manners, arts, and agriculture, while he is still seen *as* a member of a category who cannot have these things in any form. The merely gathering and beastly forest dweller of the founding story is superimposed upon and identified with the actual men and women who come in darker shades and wear fewer clothes (in the latitudes so far explored) than we, and who do all sorts of things that we find both familiar and admirable—yea, even unto the superior rate of commodity production. But despite all, we're civilized and they aren't. *C'est tout.* At this point in the sixteenth century, the contradictions are merely recorded; there is not yet the anxiety that will later require them to be dealt with, to be explained away. Heriot does not feel obliged, as later colonialists will, to explain that small-plot, slash-and-burn cultivation does not really count as agriculture. There is not yet the anxiety that will endow the fiction with another, and greater, form of determining power: to block perception altogether. Later witnesses will cease to see whatever manners, arts, and agriculture may be practiced by various indigenous communities.

Or, if they are seen, they will be eliminated in subsequent accounts. This is precisely the fate of savage agriculture in the pages of the *Grands voyages*, a compendium of narratives of exploration and conquest from all Europe, issued in thirteen volumes between 1590 and 1634 by Theodor de Bry, his sons and successors. The work is famous for its hundreds of copperplate engravings of savage life from Virginia to Tierra del Fuego. An anthropologist has analyzed the codes of these visual depictions, and demonstrated, not surprisingly, their basis in European, specifically Protestant, conventions, values, and stories, showing how these portrayals alter as European settlement proceeds (Bucher 1981). Though the savage bodies themselves change greatly, from idealized types to monsters, there is not a single picture of their agricultural activities—not even when, as in the case of the Tupinambá of Brazil, these were shown in the woodcuts that were de Bry's own sources. The elimination is systematic, in order to create the lack that justifies their subjection (Bucher 1981: 110, 171).

This lack is a fiction (our legend of the savage past) that produces a fictitious lack (present savages have no agriculture). As the anxiety of colonial domination mounts, what happened to indigenous cultivation in the pages of de Bry will happen on a much larger scale to the observations of pioneer ethnographers (Jesuits in seventeenth-century Canada) in subsequent histories (supposedly) based upon them. What was seen will simply disappear, blocked out by what the story has told us we already know.

§♙

Chapter 11

THE EPIC OF JUSTIFICATION

Edmund Spenser

A laboratory in which one can see the anxiety growing, and being incorporated into the founding legend, is the epic poem and the whole career of Edmund Spenser. His retelling of Geoffrey's version of the story in book 2 of *The Faerie Queene* enshrines in the most prestigious literary tradition of the period the aims, motives, methods, and justifications of European colonialism as it had gotten well under way by the end of the sixteenth century. Responses to the actual inhabitants of the territories that Europe was taking over are written into the story of all those past takeovers. The foundations that England in particular was attempting are inscribed in the story of England's foundation. Like Ronsard, Spenser is attempting the definitive national epic, and is using as a part of his material the local variant of the historical descent from Troy whose veracity is questionable. Like Camoens, he wishes to immortalize the contemporary deeds and policies of his nation. Like the Italian poets, he selects a framing structure of chivalric (local and Arthurian) narratives. Unlike all of them, he gives this structure allegorical significance. Like all of them, he imitates Virgil.

Spenser's work is thus a consciously designed culmination and résumé of Renaissance ambitions—of the whole period's two major forms of imperialism: literary and real. It is Spenser's participation in the latter form that gives the edge to his rendition of the founding story. For he was also a colonial administrator, not, like Camoens, in new and distant lands, but in Ireland, where he began service in 1580 as secretary to its governor, Lord Grey, was given estates, and had become sheriff of Cork by the time he died in 1599. Serving her majesty's government was equally the aim of his poetic career, which, from his first full published work, *The Shepheardes Calender* (1579), took the form of furthering her majesty's personal mythology as the Virgin Queen. As Gloriana, she is also the conceptual center of the design of the epic, which he dedicated to her—"the most high, mightie and magnificent empresse . . . Queene of England Fraunce and Ireland and of Virginia"—and which he traveled to London to present to her personally in 1590. The ambition is quintessentially Virgilian, the most thoroughgoing of all such efforts in the period. For Spenser's imitation of Virgil is not merely textual, but rather the sustained attempt of an adult lifetime to reproduce the simultaneously literary and political career, to recreate the symbiotic relation between prince and poet, ruler and celebrator of empire, modeled on Augustus and Virgil. Ronsard had his fling at this, too; but it was cut short by the early death of Charles IX. Not only did Spenser's attempt last longer, it started earlier in his career and was more systematic.

He began, as Virgil had done, by publishing pastoral eclogues which, like Virgil's, blended the ancient themes of amorous debate and singing contests with comment on and dramatization of contemporary social and political (mainly religious) conflicts. *The Shepheardes Calender* was also fitted out with summaries, glosses, and explanatory prefaces supplied by one "E.K." Most of this apparatus (plausibly ascribed by recent scholars to the poet himself: see Schleiner 1990) was necessitated by the diction Spenser confected as part of his whole complex of nationalist ambitions. He wished, typically for transalpine poets in the sixteenth century, to dignify the mother tongue, to prove that the vernacular was capable of being as "stately" a vehicle of culture as Latin was.

To this end, Spenser concocted a poetic idiom derived from the greatest English poet to date, Geoffrey Chaucer. Owing to the enormous changes in the vocabulary and pronunciation of the language since Chaucer's death in 1400, this idiom indeed required explanation, which it got, along with lots of puffery, from E.K.: "it is one special prayse, of many whych are dew to this Poete, that he hath laboured to restore, as to theyr rightfull heritage such good and natural English words, as haue ben long time out of vse and almost cleane disherited" (1912: 417). Spenser would create a national literary language, an "illustrious" vernacular such as Dante had dreamed of for Italy and the Pléiade for France, in which to celebrate the national destiny. And he would create it on the most honored local model, by drawing words from the Chaucerian "well of English vndefyled" (*FQ* 4.2.32) to pour out in his domestication of Virgil's imperial theme. The deliberate archaism of this language did not universally please (Sidney had doubts about it, and Ben Jonson loathed it), and did not establish an idiom usable by other poets (except for a few minor imitators). But the impulse behind it—to domesticate the classical and classicize the domestic, to give English culture the lustre of the Roman—was generally shared and instantly admired, making Spenser something of an overnight sensation. Even today, editions of his texts and scholarship about him conventionally continue to pay tribute to Spenser's archaizing linguistic nationalism by reproducing its spelling.

Spenser asserts the smooth Virgilian transition from eclogue to epic at the very beginning of *The Faerie Queene* in lines that are an adaptation of the canceled beginning of the *Aeneid* itself. "He am I," wrote Virgil, "whose song was once on slender reed / Composed" (*Ille ego, qui quondam gracili modulatus avena / carmen*). And Spenser:

> Lo I the man, whose Muse whilome did maske,
> As time her taught, in lowly Shepheards weeds,

Am now enforst a far vnfitter taske,
For trumpets sterne to chaunge mine Oaten reeds . . .

(Proem, bk. 1)

Spenser does not, however, structure his poem in the rather slavish way that Camoens and Ronsard constructed theirs, by reproducing the prophesied peregrinations and divine persecutions of a single Aeneas-like hero. The episodic epics of Ariosto and Tasso are his immediate models, and he is drawn to them largely because they provide precedent for using medieval narrative materials. For he wants to use what England already has (in bk. 4 he actually completes one of Chaucer's unfinished *Canterbury Tales*) to glorify the idea of what she might, under Elizabeth, become.

One of the things she already has is her founding history as told by Geoffrey of Monmouth. Like Ronsard with respect to Lemaire, Spenser wavered a bit as to how veracious this was, and seems finally to have decided that it wasn't very. But when he raises the issue in the epic itself, he quite skillfully (we'll see in a moment) fudges it by subsuming it under larger questions of both imaginative and geographical truth. For Spenser was not willing to relinquish, in the poem, the age's assumption that epics were true. In the letter to Raleigh appended to the first edition of the poem, which outlines its structural framework (the quests of Gloriana's knights), identifies a few of its allegorical characters (as these do appear in the text), and sketches a supposedly Aristotelian allegorical scheme (which does not appear there), Spenser admits the fiction and still insists that it's "historicall." He claims to follow the Italians, Homer, and Virgil—the "antique Poets historicall"—in using fiction to implement and enliven a moral purpose. "Historicall" is here the synonym of epic, what distinguishes it from other fictions: some basis, however remote, in fact.

That Spenser was anxious to include lots of facts in the poem, perhaps to balance its abundance of evident fables, is readily seen in book 5, where the veil of allegory gets very thinly stretched in the effort to justify the fine details of Elizabeth's actual policies and deeds, both domestic (the trial of Mary Stuart) and foreign (in the Netherlands and Ireland). The poet's dramatization of literal event here carries to extremes the aim of prince-pleasing. But the aim was to remain only partly realized, for Spenser's politics and patrons prevented him from achieving the Virgil/Augustus symbiosis on which he modeled his career.

He was attached, successively, to the parties and policies of the most bellicose Protestants at Elizabeth's court—Leicester and his nephew Philip Sidney, Raleigh, and Essex—whose views were never allowed to prevail over the caution of the Queen herself and the opposition of her chief minister, Lord Burghley. Spenser's hostility to the latter is recorded in *Mother Hubberd's Tale*, written apparently while he was hanging around London waiting for his reward after presenting the first three books of his epic to the Queen. He did get a reward, a considerable one and the only one that Elizabeth ever gave to any of the vast chorus of poets who sang her personal myth: a pension of £50 per year (Judson 1945: 155). But Burghley seems to have held up its payment when he could, and the gossip of the day was replete with stories of his general scorn for poets and of the shifts to which Spenser was obliged to resort to collect the Queen's bounty. Otherwise, Spenser's relegation to colonial service in Ireland was of a piece with the Queen's treatment of the whole group who advocated more militant policies than she wished to pursue. Leicester she allowed to take his own private army to fight Spain in the Netherlands (where his nephew famously perished); Raleigh's adventures in the new world she encouraged; and Essex she finally made military commander in Ireland. She kept their loyalty (save that of the hapless Essex) and got them away from the court by the simple expedient of letting them do on a small scale what they wanted her to do on a large one. England never had a shrewder monarch, nor one less likely to privilege a poet for providing the kind of public relations at which she herself was a master.

So the Virgilian project of Spenser's life becomes another incomplete monument to Renaissance ambitions, another example of the pathos and impossibility of creating oneself in the image of Roman greatness. A century later Alexander Pope will repeat the project, which will have both more temporary success and more corrosive failure. Given the Virgilian design, our founding legend has a necessary place in the imagination of both poets. Pope left a detailed plan, and even a few blank verse lines, for an epic on Brut that he never wrote. And Spenser, of course, versifies in summary virtually all of Geoffrey's history in books 2 and 3 of *The Faerie Queene*.

The main context of his retelling the legend is the education of Sir Guyon, the emblem of temperance. For history was proverbially regarded as a rich source of lessons in that Aristotelian virtue. And here arises the problem of the dubious veracity of Geoffrey, debate about whom had become considerably more sophisticated since the twelfth century. Italian humanists and philologists had produced a recognizably modern conception of history, one that was critical of sources, skeptical of evidence, and attentive to all nuances of linguistic use and semantic change (see Kelley 1970). One such Italian, Polydore Vergil, had been appointed by Henry VII, and continued under Henry VIII, to write the "official" history of England. His book, *Historiae Anglicae libri XXVI*, published in 1534, raised a storm of controversy by simply dismissing Geoffrey from serious consideration. English scholars of Spenser's day were bitterly divided on the issue: John Leland was furious at the foreigner's having thus impugned the most renowned native source, while John Selden added ridicule to Vergil's contempt, summing up Geoffrey as "bardic imposture" (Ferguson 1979: 36–37, 106). Whatever Spenser's own conviction, he could not in this climate present Geoffrey's material as straightforward fact; but neither was he willing to forgo the venerable claim of epic to "historicall" truth.

In this dilemma, it is the discovery of the new world in the western hemisphere that provides him with another, subtler way of making the claim. He thus begins the second book:

> Right well I wote most mighty Soueraine,
> That all this famous antique history,

Of some th'aboundance of an idle braine
Will iudged be, and painted forgery,
Rather then matter of iust memory,
Sith none, that breatheth liuing aire, does know,
Where is that happy land of Faery,
Which I so much do vaunt, yet no where show,
But vouch antiquities, which no body can know.

But let that man with better sence aduize,
That of the world least part to vs is red:
And dayly how through hardy enterprize,
Many great Regions are discouered,
Which to late age were neuer mentioned.
Who euer heard of th'Indian *Peru*?
Or who in venturous vessell measured
The *Amazons* huge riuer now found trew?
Or fruitfullest *Virginia* who did euer vew?

Yet all these were, when no man did them know;
Yet haue from wisest ages hidden beene:
And later times things more vnknowne shall show.
Why then should witlesse man so much misweene
That nothing is, but that which he hath seene?
What if within the Moones faire shining spheare?
What if in euery other starre vnseene
Of other worlds he happily should heare?
He wonder would much more: yet such to some appeare.

(Proem)

The final two stanzas of this prologue go on to claim that his Faerieland is a "faire mirrhour" in which the Queen can see her own kingdom and her "great auncestry"—though not directly, since the dazzle of her glory requires a veil to prevent blinding the "feeble eyes" of readers. The arch hyperbole of this compliment thus justifies the poet's allegorical method, and his truth-claim is neatly modulated through the usual ambiguities in the Renaissance usage of "mirror," which meant both a reflecting surface and an ideal pattern or image. Mirrors show us both what is and what ought to be, and Spenser is eager to have it both ways. His fiction is both feigned moral exempla and factual reflection of those great ancestors. Spenser's full awareness of what is at stake, and how dubiously, in this genealogical claim is shown by his evocation of the problem of evidence in the first stanza. What's the proof for fairyland if nobody living can go there, and if it is only attested by "antiquities" that nobody can know? The word was, we recall, the very title of Annius's book, and indicates the highly disputed kind of sources that he produced and that Geoffrey claimed.

So Spenser will suggest a proof not dependent on sources and will raise the problem to a different level by evoking the geographical and astronomical superiority of the modern world to the ancient. It is this that gives new point to the old resolution of the problem of how fiction can be said to be true. For here are realities heretofore concealed from "wisest ages." Hakluyt's pages resonate with the pleasure this age took in the discovery of the globe that allowed it literally to know more than the classical world it otherwise so ambivalently worshiped. Spenser uses Peru, the Amazon, and Virginia to open new espistemological vistas that do not stop there, but continue from earth into the outer space of such trendy speculators as Giordano Bruno. Bruno had lately visited England and been a guest of some of Spenser's acquaintance and would soon be famously burned at the stake for, among other heresies, his hypothesis of plural worlds and plural universes. These exciting prospects would be actually glimpsed by Galileo's telescope in the next decade, and here furnish Spenser with the implicit analogy to his own fictional fairyland that asserts, without really asserting, its actual truth. If all these "other worldes" have existed and might possibly exist, why not the one I've made up? Left in ignorance of other continents for so long, how can mere human beings ever be sure that fables may not be facts? It's cleverly suggested, a witty implication that might make Spenser the philosophical equal of Uchendu: "There is no story that is not true."

Spenser's story, at any rate, has just that dimension of truth invoked by his analogy of those new worlds, which introduces the book of the poem that will recount the discovery and the founding of his own world, Britain. For the facts of nascent colonialism—those responses of Englishmen to the fauna of the new world, themselves conditioned by fables, as well as the commodity-producing motive for colonization—become part of Spenser's version of Geoffrey's fable. The present experience of new foundations is here altering the way the story of the old foundation is retold.

The first alteration is in the order of its telling. Spenser begins the story, his versified résumé of Geoffrey, with its climax, the arrival of Brute in the promised land. All his earlier wanderings will be perfunctorily alluded to in the next book; what is given pride of place is the encounter with the indigenes. The setting of the résumé is that Sir Guyon and his rescuer, Prince Arthur, have climbed to the topmost story of the House of Alma (an allegory of the human body), where in the chamber of Memory they read the histories of their respective nations: Guyon of Faeryland and Arthur of Britain. Spenser signals the importance of the episode by the conventional epic request for inspiration: "words and sound, / Equall vnto this haughtie enterprise," which is to recount "the famous auncestries / Of my most dreaded Soueraigne" (*FQ* 2.10.1). And the story begins with the arrival of the culture-bringers:

> The land which warlike Britons now possesse,
> And therein haue their mightie empire raysd,
> In antique times was saluage wildernesse,

Vnpeopled, vnmanurd, vnprou'd, vnpraysd,
Ne was it Island then, ne was it paysd
Amid the *Ocean* waues, ne was it sought
Of marchants farre, for profits therein praysd,
But all was desolate, and of some thought
By sea to haue bene from the *Celticke* maynland brought.

Ne did it then deserue a name to haue,
Till that the venturous Mariner that way
Learning his ship from those white rocks to saue,
Which all along the Southerne sea-coast lay,
For safeties sake that same his sea-marke made,
And namd it *Albion.* But later day
Finding in it fit ports for fishers trade,
Gan more the same frequent, and further to inuade.

But farre in land a saluage nation dwelt,
Of hideous Giants, and halfe beastly men,
That neuer tasted grace, nor goodnesse felt,
But like wild beasts lurking in loathsome den,
And flying fast as Roebucke through the fen,
All naked without shame, or care of cold,
By hunting and by spoiling liued then;
Of stature huge, and eke of courage bold,
That sonnes of men amazd their sternnesse to behold.

But whence they sprong, or how they were begot,
Vneath is to assure; vneath to wene[1]
That monstrous error, which doth some assot,
That *Dioclesians* fiftie daughters shene
Into this land by chaunce haue driuen bene,
Where companing with feends and filthy Sprights,
Through vaine illusion of their lust vnclene,
They brought forth Giants and such dreadfull wights,[2]
As farre exceeded men in their immeasurd mights.

They held this land, and with their filthinesse
Polluted this same gentle soyle long time:
That their owne mother loathd their beastlinesse,
And gan abhorre her broods vnkindly crime,
All were they borne of her owne natiue slime,

1. "Is hardly to be ascertained; difficult to know"
2. "creatures"

Vntill that *Brutus* anciently deriu'd
From royall stocke of old *Assaracs* line,
Driuen by fatall error, here arriu'd,
And them of their vniust possession depriu'd.

But ere he had established his throne,
And spred his empire to the vtmost shore,
He fought great battels with his saluage fone,
In which he them defeated euermore.

                                        (2.10.5–10)

The battles are quickly summarized, and they are not sport, as they were for Geoffrey, though they include Corineus's feat of throwing Goëmot (Gogmagog) off a cliff. After a stanza on place names the scene concludes: "Thus *Brute* this Realme vnto his rule subdewd, / And raigned long in great felicitie" (2.10.13), and off we go into the catalogue of Britain's real and imaginary kings.

Compared to his predecessors, Geoffrey and Virgil, Spenser's version of the encounter with the indigenes has one exclusive and obsessive purpose: to slander their character in order to justify wiping them out. Since Geoffrey's emphasis was on the culture that the culture-bringers brought, he could dispose of the giants rather casually, not needing to tell us much about them. Spenser, on the contrary, takes the culture for granted, evoking it only by negative contrast (what the land is now that it wasn't then), and focuses wholly on the giants. Spenser reproduces the three essential features of these original inhabitants of the place destined for empire (which Virgil found in mythic fauns, nymphs, and men born from tree trunks) and adds, with a vengeance, a fourth: their "filthiness," moral and sexual. They live by hunting (and pillaging); they are autochthonous (even their mother earth can't stand them); and not only are they uncivilized noncultivators, they are bestially immoral. Such a condition might safely be assumed of those who have no *mos* or *cultus*; but neither Virgil nor Geoffrey saw fit to expatiate on it. Spenser repeatedly asserts it, and can only assert it, admitting it to be but conjecture. In the absence of information about the giants' origins, the conjectures are of unspeakable practices and unnatural acts. The more to condemn them, the giants are quite ambiguously associated with "half beastly men," thus rendering them just not subhuman enough to escape moral strictures. In terms of strength, they're superhuman. The intensity and gratuitousness of Spenser's denunciations is a precise measure of the anxiety aroused by Europe's real encounter with real indigenes in the new world.

This connection is made clear in the text only at the end of stanza 9, where Brute's only action is stated in negative terms: he deprived the giants of "their unjust possession." This is the same figure of speech employed on the same word that Sir George Peckham used to describe the case where European settlers would be "unjustly repulsed" by native North Americans. In this single transferred epithet lies the new urgency, and the new stridency, of the old legend. As one might think the repelling of intruders sufficiently just, so logically there is nothing unjust about the possession of a land by its aboriginal inhabitants. But the giants' possession is unjust because they themselves are so, and the whole point of Spenser's version of the legend is to make them so. And then to transfer the "injustice" from their behavior to their land-tenure renders the taking-over of that land, as well as their extermination, "just."

The land itself, of course, is personified in order to increase the offense: the "soil" is "gentle," and their tenure has only "polluted" it. The land is feminized (as mother earth) differently than it was by Geoffrey, so that all the fiendish sexual licence that incurs their mother's abhorrence implies that the giants are incestuous rapists. Hence Brute can perform by his conquest an appropriately chivalrous act of rescuing a damsel in distress, saving this mother from her hideously unnatural children. Rhetoric defies logic, and the highest degree of sexual taboo is evoked in what is thus revealed as the desperate aim of this retelling of the story: to justify dispossession, to legitimize extermination. The discourse of colonial foundation in practice is here reincorporated into the legend of imperial foundation that provided its blueprint.

In the Virgilian blueprint, as well as in many subsequent travelers' accounts, the aborigines are strongly identified with the land itself; they spring from it or blend with it in various nondominating ways because they don't clear it, cultivate it, and build towered cities on it. Geoffrey's giants, we recall, were driven by the invaders into caves. But with Spenser and his age's new imperialism of commercial production, this identification, still necessary as part of the very definition of the savage, modulates into a now equally necessary separation. The savage is, after all, to be made to produce commodities as we do and for our markets—or else; so he must also and simultaneously be perceived as alien to his land, a useless excrescence upon it.

In the pages of Hakluyt, this separation is effected by the constant observation of the grandeur, opulence, and enormous productive potential of the land itself as contrasted to the poverty, ignorance, idleness, etc., of the small and skimpily provided bands of people who are so signally failing to exploit it. Our very ability to exploit it constitutes a kind of title for such writers (and they are legion) as Peckham: we have the know-how to make grain fields out of waste forest; we can make the desert bloom; we therefore deserve to have it. Since our object is to take the savages' land away from them, it requires that they be separable from what in the first instance constitutes them as a category. Spenser presents all this very adroitly by his sexualization of the relation between the indigenous giants and their mom. She, the local place that gave them birth, herself becomes revolted by them and rejects them. Brutus wipes them out and makes her the seat of empire, the site of commodity production it is her glorious destiny to become.

Until he does so, while this female island is being "unjustly" possessed—or shamefully raped—by her own offspring, she doesn't deserve even a name. In Geoffrey, Brut names the land after he and his tribe have changed its face, have made it an object of use by dedicating it to settled agriculture. So too in Spenser: "unmanured," uncultivated, it remains "unpraised," unappropriated by language.

But now there's a further and more important use; the old commodity has become the new: the land is "desolate" not just because uncultivated, but because it serves no market, is unsought by "merchants far, for profits." The utility of the land (whose beauties are not here listed, as they are in Geoffrey) is less intrinsic than negotiable. It gets even its first name, Albion, from its integration as a navigational aid into a system of "trade." And the commercial emphasis slides directly into the imperial: Spenser wastes no time on the edification of the island itself or, at this point, of its capital. Instead, Brute's descendants race off to "subdew all Germany" (2.10.23) and with "victour sword" to open "the bowels of wide Fraunce" (2.10.24).

That image—another form of rape—is an appropriately brutal reduction of the Virgilian founding legend to the circumstances and purposes of Europe's worldwide expansion in the sixteenth century. The narrower but parallel circumstances of the poet's colonial experience in Ireland elicit a similar form of reduction in the application of the legend's definition of the civilized and the savage. As a civil servant, like Camoens, Spenser made history as well as literature, and left a document defending the policies of his superiors in Ireland, where he himself lived on a frontier both military and cultural.

The document, *A View of the Present State of Ireland* (completed in 1596 but not permitted publication until 1633), is described by an historian as an elaboration and summary of all the justifications for military conquest on the basis of cultural superiority put forward by Elizabethan Englishmen (Canny 1973). It begins by invoking the contrast between the "goodlye and commodious soyle" of the island and the "salvage nacion" of its native inhabitants (Spenser 1934: 3). The Irish are classified, exactly as the Americans, on the basis of the way they use and fail to use their land. The classification can be supported here by the entire version of European history disseminated by Annius's legend of Noah. Spenser seeks at some length to establish the Scythians as the ancestors of the Irish, for the Scythians were herdsmen who required Noah to teach them plowing—and all else. And the Irish are pastoral seminomads, changing their dwellings as pasture is exhausted. This way of life is simply awful: it encourages outlawry and more licentious barbarism than living in towns, makes the Irish intractable to the civility of English law, and even gives them a taste for "freedome" (65). The remedy, Spenser proposes, is to require by law that anyone who has twenty cows *must* also "kepe a plough goinge, for otherwise all men would fall to pasturaige and none to husbandrie . . . looke into all Countries that lyve in such sorte by kepinge of Cattle and yow shall fynde that they are bothe verie barbarous and vncyvill, and also greatlie geven to warr." Peace and civility will thus be imposed by statute, as subsequently will learning and "liberrall scyences" (204). Spenser is perfectly aware that this transmission of our culture by force entails the eradication of theirs, which is but rude and brutish behavior anyway. And he is equally lucid about the kinds of force necessary to accomplish deliberate ethnocide: the natives are to be first subdued, then their structures of kinship and political allegiance are to be extirpated by dividing and resettling them in different parts of the country where they will be installed as tenants of English landlords, where the use of their language, dress, and customs will be forbidden and where their children, at length, will have their "salvage nature" softened and tempered by obligatory schooling (205). Though there is still argument about the details of Spenser's recommendations (Canny and Brady 1988), their aim is uncontested, and their justification is clearly the founding legend of our civilization.

Just what and how much force Spenser saw as required to accomplish these aims is also a matter of debate; but its logic is not in question. The *translatio imperii, commercii et studii* is here achievable only by war. Events were soon to prove that Spenser's estimate of the troops necessary to quell Tyrone's resistance was overoptimistic. He thought 8,000 would do the job (128); a few years later Essex was given 19,000 and failed. The assumption of superiority our legend gives us over less technologically advanced societies will often produce this pattern of initial underestimation and subsequent increase of the force required. Even the nature of colonial wars is inscribed in all the stories the legend tells. Our enemies in such conflicts are after all necessarily protecting their homeland; they rely on popular support and use every resource to compensate for their inferior equipment: concealment and ambush, surprise hit-and-run attacks, sabotage, and, when cornered, terrible ferocity. They have no military manners any more than civil ones. Spenser was appalled by the battle shriek of the kerns. Virgil's Rutulians were sometimes equally gauche. Geoffrey's giants wouldn't let the Trojans have a worship service in peace. Our enactment of the legend as invaders of course elicits from our adversaries behavior that makes the legendary description of them a self-fulfilling prophecy. Barbarians behave barbarously, especially in self-defense. We drive them into caves and can then express contempt for them as cave-dwellers.

This is precisely what will occur with melancholy and predictable frequency as western Europe takes over most of the planet. An anthropologist has recently begun to theorize this phenomenon, the way in which European intervention produces the violence that we then observe and condemn (Ferguson 1992: 91). In North America, scores of sedentary, partly or wholly agricultural, native tribes will be driven off their land and obliged to find other livelihoods. Some will take to one form or another of hunting, whereupon we can scorn them as the lowest form of savage and attribute that condition to their "nature," forgetting that it was we who reduced them to it. Though Spenser uses "savage" and "barbarian" interchangeably to describe the Irish, he favors the latter term, which will have a long afterlife in subsequent rationalizations of the plot of the legend. For "barbarian" will become the most usual term for a nomadic, herding culture, a middle term between the savagery of hunter-gatherers and us. Spenser's *View* also demonstrates, even prophesies, with great clarity, the full consequences of the new deployment of these old categories: the strategy of ethnocide.

Thus, by 1600, the "historical" epic of the Renaissance has rewritten the founding story of Virgil to include in the old imperial plot the new commercial motive and its contemporary adventures. The European literary/historical perception of the frontiers and indigenes in its own past (and present) has been reproduced as its perception of the frontiers and indigenes in the new world. The scenario of the descent from Troy has acquired a newly obsessive legitimizing function: not merely to qualify a dynasty or region as civilized, but ever more actively to deny that title to noncultivators. That civilization comes from elsewhere; that it consists in dominating the land, planting fields and towns upon it, and extracting profit from it; that any nondominating human identification with uncultivated land is ipso facto primitive and savage; and that therefore the dispossession and/or destruction of such savages, in the name of all the foregoing, which is progress, is morally justified—such is the scenario of the transmission of empire and learning that is continually retold in the legend and continually enacted in the world.

Each part of the process entails the other: what is performed gets written; scripts are written to be performed. The performances at the Globe were fictitious; those on the globe were not. But they were both scripted performances: neither could have occurred without the playwright, whether individual or collective. Our legend both casts us as the heroes of its plot and vindicates that role. Both the role and the vindication will shortly be cut loose from the legend as history to take on the power of more authoritative discourses.

Chapter 12

୨➤

SPECTACLES AND SERMONS

Pageants and John Donne

W hile the Trojans were making in the sixteenth and seventeenth centuries their gradual exit from the stage of serious history, they still enjoyed frequent appearances on more popular stages. These consisted, first, of the iconography produced for, and the various spectacles—processions, tilts, entries—produced by, royalty. Painters of Queen Elizabeth appropriated various iconic devices used by Emperor Charles V that linked them both to ancient Rome and Troy; the same devices served equally for Charles IX and Henri III of France (Yates 1975). Ceremonies of royal entry into Paris in 1549 and 1571 ushered the different monarchs through the Porte Saint-Denis adorned with statues of the Gallic Hercules, Francion, and Pharamond (Graham and Johnson 1974: 37). Among the emblems of virginity—Mary and the vestal Tuccia—evoked in pictures of and poems about Elizabeth, the most obvious was that of Astraea, the goddess of justice who ruled on earth during the golden age of Saturn, the ultimate *civilisateur*. Genealogies continued to be turned out, solemnly linking the ruling monarch to the relevant Trojan forebear. The "great ancestry" of Brut that Spenser sang of Elizabeth was produced in more prosaic form for her successor, James I, by Thomas Lyte, for which service he was rewarded with a Hilliard miniature portrait in gold set with diamonds (on display at the British Museum).

Second, and unique to England, was the deployment of the entire legend— from Geoffrey through Annius to Spenser—in civic pageants mounted by the guilds of the city of London. From the coronation celebration of Elizabeth in 1559 right up to the end of James's reign in 1625, these pageants make continual allusions to, and one is centered on, the events and characters in the legend of Brut, the founding ancestor of Tudor and Stuart alike (Bergeron 1971: 303–304). The guilds that paid for them, often at no small cost, employed such professional dramatists as George Peele, Thomas Middleton, Thomas Dekker, and John Webster to design their tableaux and write their dialogue. The occasion of most of these pageants was the installation of a new Lord Mayor; they are less concerned to flatter the monarch than to celebrate the real power and motive of modern history: the industrial and commercial expansion over which the guilds presided. These "right worshipful companies" had evolved far beyond the associations of artisans and small-scale merchants in which they had their medieval beginnings. The Merchant Taylors and the Merchant Adventurers in particular, two of the richest and most powerful, were not composed of people who actually sewed garments or went on voyages to peddle their goods. Their members were big businessmen, wholesale dealers in commodities and import-export traders. The shows the dramatists designed for their delectation made visible even to the illiterate citizenry the links between material and cultural production of all kinds.

Middleton in 1613 had his show presided over by mother London, costumed like Rome and the ancient goddesses of grain, "on her head a model of steeples and turrets" (Bergeron 1971: 179). In his pageant of 1612, called *Troia-Nova Triumphans*, Dekker welcomed the new mayor, Sir John Swinnerton of the Merchant Taylors, from his barge with a figure of Virtue leading the seven liberal sciences (the trivium and quadrivium) and attended by numerous other personifications of the motives ("Desire") and agencies ("Industry") of productive energy, including an old man with a spade "as the *Embleme* of *Labour*." Virtue exhorts the twelve major guilds, in verse, "*To guard* this new Troy" (Dekker 1612: 235–36). In such self-congratulatory spectacles as these, the merchant gentry of the nascent empire mobilized all the resonances of classical myth to present itself as the heir, patron, and preserver of the entire civilization transmitted from Troy through Rome to London.

The one pageant of the period wholly devoted to the universally familiar legend of Brut was produced by Anthony Munday in 1605 for Sir Leonard Holliday of the Merchant Taylors. The show begins with seamen coming ashore from a ship called *Royall Exchange*, exulting in their "rich returne, / Laden with *Spices, Silks, and Indico*." Punning on "holiday," they distribute fireworks, pepper, cloves, and mace to the happy crowd. Munday's text (4–13) then summarizes the initial dialogue: Britannia tells Brute, "her Conqueror," that,

> for his conquest of her virgine honour . . . she reckons it to be the very best of her fortunes. *Brute* shewes her what height of happiness she hath attained unto by his victorie, being before a vast Wildernes, inhabited by Giantes, and a meere den of Monsters. *Goemagot* and his barbarous brood, being quite subdued, his civill followers first taught her modest manners, and the meanes how to raigne as an Imperial Lady, building his *Troia nova* . . . and beautifieing his land with other Cities beside.

The wrestling match of Gogmagog and Corineus (very popular, this; it had appeared in earlier shows), the founding of Troynovant, and Brute's division of the kingdom among his three sons are all described. At one point Brute addresses Britannia in rime royal:

> Thou that before my honord victorie,
> Wert as a base and oregrowne wildernes,

> Peopled with men of incivility,
> Huge and stearne Gyants, keeping company
> With savage monsters, thus was Albion then,
> Till I first furnished thee with civill men.

All the characters—the sons, Troyanova, personifications of the island's rivers—then praise King James as the "second Brute" for reuniting the kingdom. The show, called *The Triumphes of Re-United Britannia*, concludes with various gods and goddesses arriving in a chariot of Fame to sing the praises of James and Sir Leonard and to recount the history of the Merchant Taylors. The Company, we learn, received its present charter and title of "merchant" from Henry VII,

> ... for they traded, as no men did more,
> With forren Realmes, by clothes and Merchandize,
> Returning hither other Countries store,
> Of what might best be our commodities.

A more thorough and compendious staging of the legend in the public streets could scarcely be imagined. Produced by, and framed by images of, the commercial energies that empowered the legend throughout the Renaissance, the pageant perfectly dramatizes its Spenserian meaning. The expanders of commerce are the bringers of culture; mercantile imperialism *is* civilization. Munday was in fact a scholar of the subject, and lards his published account of the show with marginal citations of, among others, Annius, of whose text he will publish his own résumé in 1611. From Spenser Munday appropriates the emphasis on the beastliness of the giants, their utter intractability to civility, and performs a neat variation on the epic poet's sexualization of Brut's conquest. Spenser had Brut rescuing the British *terra* from incestuous rape; Munday presents him as the polite ravisher of a grateful virgin, filling her with "civill" progeny. Wrestling and rape serve as the usual figures for the violence implicit in the culture-bringing foundation. Sport and sex need no justification, and barbarous ignorance deserves none. The occasions are festive, after all: apprentices get the day off; fountains flow with real wine and beer, and the mood hardly encourages any anxious reflections.

Other occasions and other moods do. It is worth examining one of these to see how Spenser's anxiety to justify dispossession is modulated into calm and confident argumentation when the issue of actual and present colonizing is addressed by one of the most eloquent clergymen of the age. Here, the motive of commercial profit is completely condoned by being subsumed under the spiritual profit enjoined upon all Englishmen by the established Church.

On 13 November 1622, Dr. John Donne, Dean of St. Paul's Cathedral in London, preached a sermon to the "Honourable Company of the Virginian Plantation." His text is Acts 1:8: "But yee shall receive power, after that the Holy Ghost is come upon you, and yee shall be witnesses unto me both in Jerusalem, and in

all Judea, and in Samaria, and unto the uttermost part of the earth." Like the ba-
roque poet he was, Donne ingeniously applies each key term of this verse to the
enterprise of the shareholding company directors who were his audience, and who
were so delighted with the performance that they had the sermon printed. It was
splendid self-advertisement. By the time Donne finishes with the text, its message
reads like this: "You'll have solid profits, not right away, but only after you give
spiritual matters (converting the heathen) first priority, and so become good Christian examples (witnesses) to other investors in the City (Jerusalem), agents of rec-
onciling their interests to those of the country landowners (all Judea), warriors
acquiring souls and territory from hostile, papist powers (Samaria) in North America (the uttermost part of the earth)."

It takes no little ingenuity for Donne to include in the "power" Christ promised the Apostles the temporal and financial clout that He specifically excluded.
The poet/preacher begins by asserting the identity of the Apostles and the stockholders as propagators of the Gospel: "Beloved, you are *Actors* upon the same Stage
too: the uttermost part of the Earth are your *Scene*" (Donne 1622: 265). He then
makes perfectly clear that the promised power is "not a temporall Kingdome; let
not the riches and commodities of this World, be in your contemplation in your
adventures" (266). Donne stresses at some length that "this first word, *But,* excludes
a temporall Kingdome" (267). But only temporarily, as it turns out: to give "riches,
and commodities . . . is not *Gods* first intention; and though that be in Gods intention, to give it you hereafter, you shall not have it yet; thats the *exclusive* part;
But; there enters the *inclusive, You shall receive*" (266). And what you shall receive
may well be riches; their inclusion is allowed for on the condition that they not
be desired. The stockholders must not want "to be *Kings,* to devest *Allegeance,* to
bee under no man;" nor should "those that adventure thither, propose to themselves present benefit, and profit, a sodaine way to bee rich, and an aboundance of
all desirable commodities from thence. . . . Whom liberty drawes to goe, or present profit drawes to adventure, are not yet in the right way" (269). However, with
the proper motive, these undesired things will follow right along: "Onely let your
principall ende, bee the propagation of the *glorious Gospell,* and though there bee
an *Exclusive* in the *Text,* . . . yet there is an *Inclusive* too; . . . something equivalent
at least" (271). And the equivalent is already, even before its fullest achievement,
nicely compensatory:

> *No Kingdome,* not *ease,* not *abundance; nay nothing at all yet;* the Plantation shall not
> discharge the Charges, not defray it selfe yet; but yet already, now at first, it shall con-
> duce to great uses. . . . It shall sweep your streets, and wash your dores, from idle per-
> sons, . . . and imploy them: . . . already the imployment breeds Marriners; already the
> place gives essayes, nay Fraytes of Marchantable commodities; already it is a marke
> for the Envy, and for the ambition of our Enemies. (272)

And in order thus to get what you musn't want, it isn't even necessary *not* to want
it at all, but merely to put such desires in second place: "if thou doe but *Post-pose*

the consideration of temporall gaine, and study first the advancement of the *Gospell* of *Christ Iesus,* the *Holy Ghost* is fallen upon you, for by that, *you receive power,* sayes the *Text*" (274).

So says the text, anyway, in Donne's quintessentially Protestant interpretation of it. One kind of power follows, as night follows day, the other. Worldly prosperity as bait for and ratification of spiritual sanctity may well, as Weber and Tawney claimed long ago, have given the Calvinist nations (Holland and Britain) the edge in capitalist development. Donne works the idea in here as part of his orchestration of the more psychological Protestant paradox that we get what we want by not wanting it—softened to the more palatable form of merely not wanting it as much. This is the Protestant variation on the ancient Christian paradox that we find our life by losing it.

Exactly what, in this context, may be found, and founded, Donne now specifies, distinguishing between "a *Power* rooted in *Nature,* and a *Power* rooted in *Grace*; a power yssuing from the Law of *Nations,* and a power growing out of the *Gospell.*" The former we have met before, in the discourse of Sir George Peckham, the principal investor in Newfoundland. Donne's development of it is worth hearing at length, since it not only recapitulates the legend's justification of dispossession, but links its secular terms to the divinely apostolic mission. Neither Noah nor the Trojans are mentioned; but both are there as *civilisateurs* in the way that spiritual power is made chronologically to follow, and psychologically to precede, real power. Donne is telling his audience—all of expanding Europe—what it will never tire of hearing:

> In the Law of *Nature* and *Nations,* A Land never inhabited, by any, or utterly derelicted and immemorially abandoned by the former Inhabitants, becomes theirs that wil posesse it. So also is it, if the inhabitants doe not in some measure fill the Land, so as the Land may bring foorth her increase for the use of men: for as a man does not become proprietary of the Sea, because he hath two or three Boats, fishing in it, so neither does a man become Lord of a maine Continent, because hee hath two or three Cottages in the Skirts thereof. That rule which passes through all *Municipal Lawes* in particular States, *Interest reipublicae ut quis re sua bene utatur, The State must take order, that every man improove that which he hath, for the best advantage of that State,* passes also through the Law of *Nations,* which is to all the world, as the *Municipall* Law is to a particular State, *Interest Mundo, The whole world, all Mankinde must take care, that all places be emprov'd, as farre as may be, to the best advantage of Mankinde in generall.* Againe if the Land be peopled and cultivated by the people, and that Land produce in abundance such things, for want whereof their neghbours, or others (being not enemies) perish, the Law of *Nations* may justifie some force, in seeking, by permutation of other commodities which they neede, to come to some of theirs. Many cases may be put, when not onely *Commerce,* and *Trade,* but *Plantations* in lands, not formerly our owne, may be lawfull. And for that, *Accepistis potestatem,* you have your *Commission,* your *Patents,* your *Charters,* your *Seales* from *him,* upon whose acts, any private Subject, in Civill matters, may safely rely. But then, *Accipietis potestatem, You*

shall receive power, sayes the *text*; you shall, when the *Holy Ghost* is come upon you; that is, when the instinct, the influence, the motions of the *Holy Ghost* enables your Conscience to say, that your principall ende is not gaine, nor glory, but to gaine Soules to the glory of GOD, this Seales the great Seale, this justifies Justice it selfe, this authorises Authoritie, and gives power to strength it selfe. (274–75)

Donne's alliterative wordplay and rhythmic incantation, adorned with the flourishes of legal Latin, make the persuasive music that sings the seamless progress from one *potestas* to another: the monopoly charter already received from the King of England will be totally fulfilled, exponentially increased, by the psychological charter from the King of Kings. A clear conscience will conquer the world, justly; since its primary aim is glory, not gain, it will get both gain and glory. And even the gain that must remain the secondary objective is lawful (should anyone worry), legitimized even without the greater glory that comes after by the legend's picture of the "civilized" use of land, that is, making it maximally productive in our terms, the terms of the legend. The takers-over of *terre gaste*—and even not so *gaste*—are the founders, the Trojans, the investors, the colonists, the consumers: we, all of us. Even though

> there may be divers in this Congregation, who, though they have no interest in this *Plantation*, yet they may have benefit and edification, by that which they heare me say, so *Christ* spoke the words of this *Text*, principally to the *Apostles*, . . . but they are in their just extention, and due accomodation, appliable to our present occation of meeting heere: . . . so these words which he spoke in the *East*, belong to us, who are to glorifie him in the *West*. (266)

And so the words of *this* text duly consecrate a further passage from east to west, a continued transmission of dominion and culture from Troynovant to the twenty Troys that will be founded later in the United States, Canada, and Jamaica. Donne will make more of this passage in his peroration.

But first he continues his geopolitical application of the biblical locations. "Let those of the *Citie*, who have interest in the Government of this *Plantation*, be *Witnesses* of *Christ* who is *Truth it selfe*, to all other *Governours* of *Companies*, in all true and just proceedings" (276). Donne spells out his opening analogy between Apostles and investors:

> preach in your just actions, as to the *Citie*, to the *Countrey* too. Not to seale up the secrets, and the misteries of your businesse within the bosome of *Merchants*, and exclude all others: to nourish an incompatibility betweene *Merchants* and *Gentlemen*, that *Merchants* shall say to them in reproach, you have plaid the *Gentleman*, and they in equall reproach, you have playd the *Merchant*; but as *Merchants* growe up into worshipfull Families, and worshipfull Families let fall branches amongst *Merchants* againe, so for this particular Plantation, you may consider *Citie* and *Countrey* to be one body, and as you give example of a just government to other companies in the *Citie*, (thats

your bearing witnesse in *Ierusalem*,) so you may be content to give reasons of your proceedings, and account of moneyes levied, over the *Countrey*, for thats your bearing witnes in *Iudea*. (277)

The analogy yields a remarkable lesson in sociology: bearing witness to Christ means healing class antagonisms at home by unifying the economic interests of the commercial bourgeoisie and the landowning aristocracy. Donne reminds his hearers of the actual (and long established) traffic between these classes, and hints at the necessity to solicit aristocratic investments in trade when he identifies the giving of reasons and accounts (to the country party) as the acts of these apostles. The justice of their proceedings is their Christian witness; they're doing the work of the Lord by producing a cogent prospectus and an accurate annual stockholders' report—as if the Lord were a celestial Securities and Exchange Commission. And Donne is not through yet.

As the board of directors' proper business practices serve the Lord, so too does the nature of their enterprise, the expansion of their nation overseas. Here, every convert gained for English Protestantism is a true witness-bearer against the heretics, schismatics, and miracle-mongers—"the *Samaritans* . . . of our times," who are of course the Roman Catholics (278). And this witness will be borne in an arena larger than the world known and available to the Apostles, in "this world which hath been discover'd since" (279). There, in the uttermost part of the earth, the "*Apostolicall* function" of "those . . . that goe, you, that send them who goe," becomes literally greater than that of the Apostles themselves.

Donne begins his peroration by exhorting his audience to the task:

Preach to them Doctrinally, preach to them Practically; Enamore them with your *Iustice*, and, (as far as may consist with your security) your *Civilitie*; but inflame them with your *godlinesse*, and your *Religion*. Bring them to *love* and *Reverence* the name of that *King*, that sends men to teach them the wayes of *Civilitie* in this world, but to *feare* and *adore* the Name of that *King of Kings* . . . for the next world.

This done, says Donne, resuming in a coda the earlier theme of the passage from east to west, "You shall have made this *Iland*, which is but as the *Suburbs* of the old world, a Bridge, a Gallery to the new; to joyne all to that world that shall never grow old, the Kingdome of heaven" (280–81). The island on the periphery, farther out even than the Hesperia to which Aeneas was told to sail, is to become the metropolis, the new center, out from which oriental civilization will irradiate western barbarism.

Or rather, Donne most adroitly concludes, has already begun to do so. He ends with supreme flattery of his audience, made by denying his own rhetoric of exhortation throughout the sermon. He announces that his own procedure has been the opposite of the prophets':

As their way was to procure things to bee done, by saying they were done, so beloved I have taken a contrary way: for when I, by way of exhortation, all this while

have seem'd to tell you what should be done by you, I have, indeed, but told the
Congregation, what hath beene done already: neither do I speake to move a wheele
that stood still, but to keepe the wheele in due motion; nor perswade you to begin,
but to continue a good worke, nor propose forreigne, but your own Examples, to do
still, as you have done hitherto. (281)

This is the final brilliant reversal—on a par with his initial insistence that Christ
excluded a temporal kingdom only to include it later—to say that all he put in the
future is really in the past; all that was conditional is really present. How pleasant
to hear from the grandest pulpit in the land that your priorities are in order, your
motives pure, your behavior just, your (eventual) profits assured.

I trust it is obvious that in listening to John Donne preach, we are witnessing
the formation of the ideology of the emergent class, the financiers of commerce
and industry who are being told to (do what indeed they have already partly done)
ally themselves with the still dominant but rapidly fading feudal aristocracy. The
motives and aims of this emergent class are receiving the blessing of the local variant of Europe's official religion. Just as Virgil became a Christian prophet, and
Noah a proleptic Trojan *civilisateur*, so now the English merchant gentry has become the apostles of the Gospel itself. As a sociologist, Donne is exceptionally
acute. For he perceived, beneath the apparent conflicts of social attitudes and styles,
the existence of the economic alliance whose development he advocated.

For the purposes of trade and colonization, the alliance was already complete;
the more than thirty joint-stock companies formed for these purposes united in
their membership, in a way unprecedented in Europe, aristocrats, gentlefolk, and
commoners (Rabb 1967). The "governors" of the Virginia Company, who ad-
journed their afternoon meeting to go hear Donne preach, comprised on that day
five peers, eleven knights, and thirty-two commoners (Kingsbury 1906: 2.122–23).
This crucial alliance, harnessing the prestige of the old order to the capitalistic energy of the new, is adduced by historians as furnishing Britain with her key advantage over her larger and richer rival for empire, France. No such community of
interest united the French nobility and bourgeoisie; there, the merchants—even
the big-time ones—were not gentry; trade remained traditionally contemptible,
something that the monarchy allowed to occur but didn't want to pay much attention to. In England, by contrast, the encouragement and regulation of trade had
not been wholly neglected by government even in the Middle Ages, and became
a positive preoccupation from the early years of Elizabeth's reign. And it was trade
that led, inexorably, to plantation and thence to empire. And it was trade that got
incorporated into the founding legend in its epic retellings by Camoens and
Spenser. And it is trade, as the shareholder's yield in a colony-founding company,
that is sanctified by Donne as the achievement of the kingdom of God.

The sermon, mobilizing the rhetorical resources of one of the greatest writers
of the age, is nonetheless as pure a form of propaganda as the costly spectacles
mounted in the streets of London by the same emergent class, in order to exhibit
itself as bringing prosperity to the nation by bringing culture to the wilderness.

That place of savagery was once our place—Albion before the providential rape of Brute—but is now their place, that vast expanse of territory whose native inhabitants do not know how to cultivate it properly any more than they know how to worship the one true God. They're just us, before we got civilized. The point is made both graphically and verbally in de Bry's *Voyages* when he juxtaposes an engraving of the ancient Picts (who painted their bodies) to one of the Americans in order, he says, "to show that the inhabitants of Great Britain in the past were as savage as these of Virginia" (quoted in Bucher 1981: 36). The legend projects its version of our own past on the present we now share with the savages; it defines what "primitive" is—simply what the legend says we used to be. Hence the outpouring of speculations in the sixteenth and seventeenth centuries that the Indians of America are but earlier forms of us: they're Homeric Greeks, or the lost tribes of Israel, or merely prototypical humanity in a state of "nature." They are what our stories tell us we were.

One of the things they were, and we might well have been had the shoe been on the other foot, is resentful of those who had come to dispossess them. When Donne exhorts the investors in Virginia to treat the natives with "Civilitie . . . (as far as may consist with your security)," he is being more than a little disingenuous. For there wasn't any more security: the famous massacre of 22 March 1622 had already occurred, in which the Indians, after years of uneasy coexistence, had made their "treacherous" attack on the Jamestown settlement, killing 347 souls. News of this event had reached London in May; on 3 July, the Virginia Company enrolled Dr. Donne, routinely among others, as a "freeman" entitled to its privileges—that is, made him a member of the Company by awarding him a share (worth £12.10s) in it (Kingsbury 1906: 1.155; 2.76, 89). Not only was "security," hence any excuse for "civility," at an end, but the whole crucial question of motive, the priority of converting the heathen that Donne makes the central consecration of the merchants' aims, had already been revealed to be as negligible for them as it was for Sir George Peckham. The Virginia Company records describe their appropriation of funds to establish a "college" to educate and convert the young Indians; but this money "was actually used as part of the financing of the iron works set up in 1620" (Kupperman 1980: 165). These had also been destroyed in the massacre of March 1622. So Donne was preaching his sermon at a moment when the Company had particular reasons to be grateful for it, a moment, like all moments, that is recorded not just because it was there, but because to record it serves the interest of the recorder.

And the particular priority of motive Donne alleges is particularly hollow. All the contemporary talk about conversion/civilization is, in the light of actual behavior, the merest hypocrisy. Even some participants, who were also sincere Christians, were undeceived about this. Captain John Smith wrote of New England in 1616: "I am not so simple to thinke, that ever any other motive then wealth, will ever erect there a Commonweale," and in 1631 accused the Virginia Company of making "Religion their colour, when all their aime was nothing but present profit" (Kupperman 1980: 165–66). The editor of the Company's copious documents, who spent over thirty years transcribing them, was also concerned to counter their propaganda: "the theory that the chief motive of the enterprise was religious is not supported either by the spirit or by the data of the records" (Kingsbury 1906: 1.98). So Donne is no worse than anyone else; indeed, he is rather better in his rhetorical skill and comparative restraint than his fellow-clergyman Patrick Copland, who preached even more fulsome sermons to both the East India and the Virginia Companies, and was rewarded more fulsomely than Donne by the latter; he got three shares (Wright 1943: 108–109).

Donne's contribution to the ideology of empire is one of the most skillful of innumerable such efforts, made by both clergy and laity, to identify commerce and piety, to give Christian consecration to the Renaissance motive and means for transmitting dominion and culture. Biblical stories from both Testaments lay ready to hand to be used as Donne used the mission of the Apostles. First among these, and already incorporated into the legend, was the figure of Noah as civilizer, and the Lord's repetition to Noah of his injunction to Adam and Eve: to be fruitful, multiply, and fill the earth. For military takeover and exploitation of desirable agricultural territory, there was Joshua's invasion of Canaan, the land of milk and honey—an image as frequently invoked by the Puritan settlers of New England as was, with a more political edge, that of Moses leading his people out of bondage to the promised land. And then there were the parables of the New Testament that explicitly figured spiritual as financial gain: those of the pearl of great price, the talents, the unjust steward. In short, no story ever told in the occident since the dawn of the Christian era has lacked legitimizing analogues drawn from its sacred book, which, like nature itself in the words of Stephen Jay Gould, is "sufficiently rich and multifarious to say yes . . . to any human vision" (1978: 85).

Part IV

FROM HISTORY

TO SOCIAL THEORY

The Death and Rebirth of the Legend

Chapter 13

EXIT HISTORY PAST

Neoclassic Historiography in England and France

T he vision mediated and defined by the legend of Trojan descent is that of those twinned, contrastive categories, the civilized and the savage. As we have noticed, scholarship in the form of our "modern" and critical notion of history had been repudiating the legend since the beginning of the sixteenth century. But it died hard. Kept strugglingly alive not only by dynastic and commercial ambitions, but also by the sheer weight of its antiquity, the legend faded slowly, fitfully, with a reluctance that testifies to its centrality in the west's vision of itself.

Its British version, the story of Brut, was still confidently presented as "knowne History" by Anthony Munday (who dramatized it for the Merchant Taylors) in his compendium of Annius (Munday 1611: 470). Munday claims to retell it in the words of Henry Lyte, who performed for Queen Elizabeth the same genealogical service that his son, Thomas, performed for King James. The Lytes were genuine antiquaries (convinced that their own family descended from Brut), if not outstanding intellects. In Munday's account, as in many others, what was fact for Britain became merely the "idle fancies" of those "loudest liars," the French. Munday retells the Frankish legend, too, hotly denying that Francion was the son of Hector and that Valentinian ever called them fierce; the French are merely a Germanic tribe (306–16). It is a nice example of the new, critical history being selectively applied as nationalistic propaganda.

In the mid-seventeenth century, a riper scholar and genuinely outstanding intellect expresses frank uncertainty and ambivalence about the veracity of the legend. John Milton, beginning his *History of Britain* (not published until 1671) about mid-century, confesses that he cannot omit recounting the story of Brut. Milton is far from swallowing Geoffrey, or any source, whole. Taking his cue from Livy, he selects what to recount from ancient tradition, and labels it clearly. Some of it he simply refuses, making, for example, very short work of King Arthur—of whose career he had earlier thought to fashion an epic. Milton dismisses all the imperial conquests

119

attributed to Arthur and emphasizes the difficulties of even identifying the place-names in his legend (Milton 1671: 166–71). But even the revolutionary regicide has a curious respect for the founding story as Geoffrey told it. Though rejected as "Fable" by the most judicious authorities, the story is reluctantly accepted by Milton as: "Descents of Ancestry, long continu'd, laws and exploits not plainly seeming to be borrow'd, or divis'd, which on the common belief have wrought no small impression: defended by many, deny'd utterly by few" (3).

Milton will summarize the tale, apologizing all the while, as an antiquity whose only confirmation is perhaps that of social consensus. Acutely perceiving the object of "the whole *Trojan* picture . . . to make the *Briton* of one Original with the *Roman*," yet, he insists, "those old and inborn names of successive Kings, never to have been real persons, or don in their lives at least som part of what hath bin remember'd, cannot be thought without too strict an incredulity" (8–9). So he begins with Aeneas. It would be hard to imagine a mind less credulous than Milton's; but even though the story is dubious, it's too good a story not to be true. The Miltonic excusing comes close to the insight of Uchendu. An additional Miltonic reason for recounting what he explicitly says is false is that the story has been graced with the epic imprimatur of Spenser. Milton denies, even while quoting his illustrious predecessor's version of, the conquests of Brut's sons in Germany and France (19–20); he narrates the wrestling match only to call it "a grand Fable . . . dignify'd by our best Poets" (16–17). Popular belief and literary dignity: the high and low levels of culture unite for Milton to preserve in a carefully phrased limbo of the could-have-been the story of transmitting the culture.

But Milton still chose another subject for his epic, and subsequent English historians either maintained the legend in a similar limbo, or briskly consigned it to outer darkness. The outraged controversies of the previous century were long finished—even when Milton was writing; hence his own ambivalence on the subject. This ambivalence lasted, for some, until the age of Swift and Pope. William Wynne, writing the history of Wales in 1697, uses a metaphor to describe the legend of Brut that is repeated by Aaron Thompson, who translated Geoffrey in 1718: against what even they take to be the skeptical consensus, they insist that there is some "foundation" of truth in the fabulous "ruins" of the story (Kendrick 1950: 100–102). For others, the fiction was total and unsalvageable. "King Brutus" was silently dropped from an official Oxford chronology of British monarchs in 1675; and Sir William Temple dismissed the Trojan Brut in 1695 as a "forgery" (Kendrick 1950: 111).

Another contemporary, James Tyrrell, in *The General History of England*, carries the ambivalence about as far as it can go. He summarizes the story, but only after having cited the scorn of William of Newburgh for Geoffrey, rehearsed the confusions in Geoffrey's known source (the chronicle of "Nennius"), and attributed its staying power to the "vanity" of the Romans, which is shared by "almost all other Nations of *Europe*" (Tyrrell 1698: 6–7). In the summary, he quotes some of Milton's ambivalence and dismisses the wrestling match as a tale "fit" only for "children" (9, 17). This is the very voice of modernity and enlightenment; we're growing up and putting away childish things. But he still *tells* the story. He doesn't waste much time on it, though, and his expression of relief as he begins the next episode is determinant for the future. Having arrived at the conquest by Julius Caesar, Tyrrell compares his journey, and the reader's, to that of a traveler obliged to pass on through the dark night of "Ages of Fictions" welcoming the break of day (19).

Post tenebras lux ("after darkness, light"—the motto of reformed Geneva): this self-congratulatory slogan inherited from the Renaissance by Protestantism and passed on to the libertines of the *siècle des lumières*, is fairly replete with irony as applied to our founding legend. To begin with, the bringers of light are just those folks who gave us the darkness of the legend; both come with the Roman conquest. But that conquest, to Tyrrell and henceforward, is real history: indisputable, confirmed, memorized by all schoolboys then (and until just yesterday) from Caesar's own account of it in the *Gallic Wars*. The winner writes the real history; that's where it starts. And that's just where the history of Britain really starts for Tyrrell, where it had already started for other writers, where it will start for David Hume. And that's of course where the history of the rest of the world starts, for us, with its "discovery" by Christopher Columbus. We won it, so we can write it. Western Europe dismisses the legend as it reenacts it, jettisoning the Trojans as it assumes the mantle of the Romans. It's no longer necessary to invent ourselves as siblings to the greatest empire of the past; we can now admit that the Romans are our fathers because we are in the process of politically becoming them. In the spheres of high culture, this is called neoclassicism. As an artistic style of no little rigidity, it ushers in and dominates the century during which the imperial European powers struggled for and consolidated their domination of the globe.

Robert Brady begins his *Complete History of England* in 1685 with the Roman conquest of it, for the simple reason that "To the Romans originally all *Europe* is obliged for the *Civility, Literature, Laws* and *Government* it now injoys" (i). The particular genius of the Romans, he goes on, was to reproduce themselves by founding colonies. How appropriate that we should now assume their perspective, and begin our story as their colony, now that we have colonies of our own. A bit more than two centuries later, a fictional character will begin his story of colonization in Africa with just the same perspective. Marlow, sitting in a boat anchored in the mouth of the Thames, begins by recalling that "this also has been one of the dark places on the earth," and goes on to compare the fear and bewilderment of the sophisticated Romans confronted by the barbarous Britons with what he will feel while steaming up the Congo. Conrad's story reminds us that the *Heart of Darkness* is historically transportable, that Europe finds in Africa what it brings there. And what it brings there was once here, in two senses: historical transportation—they, the primitives, are what we were—is psychological projection—they horrify us because we horrify ourselves. Conrad brings back the darkness (in some new senses, as we shall later observe) that the neoclassical luminaries expelled. Brady begins his history with the civilizing Roman invaders, skipping all the obscure stuff that went before. A couple of generations later, David Hume, writing *The History of England*, skips it too, and explicitly consigns it to the deserved obscurity of barbaric darkness.

The legend of Trojan ancestry ceases to be needed as an assertion of cultural fraternity with ancient Rome only when actual events—the ongoing acquisition of a commercial empire—make it possible to admit Rome's paternity. We can acknowledge our fathers only when we are in process of acquiring their power. Then we can start identifying with them, and stop rebelling against or trying to displace them. The displacement of the Romans was a primary function of the legend for the Middle Ages, and reached a kind of fever pitch in the Renaissance efforts of Annius and his horde of imitators to interpose yet further displacements—Hercules of Libya and the whole line of Gallic kings—between us and and the Trojan displacers of the Romans, all designed to show that we had no fathers, that we (modern western Europeans) are really our own fathers. Now, at the turn of the eighteenth century, we're slowly coming of age. So all the old displacements can be read out of the discourse of veracious history as we come to identify with the real father; the grandeur that was Rome is now us. Our civilization is Roman. With this acknowledgment comes, of course, a disquieting awareness of our own mortality: for our actual father, who once lived (as opposed to that mythically remote and always already dead one in Troy), is dead. It is no accident that the greatest work of history in the eighteenth century is Gibbon's *Decline and Fall of the Roman Empire*. To admit that we were not self-created is also to admit that we are not self-perpetuating; we too must die. But we can indeed reproduce ourselves as the Romans did, have children as our fathers did; we can found colonies. So the legend is expelled from our history by being incorporated, as it were, into our psychobiology, the identification of our modern western selves with the ancient father who created the legend in the first place. It remains a constituent part of what we are—only a different part.

The expulsion of the legend from history proceeded in the same gradual and fitful way in France as it did in England. In France, however, the fitfulness was more extreme and the order of the procedure rather different. There, the legend was more fully discredited in the sixteenth century, only to be aggressively reasserted in the seventeenth before arriving at roughly the same terminus—in limbo or outer darkness—as in England. The sixteenth-century French scholars who attacked the veracity of the legend were more numerous, more prestigious, and more thorough than their counterparts across the channel. Pasquier doubted the legend; Vignier refuted it; Hotman, following Beatus Rhenanus, ridiculed it; and Belleforest, summing up the learned consensus, confidently rejected it (Huppert 1970: ch. 4). By 1572, in fact, the year when Ronsard first published *La Franciade* (hence his ambiguous prefatory truth-claims), the legend was virtually disproved. Belleforest, up-to-the-minute in his reading, even enlists the poem to trash the legend. He begins his chronicles of France by attacking Trithemius, whom he takes as the primary villain, for inventing the "fabulous stories" of Trojan origins. They accord with nothing known from the writings of ancient historians, and their chronology is silly. He compliments Ronsard as the chief of the poets who made the Trojans historical, and cites his tale of Jupiter's intervention to save Astyanax so that he could become Francus—this "in order to make us understand that all that is sung of the Trojans is only foolishness" (Belleforest 1573: fols. 1–1ᵛ). Germany, and not Phrygia, is where the French really came from. Belleforest's tone is crisp and businesslike. Reflecting the interests and attitudes of the whole school of local legal historians who preceded him, he adduces as evidence the presence of German words in the oldest texts of Frankish laws (fols. 2–3).

But all of this "modern" lucidity is in its turn assailed in the next century by historians who "relapse into fiction" under royal patronage in order to provide propaganda for absolute monarchy (Huppert 1970: 85–86). A typical example of this effort is Jacques de Charron's *Histoire Universelle*, of which his printer made a popularized abridgement in 1629, dedicated to King Louis XIII. This little book, in large type, simple language, with portrait engravings and thumbnail biographies of every monarch named, is called the *Genealogical History of the Kings of France from the Creation to the Present*. The genealogy is a continuous line, beginning with God (whose portrait is a blaze of light infusing the stellar, oceanic, and terrestrial worlds) and ending with Louis. The line is taken, the preface informs us, from Berosus, Manetho (another of Annius's "sources"), and Hunibald, "whom some among the moderns wish to reject as false and invented." But they're the *real* sources, supported by such as Annius, Trithemius, and a long list of names, mostly medieval, including Vincent of Beauvais, Paul the Deacon, and Gregory of Tours. The genealogy given follows pretty exactly that of Annius as deciphered by Lemaire de Belges.

The motives for reasserting it are suggested by the alternative interpretations Charron gives to the original division of the world among the sons of Noah: "Shem got the Orient, or as some say, the government of spiritual matters; Japheth all the Occident, or as others say, the lordship of all the earth; and Ham Africa, or as others say, the coastal places sequestered from the true habitation of men" (Charron 1629: 22). Thus to extend the occident to all the earth, and thus to marginalize, while expanding, Africa into a figure for mysteriously subhuman coastlines reflect both the ambitions and the deeds of European monarchs and their global explorers since Annius. A lineal descendant of Japheth and of Troy can now claim all the world, especially those remote parts of it where real habitation (ours) doesn't exist. And to show Louis as this claimant is the whole point of the exercise. The Gallic Hercules and Francus provide the pure pedigree for French royalty that Brut provided for the English. Charron performs in print, exclusively for the monarchy, just the same kind of puffery that the Jacobean dramatists had performed in the public streets, for both the monarch and the merchant gentry of London.

Puffery reached loftier summits (or lower depths) under the next lineal descendant, the Sun King, who reigned from 1648 to 1715 and whose vast patronage of the arts was inversely counterbalanced by a most repressive censorship of print in general (Mandrou 1973: 160). Small wonder that historians relapsed into fiction in a climate where "critical historical analysis in itself was deemed potentially subversive of Louis XIV's absolutism." Historians patronized by the crown produced official mendacities, with the exception of one royal historiographer "who proves the point because he was dismissed for an excess of independence in publishing his views" (Klaits 1976: 192–93). This was François de Mézeray, author of two enormous histories of the nation, issued in 1651 and 1668.[1] Released from royal service, he never criticized the régime, but passed his old age preparing a corrected second edition of his first work and writing a new first volume on the very beginnings of the nation. He died in 1683, and the second edition appeared two years later.

It demonstrates that even the considerable efforts of the grandest Bourbon of them all could not stifle the modern historical voices first heard in the previous century. From beyond the grave, Mézeray makes the old legend unavailable for legitimizing purposes by rejecting most of it and arriving at the same positions as his English contemporaries: skeptical, if nostalgic, dubiety about Japheth and the Trojans, along with enthusiastic embrace of the Romans. The *Histoire de France avant Clovis* is a detailed consideration of the numerous hypotheses and speculations about the origins of the French. Mézeray begins by stating his preference for the hypothesis that they were a mixture of Romans, Gauls, and Germans—before which time Europe was populated by Celts, whose origins are wholly obscure. He then pleasantly repudiates the legend by announcing that he will "completely refrain from seeking what grandson or great-grandson of Noah was the chief of this group, or whether there was a Celta to give them their name, and other antiquities which have little foundation and no utility." He pokes more fun at the etymological fantasies in the legend's riot of eponymous heroes, adduces its nonconfirmation by any classical source, and discards it: these "twenty-two kings that the Berosus of Annius of Viterbo gives us in Gaul before the Trojan War . . . are fables for the most part, and for the rest are so uncertain that they're not worth talking about. One must say as much for Francus" (Mézeray 1688: 3–6).

When it comes, however, to the origin of the Franks, Mézeray drops the jokes and treats the old story as at least a plausible "conjecture," presumably because their activities in Pannonia may have been alluded to by Cicero and Strabo. So he recounts their building of Sicambria, their dealings with Valentinian, their split migration west to the Rhine and south to Turkey (the version in the *Liber Historiae Francorum*). "I know," he apologizes, "that all this is full of fables . . . but am persuaded that there are scarcely any old tales that have not some foundation in the truth" (193–94). Good modern that he is, Mézeray can adduce the tangible evidence of a stone inscription in old Buda (195). (He didn't know it, but the stone was faked in the early fifteenth century by an Italian employed as historian to the King of Hungary: Eckhardt 1943: 46–47). So, having done his best to sift what little in the legend seems verified by classical writings, Mézeray goes on to the

1. His stringent remarks in the latter work on remote but still sensitive royal practices of taxation offended Colbert, Louis's chief minister, and lost him his pension.

lengthy task of describing the barbarian invasions of the collapsing Roman empire. Here the Franks become simply the enemy, and the book ends with them, along with the Burgundians and the Goths, laying waste to libraries, schools, and magnificent buildings—all the cultural artifacts that made the Romans their incontestable superiors. "But necessarily after all, in spite of the brutality of the ignorant, the empire remains in the mind and spirit of the literate" (556–57). And this is the Roman perspective, our perspective now that we are grown up, have gotten civilized, and can treat our own barbaric origins with appropriately distant contempt.

But the last occasion on which the veracity of the legend mattered was yet a generation hence, at the very end of the Sun King's reign. It appeared to matter only because of the local circumstances: the régime's general terror of historical investigation, and its particular worries over the royal succession. The males of three generations of Louis XIV's progeny, in direct line to inherit the crown, had died within months of each other in 1711–12. Worried himself, Louis legitimized his bastard sons, and the court was abuzz with speculation as the king grew sicker in the fall of 1714. In November, a member of the Academy of Inscriptions, a scholarly antiquarian named Nicolas Fréret, made a speech (as he often did) in which he averred that the French were not Trojans, but Germans. Another member, the abbé Vertot (one of Louis's tame historians), took great offense and accused Fréret of shaking the very foundations of the régime. The following month, Fréret was sent to the Bastille by a letter of cachet, where he remained (studying Chinese and writing) until June 1715. Perhaps on the strength of this offense, Fréret enjoyed a quite undesired and undeserved later reputation as an anti-Christian freethinker (see Simon 1961). Since he said no more, and with no more information than that deployed almost a century and a half before by Belleforest, it seems evident that advocating German ancestors was not what the court wanted to hear. The Academy itself had been created by Louis in 1663 for the express purpose of telling the court what it wanted to hear. Its task was to research classical motifs and icons to be struck on the medals commemorating the events of his reign. He wrote to its first members: "I confide to you the thing in the world most precious to me: my glory" (Mandrou 1973: 159).

It is perhaps appropriate that the last role to be played by the Trojan connection on the stage of what counted as history should be in a comedy of megalomaniac farce. The legend had always been propaganda, and it had achieved and reachieved epic dignity. It had helped to transform a landscape and been incorporated into the dynamic ethos of commercial colonization. And now it has shrunk to a royal sledgehammer crushing a pedantic pea. The jailing of Fréret is, so far as I know, the final dynastic hiccup in the often troubled, but now complete, expulsion of the legend from the domain of history past. The dignity that the Trojan connection had furnished for a millennium to feudal and monarchical Europe was needless, now that Europe was imperial.

But what was still needful, and what indeed remained, in now imperial Europe, was the whole picture of civilization that the legend had preserved, disseminated, and recreated. That all our forms of culture come from elsewhere (the east) and are transmitted to us, not produced by us; that all depend on settled, intensive cereal cultivation; that their validating results are cities, writing, and (now) large-scale commerce; that other societies which farm differently and so do not achieve these results are ipso facto primitive and savage: this definition of what civilization means (in and to the west) is (and largely remains today) unchanged. The mythic meaning, and the enacted fact, of the legend are mutually intensified by shifting our identification from the Trojans to the Romans, from the characters in the myth to its authors.

The shift that declares the Trojan ancestors unhistorical ends one cycle in the life of the myth only to begin another. Only an inelastic myth ever dies; and in our founding story of transmission and displacement as necessary civilizing processes there is considerable elasticity in the identity of the invading culture-bringers. As long as culture remains what must be brought, the bringers may alter. Indeed, they must alter as transmission proceeds, just as they did in Virgil: from Saturn to Hercules to Evander to Aeneas to Augustus. One foundation follows another. But when our actual colonization of the new world allows us to assume the Roman mantle and acknowledge our Roman paternity, there is one crucial change in the purpose and function of our continued deployment of the myth.

This change first surfaced in Spenser's version of Geoffrey; but it's now about to be diffused through the new "modern" history into law. Geoffrey used the legend as did its earliest medieval chroniclers: as an entitlement to civilization. Spenser used it as a justification of dispossession. Medieval writers wished to characterize themselves as descended from culture-bringers, in order to regard themselves as culture-havers. Spenser, taking this for granted, wished to characterize the indigenes as savages. Now, no longer requiring entitlement to civilization themselves, European historians can follow Spenser's example and employ the myth no longer as a claim *for* themselves, but as a claim *against* the "primitive" others.

Such a claim is made possible by the easiest kind of historical retrospection: in the members of primitive societies where we're now planting our colonies, we recognize the savage barbarians we can now admit that we once were. What Michel Foucault has called the tyranny of the biological model that governs our conception of history finds in this process one of its most powerful and consequential expressions. We read the collective as we read our individual pasts; we impose on our institutions and ideas the organic model of our bodies. Since these have birth, youth, maturity, decline, and death, our collectivities and abstractions are seen in the same way, as necessarily, indeed "naturally," going through the same stages. Having now admitted that our collective childhood was savage, it's easy for us to see savages as children. Legally, they are about to be classified as infants: incapable of speech, they will soon be regarded as incapable of ownership or contractual obligation. And this is made possible, indeed inevitable, by ruling the myth out of history and at the same time rehistoricizing it in different registers: here, that of sociopolitical development. The myth is dead; long live the myth.

Chapter 14

ɔ◖

ENTER HISTORY PRESENT

Providential Historiography in the Eighteenth Century

The rehistoricization of the myth is implicit in the late seventeenth-century historians examined so far, and becomes even more apparent in the work of some rather eccentric scholars in the next century. Their oddness, however, merely throws into high relief a process that will be carried on in other discourses that will become typical, normative, and determinant, as westward the course of empire takes its way. The oddness consists in being very "modern," quite like their immediate predecessors, in deriding the likes of Brut and Francus as fables, while being as driven as Annius himself was to recuperate all classical mythology into a euhemeristic and more or less providential view of the European past. The typicality consists in linking this past, thus seen, to the present of the peoples whose territories we are colonizing.

All this takes place in the context of feverish and acrimonious speculation about the age of the world—itself a product of the clash between the modern, critical history empowered by embryonic empirical science and the traditional biblical chronologies (see Rossi 1984). The problem was how to reconcile the biblical accounts of creation and the flood, along with the traditional history of nations that had developed from them, with the growing body of information amassed by antiquarian researches into the pre-Roman origins of the major European nations. In the seventeenth century, a school of thought called "pre-adamite" had arisen to maintain that the world was far older than the 4–6,000 years that had been calculated from the (far from exact) figures mentioned in the Old Testament. Such thinkers were often perceived as libertines who threatened to undermine all belief in the sacred book. Barrels of ink would be spilled in this kind of debate, of course, until this century. Trying to save the Bible as a repository of literal, scientific truth did not become rationally impossible until after Lyell's geology and Darwin's biology (nor is the issue dead even today; it's just become subrational). Amid the accusations of who is more pious (or atheistic) than whom, the question of the origins of European nations is engaged in this discourse in ways that perpetuate the terms of the founding story while denying it as history.

The denial serves, as usual, to align the writer on the side of modernity—that is, with certain classical writers, who are mutually verifiable sources, as opposed to more recent fantasists. Paul Pezron, a Dominican Abbot and a Breton, published in 1703 a work arguing that the Celts (alias the Gauls) are everybody's ancestors and that this is perfectly consistent with the Bible. The Annian design, as well as the Renaissance ambivalence about classical antiquity, are apparent in the subtitle of the rapidly made English translation: *The Antiquities of Nations . . . particularly of the Celtae or Gauls . . . the same people as our Ancient Britains . . . containing Great Variety of Historical, Chronological, and Etymological Discoveries, many of them unknown both to the Greeks and Romans.*

But the preface of the work, which summarizes its entire tissue of assertions, wholly repudiates the "Impertinencies" and "Extravagancies" introduced "after Annius Viterbus, a Fabulous Author, if ever there was." The voice of modernity continues: "As the present age has a Relish of that which is Good Sense, we are to have Recourse for it to the Right Sourses, the Ancient Authors" (Pezron 1706: iii). These latter, however, are as likely to be church fathers as ancient pagan historians, who are nonetheless pressed into service as needed. What all these sources say is that Gomer (Japheth's eldest son) was the father of the ancient Gauls in the eastern Mediterranean, who took the name of Titans and migrated north and west, becoming Celts in central Europe and Gauls between the Rhine and the Atlantic. Scripture calls these people Giants; their early leaders, "Uranus, Saturn, and Jupiter, were not Gods, as the Greeks and Romans vainly believed, but Potent Princes and Mortal Men." All this is manifest from their names, which are of Celtic origin, the language spoken by the Gauls in Caesar's time and preserved today in Bretagne. The Bretons and the Welsh "have the Honour to preserve the language of the Posterity of Gomer" and of those princes "who passed for great Deities among the Ancients" (iv–xiii).

Pezron buttresses these assertions with lists of those names and terms which he claims were taken over into Greek, Latin, and German from Celtic. Though many of these seem fanciful, other of his guesses have proved accurate: for example, his identification of St. Paul's Galatians with Celts who wound up in Asia Minor about 270 B.C. (15). And though Pezron's motive—to defend scriptural "history" against both ancient and modern versions—is just that of Annius, his historical chronology compels rejection of Annius's, and does so in the interest of the new willingness of Europeans to admit that their culture is indeed a near-eastern inheritance. Excoriating "modern authors" for claiming ridiculous migrations of Japheth's sons into all of western Europe, Pezron insists that these worthies never left Asia. Consequently, that "Part of the World ought to be looked upon as the Cradle out of which these numerous Nations came, that in After-Ages peopled all *Europe*" (12). So Pezron's Celtophilia can have it both ways: we (western Europeans) are not our own ancestors (as Annius claimed); but although our ancestors were located elsewhere (in Asia), they were really us (that is, Celtic). Down with the Annian list of Gallic kings (and Trojan ancestors); long live our ancient forebears, who were nonetheless ancestral to the Greeks and Romans whom we now acknowledge as our forebears. Pezron denies the adventures of Noah's progeny in Europe only to affirm the meaning that Annius attributed to them, even to intensify it. The gods of classical mythology are but Celtic heroes in disguise.

The English historian most inspired by Pezron was Thomas Carte, an outspoken Jacobite who spent much of his working life in Paris writing a huge and predictably biased *General History of England* (1747–1755). Frankly summarizing Pezron as the supreme authority on the original inhabitants of Britain, Carte abjures any reliance on Geoffrey's "romance . . . it being so manifestly fabulous in the main" (vi). His summary of Pezron, however, makes clear his modern (i.e. classical) allegiances as well as his assimilation of our ancient Celtic ancestors to their contemporary "barbarian" equivalents in the New World. Carte is concerned to dramatize the present relevance of Pezron's rather dry and polemical assertions about the sons of Japheth—Celts all—and their gradual expansion out of Asia Minor. Having first "planted" Phrygia, they moved into Thrace, thence into Russia and along the Danube and the Rhine to the Atlantic. Their two subgroups were called "*Thrax* and *Bryx*," since, Carte assures us from the highly evolved modern position, "all ancient languages are simple, and consist for the most part of monosyllables." He doesn't, of course, mean Greek or Latin, which are the much later forms of what everybody's ancestors once spoke. The "primitive" is ipso facto the simple. They were best known as Phrygians, these colonizers of the occident, the "first planters of *Europe*" (8–9).

No legends for Carte—he's put fables far behind him even as he reproduces something practically indistinguishable from the *Liber Historiae Francorum*. The Trojans, indeed, are gone—or rather have not yet appeared in this newly extended backward chronology—replaced by semibarbarians whose function merely replicates and intensifies the one they had for Annius: to give us a title, if not to civilization (we no longer need that, being the heirs of the Romans), at least to enormous antiquity. This is the final point of his employment of Pezron, to claim that the Celtic settlement of Britain took place about 2,000 B.C. Thus the fabulist Geoffrey, he concludes, defrauded the Britons of some nine hundred years of their true antiquity merely because he was so "enamoured" of the *Aeneid*, and thus ignored their true descent from a race of heroes so potent as to have been reverenced by the classical world as gods (21). Carte also rehearses all the negative evidence against the Trojan connection: it has no "support from any ancient genuine history"; the Britons, without letters or writing, couldn't possibly have preserved "any such regular series of historical events" as Geoffrey gives; no such thing is found in Gildas or Nennius, who gives wholly inconsistent accounts of Brute; and Hunibald is worse. All this stuff passed current only "in an ignorant age" idolatrous of Virgil and eager to flatter itself. The notion, however, of British descent from the Phrygians gained its plausibility, Carte triumphantly admits, "because it was really the case" (16).

So the exchange of the old form of the myth for the new form is perfect: the civilized Trojans have become their (and our) own barbarian forebears. But what they do that is identical is what makes it the same myth: they found colonies. The folks who were the Phrygians and Gomerians blended, in the west, into the Allobroges, the Belges, and the Britanni; this (always Celtic) mixture settled the island of Britain once there was leisure for it, that is, after the reign of Jupiter brought a measure of peace, and the ensuing régime of Mercury in Gaul and Spain could think of "sending out colonies . . . encouraging commerce (the never-failing means of making a people rich)" (20–21). Carte has earlier expatiated on Pezron's account of Jupiter, who reduced the Gomerian (Asian) branch from their giant or Titanic insolence to "order and civility." "This prince applied himself . . . to the administration of justice, the suppressing of rapine and violence, the civilizing of his people, the improvements of commerce, and the encouragement of arts and sciences." In Europe in the next generation, Mercury continued this effort: of his measures "for civilizing the *Celtae* . . . there was none on which he was more intent . . . than the encouragement he gave to commerce; and the means he used to link them together in society and friendship by a mutual intercourse in the way of merchandise." Hence, of course, his name and his classical signification as the god of gain and commerce (13–14).

What Spenser read into the legend as epic, thanks to Brut, Carte now reads back into Brutless history, thanks to the Celts (as disguised deities). Could there be a clearer case of present values and interests determining our view of the past? Maybe; other candidates will soon present themselves, all of them exfoliating from what is now the principal interest of the eighteenth-century occident: the amassing of profits from colonies. Thus Carte takes care to make psychologically plausible the Celts' colonizing passion by appealing to this more recent history. "The humour of making plantations in remote parts of the world" would, he says, seem odd and arduous, "were it not for the fury" with which later Europeans went on crusades and the like fury with which, "within the one hundred and fifty years last past, men exposed themselves to the horrible dangers and hardships . . . in their voyages for discovering a . . . passage to the *East-Indies*" (10).

Carte draws even more striking parallels between the former colonizing of pre-Roman Britain and the present colonizing of the new world. The venerable name of Troynovant (for London) he explains by an emendation: the name was really Tre-novant and meant in Celtic (a language of which Carte has earlier admitted ignorance) simply the "town of the newcomers"—that is, the Belgic immigrants to Kent. All this settling "seems to have been done, without giving more umbrage and offense to the old natives, than our late settlement of *Georgia* hath done to the *Creak Indians*, there being still woods enough for those, who did not care to fall into the Belgic way of living, to gratify their passion for hunting" (25–26). Whoever the "old natives" were, what they did was hunt, since that's what primitives do, since the savages we now know do (supposedly) just that. Once settled, the Bards and Druids used no writing, since they lived remote from "the east, whence light breaks on the earth," that place which alone "first gave birth to letters." Moses invented these, of course, whence they passed, via Cadmus, from Phoenicia to Greece. Though the Phoenicians traded with the Britons, they did not pass on to them their literacy—for reasons that Carte adduces most pertinently from contemporary experience. Because the Phoenicians "made so extraordinary a profit" from their trade with ancient Britain, "they took all . . . pains . . . to conceal from the world the course of the navigation thither." Their aim naturally being gain, "it cannot be thought, that they should take any more care to instruct and improve the *Britains* in knowledge, than we have done in the case, either of the inhabitants we trade with on the coast of *Africa*, or of the *Indians* that live on the back of our plantations in *America*" (37–38). Carte finds this policy comprehensible, but in the long term "contrary to their interest"—since continued ignorance does nothing to expand the market.

The motive of making commercial profits, it would appear, might actually *prevent* the bringing of culture which the Renaissance versions of the legend had identified with it. Ideally, though, the identification remains: more profits are obtainable if at least some culture is brought. The expansion of markets requires an awareness of what is available, after all. In any case, Carte manages to find in the past of the Celtic Phrygians the same energetic "plantations" that Europeans were busily performing in the present. And whatever the possible conflicts between the motives of profit-taking and culture-bringing, culture remains that which must be brought—somehow by somebody, here the culture heroes who were really our ancestors the Celts, whose greatness was purloined and deified by the Greeks.

The ultimate systematization of this Annian objective—to present biblical history as the only true history—was achieved by an exact contemporary of Carte who sometimes passes as one of the first social theorists in the modern world. This is Giambattista Vico, whose *New Science* appeared in its final form in 1744. Vico's aim is to construct a history of all nations that will vindicate its direction by divine providence, taking the Old Testament as the only accurate source and interpreting all pagan writings as shadowy fables. The interest of his system with respect to our legend of civilization is that, along with many other historians and philosophers of the Enlightenment, it transfers the myth from one register of discourse to another, from history as veracious event to a global theory of all history, from story to historiography. And in this latter form, the myth will pass before the end of the century back into the writing of present history, that of the Americas.

By conferring the unique privilege of historical authority on the Hebrew Bible, Vico accomplishes for our (western European) history what Brady and Tyrrell and Hume accomplished for it by beginning it with the Romans and what Pezron and Carte accomplished by asserting its Celtic origins. That is, we now see ourselves not as the direct heirs of the original culture-bringers (the sons of Japheth and of Troy), but rather as the highly evolved descendants of the savages to whom culture was brought. This possibility was of course always there in the ancient versions of the legend and was carefully, strategically, preserved by Virgil, to acknowledge the mixture of Etruscans, Latins, and others that finally became Romans. Some medieval uses of the legend as entitlement had, however, foreclosed this possibility: Brut didn't intermarry with the giants, but exterminated them. Other versions of the legend preserved the possibility, for example, in the various wives that Francus and his siblings were said to have acquired in their peregrinations. But now, whether as barbaric gentiles awaiting the Mosaic illumination, or savage Celts awaiting the Roman one, or Phrygians having received their own, there is the same assumption that we too were once savages. The crucial consequence of this quintessentially modern notion of "development" (or, naturally, "progress") is that it allows us to assimilate the savages in our present world to our own past, to know, understand, and prophesy what must be their history, simply because it was ours.

Vico, insisting that all stories of origin save that of Moses are false, thus interprets them as fables from a barbarous age that encode the stages of development by which human society passes from hunting and gathering to settled agriculture. He offers these readings in the fourth part of his massive work, called "Poetic Economy." In the beginning, that is, after the Flood, the offspring of Noah's three sons were called in the fables "giants," because they led strenuous lives in forest-covered places. These prehistoric times—in contradiction to all classical imaginings of any Golden Age of justice and wisdom—were "full of arrogance and savagery because of the fresh emergence from bestial liberty, in the extreme simplicity and crudeness of life content with the spontaneous fruits of nature" (Vico 1970: sec.522). Millennia were required for these childlike people "to be tamed from their feral native liberty" by progressing through a long period of family discipline to obedience to the much later civil states. The agent of this transformation was simply "divine force," which was alone sufficient "to reduce these giants, as savage as they were crude, to human duties" (sec. 523). This is Vico's reading of the myths of Orpheus and Amphion.

Gradually the giants were literally reduced in stature as they were reduced to rule, by divine providence working through all their pagan religious observances, which Vico catalogues at length. They cease wandering in forests, gather in cleared spaces, begin to plant, cooperate in using water, and learn to bury their dead. Hence, says Vico, the literal truth of what he cites as a Roman burial rite: "we are sons of this earth, we are born from these oaks" (sec. 531). Here of course is the Virgilian description of the indigenes; only now these autochthonous savages are ourselves in an earlier form. Vico, by training a philologist, makes much of the Latin vocabulary of the family "tree," its stocks (*stirpes*) and shoots (*propagines*). And he summons all of classical mythology in order to document the passage from savagery to civilization.

The passage is made, of course, by means of agriculture. Apollo's reputation for wisdom is validated by his conversion of Daphne, "a vagabond maiden wandering through the forests (in the nefarious life)" to a laurel tree, "which is ever green in its certain and acknowledged offspring." Vico's ingenuity is fully equal to that of the whole allegorizing tradition, which he, like Annius, despises; and, like Annius, he labors to be convincing—not by faking his evidence but by offering rational explanations in the "modern" mode. Thus, he assures us, "the pursuit of Apollo was the act of a god, and the flight of Daphne that of an animal; but later, when the language of this austere history had been forgotten, Apollo's pursuit became a libertine's, and Daphne's flight a woman's" (sec. 533). In the age of heroes, thus dimly witnessed by the ancient myths, the gradual development of agriculture is recorded in the labors of Hercules. The beasts he slays (dragons, lions, etc.) are figures of the untamed wilderness; the golden apples of the Hesperides are the ears of grain produced by clearing it (secs.539–48). Other deities encode the same process: Vulcan is he who burns the fields to clear them; Saturn is he who sows; Cybele the cultivated land itself. She "is depicted as seated on a lion (the enforested earth which the heroes reduced to tillage)," and is the goddess of the first cities as well as the earth mother (sec. 549). Colonies, observes Vico, were originally groups of "workers who till the soil (as they still do)." Many of them were founded by the Gallic Hercules, with the chain of gold issuing from his mouth, "hitherto . . . taken as a symbol of eloquence, but the fable was born at a time when the heroes had as yet no articulate speech"; so the gold really signifies, as it does everywhere, grain (sec. 560). And so it goes: the golden apples merge into the gold of Pluto and the golden bough by which Aeneas descends underground, which, extending the metaphor of apples for ears, signifies the whole harvest. The ruler of the underworld, Pluto/Dis, "the god of heroic riches, gold or grain" is the abductor of Proserpine/Ceres, "goddess of grain" (sec. 720). The association is perfectly logical, "since tilled fields make the true wealth of peoples" (sec. 723).

So they do—in our culture, in its founding legend, and in Vico's remarkable farrago of untenable hypothesis and plausible conjecture. He dismisses, of course, the founding story about the Trojans as but a Greek "conceit" foisted off on the Romans (secs. 770–73). Real history, for him, has no founders, merely the anonymous "heroes," who arose from savagery to a kind of feudal familism, thanks to God. They became the first "nobility," ruling over others, and thus established the political principles that later developed into commonwealths. And in their savage state, they are everywhere compared to the indigenous peoples in Europe's present. Homeric kings, the heads of feudal families, "are still found in great numbers in Arabia . . . and in the West Indies the greater part were found in this state of nature to be governed by such families, surrounded by slaves," much as must have been, Vico continues, the family of Abraham (sec. 557). Roman historians describe the use by "barbarian nations" of fire-hardened wooden spears, "similar to those the American Indians were found to wield" (sec. 562). Elsewhere Vico claims the universality of sky gods as sources of law to be proof of divine providence, which in this instance includes the "Peruvian Indians" (sec. 480).

The alleged practices and beliefs of both present and past barbarians turn out to be identical in Vico's pages, each being used to corroborate the other. Thus, the practice of burial, which entails for him the belief in the immortality of the soul, is seen as a crucial step away from the bestiality of our origins, when men went about "like swine . . . in uncultivated fields and uninhabited cities." That burial "was the consensus of the ancient barbarous nations may be inferred from what we are told of the peoples of Guinea . . . Peru and Mexico . . . Virginia . . . New England . . . Siam" (sec. 337). Such practices must corroborate each other in Vico's whole deliberate exposition of universal history directed by the one true God. He calls this "an ideal eternal history traversed in time by the histories of all nations" (sec. 114). It might (and soon will) be Hegel talking; once we get the "idea," we have the key, not just to all mythologies, but to all history: we can infallibly predict it. Our passage from childish bestiality to agriculture, legal order, and commerce becomes the only possible history for anyone. And contemporary barbarians become thus perfectly explicable as our own primitive selves: they're just younger. Vico (who is nothing if not repetitious) makes the entire biological metaphor into one of the first "principles of the ideal eternal history traversed in time by every nation in its rise, development, maturity, decline, and fall" (sec. 243).

There's only one trajectory, that of the human life cycle, and the content of its stages is that of the picture of civilization in our founding legend. The legend is rejected, of course; the story of journey, arrival, and conquest is replaced by a theory of universal social development. But the picture is the same: our founding culture-bringers have become our barbarian paterfamilias, who wrought they knew not how by divine providence. And what they wrought is just what we've acquired: agriculture, cities, writing, and commerce. The process of their acquiring it is what Vico reads out of classical mythology, the only surviving witness of a period that is "as if empty of history" (Rossi 1984: 180). The phrase is exact, and also precisely describes the status to which our culture relegates all those indigenes who do not till the soil and build on it and use writing as we do. The people we are dispossessing and colonizing are without history, as we were in the fabulous age of "heroes" that Vico reconstructs as our own savage past.

And Vico describes his own effort of reconstruction—his manner of appropriating the myths, debunking them as repositories of occult wisdom, and revealing the history they really contain—as itself a colonial takeover, a dis- and re-possessing of territory. Should we not, he rhetorically asks, "make ourselves possessors of the things of the distant past which have hitherto belonged to nobody, ownership of which can consequently be conceded legitimately to whoever occupies them?" (Rossi 1984: 181). Indeed—we can "occupy" by interpretation just as we can by invasion, and in the case of indigenous peoples the former inevitably accompanies the latter. Vico chose his metaphor advisedly, for the other major context of his speculations (distinct from but related to the age of the world) is the formal legitimation of just those actual dispossessions and occupations.

This effort was that of the theologians and legal theorists who strove to do explicitly what Vico does implicitly: to assimilate the savages of the present to a universal concept of "natural" law that would justify our treatment of them. This was not Vico's concern; he can merely assume that "ownership" of what was unoccupied is "legitimate," using as a figure of speech what other thinkers had labored to defend. The forms their defense took, however, accomplish just what Vico accomplished, and by the same means: what he made a theory of providence in history, they made a theory of nature in jurisprudence. Both theories were but redeployments, inscriptions in more authoritative registers, of the picture of civilization mediated by the founding legend that was no longer our history, but was rapidly becoming someone else's.

Chapter 15

MYTH IN LAW

From Victoria to Locke

When we Europeans felt we were barbarians, the Trojan legend told us we weren't; now that we know that we were barbarians but aren't any longer, we can drop the legend from our history, and use it henceforth to determine the history of the barbarians we've so lately discovered. The use of the legend in its most prestigious form, the epic of Virgil, to determine the fate of the indigenous populations in the new world is clearly visible in the formation of a special branch of law. This would eventually become international law, and was created expressly to deal with the accelerating conflicts among the major powers of Europe, due in large part to their competing claims over territory and trading privileges in the new world, and with the vexed question of the respective "rights" of the colonizers and the colonized.

It was to the fledgling attempts to form this body of law that Sir George Peckham was alluding in the 1580s when he cited the opinion of some not "meanly learned" that it was "scarce lawfull" for Europeans to plant colonies and Christianity by violence (see ch. 10). The most tireless expresser of such an opinion in the sixteenth century was the great Dominican, Bartholomé de las Casas, who devoted his life to criticizing and attempting to improve the Spanish treatment of the Indians in the new world (see Todorov 1984). But the earliest surviving formal effort to bring colonial invasion, dispossession, and enslavement before the bar of Christian moral law was that of a theology professor at Salamanca, who lectured his students on the subject in 1539 (their date was long mistaken: see Haggenmacher 1988: 34). In these lectures, not published until 1557, Francisco de Victoria, in the dry late scholastic style of numbered questions and answers, propositions and corollaries, manages to reject almost all contemporary justifications for the Spanish takeover of America but one. And that one, derived in part from the *Aeneid*, will become the central focus of debate for theorists of natural law up to and including Vico.

Victoria begins by asserting the right of theologians, and not jurists, to inquire by what just title the Spaniards have taken their American territories away from their native inhabitants. Since barbarians come under no human (i.e. European) law or ruler, what concerns them can only be judged according to divine law (Victoria 1917: 119). Neither their grossest sins nor their heretical unbelief debar them from ownership or sovereignty. Nor can their alleged "unsoundness of mind" justify their subjection, since they have "reason" after their fashion, shown in their practice of "orderly arranged" politics, marriage, magistracy, systems of exchange, and so forth (123–27). Therefore they have dominion over their lands and the Spaniards no warrant to deprive them of it (128).

The thornier question for Victoria is whether the natives' refusal of peaceably offered Christianity justifies conquering them. At some length he concludes not: since neither prince nor pope can claim temporal lordship of the globe, the natives cannot be attacked and dispossessed for refusing their behests; they're not bound to believe even the truth. Nor are there grounds for coercing them even for violating the "law of nature" by committing all sorts of sexual deviance and cannibalism (137–48). Victoria regretfully concludes that there is no moral "title" at all for what has been done to them (149).

So divine law, in Victoria's liberal view, can justify nothing about colonial takeovers. His whole examination comes down to the point that we Christians have no right to bash people around merely because they're unbelievers. Next, however, he asks if there are any lawful "titles" by which we may do so—that is, derivable from the "law of nations," whose definition he quotes from the *Institutes* of Justinian: "what natural reason has established among all nations is called the *ius gentium*" (151). And here appears the extreme utility of universalism: since the aborigines are sovereign over themselves in their place, they are not subject to our institutions. So we must find something to which they and we are both subject, some principle more universal even than Christianity. Hence the ancient Roman notion of what is common to all *men*—here applied, by strategic misquotation, to all *nations* (Justinian's *homines* becomes *gentes*)—comes into its own. And what is thus common, Victoria spins out somewhat laboriously, is a principle of "natural society and fellowship."

What this means is that all people have the right to travel, visit, settle, trade, and mine in the territories of others—so long as they do no harm. Here is something that can apply to Christians and unbelievers alike; it is ethnically neutral, color blind, in a word, universal. The evidence for the principle is drawn from a cento of references to mostly ancient writings of all kinds, including myths and fictions. The key citation is of *Aeneid* 1.539–41, where Ilioneus complains to Dido of the hostile reception the storm-driven Trojans received from her coast guards:

> What race of men is this? And what the land,
> So barbarous that it allows this custom?
> We are refused the hospitality

Of seacoasts; they cry for wars, forbidding
Us to rest even on the utmost borders.[1]

Victoria doesn't quote the lines, but merely alludes to "the Poet" everybody knows as one "proof" of the universal principle that obliges everyone to welcome harmless visitors, as indeed Dido proceeds to do, even inviting the Trojans to settle in her city.

From such precedents as this Victoria deduces the universal right to travel, visit, settle, trade, and mine. If any of these is refused, when asked nicely, then it may be fought for, since defense of one's rights is the only justification for war (151–55). Only if the Indians refuse traffic, or forbid the Gospel even to be preached (no matter whether they believe it), do the Spanish have just reason to conquer them (157–58). The forcible halting of human sacrifice or cannibalism is also lawful, as is participation in the Indians' own wars when requested (159–60). And even in these cases, the violence should be minimal, taking account of the Indians' inferior intellects and means. Though not "wholly unintelligent," they still lack arts and manufactures, "proper laws," and "careful agriculture"; they're "infants" who may be ruled for their own good, provided, adds Victoria, it's really in their interest and not for our profit (160–61).

So what Christianity can't do for this pious idealist, the "law of nature" can: produce a universal principle, claiming its grounds in Roman law and finding its precedents in myth, that will, under circumstances carefully limited by Victoria but infinitely extendable in later thinking, justify the dispossession of the indigenes. And what a principle it is: under the rubric of the relational bonds of common humanity, from the postulate of "natural sociability and fellowship," will proceed just the kind of "right" that Peckham invoked: our right to settle their territories and carry on trade. In the light of what happened in the new world, the application of this principle to those peoples is almost too painfully ironic to contemplate. In the name of natural sociability we can have Mayan women devoured by dogs and exterminate entire cultures. The natural law theorists to follow are all quite as well-meaning and pious as Victoria; but what they are theorizing and justifying is the continued territorial expansion of Europe around the world. And they are doing so by assuming the categories in our founding story, that comfortable (for us) division between the civilized and the savage.

Further systematization of Victoria's principles is offered by Alberico Gentili, a naturalized professor of civil law at Oxford. In his treatise on the law of war, published in 1588, he makes the opposite jurisdictional claim to Victoria's: since war can be justified neither as "natural" (because people must be taught to hate, being naturally sociable) nor as religious, it is the proper business of lawyers—not theologians—to find its justifications and prescribe its rules (Gentili 1933: 55–58). And

1. quod genus hoc hominum? quaeve hunc tam barbara morem
   permittit patria? hospitio prohibemur harenae;
   bella cient primaque vetant consistere terra.

the sole justification for war is (as for the whole Roman legal tradition, which ruled out all forms of aggression and all motives of glory or dominion) defense of one's own "rights": when something "is refused us which Nature herself has bestowed upon mankind." The use of force is always and only justified to repel force (58–59). There are other classes of wars, though, presumably less justified, which arise from "expediency." Prominent among these are conflicts caused by the emigration of whole peoples, made exiles by conquest, population pressure, disaster, disease, or persecution (79). In these cases, there's sort of a quasi-right to territory elsewhere: the good example is Aeneas's polite approach to Latinus in Latium (7.229) and his response. In addition, "the seizure of vacant space is regarded as a law of nature"; even if claimed by some sovereign, if it's empty, it can be lawfully occupied, since the "law of nature . . . abhors a vacuum" and the earth was made to be peopled. And even if it's not quite empty, again to accommodate exiles, "a slight loss ought to be endured" (80–81). The good example, again, is the final settlement of the Trojans in Latium (12.190).

Gentili's proof texts throughout are proverbs and verses from ancient poets and dramatists. These are the precedents that establish just what "Nature herself" has given us, to wit: "rights" of passage, harbor, provisions, commerce, and trade (86–88). Classical tags about the value and need of commerce are adduced in profusion to prove a right to it that justifies war if it's prohibited (88–89). At this point, as at several others, Gentili is loading the dice of his principles to tilt them toward the English and away from the Spanish. The latter alleged this right to commerce as a justification, he adds, but what they were really after was dominion.

So: the law of Nature mandates free trade—*ergo*, any restriction thereon is a just cause for war. With this syllogism, legal theory passes, as usual, from the high idealism of what ought to be to the real description of what is. As the editor of Gentili's text reminds us (28a), Queen Elizabeth cited the *ius gentium* to the Spanish ambassador when he complained about Drake's piracies in 1580: the sea is free, she said, and the Spanish invite reprisals by refusing other countries' right to trade in their dominions. From the English Navigation Acts of the 1650s (against the Dutch) to the American War of Independence in 1776, virtually all the numerous wars waged by European powers in Europe and around the globe had the enlargement of trading privileges and terms as a primary objective. None of the contending powers during this period permitted anything like "free" trade. Nor do they yet—only now the arena of conflict has shifted (though not entirely) from warfare to the international conference tables of the WTO (World Trade Organization—formerly GATT, General Agreement on Tariffs and Trade), UNCTAD (United Nations Conference on Trade and Development), the European Community, and an endless succession of bilateral and multilateral negotiations and protocols, including (since 1990) the whole happy scramble to integrate the second world (the formerly evil empire) into the first (us). Free trade is the ideal (as for Adam Smith), decreed by Nature herself. But the real is that it's never free. So all the wars that ever Europe fought against restricting it are just and justified. And all the wars that Europe will fight, against the hapless savage who is reluctant to stop planting yams (which he can eat) and start planting cotton (which we can sell), are justified by the same principle: the savage is restricting our right to trade; he's not sociable.

Gentili summarizes the Virgilian passage adduced by Victoria as proof of the universal right of access to the sea, its coasts and inlets: "What barbarians deny the hospitality of the strand?" (90). The rest, and largest part, of Gentili's treatise derives rules for the "proper" conduct of wars from the usual fictional and proverbial sources. The military behavior of pious Aeneas is a frequent source of good examples. One particular form of proper conduct summons up another variant of the founding legend in order to invoke the distinction between the civilized and the barbarian. The rule Gentili prescribes here is that the decent burial of fallen combatants must always be allowed for and the abuse of corpses always prohibited; in no case should even enemy bodies be injured. Let us recall an event from the subsequent history of Gentili's adopted country: at the Restoration of Charles II in 1660, the bodies of those regicides who had died since 1649 were disinterred from Westminster Abbey. Their skulls were impaled in Westminster Hall, and the rest of their rotting fragments were hung on Tyburn Hill, where apprentices amused themselves by cutting off their toes (Hutton 1987: 134). Of the abuse of corpses, Gentili says: such a "barbarous practice" is never lawful; it is "worthy of the early uncivilized days; and it was done away with by Hercules, who was, as they say, the reformer of barbarous customs" (283).

I have not juxtaposed those corpses and this judgment merely to illustrate that our behavior customarily violates our principles or that it constantly erases or reverses our prized distinction between what is and isn't civilized. I have done so rather to suggest the futility of what this kind of legal discourse forbids, in contrast to the enormous effectiveness of what it permits. It compiles ever-longer lists of prohibited (but unpreventable) practices in the name of an ideal so abstract, a principle so construable, as to prohibit nothing. And the authority for the principle is a supposed universalism derived in very large part from the fictions of the ancient Mediterranean world, including that of our founding legend.

Victoria and Gentili typify the beginnings of this discourse, which expands to take on philosophical and supersystematic pretensions in the works of its major practitioners in the next century, Hugo Grotius and Samuel Pufendorf. It expands also into dimensions of prolixity that were and remain the despair of its always admiring translators. For it is often impossible to follow the thread of any argument through the dense, columnar thickets of quotation and reference. The various translations I have seen of both men's work, from the seventeenth to the nineteenth centuries, all comment on these difficulties and deal variously with them: by summary, omission, or typography. The prolixity is a kind of overkill (as was Peckham's list of legitimizing conquests), the sign of an irresistible anxiety or need. The sheer multiplication of examples and authorities for almost every point, regardless of its importance, rapidly comes to seem an end in itself. This verbosity is not, I think, the generic pedantry that may accompany any form of erudition; it is part of the peculiar discursive operation being performed: to justify anything while appearing to prohibit a great deal.

The selection of authorities is consciously purposeful for Grotius: they are to make the "law" as rigorously objective as mathematics. He solemnly declares that he writes without reference to any present controversy or situation, considering "rights" in pure isolation, like numbers abstracted from any body or fact (Grotius 1853: 1.lxxviii). And sure enough, one can find in his massive tomes not the slightest allusion to any contemporary events or people; the endless sources are all classical. What is more, the sources are graded: the most authoritative are the histories of "better times and nations," that is, the ancient Greek and Roman; poets and orators are less weighty and are used for ornament. What is sought in the sources is agreement, since natural law is proved mainly by consensus, what most people have thought, and the law of nations can be proved in no other way (1.lxxi-ii). Here is another voice of modernity: the enterprise is one of objective and empirical science. Grotius is going to demonstrate in this new way what previous thinkers took for granted, that (in Hooker's words) "the general and perpetual voice of men is as the sentence of God himself."

Grotius wrote his text in Paris, in the diplomatic service of Louis XIII, to whom the first edition of 1625 is dedicated. He had escaped to France from imprisonment in his native Holland as an Arminian heretic. Widely honored throughout Europe for his vast learning, he ended his days in the diplomatic service of Christina of Sweden. Though he thus had good and obvious reasons for wishing his work to appear wholly objective, disinterested, and inoffensive to contemporary monarchs, his protestations do not make it any less relevant to contemporary concerns than the straightforwardly interested inquiry of Victoria. His key principles are indeed Victoria's, only presented in the new way, with a prolix apparatus and an announced procedure pretending to an objectivity that is itself a form of self-protection.

The principle that grounds everything for Grotius is that the nature of humanity is social; he finds various Latin and Greek terms for this, one of them being what the Stoics called "the domestic instinct or feeling of kindred" (1.xli). Contemporary English translators liked to render this as "desire for communion." As a good empiricist, Grotius evokes and disposes of several ancient writers who contested the universalism he is advocating. The skeptic Carneades is chief among these; he denied any universal basis at all to law, which he saw merely as that which was useful or profitable for a given state at a given time. What is the present issue in this discourse is here displaced into the past. And the past opponent is well selected (Pufendorf will deal with him too): his opinion is indeed fatal to the enterprise, which is to assert a universalism that can have no exceptions, no local variants, but must cover all the inhabitants of the planet. So Grotius must insist that Carneades' view is false, that all law derives from a universal human nature. This is defined, as opposed to the nature of animals (the opposition demonstrating how little attention must have been paid even to the animals in the barnyard), as a desire for "mutual society." This implies the preservation of society, from which unfold the constituent parts of natural law: abstinence from other people's property, obligation to keep promises, reparation for damages done to others, and recognition that punishments are deserved for failing to do any of these things (1.xliv). For Grotius, all these add up to "justice." He is aware that other and larger ethical questions congregate around the notion of *jus*, and is explicitly ruling these out (since moral customs are so various as wholly to defy universalization). The proper concern of the justice of natural law is, in a nutshell, "that what belongs to another is left to him or gets compensated" (1.xlvi).[2]

Nature has thus bestowed upon all humanity our notions of private property, alienable ownership, and the individual responsibility for language and action that is enforceable by contract. It has occurred to no one yet (except perhaps the prescient Carneades, who survives only in fragmentary reports of other writers) that all these things are culture-specific. We've learned only lately that the Iroquois of New York and the Algonquin of Virginia had none of these notions in the seventeenth century when they were "selling" their lands to us Europeans. They never imagined that land could, in any of our routine senses, even be "sold." They entertained a very different relation to the land—not, of course, a "civilized" one.

The central aim of universalizing our notions of property and contracts is so important to Grotius that he extends it beyond what many later writers (among them Pufendorf and Vico) found religiously acceptable. For he makes his science of law independent even of God. Though he is careful to insist that the revelations in Scripture are higher and holier than any precepts drawn from classical antiquity, he maintains that the Bible merely confirms the natural law of humanity that existed before and irrespective of Christianity. He goes yet farther, in the name of the new science, to insist that God can no more alter natural law than He can make two plus two not equal four (1.12). God allows himself to be confined to the "rule of reason"—that is, of noncontradiction in language: for if He didn't, we couldn't speak of the possibility without contradiction; we could make no sense.

How obliging of God to do no more and no other than human language can rationally describe. How admirable of Him to maintain with us this form of binding contract. To limit the traditionally ineffable and unknowable Creator to the linguistic systems, verbal or mathematical, that we can understand was regarded by Grotius's subsequent critics as impiety verging on blasphemy. But it demonstrates rather the bold consistency, even the obsessiveness, of what the discourse of natural law was striving to accomplish: to make the entire world, in time and space, subject to its formulations, to make it possible to judge everything and everybody in it by the customs of our ancient and tortuously transmitted civilization. Nothing is to remain outside this discourse, or other from it; it recognizes no others, and so it absorbs that ultimate and transcendent Other who is God. And its for-

---

2. The Latin here, garbled in all the translations I have seen, is: *ut quae jam sunt alterius alteri permittantur, aut impleantur.*

mulations are now centered, not accidentally, on our conception of property. That no exception to them is to be made even for God reveals the power that this discourse dreams (and will achieve). While the Dutch Protestant Grotius was making God a party to our notions of science and contracts, the English Protestant Donne was presenting Him as a celestial overseer of stock-offerings. God continues to evolve in the same direction, and before the end of the next century he will become indistinguishable from the operation of the market—from which in truth nothing and no one will be allowed to be other.

Meanwhile, Grotius fills hundreds of pages with the usual prescriptions of his predecessors. Defense is the only excuse for war: "a just cause of War is injury done us, and nothing else." But it's a pretty large excuse, covering not merely physical and territorial integrity, but the recovery of property and revenge or punishment (1.204–205). Even larger are the prospective gains in a war justly undertaken: these are called "rights of conquest" and amount quite simply to winner-take-all. Land, goods, governments—all are the victor's to do with as he likes; also his are any "incorporeal rights" (privileges, debts, powers) possessed vis-à-vis other nations by the loser, whose people may be lawfully compelled to anything, including changing their language and their way of life (3.164–65). The latitude of what is permitted by the universal principle of human nature is indeed wondrous, and is here made explicit—albeit with comfortably remote ancient examples—in a form appropriate to colonial conflicts. Because we're naturally sociable, we can legally commit ethnocide. All we have to do is construe our natural right to free trade as being injured. No problem.

Soon enough, though, there would be a problem for this discourse, a problem which its next practitioner must confront so that he can reassert its all-licencing chain of pseudo-reasoning that allows us to wipe out communities in the name of our desire for community. The problem is Hobbes. Baron Pufendorf will be driven to greater prolixity than Grotius in the effort to preserve our natural sociability from the total denial it receives in *Leviathan* (1651: 1.13). The crisp candor of Hobbes is a refreshing interlude between the turgid outpourings of the natural lawyers. No enemy at all to universalism, Hobbes merely reverses the meaning that the sociable theorists wish it to have. For him, famously, the "natural" condition of mankind is the war of each against all. We desire eminence or gain—anything but association—and we live in continual, bestial, and violent competition with our fellows. "It may seem strange to some," Hobbes allows, "that Nature should thus dissociate, and render men apt to invade, and destroy one another." But the doubter is invited to reflect on his actual behavior. Even in the present world, furnished with "Lawes, and publike Officers," let him think "what opinion he has of his fellow subjects, when he rides armed; of his fellow Citizens, when he locks his dores; and of his children, and servants, when he locks his chests."

The state of nature for Hobbes is savagery as our founding story defines it, and his clinching example of it, after this evocation of our routine urban forms of distrust, is the place in the present world where folks live as we presumably did when in that state. "For the savage people in many places of *America*, except the government of small Families, the concord whereof dependeth on naturall lust, have no government at all; and live at this day in that brutish manner." They are (and we once were) wholly without *mos* and *cultus*: "The notions of Right and Wrong, Justice and Injustice have there no place. Where there is no common Power, there is no Law; where no Law, no Injustice." And so, weary of combat and fear, men at length consent to "articles of peace" suggested by reason. "These Articles, are they, which otherwise are called the Lawes of Nature." They consist, we learn in subsequent chapters, of justice, equity, modesty, mercy, and so forth—all the principles by which people live tranquilly together. But they are of course not innate; they are learned and above all *enforced*. Their necessary enforcement is the *raison d'être* of Hobbes's absolute monarch. If there were no power to compel us to obey these laws, we'd be brutes again.

The idea that we must be politically coerced to be anything other than brutes made Hobbes the same kind of moral bête noire for the Enlightenment that Machiavelli had been for the Renaissance. For both thinkers made the pure struggle for power self-justifying. And such a doctrine was simply too brutal to be acceptable during periods when the exercise of power, as measured (brutally) by the number of wars fought, was naked and unprecedented. In the history of Europe from the fall of ancient Rome to now (a total of about 1,500 years), the period from 1500 to 1800 (one-fifth of the total) accounts for the following percentages of all wars ever fought by the major powers: England and Great Britain, one-third; France, 40 percent; Italy and Spain, more than 40 percent (see Kohn 1987: Index).[3] In other words, the period when Europeans were fighting each other, as well as others, largely to consolidate their grasp of the globe contains roughly twice as many wars as the proportion of time it occupies. The discourse of natural law, of course, has the justification of war and the rationalization of its conduct as the central focus. War is its subject because the intensification of war is its context. And its aim is to sanitize the subject, to legitimize the practice of war now and everywhere by finding its universal principles laid down in the stories and philosophies of Mediterranean antiquity. The principles selected—of sociability and community—require the elaborate legitimation of war as an aberration from them. Hobbes's aim and procedure are just the reverse: war is itself the principle, so the power that stops it is ipso facto legitimate.

Pufendorf, a professor of jurisprudence at Lund and Berlin, first published his thick folio (which got thicker in succeeding editions) on the laws of nature and nations in 1672. Hobbes wasn't his only problem. The other major one was to avoid the pitfall into impiety of Grotius but still maintain the applicability of all the justifications and precepts and prohibitions to heathens and Christians alike by keeping the ground of all in a universal law of nature. Pufendorf deals with both problems by greatly enlarging the discussion of the classical texts where he is careful to place them. He can then declare that Cicero, and the Bible, have solved them

---

3. Holland and Portugal cannot be included, since their wars are not tabulated by Kohn until their formation as nations, more or less, in the fifteenth century. My calculations are obviously approximate.

already, and continue to deplore Grotius's theology and deny Hobbes's contentions while using what suits him from both men's work.

Pufendorf is thus obliged to foreground the question of whence the law of nature is derived (God or human consensus) and of what it consists (warfare or benevolence). He begins book 2 with the latter question, quoting most of the ancient sources for Virgil's description of the indigenous inhabitants of Rome as wholly lacking *mos* and *cultus*. He quotes them, of course, because they exemplify the claim of Hobbes that our natural state is savage violence. He then leaves this question in suspense and reviews in detail the ancient opinions against there being any universal consent of mankind. The skeptics, and Sextus Empiricus in particular, are richly employed (Pufendorf 1703: bk. 2, ch. 3, sec. 7).[4] He evokes the difficulty of discriminating the innate from the habitual: "meer Use and Custom when it hath born a long and an unquestion'd Sway, frequently puts on the Face and Semblance of Natural Reason" (2.3.9). The review ends by alluding to the conclusion of Carneades, that "the diversity of Laws and Manners" has led some to deny that law is natural, maintaining instead "that all Law first arose from the Convenience and the Profit of Particular States."

"Profit" will be Pufendorf's wedge of refutation here, permitting a quick shift to the authority of Cicero, whose equation (in *De officiis*) of "profit" and "honesty" provides Pufendorf with his needed definition of natural law. He distinguishes simply between short- and long-term profit: the actual laws made by states for some punctual advantage are the former; only what conforms to the law of nature can be the latter. Duration of "profit" (on some unspecified scale) is what permits the distinction between laws that merely secure a "private advantage" and those that have their origin in the general good. Cicero's unification of the profitable and the honest is buttressed with numerous quotations from Scripture (mostly from Proverbs). Real, long-lasting profit can never be at the expense of others, since, in the state of nature, "Nature hath never given any Man so large a Privilege, as to let him exercise any kind of Right against others, the use of which they are not allow'd to turn against *him*"—this would be the war of "all against all." Thus Hobbes's thesis becomes an (unthinkable) alternative already exploded by Cicero: only those laws are just that conform to the law of nature (and thus allow us to discern it). Only they conduce to our "safety," which is assured only by "society and friendliness." Justice is necessarily the common good, and leads us to tranquillity; the unjust never prosper, or if they do, they suffer psychologically. Tags from Quintilian, Demosthenes, Epicurus, and others are adduced throughout—all to equate the just with the common good (2.3.10).

Hobbes thus evaded, Carneades is next: Pufendorf reports (from Lactantius) his equation of justice with folly, on the grounds that if the Romans were to be just, they would dissolve their empire, giving back the territories they rule to their original possessors. Not so: since real profit is not "what seems advantageous to such

---

4. For various reasons, I have used two different editions of this text, and so cite it in the form that permits reference to both, or to any.

or such a Man at such a particular time, to the prejudice of others; but what is of Universal and Perpetual Benefit and Expediency." And in the long term, the Romans lost their (apparently ill-gotten) empire. Hence, long-term profit equals justice and the common good equals the "Law of Nature . . . by which the Safety of Mankind is secur'd." And to know this law, natural reason is quite sufficient (2.3.11)—since it's knowable by a process of elimination (of whatever good isn't common) over time (however much it may take).

If all this seems illogical at best and circular at worst, that's because it is. The opponents are scarcely engaged, let alone refuted; they're drowned in a barrage of assertion and miscellaneous quotation, in which Pufendorf is careful to include as much Scripture as possible. For although natural reason can supposedly find out natural law, it does so only by ex post facto inference, and so cannot establish it. It is nonetheless always obeyed, even though most men cannot articulate it, just as a rude "mechanick" must conform what he builds to the rules of mathematics without knowing any (2.3.12). And here is the necessary, normative universal, which Pufendorf goes on to establish not by consensus but by God, contra Grotius. Grotius's idea that natural law binds God and could exist without Him is, says Pufendorf, against reason; "since law necessarily supposes a superior" power to impose it (2.3.19). And since no sovereign imposes an end without supplying the means, God made the nature of things available to our reason. This, Pufendorf triumphantly concludes, is "Proof of Man's being oblig'd to a Social Life by the Command of GOD" (2.3.20). The assumption here that law can only be imposed by supreme authority is borrowed from Hobbes, retheologized, and used to trounce Grotius. Hobbes's monarch becomes Pufendorf's God; the resultant law of nature is full, perfect, and confirmed in Scripture, which is copiously cited throughout, along with sundry tags and proverbs to show us that there is poetic justice in the world.

The system thus established, Pufendorf proceeds to apply it to every situation and practice he can think of, not omitting the contemporary. Under the "general duties of humanity" appears that of hospitality, duly cited from the *Aeneid*, 1.539 (Pufendorf 1934: 3.3.8). But Pufendorf limits this duty to short-term provisioning, and dissents at length from Victoria's use of it to justify the Spanish conquests and occupations. Long-term settlements are to be judged rather by their motives in particular cases, since such "social" rights as hospitality "cannot prevent a property-holder from having the final decision" about whether to share the use of his property. Again, the final deals between Aeneas and Latinus (11.316, 12.192) are models (3.3.9). Other practices that Pufendorf finds fully sanctioned by the law of nature are the obtaining of monopolies by chartered corporations (5.5.7) and the taking of interest for the use of money—the prohibition of usury being merely a local regulation among the Jews (5.6.9). Founding colonies is fully sanctioned, too, especially in order to remove starving, useless, or suspicious citizens from the home country (8.11.6), and regardless of whether they are left to govern themselves, or are governed from the metropolis, this being the Roman practice, "imitated by most of the present-day nations of Europe" (8.12.4).

The primacy Pufendorf gives, as Grotius did, to property rights suggests why in later colonial discourse the natives will be found incapable of having them (vs. Victoria, who insisted they did). The natural law that sanctions private property was to become a key notion in the political theory of one of Pufendorf's admiring readers, John Locke. The philosopher (a friend and associate of the historian Tyrrell) who provided the self-description of our occidental modernity as liberal individualism regarded Pufendorf's *De Jure Naturae* as the "best book of that kind" (Laslett 1970: 142). In his greatly influential "Essay . . . of Civil-Government" (first printed in 1689) Locke explains the emergence of society from the state of nature in terms that also assume (as Hobbes did) the historiography that the legend had become in the past century, in which the savage present is but our own past. Locke sees civil government arising to regulate the possession of property, which is acquired by the individual's labor in producing goods from the earth. This labor creates both ownership and value; Locke exemplifies the point by observing that ten acres of Devonshire are worth more than a thousand in the "uncultivated wast of America." He specifies that "wast" is where there is no "Pasturage, Tillage, or Planting." (The corollary that untilled land is therefore unowned will be deduced in the next century.) The "law of nature" that thus confers ownership also limits it, Locke says, to such goods as can be used before spoiling. But of course, once surplus is produced, it is exchanged by barter, and then for money; hence the use of the goods is greatly extendable. Such extended use is not possible where there is no "Commerce," and hence no need for property. "Thus in the beginning all the World was *America*, and more so than it is now; for no such thing as *Money* was any where known" (secs. 27–50, in Laslett 1970).

Locke well learned how to employ in political economy, where it will have a long afterlife, the discourse of the natural lawyers: the seeming prohibition that can justify anything. For the "natural" limit that Locke sets to the acquisition of private property turns out to be no limit at all, as he insists: it does not concern size or amount, but is determined only by use (sec. 46); and by means of commerce, use can be multiplied indefinitely. So natural law thus prescribes the holding of goods in common for American savages (such as we were) and permits us (as we now are) to amass as much property as we can, which in turn mandates a government by the elected representatives of property owners. God and Nature take pretty obvious sides in this discourse, functioning as the conceptual rationalization for what the savage lacks that we have, finding equally "natural," because part of a single history, his deprivations and our appropriations.

The putative limits of what the universal law of nature permits extend ever wider, farther, and longer in the eight books of Pufendorf's folio. But the most interesting of these obsessive extensions is the amount of initial space yielded to the claims against universalism, especially all the classical citations that emphasize the radical, irreducible differences among human communities. These must be mentioned (even more of them than Grotius did), anecdote after anecdote of them, only to be rather brusquely denied. The discourse must contain these differences, reproduce them, in order to subsume them under the all-covering natural law. And what this amounts to is the kind of grand tautology that the age of Leibniz never wearied of repeating: what succeeds is success; if it still exists, it must be just. As the next (after Spenser) Virgilian poet in English will express it, "Whatever is, is right."

This discourse of containment and subsumption will characterize a good deal of eighteenth-century literature. It developed from the pan-European effort of these scholars to find what Victoria sought and where he found it: a universal older than Christianity, a covering law as scientific as mathematics, that will globally apply. The law of nature as God's expression through "the general and perpetual voice of men," which could be assumed by such Christian philosophers as Aquinas and Hooker, has had in this legal discourse to be lengthily reasserted and tortuously reestablished. Such reestablishment was necessary because there is now more than one voice, whose generality can no longer be assumed, whose heterogeneity must at all costs be denied, and whose perpetuity will perish.

Victoria, Gentili, Grotius, and Pufendorf, though by no means the only, are fairly representative and influential formers of this discourse, whose consistency of aim and procedure (despite their disagreements) is the more impressive given the variety of their nationalities, religions, and intellectual training. From Spain to Scandinavia, from late-medieval scholasticism through the new science of the Renaissance to the assured optimism of the Enlightenment, they speak in one voice: Latin, the waning but still hegemonic language of learning in cultured Europe. This is the voice of that single natural law to which all are subject, the voice of the Roman empire become us. The unquestioned hegemony of this voice is such that the actual obstacles to communicating with other, wholly unknown voices of indigenous populations around the world receive no attention whatever in these texts (on the way in which such obstacles were both confronted and ignored in the earliest texts of Spanish conquest, see Greenblatt 1991: ch. 4). Even when such communication is presupposed, as it must be, in all the prescriptions to make clear to them our harmless intentions, explain to them our natural rights, ask them nicely for provisions—the crucial question of how any of this is to be understood is simply ignored. In practice, it was famously ignored by Columbus, who regarded his duty done when he had his notary read to the bewildered Caribbean islanders the proclamations of his Spanish monarchs. Also in practice, it was crucially important to find some kind of translator, to acquire some kind of information (see Todorov 1984). But the discourse that legalizes the activity never notices the problem. It is as if only one voice exists—which is indeed the case.

The vernacular voices of poets like Spenser and preachers like Donne had made colonial dispossession moral; but it required a whole chorus in the uniquely privileged voice to make it legal. Now that it was, the means by which it was made so—the law of nature and of nations—would be rapidly diffused through all levels of vernaculars. The most influential text of international law, however, will have a different orientation from that of Latin scholarship and will be published in French, in 1758. Before examining it, we shall see how the discourse of law as universal and historical myth had already been incorporated into both traditional forms of poetry and a new form of prose, the novel.

The formulation of the covering law—that puts us and the savages on the opposite ends of the same biological scale—is exactly contemporary with the rejection, over the sixteenth and seventeenth centuries, of the Trojan legend as history. As the story becomes unhistorical, its terms, unchanged, are rehistoricized as the *telos*, the necessary development—"modernization" would be a more recent term for it—of all mankind. The savage other is domesticated, becomes familiar, as what we ourselves used to be: so of course the same laws apply, both to judge his conduct and to write his history. By assimilating him to our own (legendary, but now both philosophical and legal) history, he will become almost invisible, rather like our own infancy, a negligible vestige of what everyone must go through and emerge from. That he might not live to emerge from it would be but the natural accident of mortality.

Chapter 16

LAW IN MYTH

Alexander Pope

The neoclassical age in England is practically synonymous with the career of its greatest poet, Alexander Pope. The extent to which this career, like Spenser's, was modeled on Virgil's is evident from the progression of publications from pastoral to epic. But Pope was a busier classicizer on more fronts than Spenser; excluded from office by being born a Roman Catholic, and excluded from active life by chronic sickness, Pope had little to do but write. He played Horace as well as Virgil, popularizing in English the critical tenets of French classicism, imitating as well as translating some of Horace's didactic and satirical verse, translating Homer (Dryden had beat him to Virgil), editing Shakespeare, and generally setting himself up, with his Tory coterie, as the arbiter of the newly refined and correct taste of the age. So successful was he at this, that a character in his friend Fielding's *Joseph Andrews* tries to test the sophistication and bona fides of Parson Adams by asking him to describe the latest thing from the pen of Mr. Pope. Ironically—and the age is nothing if not ironic, in all possible ways—the test fails, since Parson Adams does not read vernacular literature, and so must prove his cultural status by rapping out a hundred verses of Homer in the original Greek (Fielding 1980: 177).

Not merely an arbiter of literary taste, Pope was also a pioneer of literary marketing, devising for his Homer a method of subscription publication that brought its considerable profits to him, instead of to its publisher. With some of these he had a Palladian villa built for himself on the Thames at Twickenham, where, like Horace and Cicero, he entertained his literary/political circle, which included such aristocrats as Viscount Bolingbroke, who had held various high offices under Queen Anne. Pope's closeness to this Tory ministry (the last for generations) was the apogee of the poet/empress symbiosis that was the aim of the Virgilian career. The poem that celebrates this moment, which was also the apogee of Anne's reign, is the fullest expression to date of Britain's imperial ambition and the discourse that justifies it. Before examining what Pope wrote, however, a look at what he didn't write will reveal the depth of his imperial literary ambition and his thorough comprehension of the founding legend.

The unwritten poem is a full-scale epic called *Brutus*, a detailed summary of which is preserved, ostensibly from Pope's own notes, by his first serious biographer, Owen Ruffhead (whose reliability is confirmed by his last one: Mack 1985: 925). The epic was to be in blank verse, and from the few opening lines that survive, one can hear why Pope in his actual publications stuck to the heroic couplet. But one also knows why he had to try blank verse: Milton had made it the epic verse form in English. Pope is planning to do just what Spenser did, to tell Geoffrey's founding story with the resonance in style and diction of the greatest native predecessor; Milton takes Chaucer's place. But Pope's plan is far more rigorously Virgilian than Spenser's, with Milton in the role that Homer played for Virgil. Entire episodes are modeled on *Paradise Lost*: for example, an early debate between Brutus's captains about where the Trojans should settle (Ruffhead 1769: 411–12) almost reproduces the debate in pandemonium of *PL* 2. Like Spenser, however, Pope also designs his version of the founding legend as a moral justification of the whole colonial enterprise, and duly incorporates in it the anxieties produced by its enactment.

The most striking thing (and the most un-Virgilian) about Pope's unachieved national epic is the hero's self-consciousness of being a *civilisateur*. Brutus's reason for sailing into the uncharted ocean in search of a "new country" is "that he entertained no prospect of introducing pure manners in any part of the then known world; but that he might do it among a people uncorrupt in their manners, worthy to be made happy; and wanting only arts and laws to that purpose" (411). This aim prevails in the debate, and "that night, Hercules appears to him in a vision . . . encouraging him to persevere in the pursuit of the intended enterprise" (412). This endorsement by the great culture-bringer of classical myth is immediately confirmed by

> the supreme God in all his majesty, sitting on his throne in the highest heaven. The superintending angel of the Trojans empire (the *Regnum Priami vetus*) falls down before the throne, and confesses his justice in having overturned that kingdom . . . but adds, that after having chastised and humbled them, it would now be agreeable to his mercy and goodness, to raise up a new state from their ruins, and form a people who might serve him better. That, in Brutus, his Providence had a fit instrument for such a gracious design. (413)

God sends the angel off to assist Brutus in the "reduction" of Britain. Our hero, as pious as Aeneas, is constantly aware, as Aeneas never is, of the providential *telos* of the enterprise. His followers want to settle on the uninhabited Canary Islands: "What more, say they, can we wish for ourselves, than such a pleasing end of all our labours? In an inhabited country we must, perhaps, be forced to fight, and destroy the natives; here without encroaching upon others, without the guilt of a conquest, we may have a land that will supply us with all the necessaries of life."

This counsel is qualified as "laziness," and Brutus rejects it as "narrow and selfish . . . incompatible with his generous plan of extending benevolence, by instructing and polishing uncultivated minds. He despises the mean thought of providing for the happiness of themselves alone, and sets the great promises of heaven before them" (413–14). This Aeneas might as well be Jupiter himself.

According to this instrument of providence, polishing minds is more than worth a little guilt. If cultivation entails destruction, we are to bear this burden; we're stingy if we don't. (Only we *can* bear it, since it's not we who are destroyed.) The unrealized project thus outlines how the discourse developed by the natural lawyers works: by containment and subsumption, producing differences or objections to be erased by a higher, unifying principle: here generosity and benevolence. Brutus demonstrates this by allowing "the old men and the women, together with such as are timid and unfit for service, to enjoy their ease there, and erect a city" (414). He gives "his colony a form of pure worship, and a short and simple body of laws, orders them to chuse a government for themselves, and then sets sail" (415). Like Aeneas, Brutus is a born founder, and rehearses for the main event.

Before it can occur, though, there will be the usual vicissitudes. Brutus's departure from the Canaries will be delayed by "the passion of some friend, or the fondness of some female." He arrives at Lisbon, which offers the contrasting example of a false foundation, attributed to Ulysses. He built the city on "wicked principles of policy [i.e. calculated personal advantage] and superstition" and was "at length driven away by the discontented people he had enslaved" (415). Driven by storm to Norway, Brutus's band are attacked by the native barbarians, but obtain some captive Britons who will pilot the Trojans to their island. Throughout Brutus prays to and receives encouraging omens (like the aurora borealis) from the Supreme God. The guardian angel is also busy trying to provide favorable weather. Next, "Brutus touches at the Orcades, and a picture is given of the manners of the savages" (416). Here he must also contend with hurricanes and volcanoes, which are figures for "some of the Titans" said to be confined by Jupiter in a northern island (417). The angel sees Brutus through all this and "then directs him to seek the south-west parts of Great Britain, because the northern parts were infested by men not yet disposed to receive religion, arts and good government; the subduing and civilizing of whom was reserved by providence for a son, that should be born of him after his conquest of England (418)."

Finally Brutus arrives at Torbay, whose weather and inhabitants alike are suited to his aim: "The climate is . . . free from the effeminacy and softness of the southern climes, and the ferocity and savageness of the northern. The natural genius of the native being thus in the medium between these extremes, was well adapted to receive the improvements in virtue, he meditated to introduce(418)." Brutus gets along fine with the Druids, who tell him about some tyrannical giants from the north, "whom he undertakes to assist them in conquering." These villains live in "*dismal Anarchy* . . . eating their captives, and carrying away virgins; which affords room for a beautiful episode," in which Brutus will rescue one from "her brutal ravisher." The biographer observes that here the poet "proposed to moralize the old fables concerning . . . *Corinaeus, Gogmagog, &c*" (419). But the more serious obstacles to Brutus's civilizing mission arise from the priest-ridden and superstitious natives as well as from the fierce ambition of one of his own kinsmen, who enslaves them. Brutus, however, vows "not to conquer and destroy the natives of the new-discovered land, but to polish and refine them, by introducing true religion, void of superstition and all false notions of the Deity, which only leads to vice and misery, among people who are uncorrupted in their manners, and only want the introduction of useful arts, under the sanction of a good government, to establish and ensure their felicity" (420). The contemporary relevance of this foundation, were it not obvious, is underscored by the biographer: "Here the poet could have had a fine opportunity of exposing the inhuman conduct of the Europeans, with respect to the Indians" (420). Could have, indeed, but the discourse that makes the exposure does so only to erase it, or, as is the case with Pope's whole scenario, to oppose nasty foundations (superstition is the code for Catholicism) to nice ones (true religion is deistic Protestantism). In the latter, just as in the discourse of natural law, any inhumanity is excused by the pious humaneness of the motive: we just want to make the others happy. Brutus at any rate quells the rebellion of his fierce kinsman, who repents and is ashamed that he was "a victim to female blandishments." The foundation is achieved: "Brutus, in the end, succeeded in his enterprize against the giants, and enchantment vanished before him: having reduced the fortresses of superstition, anarchy and tyranny, the whole island submits to good government, and with this the poem was intended to close" (421).

And with this dangling participial phrase (having reduced, . . . the island submits), Ruffhead concludes his summary, identifying grammatically the conquered land with the conquering agent. What he accomplishes by grammar, the earlier versions of the legend performed by sexual metaphor. The land participates in its own reduction and submission, desiring it or stimulating the invaders' desire for it (Geoffrey), being grateful for rescue from incestuous rape (Spenser) or for proper impregnation (Munday). The feminized land always requires a firm hand, since females in general are always both a threat to the imperial enterprise (since Dido) and necessary to its continuance (the founder must breed). Pope's design also faithfully reproduces all the past and present frontiers on and for which the legend was created. Those in the new world are present by continual implication; those in the old reflect the contemporary prejudice that descends from the Roman occupation of the island. Beyond Hadrian's wall and the Welsh Marches (one of the areas held by Pope's giants is the isle of Mona, now Anglesey) are the savage Celts, and the farther north you go the worse they get. The inhabitants of the Scottish highlands must await the civilizing ministrations of the next generation of culture-bringers.

Brutus's complete awareness of himself in this role reduces all the complexities of the *Aeneid* to the blunt purposes of the discourse of colonial justification in its uniquely English form. For the vague "good government" that Brutus wishes to impart—defined only by its opposition to anarchy (republicanism), tyranny (monarchical privilege), and superstition (the Catholic Stuarts)—is that of the famous (and unwritten) English Constitution, interpreted by Tories as achieving the appropriate balance between royal authority and the legislative power of property owners, from the Magna Charta to the Glorious Revolution of 1688. This view of local political history is enshrined in Pope's planned epic, which is careful always to use the Latin form of Brut's name, there being no doubt about either where civilization comes from or where it now resides. Thus the plan retains in the character and policies of its hero a dimension of actual history, still appropriate to a national epic, which its legendary plot can no longer claim. Troynovant is never mentioned, for London is now Augusta (Rome), and this Brutus, dreaming of Hercules and talking with angels, has the piety of a well-bred Augustan Anglican.

"Augustan" was of course the age's description of itself, coined by many hopeful panegyrists at the accession of Charles II in 1660. The restoration of the monarchy was hailed (not by the likes of Milton) as the final resolution of the English Civil War, analogous to the victory of Octavian in the Roman one, which made him Augustus Caesar. The analogy intensified for the English the kind of identification with imperial Rome that characterized the historians who were at this time declaring the story of Trojan descent but a fable. As Augustus became famous for patronizing poets and rebuilding Rome—finding it brick and leaving it marble, as Dryden put it—so the same flowering of the arts, the same refinement of public taste, was now to be accomplished in London. The great fire of 1666 gave Christopher Wren the architectural opportunity he was quick to take advantage of; and his borrowing the dome of Peter to put on Paul made the appropriate Roman statement: though a monument to Renaissance papistry, its design was classical. (The same statement would be made less than two centuries later by the capitol dome in Washington—its connotation of reverence transferred from a church to the legislature of a republic.) Other architects followed Wren, to provide the domestic accommodation for an ever-expanding merchant class. Commercial prosperity was visible in the streets of London, in its walls and towers, in ways that proclaimed it the heir to Roman civilization.

Although land revenues were down, trade was unstoppable, and registered its greatest increases in commodities from the colonies. For example, in 1663 England imported 7,400 tons of sugar, in 1720, 32,600 (Sheridan 1974: 22). Formerly a luxury item, sugar was now a staple product that went increasingly into cups (from China) of tea and coffee, which were still luxuries, but were already creating new social habits and institutions, among them the coffee houses where Dryden, Addison, and Pope ruled on the literary disputes of the age. Of the new colonies established in the western hemisphere during the seventeenth century, 60 percent belonged to England, and they furnished commodities in such abundance that England also acquired a vastly profitable trade in reexporting them (Wallerstein 1980: 102). The most remunerative of these colonies were the sugar islands of the Caribbean. Growing and processing sugar cane was done exclusively by slave labor (something approaching slave labor is still required to harvest it today: see Wilkinson 1989). The Atlantic slave trade reached its peak between 1760 and 1780. By 1650, 10,000 slaves were being shipped annually from West Africa; by 1713, 40,000; during its peak years over 60,000; the annual average did not fall below the 1713 level until 1840 (Rawley 1981: 17–18). Forty-three percent of all these slaves went to the Caribbean. During the eighteenth century Great Britain (no longer England after the Act of Union with Scotland in 1707) shipped about one-third of them, making it the world leader in the slave trade, on which profits were normal for the investments of the day, around 8 percent (Rawley 1981: 264–65). Sugar of course did more than sweeten Pope's coffee; it was reduced to molasses and distilled into rum. And these products provided the revenue that bought the firearms and trinkets that purchased the slaves who manufactured the sugar: this is the famous triangular trade linking Africa, the east coast of the Americas, and Europe, of which Great Britain enjoyed its lion's share.

The happiest forecasts of commodity production in the pages of Hakluyt had become realities—but not without energetic competition. England acquired most of her sugar islands by military actions against France, Spain, and Holland, with one or another of which she was sporadically at war (as they were with each other), from the Armada of 1588 to the Treaty of Paris (by which Britain expelled her last rival, France, from both India and North America) in 1763. Two fairly continuous periods of war ushered in the neoclassical century: the War of the Grand Alliance, known in North America as King William's War, 1689–97; and the War of the Spanish Succession, the North American phase of which was called Queen Anne's War, 1701–14. All these wars were vitally concerned with colonial possessions and trading rights, in addition to their titular issues of intra-European dynastic politics. The last two in particular were waged on land and sea in both hemispheres, encompassing actions from the Danube to Gibraltar, and from Florida to the St. Lawrence. Britain's part in the War of the Spanish Succession was ended by the Treaty of Utrecht in 1713. The nominal issue of this war was the inheritance of the Spanish crown by a Bourbon, an intolerable prospect given the already overweening ambitions of the Sun King. On land in Europe, the war was distinguished by the generalship of Marlborough, to whom his grateful nation presented a palace of classical design named after his greatest victory, Blenheim. But as strategically conducted on all its fronts by both France and Britain, the war was "an attempt to destroy each other's trade networks, especially by privateering" (Wallerstein 1980: 188). As such, it took its place in the "round of almost unending wars" between the two great rivals after 1689 "over the issues of land, allies, and markets in Europe and over supplies" of commodities—from slaves and sugar to spices, cotton, furs, and naval stores—in the rest of the colonialized world: the Americas, West Africa, India (246).

Pope never wrote the founding legend of Brutus, but he did write *Windsor-Forest*, a poem that incorporates the categories, images, and meanings of the legend into a national myth composed to celebrate the Peace of Utrecht in 1713. This separate peace had been largely negotiated (rather to the dismay of Britain's allies) by Pope's friend Bolingbroke. By its terms, Britain received from France and Spain the Hudson Bay territory, Acadia, Newfoundland, St. Kitts, Gibraltar, Minorca, and the sole right to the slave trade with Spanish America. All the dimensions of the global reach Britain is acquiring are figured in the poem, which presents itself as

a history and description of the royal park. It also presents itself as a complete Virgilian anthology, containing echoes and adaptations both verbal and thematic from
the *Eclogues*, the *Georgics*, and the *Aeneid*. Though often classed with other neoclassical topographical poems as "neo-georgic," *Windsor-Forest* is a good deal more ambitious than they, and suggests that its twenty-five-year-old author is moving at
one fell swoop from the *Pastorals* he published four years before right on through
the georgic and well into the epic. The ambition is further signaled by careful allusions to the great national precursors, Spenser and Milton. Never again, indeed,
would the moment be so propitious for realizing the Virgilian career as a member
of the imperial inner circle, singing the praises of its gracious and grateful sovereign. For Queen Anne, the last Protestant Stuart, dies in 1714, and the succession
passes, by prearrangement, to the German Hanovers, who speak no English, read
no poetry, and install the Whigs for the rest of Pope's life (he died in 1744) and
beyond.

The bitterness and satire that will mark his later career are, however, far away
from the triumphal moment of 1713. The poem begins with an epigraph from
Virgil's sixth *Eclogue*, "non iniussa cano . . ." (I sing not uncommanded), addressed
to its dedicatee, George Granville, Lord Lansdowne (a minor Tory politician and
man of letters). Its opening lines invoke the muses, as usual, but in terms that transform this literary cliché into the functional equivalent of colonial invasion:

> Thy Forests, *Windsor!* and thy green Retreats,
> At once the Monarch's and the Muse's Seats,
> Invite my Lays. Be present, Sylvan Maids!
> Unlock your Springs, and open all your Shades.
> *Granville* commands: Your Aid O Muses bring!
> What Muse for *Granville* can refuse to sing?
>
> (ll. 1–6)

The (virgin) land, feminized as nymphs of wood and water (dryads and naiads),
will "open" and "unlock" itself at the command of male authority. The literal sexuality of the transaction, submerged by centuries of imitating its gestures, emerges
anew in the choice of verbs and in the context of the legend of Brut, where she,
the land, is always the willing partner of her commander. Pope will develop this
theme, by inverting it, in a later section of the poem. He will also develop the (ideally) indissoluble association of monarchs and muses, giving about equal later space
to a catalog, first, of the poets who wrote in or of Windsor, and second, of the
kings who were born or buried in it. The association is of course what this poet
aspires to, announced here as a topic and enacted here by the language that imper-
iously commands those maids.

Only of course this would be too crude; it's not he who commands, but Granville. ("Who would refuse songs to Gallus?" is the Virgilian model: *Eclogues* 10.3).
The poet's own position is announced next, as a wish, enclosed with supreme tact
in a conditional clause, to be (thought) the equal of Milton:

> The Groves of *Eden*, vanish'd now so long,
> Live in Description, and look green in Song:
> *These*, were my Breast inspir'd with equal Flame,
> Like them in Beauty, should be like in Fame.
>
> (7–10)

The conditional can be read most modestly as an optative (oh, if only I were . . .) with the outcome foreclosed (they should be—but they won't). As a straightforward conditional inference it's a good deal less modest, challenging (the reader to make) the comparison and leaving the outcome open: if (you think) I am as good as Milton, then my groves will be as famous as his. Reading the inference in reverse makes the least modest claim of all: if I get famous, then I am as good as Milton. However we read the personal claim, the lines also have two other functions: to associate Windsor with all the resonance, epic as well as pastoral and religious, of Eden; and to assert the power of writing to confer immortality, to keep alive what has perished. The poem, paradoxically, will exert its own power most strikingly in order to dramatize various fauna in the very act of perishing.

Pope, having thus adroitly hinted his epic claim, plunges directly into a generalized description of the present landscape of Windsor. It is not in any sense a portrait of the actual place, but rather a statement of the principle that governs the discourse and an identification of its subject—what the place symbolizes.

> Here Hills and Vales, the Woodland and the Plain,
> Here Earth and Water seem to strive again,
> Not *Chaos*-like together crush'd and bruis'd,
> But as the World, harmoniously confus'd:
> Where Order in Variety we see,
> And where, tho' all things differ, all agree.
>
> (11–16)

The microcosm of Windsor exemplifies the world, according to the vaguely Epicurean notion of elements in strife; but the strife produces not chaos, but harmony, according to the standard neoclassical principle of *concordia discors*. The principle is at once theological, ethical, and aesthetic; its exposition is the object of Pope's later *Essay on Man*, where he derives from it this famous conclusion:

> All Nature is but Art, unknown to thee;
> All Chance, Direction which thou canst not see;
> All Discord, Harmony not understood;
> All partial Evil, universal Good:
> And spight of Pride, in erring Reason's spight,
> One truth is clear; "Whatever Is, is RIGHT."
>
> (1.289–94)

In the history of thought, this idea is the ancient Christian argument from design (the purposes and hierarchies God imposed on the world, only partially perceivable by us) given new life for the eighteenth century by the mathematics of Isaac Newton (in which apparent irregularities, like planetary orbits, are shown to be regular). And in the history of our domination of the planet, this idea generates the discourse of containment and subsumption. There can be no clearer declaration than Pope's that its purpose is to justify everything, and that there is no possible appeal from its verdicts. Nature, Chance, Discord, and Evil are in fact (that is, in the mind of the Newtonian God, which is not available to us) their opposites. Ideas are as they are used, and the use of this one is to make a metaphysics of an excuse. Pope makes the turgid procedures of the natural lawyers transparent. The grand tautologies of the (so-called) Age of Reason subsume all phenomena under a covering law, by which all difference becomes agreement, all heterogeneity identity. All this, all that, all whatever (as Pope's rhetoric insists)—each and every all may (indeed must) be recorded, subsumed, and subordinated (as in Pope's grammar) to a single universal: "tho' all things differ, all agree."

As announced in *Windsor-Forest*, the principle is aesthetic, and is illustrated by the varied visual aspects of the landscape. The very first illustration includes a simile not very obviously related to the phenomenon described:

> Here waving Groves a checquer'd Scene display,
> And part admit and part exclude the Day;
> As some coy Nymph her Lover's warm Address
> Nor quite indulges, nor can quite repress.
>
> (17–20)

As with the introductory nymphs, bidden to "open" and "unlock," the verbs here provide the metaphorical connection between the light and the lover, who are both admitted and excluded. To see the play of light in a wood as a sexual seduction is a bit odd in its precision, though the general association may be licensed by the standard lovemaking in idealized pastoral. But again, the feminization of the land itself suggests its role in the founding legend, which is amply confirmed in the rest of the description. Windsor is not only the microcosm of the world and the symbolic center of British imperial power; it is also an emblem of civilization as the legend has taught us to recognize it. After a catalogue of the variegations in the landscape (lawns and glades, plains and hills), the initial description concludes with a full revelation of its meaning, colonial and classical:

> Ev'n the wild Heath displays her Purple Dies,
> And 'midst the Desert fruitful Fields arise,
> That crown'd with tufted Trees and springing Corn,
> Like verdant Isles the sable Waste adorn.
> Let *India* boast her Plants, nor envy we

The weeping Amber or the balmy Tree,
While by our Oaks the precious Loads are born,
And realms commanded which those Trees adorn.
Not proud *Olympus* yields a nobler Sight,
Tho' Gods assembled grace his tow'ring Height,
Than what more humble Mountains offer here,
Where, in their Blessings, all those Gods appear.
See *Pan* with Flocks, with Fruits *Pomona* crown'd,
Here blushing *Flora* paints th' enamel'd Ground,
Here *Ceres*' Gifts in waving Prospect stand,
And nodding tempt the joyful Reaper's Hand,
Rich Industry sits smiling on the Plains,
And Peace and Plenty tell, a STUART reigns.

(25–42)

There is even more variety in this landscape than can possibly meet the eye, for what it doesn't have (the spices and gums of the orient) it can command. Its power is Olympian, borne by its oaken ships but based on (in the passage begun and ended by) the fruitful fields of corn, the seductively waving grain. The "industry" here celebrated is not that of manufacture, but the labor that tills the soil, making agriculture out of waste (forest) and desert (heath). Granville commands the muse; Britain commands the commodities of India; the discourse commands everything, making it agree, as Pope's description moves smoothly from beauty through sexuality to power. They're all united in the civilization that belongs to Ceres.

This civilization, however, is but the present condition of Windsor, which is immediately contrasted to its past in the next section of the poem. The terms of the contrast are predictable:

Not thus the Land appear'd in Ages past,
A dreary Desart and a gloomy Waste,
To Savage Beasts and Savage Laws a Prey,
And Kings more furious and severe than they:
Who claim'd the Skies, dispeopled Air and Floods,
The lonely Lords of empty Wilds and Woods.

(43–48)

These lords were the first two generations of Norman conquerors, who decreed the forest a royal hunting park and whose "savage laws" prescribed dismemberment and death for anyone else taking game in it. Hunting is the definition, as usual, of their savagery, and is made worse by replacing the agriculture that had been there before. The "prey" is at once the land, the game (beasts, birds, and fish), and the former farmers. (The identification of animals with humans, here as creatures of which the land is "dispeopled," will receive crucial development later.) In these bad old days,

> In vain kind Seasons swell'd the teeming Grain,
> Soft Show'rs distill'd, and Suns grew warm in vain;
> The Swain with Tears his frustrate Labour yields,
> And famish'd dies amidst his ripen'd Fields.
>
> (53–56)[1]

In this despotism, subjects are starved and enslaved to feed beasts "for sportive Tyrants" (59).

> The Fields are ravish'd from th' industrious Swains,
> From Men their Cities, and from Gods their Fanes:
> The levell'd Towns with Weeds lie cover'd o'er,
> The hollow Winds thro' naked Temples roar.
>
> (65–68)

Everything that counts as civilization for us lies in ruins: Bad laws have destroyed agriculture, cities, and religion. The "obscene" fox howls in opened graves (71–72). But only temporarily: poetic justice serves both William and William Rufus with ignominious ends (the latter from a hunting accident in this very place), and

> Succeeding Monarchs heard the Subjects Cries,
> Nor saw displeas'd the peaceful Cottage rise. . . .
> The Forests wonder'd at th' unusual Grain,
> And secret Transport touch'd the conscious Swain.
> Fair *Liberty, Britannia's* Goddess, rears
> Her chearful Head, and leads the golden Years.
>
> (85–92)

So concludes the contrastive history, in which savage hunting is yet again replaced by civilized agriculture—both here made dependent on the policies of monarchs.

Not really replaced, as it turns out, but only transformed. For Pope devotes the next five sections of the poem (93–164), remarkably, to a detailed description of the hunts appropriate to all four seasons that still take place here. Hunting is now acceptable, apparently, because it no longer destroys agriculture by setting apart the land for the exclusive use of royalty. Anyone can hunt; it has become, in a civilized landscape, a sport. The poem leaps back into the present with an apostrophe:

> Ye vig'rous Swains! . . .
> Now range the Hills, the gameful Woods beset,
> Wind the shrill Horn, or spread the waving Net.
>
> (93–96)

---

1. "Swain" was a Middle-English term, derived from Old Norse, for a young herdsman, and acquired its subsidiary meaning of young lover from its use in the neoclassical pastoral, which strove to recreate the highly stylized diction of Virgil. Pope would never write of "lads" or "lasses," but rather, in his *Pastorals*: "Blest swains, whose nymphs in every grace excel; / Blest nymphs, whose swains those graces sing so well." The swain here, of course, in the georgic mode, is a worker.

And as they thus obey the command of the poet, the sport becomes an explicit figure for something much grander. The spaniel stalks a covey of partridges:

> Secure they trust th' unfaithful Field, beset,
> Till hov'ring o'er them sweeps the swelling Net.
> Thus (if small Things we may with great compare)
> When *Albion* sends her eager Sons to War,
> Some thoughtless Town, with Ease and Plenty blest,
> Near, and more near, the closing Lines invest;
> Sudden they seize th' amaz'd, defenceless Prize
> And high in Air *Britannia's* Standard flies.
>
> (103–10)

The parenthetical announcement of the figure is a direct translation from the fourth *Georgic* (l. 176), the only one to contain a long interpolated narrative (the story of Orpheus and Eurydice). And Pope will follow the hunting episodes with the longest single section of the poem, an invented myth modeled on the Apollo/Daphne story. But the hunting in the (Norman) past that was the standard practice of savagery is now in the civilized present an actual sport and a figure for war; the craft and energy of both are admired. Most vividly described, however, are the deaths of the avian victims. First, in order of aesthetic hierarchy, the pheasant:

> Short is his Joy! he feels the fiery Wound,
> Flutters in Blood, and panting beats the Ground.
> Ah! what avail his glossie, varying Dyes,
> His Purple Crest, and Scarlet-circled Eyes,
> The vivid Green his shining Plumes unfold;
> His painted Wings, and Breast that flames with Gold?
>
> (113–18)

Then the lesser birds:

> Oft, as in Airy Rings they skim the Heath,
> The clam'rous Lapwings feel the Leaden Death:
> Oft as the mounting Larks their Notes prepare,
> They fall, and leave their little Lives in Air.
>
> (131–34)

The pheasant receives a mini-heroic and heraldic elegy befitting a "prize," or noble adversary. The smaller deaths are dramatized with compassion and a haunting exactitude, as these circling and rising chatterers and singers sink into silence, their lives suddenly as empty as the medium of their motion and speech. Such precisely evocative compassion is characteristic of Virgil's *Georgics*.

Pope expresses it here only on behalf of the birds—we must await an image
from the end of the poem to identify who they are in the metaphor of war. The
latter continues simply with a catalogue of fish, also in quasi-heraldic colors: the
"Perch with Fins of *Tyrian* Dye," the silver eel, golden-scaled carp, and crimson-
tinged trout (142–45). The stag hunt comes next and last; this prey is never reached,
the description focusing exclusively on the exciting speed of the chase, as "The
Youth rush eager to the Sylvan War" (148). Their horses pant and gallop for some
time, until the poet swiftly closes these hunting scenes with a mythological comparison that introduces a deft compliment and another form of hunting.

> Let old *Arcadia* boast her ample plain,
> Th' Immortal Huntress, and her Virgin Train;
> Nor envy *Windsor!* since thy Shades have seen
> As bright a Goddess, and as chast a Queen;
> Whose Care, like hers, protects the Sylvan Reign,
> The Earth's fair Light, and Empress of the Main.
>
> (159–64)

Anne enjoyed riding to hounds at Windsor; she rules the waves as Diana, goddess
of the moon, governs the tides.

Pope now makes up an extended little etiological myth, in the manner of
Spenser, to explain the name of a stream, the Loddon, that flows through Windsor Forest into the Thames. Lodona was one of Diana's nymphs, as beautiful as she,
and was here pursued by Pan, who, "burning with Desire / Pursu'd her Flight; her
Flight increas'd his Fire" (183–84). The chase is the focus of interest; its impending climax is dramatized by shifts into the present tense:

> Not half so swift the trembling Doves can fly,
> When the fierce Eagle cleaves the liquid Sky;
> Not half so swiftly the fierce Eagle moves,
> When thro' the Cloud he drives the trembling Doves;
> As from the God she flew with furious Pace,
> Or as the God more furious urg'd the Chace.
> Now fainting, sinking, pale, the Nymph appears;
> Now close behind his sounding Steps she hears;
> And now his Shadow reach'd her as she run,
> (His Shadow lengthen'd by the setting Sun)
> And now his shorter Breath with sultry Air
> Pants on her Neck, and fans her parting Hair.
>
> (185–96)

The first sentence orchestrates a pair of negative similes, one for each contestant.
The (extended) negative simile beginning with "not" is a trademark of Milton;
Pope doubles it with an archly balanced, perfectly symmetrical syntax that is his

own trademark. But the terms of the comparison belie the syntax: the contest is asymmetrical, the power preponderant on the male side, the outcome inevitable. As the god breathes down her neck, she prays to Cynthia to save her,

> and melting as in Tears she lay,
> In a soft, silver Stream dissolv'd away.
> The silver Stream her Virgin Coldness keeps,
> For ever murmurs, and for ever weeps;
> Still bears the Name the hapless Virgin bore,
> And bathes the Forest where she rang'd before.
>
> (203–208)

Diana pays the nymph the homage of bathing in her stream, and the little tale of Ovidian metamorphosis is over, having been used, as Spenser often uses it, to name a natural object.

Though the story is told, it is not quite concluded: Pope adds a final, striking image, borrowed and elaborated from one in the *Aeneid* (8.95–96) that describes the rowers cleaving the green woods reflected in the water on their way to the site of Rome.

> Oft in her Glass the musing Shepherd spies
> The headlong Mountains and the downward Skies,
> The watry Landskip of the pendant Woods,
> And absent Trees that tremble in the Floods;
> In the clear azure Gleam the Flocks are seen,
> And floating Forests paint the Waves with Green.
>
> (211–16)

The appropriateness of this adaptation is not merely literary—an expression of ambition, the homage of showing off—nor merely structural—a hint of the direction of the poem: as Aeneas went up the Tiber to Rome, so Pope will shortly go down the Thames to London. The image gives a finely concise picture of the discourse that identifies opposites, here by inversion: the mountains, skies, and woods dangle upside down in the water; what is absent is present; what was colorless (the "silver" stream) is now painted. Above all, the image suggests the fate of the female who loses the erotic race but frustrates its purpose. Unpossessed, she yet remains the eternal mirror into which the male gazes. The image is a male perception: what, musing, the shepherd-poet spies. Courting the muse, commanding (or failing to command) the nymph, he sees in her glass the operation of his own language. Centuries of western love poetry, the endless exploitation of erotic/linguistic play on the chases of "venery," are packed into this Virgilian image of the inverted landscape. The woman becomes part of the landscape— Daphne a laurel, Syrinx a reed—sacred or useful to the god who pursued her. In Pope, she contains the whole landscape, becomes the totality of what the male desires and can in perception possess, can in words do with what he, musing, likes:

turn it all upside down. The end of the sporting hunt is the possession of a dead animal. The end of the erotic one is the nonpossession of a dead woman, who, transformed into nature, can now be possessed. Pope's image vastly extends the possession, and as the culmination of a hunt, makes it, too, a form of death.

Lodona flows into the Thames, whom Pope now addresses as "great Father of the *British* Floods!" (219). She who, as woman, escaped possession by a lover, is now, as stream, perpetually giving herself to (dissolving her identity in) a father. The apostrophe to the latter continues in a way that makes his possessions ever more extensive:

> Where tow'ring Oaks their growing Honours rear,
> And future Navies on thy Shores appear.
> Not *Neptune's* self from all his Streams receives
> A wealthier Tribute, than to thine he gives.
>
> (221–24)

The tribute given to the Thames exceeds that of any sea or lake or even the river Po, which "swells the fabling Poet's Lays" (227: Virgil both wrote of it and was born near it). Once again, "*Windsor's* fam'd Abodes" are nobler and more radiant than Olympus (229–34). The hyperbole stresses what is obvious anyway, that routine forms of accurate detail are of no concern here, that the place is first and foremost a synecdoche for our imperial civilization. Pope knows that stories can be true even when inaccurate. He doesn't care that it was really New Forest, not Windsor, that the first Normans made their hunting preserve. Nor does he care (if he ever knew) that no navies had grown on the banks of the Thames for some time (Britain's large timber was coming from North America; in the previous century it had come from Scandinavia): it's a neat figure for British power radiating out from this center; he's used it before and will again. The vessels go forth to plant the Union Jack, capture prizes, and return laden with profits: that's accurate enough.

One begins to realize that the poem is about possession and the violence that achieves it; that possession in various forms is what links the sections as they casually ramble through history, landscape, and myth; that the place itself is both an object of possession (whose form was savage before and is now civilized) and a symbolic possessor; that the pursuit and acquisition of possessions is both what happens in the poem and what its language performs. Having realized this, one finds in the next section, which is an apparent digression in praise of the retired life of the studious eighteenth-century virtuoso, yet another series of acquisitions, this time of knowledge.

From empire to learning—no digression at all in the logic of our civilization; they always go together. But Pope moves from Jove to the retired scholar by way of an intermediate figure who alters the meaning of this fullest Virgilian set piece in the poem. Windsor, the preceding section concludes, is more brilliant than Olympus; therefore, this one begins:

> Happy the Man whom this bright Court approves,
> His Sov'reign favours, and his Country loves;
> Happy next him who to these Shades retires,
> Whom Nature charms, and whom the Muse inspires,
> Whom humbler Joys of home-felt Quiet please,
> Successive Study, Exercise and Ease.
>
> (235–40)

Virgil's passage, which inspired a whole subgenre of neoclassical verse, praises two distinct kinds of life (each of which the poet may share) by opposing both to a third. Farmers are happy with hard work and the natural riches of agriculture; also happy are those who study to know the causes of things. Both ways of life are opposed to the rat races of soldiers and politicians, urban achievers of power and money (*Georgics* 2.458–512). The genre this passage spawned renounced ambition and acquisitiveness in any form: far from the madding crowd, back to nature, reading good books, a moderate diet, freeing the mind to philosophize—all that sort of thing. The genre had been rather popular for a century, and would continue to be so until the Romantic poets, by acting it out, radically changed the nature of the game. The Renaissance and later poets who made it famous most certainly didn't act it out; for them it was a moralistic fantasy vacation from their real lives, spent scrambling for place, preferment, patrons, and the pleasures of the wicked court or city. Pope's condensed version of it here has the honest lucidity of his whole subject: the happiest man is he who serves this government and is rewarded for it (Marlborough, for example; some commentators think Lansdowne is meant, but he hardly qualified for much display of favor or love). Failing this, the next happiest is the intellectual living in retirement, and not because he's renounced anything, but because of what he gets and does. (The pleasures Virgil attributes to the farmer's labor find no mention.) He begins by gathering "Health from Herbs," and proceeds from the practice of medicine to those of chemistry, astronomy, philology, history, morality, and religion (241–56). It may be a second-best career; but those sciences are no small acquisitions. If you can't be part of the real power, you may as well acquire some other kind.

The poet now enters the landscape for the first time in his own person, addressing the muses: "Ye sacred Nine! that all my Soul possess, / Whose Raptures fire me, and whose Visions bless" (259–60). Yet another form of possession, this, which paradoxically bestows power not on the possessor but on the possessed. Pope thus begins his enumeration of the poets who have already written about Windsor, including a flattering request to Granville that he do so too. The power of the poet is to make his subject eternally reverenced. The place is numinous because possessed in song (of which the best known is Denham's "Cooper's Hill"):

> (On *Cooper's* Hill eternal Wreaths shall grow,
> While lasts the mountain, or while *Thames* shall flow)
> I seem thro' consecrated Walks to rove,

> And hear soft Musick dye along the Grove;
> Led by the Sound I rove from Shade to Shade,
> By God-like Poets Venerable made.

> (265–70)

The subject may be immortal; but the singers too must die, for their power does not extend to themselves. The music becomes a dirge as Pope evokes the funeral procession down the river of the poet Cowley:

> O early lost! what Tears the River shed
> When the sad Pomp along his Banks was led?
> His drooping Swans on ev'ry Note expire,
> And on his Willows hung each Muse's Lyre.

> (273–76)

The flattery of Granville continues with further requests that he sing the military exploits of the kings born or buried at Windsor, especially Edward III. His famous victory over the French at Crécy in the fourteenth century is evoked in language that recalls Spenser's description of the sons of Brute opening the "bowels" of France with "victour sword": "Still in thy Song should vanquish'd *France* appear, / And bleed for ever under *Britain's* Spear" (309–10). In fiction or in fact (past and present) the enemy nation, unlike the colonial territory that cooperates by timely compliance, is always to be raped. Pope then requests "softer Strains" (311) to commemorate two rivals in the Wars of the Roses, the ineffectual Henry VI and the potent Edward IV, whom, in adjacent tombs, "The Grave unites; where ev'n the Great find Rest, / And blended lie th' Oppressor and th' Opprest!" (317–18). The cliché of death as leveler takes on considerable new resonance in the context of the other deaths in the poem and the discourse that dramatizes them. For death is the universal par excellence, the covering law that does cover all, the final obliterator of difference, indeed, where all opposites dissolve into identity. Death is (in a functional sense) the goal of this discourse. It is the ultimate figure of the condition that the discourse aims to achieve.

The last king mentioned is Charles I, executed by the Parliamentary forces in 1649, which brings up England's most recent history of civil wars. Pope glances over all these as swiftly as he can, conflates them with the plague and the great fire of London, and uses them to put the queen in the quite anachronistic but nicely "Augustan" position of ending them. The poet laments the tears of Albion:

> She saw her Sons with purple Deaths expire,
> Her sacred Domes involv'd in rolling Fire,
> A dreadful series of Intestine Wars,
> Inglorious Triumphs, and dishonest Scars.
> At length great ANNA said—Let Discord cease!
> She said, the World obey'd, and all was *Peace!*

> (323–28)

The peace here invoked is domestic. A national myth summons national unity to undergo worthier scars in the acquisition of triumphs over other nations. Only with peace at home can we wage war abroad. The poem, however, goes on to a final celebration of the larger peace that was its occasion, along with an enumeration of the global benefits that will everywhere accrue. The rhetoric of this peroration centers on the figure of "Father *Thames*" (330), who arises from the river in response to the queen's word in order to be iconographically described and then to make a speech.

Engraved on the urn that depicts him is the moon (Diana/Anna) that controls his tides and the following picture:

> The figur'd Streams in Waves of Silver roll'd,
> And on their Banks *Augusta* rose in Gold.
> Around his Throne the Sea-born Brothers stood,
> Who swell with Tributary Urns his Flood.
>
> (335–38)

Ten rivers tributary to the Thames are named and described. Father Thames then turns toward the "pompous Turrets" (352) of Windsor and speaks:

> Hail Sacred *Peace!* hail long-expected Days,
> That *Thames's* Glory to the Stars shall raise!
> Tho' *Tyber's* Streams immortal *Rome* behold,
> Tho' foaming *Hermus* swells with Tydes of Gold,
> From Heav'n itself tho' sev'nfold *Nilus* flows,
> And Harvests on a hundred Realms bestows;
> These now no more shall be the Muse's Themes,
> Lost in my Fame, as in the Sea their Streams.
>
> (355–62)

The voice of modernity is harnessed to nationalism—first, in terms of writing. Henceforth, Britain will supplant the ancient empires of Egypt and Rome (Hermus was an Italian river hymned by Virgil) as a subject of discourse. And the subject will be peace, as opposed to the wars on other contemporary rivers:

> Let *Volga's* Banks with Iron Squadrons shine,
> And Groves of Lances glitter on the *Rhine*,
> Let barb'rous *Ganges* arm a servile Train;
> Be mine the Blessings of a peaceful Reign.
> No more my Sons shall dye with *British* Blood
> Red *Iber's* Sands, or *Ister's* foaming Flood;
> Safe on my Shore each unmolested Swain
> Shall tend the Flocks, or reap the bearded Grain;

> The shady Empire shall retain no Trace
> Of War or Blood, but in the Sylvan Chace,
> The Trumpets sleep, while chearful Horns are blown,
> And Arms employ'd on Birds and Beasts alone.
>
> (363–74)

Russia lately defeated Sweden; continental European powers continue there to fight; Moghuls and Hindus battle each other in their despotically barbarian manner; but the Peace of Utrecht has removed the British soldier from Spain (the Ebro) and the Ister (the Roman name for the Danube, where Blenheim was fought). He can return to civilized agriculture in this "shady Empire," where the only war is waged on game. Thus Pope announces the design of his earlier metaphor and the conscious point of all the hunting: it is a sublimation of war, whose victims are only animals. What is savage as a way of life is admirable as a pastime, a sporting recreation when the harvest is in. (Carried away by father Thames, let us forget, temporarily, that the animals are personified, and that there is another kind of "sylvan chase.")

With agriculture back in place in the shady empire of Windsor, the river god moves directly to the city and the larger empire that inexorably follow:

> Behold! th'ascending *Villa's* on my Side
> Project long Shadows o'er the Chrystal Tyde.
> Behold! *Augusta's* glitt'ring Spires increase,
> And Temples rise; the beauteous Works of Peace.
> I see, I see where two fair Cities bend
> Their ample Bow, a new *White-Hall* ascend!
> There mighty Nations shall inquire their Doom,
> The World's great Oracle in Times to come;
> There Kings shall sue, and suppliant States be seen
> Once more to bend before a *British* QUEEN.
>
> (375–84)

At the curve in the river where Westminster meets London, the new palace is where the destiny of the world's nations will be decided and delivered. Mere hyperbole in 1713, this prophecy will come true over a century later—and under another queen. This fable will be fact. Pope was no accidental prophet, for he understood the commercial motives and military means by which the British would acquire unprecedented imperial domination of the globe. These are next evoked by father Thames:

> Thy Trees, fair *Windsor!* now shall leave their Woods,
> And half thy Forests rush into my Floods,
> Bear *Britain's* Thunder, and her Cross display,
> To the bright Regions of the rising Day.
>
> (385–88)

These ships (of that no longer extant Windsor oak) bear arms and colors to the east, north, and south, and return with wealth:

> For me the Balm shall bleed, and Amber flow,
> The Coral redden, and the Ruby glow,
> The Pearly Shell its lucid Globe infold,
> And *Phoebus* warm the ripening Ore to Gold.
> The Time shall come, when free as Seas or Wind
> Unbounded *Thames* shall flow for all Mankind,
> Whole Nations enter with each swelling Tyde,
> And Seas but join the Regions they divide.
>
> (393–400)

The fabulous riches come home to the power center. But then another kind of traffic is imagined, some freer form of exchange, in which the river flows for everyone, not just for itself. Pope explains in a note that this is a wish to make London a free port, that is, to allow the ships of all nations to carry there various goods now restricted to British ships alone. A utopian wish indeed, in a mercantile protectionist economy—but a logical wish, even a predictable one, in this discourse of universalism. It is encapsulated, again, in the language, the balanced figure of the oceans joining what they divide: opposite conditions in a simultaneous identity.

The nations thus envisioned entering are not, however, identical to us:

> Earth's distant Ends our Glory shall behold,
> And the new World launch forth to seek the Old.
> Then Ships of uncouth Form shall stem the Tyde,
> And Feather'd People crowd my wealthy Side,
> And naked Youths and painted Chiefs admire,
> Our Speech, our Colour, and our strange Attire!
> Oh stretch thy Reign, fair *Peace!* from Shore to Shore,
> Till Conquest cease, and Slav'ry be no more:
> Till the freed *Indians* in their native Groves
> Reap their own Fruits, and woo their Sable Loves,
> *Peru* once more a Race of Kings behold,
> And other *Mexico's* be roofed with Gold.
>
> (401–12)

This ecumenical vision and prayer for universal peace echoes the humane sentiments of liberal opinion in the Enlightenment. It also preserves difference, but in the only form that universalistic discourse can tolerate: as comedy. The comedy is of course but the inversion of the spectacle of savage others that Londoners had enjoyed from time to time over the past century. They marveled at them, made engravings of them, as bizarre freaks. When Trinculo, in *The Tempest*, stumbles over

Caliban, who looks to him like a fish, his first thought is: "Were I in England now . . . and had but this fish painted, not a holiday fool there but would give a piece of silver. . . . When they will not give a doit to relieve a lame beggar, they will lay out ten to see a dead Indian" (2.2.30). Four Iroquois chiefs had lately been received at Queen Anne's court, where the marveling was doubtless more polite. Pope just reverses the spectacle, having them marvel at us: our odd language, color, and dress. (It seems reasonable to say that Pope does this, since the river god, who is still speaking, has lapsed into "our." If we take that possessive to denote the appearance of water gods in general, with their seaweed tresses and "shining horns" [332], then the marveling of the Indians is no joke, and the passage, though funnier, makes less sense.) The reversal is a keen touch, but it does not join what remains divided: that they should find us odd is comic only because our superiority is assumed. Their ships are uncouth; they wear nothing, or feathers, or paint.

The universalistic discourse reaches another limit to its own inclusiveness in its specification of the conquests and slavery that it wishes to abolish—of the Indians in Peru and Mexico. As in the unwritten epic there were nasty foundations and nice ones, so here there is nasty colonial exploitation—Spanish Catholic—with the nicer form only implied. Britain has no Indian slaves (just blacks) and has never (yet) conquered such organized empires as the Aztecs' and the Incas' (just bands of roving savages). The specification means that neither "all" conquest nor "all" slavery need fall under the ban. The terms of the peace being celebrated had made Britain the sole purveyor of slaves to the Spanish dominions; Pope doesn't mention the fact, but his discourse allows for it—as well it might, since Pope himself was a stockholder in the British South Sea Company, which held this privilege (Pope 1961: 192). The notoriety and pathos of the Spanish example was the extreme case that other powers could always use to defend their own colonial practices; the distinction between Spain and Britain in this respect will soon be written into international law.

Father Thames thunders to a close with a series of personified abstractions (discord, pride, ambition, etc.) thrust by peace from earth to imprisonment in hell. "There," he concludes, "*Faction* roar, *Rebellion* bite her Chain, / And gaping Furies thirst for Blood in vain" (421–22). The image recalls Virgil's *furor*, let out by Juno but shut up by Augustus in the temple of Janus—where he still roars. The poem ends in quite a different tone, a brief and quiet coda from the author himself, gracefully bequeathing the great subject of "*Albion's* Golden Days" (424) to the verse of Granville. "My humble Muse," he protests, "in unambitious Strains, / Paints the green Forests and the flow'ry Plains" (427–28). The modesty protested is false, charming, and explicitly Virgilian. Thanks to the peace, he avers,

> Ev'n I more sweetly pass my careless Days,
> Pleas'd in the silent Shade with empty Praise;
> Enough for me, that to the listning Swains
> First in these Fields I sung the Sylvan Strains.

(431–34)

Claiming humility, he asserts priority in time and in merit: first to domesticate the muse of Theocritus and Virgil in this particular place, and best as the recipient of all that praise, which, though empty, is pleasant. The contrast between the leisured singer and more active, nobler, folk (like the supremely happy politician) is taken from the end of the fourth *Georgic*, where the contrast is between the poet, "flourishing in the studious pursuits of ignoble leisure," and all-conquering Caesar. In the last line of that poem Virgil contrives to echo the first line of his own *Eclogues*, exactly as Pope does here, modifying the opening line of his own first pastoral, "Spring" ("First in these Fields I try the Sylvan Strains"). And the final statement that singing is sufficient unto itself is adapted from the end of Virgil's *Eclogues* (10.70). The transitional moments in the Virgilian career are evoked, conflated, and achieved in a poem and a place that have already made clear their epic culmination. Windsor was the site of Pope's pastorals, too, the landscape that has everything: hills, dales, plains, forests, tillage, sport, villages, monarchy; beside the river that leads everywhere: to the city that receives the rich tributes of all the world, the temple-studded and tower-adorned Augusta.

With this perfect image of civilization as our legend prescribes it, drawn directly from the complete works of its most prestigious poet, reinforced by the identification of the nascent seat of the new empire with that of the old, mediated through both the commercial practices that were expanding it and the discourse that was justifying that expansion, Pope's poem is the apex of his Virgilian career. Its conclusion leaves him nowhere to go but forward to the epic. English politics, however, deflected this trajectory—first into the translation of Homer's epic and finally into the production and reproduction of the mock-epic, the *Dunciad*, that chronicled not the foundation of civilization but its total collapse. The mordant satires of Pope's later career record in part the bitterness of once realized, then shattered hopes, the pathos of the imitation of Roman greatness as the Renaissance invented it and Spenser experienced it. In 1738 Pope published a witty trifle disclaiming, in the plangent form of an "Epitaph, For One who would not be buried in Westminster-Abbey," all the forms of ambition so manifest and so briefly achieved twenty-five years before:

> HEROES, and KINGS! your distance keep:
> In peace let one poor Poet sleep,
> Who never flatter'd Folks like you:
> Let Horace blush, and Virgil too.

Yet the ambition never died; it underlay the corrosive irony of what he continued to publish, and emerged explicitly (apparently at this mature period of his life) in the plan for *Brutus*. If neither of the first two Georges was anything like an Augustus, if the South Sea slave-trade monopoly had burst in the bubble of bankruptcy in 1720, Pope could still turn in his imagination to the legend that long predated the Roman identification, and could still dream of playing Virgil to the Trojan civilizer of his native ground.

What happens to and on and for that native ground in *Windsor-Forest* suggests, moreover, as Virgil himself had done, the cost of our imperial vision of civilization. To a greater extent even than in the *Aeneid*, that cost is death. Kings, partridges, pheasants, lapwings, nymphs, poets—all are depicted either as possessors or objects of possession, and all become the objects of spectacle as their deaths are dramatized in the text. The most dramatic are those of the birds, whose plumage and free flight link them, of course, to those "Feather'd People" whose freedom to pursue "their Sable Loves" is wished for in father Thames's peroration. The link reveals the empty piety of the wish, and the link is made by Pope's own figural identification of hunting and warfare. The discourse joins what it divides: In this shady empire, the only chase is of beasts; but in the poem beasts are people. And the feathered people are the objects of the most intense spectacle, who, by comic inversion, become us. The language makes us our own victims, just as Virgil's in the *Aeneid* identified the fertility and justice of Saturn's golden age with the agent of its destruction, Saturnia. Thus victim and victimizer, possessor and possessed, become the same even as Pope insists on their difference. He coined an aphorism to describe the hunting of hares by hounds: "Beasts, urg'd by us, their Fellow Beasts pursue, / And learn of Man each other to undo" (123–24). Men learn it, too: we recall that the Iroquois were being constantly urged by us, the British and the French, to fight each other in our interests. The logic of the discourse is inexorable, joining what is divided, erasing difference, subsuming all under the ultimate universal. Lesser universals, such as the supposed sociability of mankind that free trade will usher in, may be advocated, but they are not what the poem enacts. The poem produces death, obsessively, in the effort to contain and transcend it; but death overflows any protestation of exemption, covering all. Death is the logic and the logical consequence of our empire of possession, which is political, sexual, and discursive at once.

Chapter 17

୨╮

CONCEALING AND REVEALING

Richardson's Fiction and Vattel's Law

The chase for sexual possession of the female by the male, an immemorial motif in western literature and art, has never before or since the eighteenth century received the single-minded, exclusive to the point of claustrophobic, development that it got from Samuel Richardson. This pursuit, of one woman by one man, constitutes the entire plot of his two best-known novels: *Pamela*, where it ends happily, and *Clarissa*, where it doesn't. This concentration is not, I think, explicable merely by the vagaries of individual psychology, by Richardson's own piety, prudery, or prurience. Nor is the epistolary form of both fictions merely the result of Richardson's own occupation as printer and author of various didactic manuals, among them one on how to write letters. The function of writing for Richardson's sorely beset heroines is consistently crucial to the plot and its outcome. Despite the often-ridiculed implausibility of the circumstances in which both heroines manage to dash off copious, play-by-play accounts of their seducers' assaults, the circulation of what they write is an integral part of the combat in which they are engaged. Much time and ingenuity are spent by various characters in the novels to ensure and to prevent such circulation, control of which is a constant preoccupation of the seducer. Writing is thematized as the most potent weapon women have against the odds of sex and class (the male antagonist being always socially superior to his intended victim): it's the pen against the phallus.

Thus opposing the object to the symbol of the object, and placing the latter in women's hands, puts the old combat on a newly equal footing and gives it a new suspense, which Richardson remorselessly exploits, volume after volume. The sex war is of course discursive on both sides, waged always in language. But the male, though he occasionally writes, uses speech as his chief weapon; the female, though she must constantly speak in self-defense, uses writing as hers. The sheer prolixity of the ensuing discourse, as well as its necessary repetitiveness—he attacks, she repels, over and over; the tactics are ingeniously varied, but the goal is always the same: possession of her body—make it analogous to the discourse of natural law. There we

173

found the ceaseless multiplication of (often fictional) precedents for an ever-longer list of prohibitions derived from a principle that permits anything. Here we find the ceaseless multiplication of strategically identical situations aiming at a goal (sex out of wedlock) totally impermissible to the principles of the heroine. Richardson makes fiction of the condition that the natural lawyers had to justify, the warfare that Hobbes scandalized everyone by regarding as "natural." In Richardson, too, it's a war of each (man) against all (women); but, as in the discourse of natural law, it can't be seen as "natural" or self-justifying, but must be an aberration from the pious and benevolent sociability postulated as the human norm. The intense concentration of his fiction on sexual warfare as well as the particular discursive form it takes—not to mention its vast and immediate popularity—are explicable, even predictable, as part of the whole neoclassical effort to contain and subsume the violence of European conflict and expansion around the world.

The discourse of *Windsor-Forest*, for example, offers a virtual blueprint for both the theme and the outcome of *Clarissa* (1748). In Pope's reworking of the Apollo/ Daphne story, what he intensely dramatizes is the breathless chase. He also announces its psychological principle: "*Pan* saw and lov'd, and burning with Desire / Pursu'd her Flight; her Flight increas'd his Fire" (183–84). Another hoary cliché— that men want most the woman that's hardest to get—but it provides Richardson with his best villain and his most gripping plot. His creation of Lovelace has been often praised for its detailed working-out of just this principle, the way his desire becomes more intense and determined as it is thwarted, with social insults adding the pursuit of revenge to that of sexual possession. And as Pope's whole poem figures death as the consequence of possession, so it literally occurs in the novel. Lovelace rapes Clarissa, and the violation destroys her; she pines away (at length, and not before she arranges for the collection of all the letters that compose the novel) into a pathetically pious death. What she has written—her will and letters for everyone—lives after her to provide the dénouement. Poetic justice is complete when Lovelace is killed by her cousin in a duel.

Pope's poem, of course, presents the sexual pursuit as a figurative equivalent of other acquisitions: game, land, commercial wealth, knowledge. Richardson does no such thing, but plunges deeply into the simultaneously social and psychological ramifications of that single pursuit. Still, there is one small feature of the novel that hints at the larger, imperial dimension of its warfare. This is Lovelace's occasional quotation of Virgil, usually jocular, which sometimes makes the direct connection between one form of conquest and the other. He explains to his friend Belford that he is not going to seduce the teenage daughter of his innkeeper because her grandmother asked him not to: "Many and many a pretty rogue had I spared, whom I did *not* spare, had my power been acknowledged, and my mercy in time implored. But the *debellare superbos* should be my motto" (Richardson 1962: 53). The phrase is from Anchises' invocation of the noble mission of Rome (*Aeneid* 6.853): to spare the suppliant and "vanquish the proud." Like the ancient association of the two kinds of venery, such sexual imperialism had been exploited by many poets and playwrights since the Renaissance. Appropriate, and finally destructive, as it is to Lovelace's character, Richardson develops it no further. The only place that the wider colonialized world occupies in his fiction is one predicted by such early boosters as Sir George Peckham and approved by the natural lawyers: a dumping-ground for undesirables—in Richardson, a wastebasket for ladies who have lost their virtue, where, nonetheless, they can make their fortunes. Clarissa's atrocious family propose sending her to Pennsylvania (438). During the eighteenth century Georgia and Australia were founded, of course, as penal colonies.

What makes Richardson's fiction ideological, and what makes ideology most subtle and pervasive, is not the kind of direct apologetics, the explicit exposition or legitimation of the attitudes and practices of mercantile imperialism, to be found in all the kinds of discourses so far examined: history, pageant, preaching, philosophy, law, poetry. Taking "ideology" in its most neutral dictionary sense as a body of ideas reflecting the interests of a social group, large or small, is simply to describe how the formation and deployment of our founding legend has always worked—for ancient Rome, for medieval dynasties, for Renaissance monarchies, for modern adventurers. To take it thus is to refuse its pejorative uses, by Marxists and anti-Marxists alike, to mean little more than the false opposed to the true. Whether as false consciousness or as any leftist opinion, the word thus used is but a smear-word for what the user disapproves of. (The history and scope of the word's meanings are concisely analyzed in Williams 1976). In its neutral sense, the term, though broad, still specifies a range of discursive activities that are worth some trouble to discriminate. It can still direct attention to processes that ought not to be overlooked—precisely, indeed, to the process of overlooking.

The first process indicated by "ideology" is that of the social foundation and functioning of thought. The Greek components of the word (coined by a Frenchman in the late eighteenth century) mean the study of ideas, in the only place where they are available to us for study, in words and material artifacts. For if ideas exist where transcendental theories say they do—in a Platonic heaven or the mind of God—we can hardly glimpse them there; they are beyond rational interrogation. We can study them only where we can find them, in the form in which they come to us, which is above all in languages. And language is a supremely (perhaps the supreme) social phenomenon. It is also supremely historical, like society itself, constantly changing. The ideologues, as they were originally called (Vico was their precursor), thus focused, as Renaissance philologists did (Vico inherited their discipline), on extracting principles from an examination of the history of societies and their languages. These principles were envisioned as the basis of a new metaphysics opposed to the ancient one, derived not by deduction from axioms, but by inference from a kind of empirical research. This is the root of the polemical contrast that since degenerated into the false versus the true. But the contrast is better construed as rejection than as opposition; for, as is notorious, transcendental propositions (like the existence of God) cannot be disproved. Likewise, they can provide no explanation (but merely assert a final cause) for what happens in the world. The rejection of the transcendental, the essential, and the timeless *as the locus of explanation*, in favor of the material, the contingent, and the temporal remains the method of all subsequent uses of "ideology."

The rejection implies the second process indicated by the term, which is to detect, in transcendental assertions of any kind, what ordinary, mundane motives and interests are being both masked and revealed. Again, this is not a matter of separating the false from the true, or the real from the unreal, but rather of seeking to explain a use of language, a body of ideas, in the context where it arose, was communicated, and where alone it may be comprehended: as part of the purposes of human communities in and over time. My inquiry into the stories of civilization that compose our founding legend is ideological in this basic sense; the texts in which I trace its development and diffusion are ideological too. For in this sense, there is no text that is not ideological, none that is produced in a vacuum, unrelated to the way of life, mode of production, system of values of both the community in which it arose and those in which it is reproduced. There are many texts, however, that in very different ways claim the privilege of such a vacuum, and seek to situate themselves in a uniquely authoritative position wholly outside the interests and purposes of social groups. Such texts—a fair number have already been discussed—in our culture fall into two main categories: those that claim to record divine inspiration or revelation, and those that claim universal validity by virtue either of the principles they adduce or the objective procedure they follow. Roughly these: Scripture and some poetry; some philosophy and positivistic science. Now, to take their claims literally, by allowing them unique authority, means that how they work, how their language functions both in the text and in the world, cannot be studied, cannot even be seen. To make their operation as texts fully visible, to understand it, necessitates a concept like ideology, and a process like detection, to uncover what they conceal or omit.

The extent to which uncovering is required points directly to what might be called an ideological continuum of texts. That is, a scale ranging from those that frankly promote their social interests, to those that deny having any at all: from propaganda to divine revelation and certain forms of science and scholarship. Peckham's prospectus for investors in the Newfoundland venture is a good example of the former, and Grotius's treatise on law of the latter. Between these extremes fall most texts, many that admit or even analyze their allegiance to social interests, many that appear to ignore the matter, and many that address or assume one set of social interests while embodying another. Texts that belong to the canonized category called literature (as well as those in other categories, like philosophy) can fall anywhere along the scale. Those literary texts that derive from or consciously seek to imitate Virgil fall toward the top (propaganda) of it; so does some of the newer (in the eighteenth century) prose fiction, like Defoe's. The social allegiances of these texts—although they may be presented, qualified, and analyzed in highly complex ways, as in Virgil himself or Pope—are visible, obvious, susceptible to summary.

The kind of formulation such summary takes introduces the other major meaning of "ideology," the primary one in the neutral dictionary definition, which is those particular interests that a body of ideas (or a verbal assemblage of images and actions—a story) reflects. The word moves from denoting a method of investigation to summarizing its results. And so we may speak of the imperial ideology of Virgil or of Pope, and describe the social allegiances of Defoe's fiction as the ideology of possessive individualism, of bourgeois capitalism, of economic man, of colonial domination. This motion of the term has caused no little confusion and is both analogous to and different from that of another Greek confection of the same period, "biology." When this, instead of "natural philosophy," became the name for the study of life, it too indicated a different method of investigation, one that focused more on process than on classification. It too, in a large and neutral sense, designated all life-forms as "biological" (as all texts are "ideological"), as going through cycles of development and reproduction. And it too came to indicate the results of the investigation, the body of knowledge—theories, facts, procedures— now called biology.

But here enters the divergence from ideology, seen most clearly in the different relation adjectives have to each noun. For "imperial" ideology does not mean in the same way as "molecular" biology does. Though both adjectives identify a particular subject with which the -ology deals (empire or molecules), the former constitutes a kind of judgment, draws a kind of conclusion, that the latter doesn't. In the context of the communally established discourse we call science, to qualify a branch of inquiry by its subject matter is (at this level of labeling) unproblematic (though just what constitutes a molecule may be a problem at other levels). The qualification simply defines the subject matter; it's where we begin. It's a given. But in the context of what are sometimes called the human sciences, the subject matter is always problematic. To define and qualify it are the goal and result of a particular inquiry; it's where we end. It must be uncovered. But the end of such an inquiry, unlike the results of a particular experiment, does not necessarily (though it may) add to the body of information and procedure that the -ology denotes.

Thus, while ideology is obviously not a science in the sense of biology, neither is it (except as a smear-word) wholly random and vagarious. A science is a disciplined inquiry whose procedures of verification and falsification are, by definition, mutually sharable. Ideological inquiry must employ procedures of verification and falsification that become sharable only by argumentation. Scientific method is agreed upon, is what constitutes science; hermeneutic method (any mode of interpreting texts) isn't, but is always to be established. Still, it is, or ought to be, somehow methodical: it forms and tests hypotheses, according to which it selects data; it offers generalizations on the basis of empirical evidence. In other words, it aims at explanation, and can arrive at it in two basic ways, often combined: argument and narrative. Narrative, it must be observed, is by no means unscientific: to explain the existence in time of life, the earth, or the cosmos, biologists, geologists, and physicists tell stories. Evolution, plate tectonics, and the big bang are stories that have replaced the ancient etiological myths of Deucalion, Cronos, and Zeus—better, more cogent and complete and testable stories, we are sure, but still stories, and still subject to revision and rewriting, still as elastic as live myths. For creatures whose existence is temporal, narrative is the primary mode of explanation.

Hence, to examine what kind of explanation of what kind of phenomena is offered, or not, in the kind of stories that have become an artistic (or scientific or philosophical) tradition is an ideological inquiry. And it is perhaps most useful when applied to texts in the middle or lower ranges of the continuum, those whose social interests are not so obvious, or are apparently confined to a rather narrow range: in the present case, the novels of Richardson as contrasted, say, to those of Defoe. The pragmatic, energetic, self-made, and self-scrutinizing protagonists in the pages of Defoe have long been recognized, as has his own mercantile and journalistic career, as paradigmatic of a commercial bourgeoisie rising to dominance. Richardson, too, has been seen as paradigmatic of such social motion, but on a much narrower, domestic rather than global, scale. Seeing his obsession with sexual warfare as a sort of displacement of the global warfare ubiquitous in the eighteenth century enlarges the scale somewhat and helps to explain why his fictions were written at this period, as well as to relate their discursive form to that of the frankly colonial ideology of the natural lawyers.

But Richardson also exemplifies a profounder ideological effect than these, which, indeed, do not directly arise from the explicit and detailed focus in his novels on the psychology of his characters. And the profounder ideological effect is precisely psychological, affecting both characters and readers. It requires detection, since it is and is designed to be unnoticed. One example of its occurrence in his first novel is the best I know of what "ideology" most cogently and interestingly means. The example consists simply of an incident narrated at the end of a conversation in *Pamela* (1740). The incident is the death of a black boy. Even specialist readers of the novels of this period will not, I trust (guessing from experience), recall either that there is a black boy in this text or that he dies. And that is the point.

The text tells, almost entirely in her own letters and journals, the story of a maidservant whose master attempts first to seduce her, then to propose that she become his kept mistress. Virtuously resisting all such efforts, she writes them all down, along with her clever stratagems and anguished reflections. After her letters succeed in thwarting a scheme or two, Mr. B. (as the master is called throughout) deprives her of pen, ink, and paper. Pamela still finds ways, partly with the help of other servants, to procure these, and goes on writing. Mr. B. acquires some of it, and is fascinated by what he reads. Hooked by the plot, he demands to see all of it, as he mockingly says, "that I shall be better directed how to wind up the catastrophe of the pretty novel" (Richardson 1980: 268). At this point Pamela is carrying the scribbled sheets of paper on her person to avoid their discovery: she used to stuff them in her bosom, now she sews them into her petticoats. To make a (very) long story short, Mr. B. is indeed "better directed" than he imagined by Pamela's writing; becoming a convert to the cause of such long-suffering virtue as hers, he defies the prejudices of all his class and marries her. Her writing is indeed her body; possessing the first leads to possession of the second, but on her terms and not his. Her terms, of course, are satisfied by the marriage vows; she goes on, now ecstatically, referring to her "master," and making her obedience to his will, which she enumerates in forty-eight articles, her whole study (467–70).

Shortly after their marriage, Mr. B. introduces Pamela to his six-year-old illegitimate daughter, whom he keeps at a nearby boarding school, and tells her the story of the girl's mother, called Sally Godfrey. Pamela has been curious about this woman for some time, having first heard her name dropped in one of the furious rages unleashed by Lady Davers, Mr. B.'s sister, in reaction to his marrying so far beneath him. (Like her brother, the lady is also converted to adoration of Pamela by reading her writing.) Furious rages, fulsome sentiments, endless expostulations, constant speculations about motives, minute analyses of every impulse, mood, look, tone, and gesture are the substance of the book throughout, the means and medium of the warfare that is its plot. Now happily concluded, the warfare has given way to articles of peace, and catalogs of other articles that peace brings: the clothes Pamela can wear and the money she can charitably disburse, especially to her own family. The bastard daughter is no issue of contention at all: Pamela loves her at first sight and wants to raise her; and Mr. B. is properly penitent and moralistic about the wild oats that once he sowed. So, indeed, as he tells it, was Sally Godfrey. She put the child in his care and went to Jamaica, to save herself from any further temptation. There, passing as a young widow with a child cared for by her husband's friends in England, she married well and happily.

Pamela listens to the story, interposing occasional questions about Mr. B.'s emotional states. He finishes the story at Sally's debarkation, giving her five hundred pounds and promising more. But Pamela wants, and gets, an account of the whole parting scene: Sally's refusal that he accompany her on part of the voyage; his impatience with the Captain's command to go or stay; their last embrace that "affected every one present"; the heavy heart with which he gazed after the ship until it disappeared. He appends the incident in question to this conclusion of the story.

"And so much, my dear, for poor Sally Godfrey.

"She sends, I understand, by all opportunities, with the knowledge of her husband, to enquire how her child, by her first husband, does; and has the satisfaction to know she is happily provided for. About half a year ago her husband sent a little *Negro* boy, of about ten years old, as a present, to wait upon her. But he was taken ill of the small-pox, and died in a month after he was landed."

"Sure, sir," said I, "you must have been long affected with a case so melancholy in its circumstances."

"I will own, that the whole of the affair hung upon me for some time; but I was full of spirits and inconsideration. New objects of pleasure danced before my eyes, and kept reflection from me."

The episode closes with "agreeable reflections" (about Mr. B.'s reform as owing to the example of Pamela's virtue) "on this melancholy, but instructive story" (504–05).

The story may be even more instructive, and more melancholy, for us than for them (or for Richardson's first readers). But it's a different story—not the story the characters assume it is (of their own emotional relationships), but the one that the grammar of the text strictly refers to. The "case so melancholy in its circumstances" that Pamela's words refer to is logically that of the preceding two sentences: the gift that died. Pamela of course doesn't mean that case, but the case of her beloved's turmoil. He understands her perfectly as referring to his own case, and responds that, well, there wasn't too much turmoil; he wasn't "long affected." The other case affects no one at all for any length of time; we read right over it. It's a negligible detail in a large and often minutely detailed book; and conversation, as we all know, hardly follows strict grammatical rules. Writing, however, does—even when it purports to transcribe conversation. Words fixed on a page have relations that can be contemplated in ways that spoken words cannot. So the grammar of the text imposes a relation that its drama and its rhetoric wholly ignore. In the latter, the case of the ten-year-old black boy, given as a servant to a six-year-old girl, who dies of smallpox does not qualify as melancholy. This case receives none of the compassion that the couple so lavishly bestow on each other, participates in none of the emotional vibrations that radiate so continually among practically all the characters in the novel. The black boy's case is not only not felt; it is not even noticed.

Yet, it is there. As readers, we have ample excuse for not noticing it: caught up in the larger story, we do what the rhetoric requires, we see it from the protagonists' perspective. They ignore the black boy's "case," and so do we. Yet, it is there. Why is it there at all? In order *not* to be noticed. It is produced to be something more, or rather less, than merely contained and subsumed (as *Winsdor-Forest* produces death); it is enunciated in order to be erased. Such erasure is the subtlest of all ideological effects, the obverse of the primary effect of stories like our founding legend. Those stories tell us what to look for and to enact; this one tells us what not to see. Those determine our perception in a positive sense; this in a negative. Like Aeneas before the unborn generals who will precipitate Rome's civil war, we're being told not to ask about that monstrous sorrow, dismissed through the ivory gate of illusory dreams, exhorted to admire Mr. B.'s moral reform and his Italian silk waistcoat (505). New objects dance before our eyes, and keep reflection from us—Mr. B.'s description of his youthful, callous nonchalance is also an exact description of how this discourse works. Like Aeneas, we're being shown what will not bear scrutiny, trained to the spectacles from which we must avert our eyes. A child, presented like a puppy dog—of exotic breed from a distant place—to another child, only it takes sick, as exotic animals will in a new climate, and dies. It's there, but not for long; it leaves no trace, has no history, and disappears unnoticed.

Black children, often costumed in an oriental fashion, were all the rage as servants in the elegant households of eighteenth-century Europe. The paintings of the period are full of them. Perhaps Richardson included the dead black boy as this sort of cultural code, another sign of the lofty circle to which Pamela has been elevated. Richardson is of course very ambivalent about that lofty circle, portraying it always as in need of the pious virtues that only the middle class can supply. But both classes are united, in his text, by their marital and mutual disregard of the dead black boy. This disregard is the ideology they share, the deliberate blind spot in the moral religiosity that explicitly unites them.

And that we readers share it too, ignoring the incident as they do, demonstrates the negative determination of perception that ideology—the nexus of convictions, values, and attitudes that springs from our social allegiances—can accomplish. Again, it is not a matter of the truth or falsity of this nexus of attitudes; ideology in this sense is not false consciousness, but *un*consciousness. It's what our stories include only in order to expunge. And ideology in its other sense, as the study of such attitudes, is what can detect them, uncover their operation in language, and allow us to perceive what that language would rather we didn't. Ideology as a systematic process of overlooking is the negative complement of ideology as a systematic process of legitimation. Both processes are about to shift into high gear as Europe in general and Great Britain in particular consolidate their grasp of the globe. Colonial ideology will have more and more to justify and more and more to overlook.

The grandest and most influential justification proceeds directly from the scholarly and philosophical tradition of natural law, deliberately reduced to a more accessible style and a living language. *Le Droit des gens* was published in 1758, in London, Leiden, and The Hague, by Emer de Vattel, a diplomat from Neuchâtel in the service of the King of Prussia (to whom Neuchâtel then belonged). In his preface he reviews his predecessors, Grotius, Pufendorf, and Christian von Wolff, and declares that he is rewriting them in a less dull manner calculated to reach the audience that counts, those with real power. In his pages, the law of nature will yield precepts and arguments for practicing diplomats. This practical aim gave the work enormous currency; it was fully translated into English two years after its first appearance, went through numerous subsequent editions throughout Europe, and was twice translated in the new republic of the United States before the First World War. Although not intended for legal scholars, the book was continuously cited in judicial decisions in both Great Britain and the United States until the beginning of this century (Nussbaum 1962: 156–64). The reasons for its popularity, and for its particular utility to the expansion of the anglophonic peoples, are not far to seek.

Vattel does not fatigue the reader with elaborate arguments and citations to derive the law of nature from some universal or other; he takes it as given and, as his subtitle claims, simply applies it. He starts right off with the definition and purposes of government. A sovereign state is one that governs itself "under what form soever," regardless of its dependency on or unequal alliance with other states. By this test, the Cantons of Switzerland count as nations, since they are voluntarily associated without ceasing to be free and independent in their own government

(Vattel 1760: 1.1.4–10).[1] Any form of sovereign, collective or individual, exists only for the good of the whole nation, not vice versa (1.4.39). Princes have power only as granted in laws and are subject to these (1.4.46). All forms of sovereignty of long duration are assumed to be by the tacit consent of the people. The English constitution is praiseworthy in all these respects. The object of a state is to procure for its individual members what is necessary and useful to life, in this order: the peaceful enjoyment of their own property, justice, and defense. Thus will men be placed "in a condition to labour . . . after their own perfection; which is their grand and principal duty" (1.6.92).

After these generalities, Vattel gets down to specifics. Laboring to perfect ourselves first requires another kind of labor. Vattel devotes an entire chapter to the first duty of the state, which is to encourage agriculture. He criticizes urban contempt for the tiller of the soil, insisting that he not be despised (1.7.80). Vattel is fully aware of the basis of our civilization, and he makes the usual law out of its myth of itself, assimilating past Europeans to present savages on the basis of how they use their land. We've heard it all before, many times (and will again); but it's here acquiring judicial force. It's also especially clear:

> The cultivation of the soil is not only to be recommended by the government on account of the extraordinary advantages that flow from it; but from its being an obligation imposed by nature on mankind. The whole earth is appointed for the nourishment of its inhabitants: but it would be incapable of doing it, was it uncultivated. Every nation is then obliged by the law of nature to cultivate the ground that has fallen to its share; and it has no right to expect or require assistance from others, any farther than the land in its possession is incapable of furnishing it with necessaries. Those people, like the antient Germans, and the modern Tartars, who having fertile countries, disdain to cultivate the earth, and chuse rather to live by rapine, are wanting to themselves, and deserve to be exterminated as savage and pernicious beasts. There are others who, to avoid agriculture, would live only by hunting and their flocks. This might, doubtless, be allowed in the first ages of the world, when the earth, without cultivation, produced more than was sufficient to feed its few inhabitants. But at present, when the human race is so greatly multiplied, it could not subsist, if all nations resolved to live in that manner. Those who still retain this idle life, usurp more extensive territories, than they would have occasion for, were they to use honest labour, and have therefore no reason to complain, if other nations, more laborious, and too closely confined, come to possess a part. Thus tho' the conquests of the civilized empires of Peru and Mexico were a notorious usurpation, the establishment of many colonies on the continent of North America, may, on their confining themselves within just bounds, be extremely lawful. The people of these vast countries rather over-ran than inhabited them. (1.7.81)

---

1. Again, book, chapter, and section numbers are given to facilitate reference to the many different editions.

Noncultivators are idle pillagers and deserve extermination. The law of nature says so. Empires, though, deserve respect, which they didn't get from the Spaniards. The British and French, however, are doing the right thing to the right people. How to determine the "just bounds" of their colonies is not specified, and will come up again.

The next ranking duties of the state are, in order, to provide for commerce, highways and canals, and a monetary system. These secured, education, arts, religion, and glory may follow after. In a subsequent discussion of the rights of a state over its territories, Vattel returns to the colonial case. In general, a nation has ownership (domain) and empire (rule) of the land it occupies (1.17.203). Uninhabited countries belong to their "first possessor," and this means genuine occupation, not merely planting a flag or receiving a papal decree (1.17.207–208). Nations can also take over part of a vast place where the natives are "erratic," since

> We have already observed, in establishing the obligation to cultivate the earth, that the nations cannot exclusively appropriate to themselves more land than they have occasion for, and which they are unable to settle and cultivate. Their removing their habitations through these immense regions, cannot be taken for a true and legal possession; and the people of Europe, too closely pent up, finding land of which these nations are in no particular want, and of which they make no actual and constant use, may lawfully possess it, and establish colonies there. . . . the earth belongs to the human race in general, and was designed to furnish it with subsistence: if each nation had resolved . . . to appropriate to itself a vast country, that the people might live only by hunting, fishing, and wild fruits, our globe would not be sufficient to maintain a tenth part of its present inhabitants.

It's therefore natural to confine "the Indians within narrower limits." And it's praiseworthy to purchase their lands (instead of just taking them over) as the English Puritans and William Penn did (1.17.209). How narrow the limits may become is again not specified; but citizens of the about-to-be-born Republic will have little trouble in shrinking them ever narrower. For the law of nature that mandates cultivation as occupation will become in nineteenth-century America the manifest destiny that decrees the westward expansion of that nation until the land runs out at the Pacific Coast. The founding legend has empowered our agrarian civilization with a definition of the savage that permits anything to be done to him; confinement is gracious, compared to extermination.

Remarkable in Vattel's text is the political employment of the notion that will later serve Kant as the categorical imperative of his ethics: an act is right if the consequences of everybody doing it (of its being universal) are good. (Kant had also read Leibniz and von Wolff.) If all nations were hunters and gatherers, Vattel has twice insisted, the earth couldn't support its population. Therefore, hunting and gathering are to be stamped out (as idle and dishonest usurpation), and our system of cultivation universalized. Something has got to be universal, and it's going to be us. There's a monomania here: the familiar, modern, and scientific drive to the (a, some, any) universal, the obliteration of difference central to the discourse of natural law. The drive is masked in an apparent logic that overlooks actuality. The overlooking is done by the initial "if." The condition hypothesized is absurd: all nations are not, and are not about to become, hunters and gatherers. There is no such danger as the one conjured up. And the inference from this false premise is also false—that all the planet must become as we are. It's no wonder that the question of exactly what bounds are just, what limits narrow, is never specifically addressed. For, despite the terms of apportionment—we can take over "part" of their vast land, confining them to smaller parts of it—the thrust of the discourse allows no serious possibility of sharing. There's no room for difference. The earth still, for Vattel, seems large; but that it might accommodate different uses even in the same place is not thinkable. For the uses are incompatible, and theirs, as the legend has long told us, is the equivalent of rapine, laziness, and general immorality. Europe feels overcrowded, and so will export and transplant itself wherever it can: this is the law of nature.

Vattel codifies and sanctifies in the name of a secular universal appropriate to the Enlightenment the legendary picture of civilization and savagery that writers in the previous two centuries, like Peckham and Donne, had attributed to the will of God. Pufendorf had it both ways, as many others will continue to do. It doesn't much matter, except to expand the grounds on which almost any form of expansion may be justified. Freethinkers and pietists, aristocrats and bourgeois, of any European nationality could all appeal to the new legal form of the founding legend as their ancestors appealed to its old historical form. The Trojans are long gone (they'll be back); but their civilization and the frontiers of its transmission are marching on.

So far, the main line of march for the British and the French has been from east to west, with India the exception for both, in two senses: not a place sparsely inhabited by roving savages, and not a colony of settlement, or even of government—yet. Clive has only just (1757) taken over Bengal, beginning the British Raj. Holland is entrenched in the Spice Islands (though ousted from North America by England years before), Spain and Portugal in their parts of the Americas. All, however, are combatively competing over the slave trade in West Africa. And Africa will become the next frontier, the enormous and savage place to which the ideology produced from the founding legend may next be applied almost exactly as it was to America.

One of its earliest applications, published in the same year as *The Law of Nations*, reverses the priority that Vattel gave to the civilizing duties of the state: he put agriculture first and commerce second. Commerce, of course, had long ago made its way into the legend, first in the epic of Camoens and then especially in English writing of all kinds. The role of commerce as the primary motor of imperial expansion is now sufficiently established to claim preeminence as a civilizing agent. The claim is made by Malachy Postlethwayt, a trade lobbyist who compiled a *Universal Dictionary of Trade and Commerce* and agitated throughout the mid-century for the formation of the Royal African Company and the advantages of trade in Africa. Now, two years into the Seven Years' War, he addresses a tract to the British government, urging the seizure of French trading forts in West Africa in order to diminish their part in the triangular trade and increase Britain's. This is the standard strategy for the warfare of the age, and he supports it by the precedent of the Dutch War of 1665, fought to protect the African trade from their interference (Postlethwayt 1758: 27–28). And he buttresses the strategy with the claim that, for him, is self-evident: "Before commerce took effect amongst mankind, the human species in general were little better than brutes of the first class: but trade and navigation exciting to the advancement of arts and sciences necessary thereto, *these* have naturally civilized men: and as they have encreased in civilized polity, commerce in general has in its turn proportionally augmented. This is fact indisputable" (96). His example of this neatly mutual augmentation of civilization and commercial prosperity is that of the North American savages, who now both provide furs and constitute a market for our manufactures. Postlethwayt could frankly care less about converting them to Christianity; just integrating them into our market will do the job fine. By itself, this will be a sufficient "incorporation of customs and usages, as may in time bring them to live like christians, whether they may turn such or not." He assumes, as the legend dictates, that otherwise they have no "customs and usages." So, if the Africans are savage barbarians now, commerce is the infallible remedy (98).

Among the many profits that would swell British pocketbooks if the French were chucked out of West Africa as he proposes, are those to be reaped from planting colonies as in North America. Only here the object is to grow "all the *spices of Asia*" far closer to home (89). He offers long descriptions of soils and climate to prove this is possible, and deplores the English neglect of all that land: "the fruitful soil lies waste, a very extended country, pleasant vallies, banks of fine rivers, spacious plains, capable of cultivation to unspeakable benefit . . . remain fallow and unnoticed: Why do not the *Europeans* enclose such lands for cultivation, as by their nature and situation appear proper for beneficial productions?" (93). The prospect was indeed irresistible; but the subsequent efforts of the British to settle and cultivate commodities in tropical West Africa revealed the bacteriological limits of the analogy with America. For the germs of that climate did to Europeans what those of the Europeans had done to the population of the Americas. The mortality rate during the first year of those who tried to settle on the Guinea coast varied between 25 and 80 percent (Wilson 1977: 9; Curtin 1964: 71).

Discursively, however, the analogy had no limits: savages remained savage and land an object of commercial exploitation—in whatever direction of the compass. The legend had told us this since the Renaissance; law was prescribing it; global warfare was enacting it; fiction was showing us how to ignore its consequences; and philosophy was making it into a theory of progress. This rehistoricizing of the legend culminates in the Scottish Enlightenment, and will produce a history of the contemporary savage determined by the legend in defiance of all available evidence.

Chapter 18

ᔔ

THEORIZING

The Scottish Enlightenment

T he thinkers of the Scottish Enlightenment, all academic intellectuals like Thomas Reid, Francis Hutcheson, Adam Ferguson, John Millar, Dugald Stewart, William Robertson—along with their better-known colleagues, Hume and Adam Smith—had enormous influence on shaping the policies and attitudes of the infant republic of the United States (Pearce 1953: 82–83). It was they, moreover, who systematically reformulated the picture of civilization in the founding legend as historiography. And they did so as the heirs of the natural lawyers, the modern historians, and the commercial boosters. They found that the universal *telos* of world history was ourselves, civilized by the Romans, and our systems of competing nationalism, private property, social hierarchy, and commodity production. They elaborated and crystallized the plot of the founding story—the (usually violent) transmission of omniculture—into the doctrine of progress. And they did it self-consciously, aware even with occasional irony that they were making our present condition the measure of all things, and all people. But irony could not disturb the serene conviction that what we are is not only right, but the only possible thing to be.

For we—and after the end of the Seven Years' War in 1763, especially we anglophones—are the winners of the imperial sweepstakes. We are also, after James Watt makes the steam engine practicable in 1764, the winners of the technological sweepstakes. This new form of energy will give a new meaning to the word "industry" and will in time alter the landscape and enlarge the dimensions of our everyday world. It will produce new forms of urbanization, labor organization, and social alienation. But neither it nor all the later forms of energy that will follow from it—the internal combustion engine and the jet, electricity and electromagnetic waves of all sorts—will basically change the operation of the systems now in place. It will just make them go faster. Energy, whether produced from water, wood, coal, oil, gas, or atoms, is not self-directing and does not dictate how it's used. It empowers whatever it's put into, and it gets put into whatever is there at the moment. The mechanical engine, for example, when it became small enough, just got put into the carriage designed to be pulled by the horse. It took years for the form of the receptacle to be modified by the new energy source. And once it was, nothing qualitative had changed. Today's sleek automobiles on their networks of superhighways do exactly what horses and carriages did on the excellent (so regarded by foreign visitors at the time) roads of late eighteenth-century England. Automobiles do more of it, more comfortably, in velocity and volume: faster and for lots more people. They produce more pollution, too; but this is still a matter of degree. The horse was also a pollutant. And the increased comfort is accompanied by the increased stress of driving the faster vehicle in more crowded conditions.

Because the new sources of energy that empowered the "industrial revolution" so obviously altered the routine daily lives of so many of us, for better and for worse, we tend to overestimate their importance and misattribute qualitative agency to the amazing, but quantitative, new instruments. We forget that mechanical power, by itself, is utterly neutral. We become terribly proud that we can command so much of it (in particular contrast to savages), and terribly angry that it appears to be overwhelming our lives. The fashion for blaming technology for whatever we found wrong with our culture reached a kind of peak in the literature and philosophy of high Modernism during the first half of this century. Hostility to "technocracy" was a leitmotif of the popular existentialism of the 50s. Insofar as the hostility was directed at the *technê* (mechanical art or skill) and not at the *kratos* (political rule or authority), it was misplaced. For the art, or machine, or energy source is not responsible for what is done with it. It's an instrument that serves a purpose determined elsewhere, by agencies human and social. Mechanical energy merely empowers something else; the power that decides what will be thus empowered is the power that counts, and the only one logically to praise or blame.

And such power of course is that of political institutions and their accompanying ideologies. The steam engine will be but harnessed to our notion of civilization and will propel it ever more rapidly around the globe. And the more easily since the notion has long since become global; it's universal and covers everybody. For this reason, we have now a splendid window into our own virtually unrecorded past: we can see it in the present condition of the North American savages. We study them now to confirm what (the legend said) we were, and to measure our enormous progress from that point. They have no other history than as the most rudimentary, the earliest—i.e. "primitive"—form of us. This narcissism is systematic, and constitutes the structure of Adam Ferguson's *Essay in the History of Civil Society*: part one establishes the "general characteristics of human nature"; part two presents the history of "rude nations"; and part three that of civil policy and arts—a logical progression on a single scale, the only one there is. Ferguson was professor of moral philosophy at the University of Edinburgh, as was Adam Smith at Glasgow, where he began his career as a professor of logic. Regardless of the traditional subjects they taught, they and their colleagues are justly regarded as pioneer sociologists. They invented (independently of Vico and with a wholly secular emphasis) social history as the study of collective institutions, manners, skills, and bequeathed that subject to their student, Walter Scott. His fictionalizings of it made him the most famous man and it one of the most popular subjects of the nineteenth century, and directly inspired the careers of (among many others) Manzoni, Michelet, and Balzac.

The Scottish thinkers were, in other words, anything but parochial. Scotland itself had for centuries been in many ways less parochial than England, having traditionally resisted its southern neighbor with French alliances, and having more recently close commercial and educational relations with the Dutch. The thinkers inherited western Europe's vision of itself and gave it back intensified as well as accelerated its passage across the Atlantic. They accomplished the *translatio studii* that followed the *translatio imperii* that John Donne had identified as the apostolic mission of the Virginia Company: to "have made this *Iland*, which is but as the *Suburbs* of the old world, a Bridge, a Gallery to the new." Only now the island of Britain is far more than a bridge; the old periphery is the new metropolis. London is not merely Augusta in the fancy of poets; it's the trading and financial capital of the world, having taken over from seventeenth-century Amsterdam, and will remain so until replaced in this century by its own former colony become empire. If London was undeniably Rome, Edinburghers in the late eighteenth century liked to think of their city, then undergoing the same kind of architectural expansion that London had after the Restoration, as the Athens of the North. The classical analogy was exact: the place in the empire that generated ideas for its metropolis to absorb and transmit—now as then. The narcissism of Ferguson's text is that of all (neo)classicized Europe.

It begins with lapidary assertions about human nature which accept with equanimity a basically Hobbesian view of it. "Mankind . . . embrace the occasions of mutual opposition, with alacrity and pleasure" (Ferguson 1767: 30). "War and dissension" are "natural" to man, who delights to exercise his powers in rivalry both individually and collectively. "Without the rivalship of nations, and the practice of war, civil society itself could scarcely have found an object, or a form." For one cannot give a sense of union "to a multitude without admitting hostility to those who oppose them." However regrettable their effects may appear, quarrel, struggle, and war itself constitute "the exercise of a liberal spirit." "Could we at once . . . extinguish the emulation which is excited from abroad, we should probably break or weaken the bonds of society at home" (36–37). The Hobbesian view is accepted because it carries none of the terror that it (quite logically) did for Hobbes; it has been tamed by passage through both the century of largely successful wars Britain has fought since 1650 and the whole neoclassical ideology of the *concordia discors*. All strife finally resolves into, is contained by, harmony—as Pope insisted. We like strife; it provides pleasure for the individual and social bonding for the nation. The discourse does not qualify these generalities by discriminating different kinds of strife, or of pleasure, or of exercise. As usual, it aims to obliterate difference of any kind; and when it must confront one, it, again as usual, erases, ignores, or subsumes it.

Rude nations are therefore highly instructive, being now what all once were. When the Romans arrived, the Britons were just as the natives of North America are today: "they were ignorant of agriculture; they painted their bodies; and used for cloathing, the skins of beasts." Before going on to describe our once common condition, Ferguson enters a caveat, to preempt the objection that savages have nothing to teach us. "We are ourselves the supposed standards of politeness and civilization; and where our own features do not appear, we apprehend, that there is nothing which deserves to be known" (114). This statement is literally true in a way that does not strike Ferguson at all; he goes blandly on to assure us that real and present savages can in fact excel the civilized in both vices and virtues (115). He insists merely on the moral sameness that allows us to find "our own features" in creatures who are otherwise, and will remain, so distant from us. He goes on defending the idea that we can learn from savage life about our past selves by adducing the support of classical historians. They "understood human nature"; so, just as Thucydides sought ancient Greek manners in those of contemporary barbarians, so we can find those of our ancestors in native North Americans (119).

The most salient qualities of their life, it turns out not unsurprisingly, are absences: what they lack that we have—for this is how we can measure our progress. Those who simply hunt, fish, and gather "have little attention to property, and scarcely any beginnings of subordination or government." But those who have herds have both the latter. The difference is "material" between "the savage, who is not yet acquainted with property . . . and the barbarian, to whom it is, although not ascertained by laws, a principal object of care and interest." Since it takes time to "define possession," "property is a matter of progress" (123–24). And property functions in this discourse as the ultimate definiens, the sine qua non, of civilization. Here it supplies a way to measure progress on a temporal continuum: having it (though not fully, since its possession isn't guaranteed by law), barbarians are more evolved than savages. Thus modern Europe fills in the ancient blank, the savage lack of *mos* and *cultus*, with what it most highly values. Property, subordination, and government are now the holy trinity of civilization; the first entails the other two.

So, having most everything in common, savages have "no distinctions of rank or condition" beyond merely "personal qualities." Ferguson is talking about the entire northern half of the new world, and so must allow for some differences. He notes that the Caribs have chiefs, and that therefore among them "unequal distribution of property creates a visible subordination" (127–28). But these are exceptions to the rule, which is established by the fiercely egalitarian Iroquois—for no better reason than that these six nations were those that the British and the French knew best, and about whom most had been written. Drawing (how selectively we'll see in due course) on these reports, Ferguson finds much to admire in savages, given their rudimentary circumstances. He praises at some length their "informal" councils and politics, their kindness and justice (neither of which result from coercion or duty), their talents and physical skills. They have potential, these folks, as they must, since they are but the primitive form of ourselves. But they "study no science," have no grasp of general principles, are sunk in "groveling" superstitions (136). In warfare, they have no conception of bravery or fair play, since they seek only the maximum destruction of the enemy at the minimum risk to themselves; their "fortitude" is "patience" rather than "valor" (138). They exhibit the same paradoxical combination of great energy and great sloth that Tacitus observed of the Germanic tribes. And like them, they must inevitably yield to the "arts and discipline" of the more civilized: as Gaul, Germany, and Britain fell to the Romans, so must Africa and America now to the Europeans (144).

It's inevitable because there is only one story, our story, and we are going to enact it again—in the usual role, now Roman, of conquering *civilisateurs*. "History repeats itself," says the proverb, conveniently attributing the power of agency to what it nonetheless identifies as discourse. It *repeats*; but "it" is a structure of words, which do not repeat themselves, but require human speakers and writers to repeat them. But "it"—history—is also, of course, a sum total of events, what happened. The proverb relies on this sense of history to displace agency and responsibility from us to it: events just reoccur, all by themselves (or by some transcendental agent: Christian providence or Hegelian idea). But the verb of reoccurrence the proverb uses incorporates the other sense of history—not what happened, but what gets written down. So the proverb, mobilizing both senses of history to replicate each other by using the verb reflexively (as a kind of passive), means:

> events repeat events / words repeat words;
> words repeat events / events repeat words.

Bringing the agentless passive to the surface produces:

> events are repeated (as events) / words are repeated (as words);
> words are repeated (as events) / events are repeated (as words).

The first pair of permutations in each set (which do not combine the two senses of "history") offer the agentless tautology that is the proverb's commonest meaning. But the second pair in each set (which combine the two senses) offer instead a conception of mutual agency. They suggest that just as what happens gets written, what gets written happens. The proverb can thus encapsulate the historical process it was Virgil's achievement to discover as the structural principle of the *Aeneid*: history is made as and by the enactment of stories, fictional or factual. It is a scripted performance.

Ferguson's scenario of it continues by outlining the trajectory from primitive savagery through slightly less primitive barbarism to us. This "progress" is measured exclusively by "extending the notion of property," which is lamentably retarded by the natural aversion of men "to any application in which they are not engaged by immediate instinct and passion" (146). Acquiring discipline, enduring tedious tasks, waiting for "distant returns of his labour" (147)—in a word, postponing gratification, is what the savage is not inclined to do. The primitive is thus, as the one universal story requires, psychobiologically assimilated to the childish. He's a careless baby—which is why we can sometimes indulge his follies and admire his nascent capacities. Savages can thus be hospitable, generous, and gentle, as can barbarians (155). On the temporal psychobiological scale, barbarians are adolescents. Having rudimentary forms of property and rank gives them but an increased potential for violence: being "guided by interest and not governed by laws" produces slavery, rapine, and terror (157). Ferguson takes this opportunity, as he often does, to rail against the Middle Ages (here against trial by combat): that adolescent period in our own history conceived by the classicizing Renaissance as, precisely, "barbarian." But here too the Olympian perspective of our adulthood can be indulgent. If barbarians lack proper government by laws, they also lack (various ancient and modern observations are cited) the corruptions of such government (161–62). They retain a kind of innocence appropriate to their lack of mature development.

When he comes to describe that development, Ferguson's viewpoint is itself maturely disillusioned, another voice of liberal and secular modernity that has rejected the fictions of the past and accepted the unloveliness of human motivations. "Nations stumble upon establishments, which are indeed the result of human action, but not the execution of any human design" (187). "To covet riches, and to admire distinction" (191) are the motives of social formation, and strife is its principle. The public interest is secured "not because individuals are disposed to regard it as the end of their conduct," but because each looks after himself. "Liberty is maintained by the continued differences and oppositions of numbers, not by their concurring zeal in behalf of equitable government" (196). The strife of competing individual interests that harmonizes into the public good operates between nations as well as within them. It is "a happy system of policy" to maintain "a balance of power" in contemporary Europe, where "the independence of weak states" is preserved "by the mutual jealousies of the strong" (203). And the same dynamic applies within states to class interests as well as individual ones: in the balance of conflicts among the aspirations of the people, the nobility, and/or the prince, "the public freedom and the public order are made to consist" (252).

The arts and policy that now constitute civilization are those, it need hardly be said, of classical bourgeois liberalism, in which the political dynamic is derived from and identical to the economic. Contests for money and for power, both domestic and international, are self-checking and self-balancing; the role of government is to permit them fairly to occur, like a referee, according to minimal rules. Hence the main object of government is to "avoid doing mischief" and let individuals act from their own "motives of interest." The only positive action of the state should be to "repress the frauds" that can destroy commerce, the activity "in which men . . . are least apt to go wrong." The trader can be mercenary and stupid "in rude ages"; but after progress he becomes punctual, liberal, faithful, and enterprising: "he alone has every virtue, except the force to defend his acquisitions." The state exists in order to protect the latter, to assure the individual's possession of his property. "The object in commerce is to make the individual rich;

the more he gains for himself, the more he augments the wealth of his country." Providing the required protection and repressing crime, "government can pretend to no more" (219–20).

All of these principles, including the one universal historical continuum (from the primitive—hunting and pasturage—to the civilized—agriculture and commerce) from which they proceed, are reiterated and extended by Adam Smith in his advocacy of free trade and governmentally unrestricted competition, *The Wealth of Nations* (1776). For the process that produces the liberty and prosperity of a whole society as the result of innumerable acts of individual self-interest, he coined the since famous metaphor of the "invisible hand" (Smith 1976: 456). Pope, speaking in ethical terms about just the same process—the automatic checks and balances in the contest among every individual's self-love, which issue in the general good—attributed it to the traditional agents:

> Thus God and Nature link'd the gen'ral frame,
> And bade Self-love and Social be the same.
>
> (*An Essay on Man*, 3.318)

What will soon be cited, approvingly or otherwise, as the rationale of capitalism, the justification of private greed as producing public benefit, has grown out of the universalistic discourse of the seventeenth and eighteenth centuries and its effort to subsume difference (and justify strife) by a covering law. The law started out as a decree of God and Nature, prescribing sociability. Pope transmutes it into a decree that guarantees sociability by achieving it, mysteriously, from the total of all possible unsociable (i.e. Hobbesian) actions. The Scottish sociologists find other labels for the decree, wishing to secularize it. It becomes an automatic process, very definitely not to be legislated by anybody. The new invisible hand is but another description of the equally mysterious hand formerly identified as divine providence. But the process so described is simply that of the placeless, timeless market. The law (supply and demand) of commodity exchange is the new will of God, and is quite as difficult to perceive and predict. But we're quite sure that it operates for the best. God in medieval mysticism was once defined as a circle whose circumference is nowhere and whose center everywhere. The market—today we call it the "free" market, the one that everybody wants to join—is as omnipresent and as omnipotent. It covers everything, and its service is perfect freedom—as that of the Lord used to be. I am pointing out that paradoxes invented to describe God were and can be transferred pretty exactly to the market. Historically, in terms of the founding story that tells us what civilization is, the market is its crowning achievement.

Consequently, the people whose profession is to operate in the market are not only bringing culture to savage lands, they are also changing the political order at home. John Millar, a professor of law at Glasgow, makes these changes clear in his *Observations Concerning the Distinction of Ranks in Society*. Before arriving at them, however, he surveys the universal (legendary) trajectory according to which "society" develops, beginning with that which has no ranks at all. He makes the same points as Ferguson only with more examples, and sums up in words that recall Ferguson's: since hunters and fishers acquire no property, "there are no distinctions in the rank of individuals, but those which arise from their personal qualities" (Millar 1771: 121).

Among all the usual absences from savage life of what makes us civilized, Millar emphasizes one that is richly ironic with respect to what Richardson's example would help to make the central preoccupation of the dominant bourgeois form of literature, the novel. This is the absence of sexual warfare. Since the days of the explorers, all forms of sexual licence had vied with cannibalism as the ultimate enormities, the terminal lack of *mos*, that characterized the savage. Now, Millar informs us, savages have little interest in sex at all, being "insensible" and indifferent to women. This, however, does not contradict the earlier consensus: they're indifferent partly because sex is too easy, all impulses being immediately gratifiable for primitives (7–9). His examples come from the usual mixture of contemporary (of which more anon) and ancient sources (like Herodotus and Caesar)—the standard procedure enabled by the identification of them now with us long ago. He can observe, with the usual indulgence, that savage sexuality has therefore no reason for shame or any affected disguise, and can contrast its "plainness and freedom" to our "luxury and intemperance" (14). The real lack that for Millar is a milestone of our progress is that savages treat women utterly without reverence. Women are but physical conveniences, beasts of burden, and laborers in both savage and barbarian societies. Their position is incomparably "improved" in our civilization, with its "attention to the pleasures of sex," which gives them "rank and consequence" and "respect." This immense refinement of our passions begins in pastoral societies, but is not maximized until agricultural ones (38–46).

What Millar here regards as evidence of civilization is a complex of attitudes toward women that will require Freud to begin unraveling and that many of us today would find the opposite of respectful. To elevate women to a pedestal as sexual objects, in a disguise that arouses desire and idealizes repression, and to make the pursuit of these pleasures, in the form of combat, an obsessive theme of artistic production—one may doubt that all this is much of an improvement. One cannot doubt, though, that Millar is linking these traditional forms of western gallantry, as an index to civilization, with the political interests of the dominant class for which he and all his colleagues are the spokesmen.

This class consists of the operators in the market, and the key word for their political interests is "liberty." When a nation advances in opulence and refinement, Millar assures us, the number of merchants, tradesmen, and artificers grows; they become independent and want liberty (185). Some among them get really rich, which puts an end to their former "simplicity of manners." The inevitable "fluctuation of property . . . in all commercial countries" erodes the authority of the "higher ranks." The newly rich have not yet acquired the socially hierarchical bonds of the aristocracy—what Millar calls "that train of dependence" of old landowners. "The hereditary influence of family is therefore diminished. Money becomes more and more the only means of procuring honours and dignities. As no one order of men continues in the exclusive possession of opulence, as every man who is industrious may . . . hope of gaining a fortune," the monarchy and nobility are undermined; privileges accrue to the people; power and wealth are more diffused (185–88).

Millar and his fellows were cool and acute observers of their own society and century. They extrapolated its trends into an historiography that is still accurate as far as it goes. Where it mainly went was to the United States, the ideology of whose founding fathers was largely formed by these Scottish thinkers and written into the American Constitution. The wholly secular government that governs best when it governs least (in the famous Jeffersonian formula); the political structure of checks and balances both within the federal government and between it and the large powers granted to the states; the liberty of competition among individual interests; the elimination of hereditary aristocracy; the extension of voting rights to all adult males; and above all the hope that every man who is industrious may gain a fortune—the desires and principles that shaped the institutions of American democracy are manifest in the pages of such as Ferguson, Smith, and Millar.

And they constitute a quite clear ideology, the program of a particular class in a particular place. For the historiography is accurate only for the development of what economic historians call the "core" countries in the world-system, those that for Millar were opulent and refined. But neither the Scots nor the founding fathers saw the historiography as anything but universal. For the former it was the summit of the single trajectory that led from savagery to civilization; for the latter it was but a bivouac on the way to that summit, which would be attained by the new nation purged of the corruptions of the old. For both, the rising to power of the economic interests of the mercantile bourgeoisie, and all the forms of culture that accompany it, are mandated by the law of nature, which prescribes to humanity a single, identical pathway by which all must progress to our condition. Almost a quarter-century before the Declaration of Independence, Bishop George Berkeley envisioned America as the new summit of civilization, the final recipient of the *translatio studii*. Berkeley, the idealist philosopher, in fact spent much of his own money and three years of his life on a plan to found a college in the Bermudas that never materialized. But scarcely more than a century after he published his poem "On the Prospect of Planting Arts and Learning in America" (1752), the grateful citizens of the new nation, having accomplished its manifest destiny by extending it to the Pacific coast, named after him a town overlooking San Francisco Bay. His name was chosen when the place became the site of a university, the *studium* that follows the *imperium*, as in the Bishop's prophetic words:

> There shall be sung another golden Age,
> The rise of Empire and of Arts,
> The Good and Great inspiring epic Rage,
> The wisest Heads and noblest Hearts.

Not such as *Europe* breeds in her decay;
    Such as she bred when fresh and young,
When heav'nly Flame did animate her Clay,
    By future Poets shall be sung.

Westward the Course of Empire takes its Way;
    The four first Acts already past,
A fifth shall close the Drama with the Day;
    Time's noblest Offspring is the last.

Chapter 19

OBSERVING

French Jesuits in North America

Having universalized the founding legend from which they drew their historiography made the Scots rather less acute observers of the savages who were its starting-point, the ground zero of ourselves. As professional academics, the Scots were indeed not observers at all, but only readers of such pioneer ethnographies as were available. Though most of these *lumières* had traveled on the Continent or in England, none save Ferguson (who was briefly in Philadelphia on an aborted negotiating mission in 1778) ever saw the new world. The major historian among them, William Robertson, who would devote three volumes to North and South America, spent his whole life in and around Edinburgh, with only one brief visit to London. Royal historiographer and principal of the University of Edinburgh for thirty-one years, Robertson was probably the most influential of all in the new world whose history he purported to write. It occurred to none of these men, of course, that first-hand observation might be a necessary, or even useful, qualification for those intending to deliver concise generalizations about savage life. They didn't need to witness it because they already knew what it was; they'd found it in Thucydides, Tacitus, and Virgil. And what they thus knew also insured that they wouldn't be particularly attentive to any contemporary account that blurred such knowledge with conflicting details, confused it with nuances, or contradicted it with facts.

For this reason, it will be instructive to review the principal reports on which Robertson, Ferguson, and Millar all relied for their information about the savages of North America. The most extensive such reports, both of which constantly appear in the citations of Ferguson and Robertson and one in Millar, are those of the Jesuit fathers Lafitau and Charlevoix. Less frequently cited is the earliest serious account of the Iroquois by Cadwallader Colden, a Surveyor-General of New York who, in the course of charting the wilderness, was adopted by the Mohawks. All three of these works are distinguished by their aim, tone, and scope from the mass of traveler's accounts and captivity narratives—this is why the Scots employ them. All are based on some years of experience traveling and living among (or trying to convert) the nations of the Iroquois Confederation and their chief enemies, the Huron, who were the native inhabitants of the main region over which the French and English were contending: from the northern shores of Lake Superior south to Pennsylvania and east to the Atlantic. The three works are, in short, the closest approach the age made, in North America, toward the more or less detailed recording of another way of life, what would later be called ethnography. The approach in all three is far from disinterested, but is nonetheless unhampered by the programmatic progressivism of the *lumières*. It can thus reveal just how programmatic this was, how determined by the universalized assumptions of the founding legend that now equated private property and commerce with civilization.

Colden's *History of the Five Indian Nations* was already anachronistic when first published in New York in 1727. For the Iroquois had become six nations in 1722, with the incorporation of the Tuscaroras who had been driven from North Carolina by colonists. The bulk of their "history," for Colden, is their military participation in the struggles between the British and the French. Colden is most impressed by their form of "government," which he calls an "absolute Republick," in which all office is held by merit, all goods in common, and all "Authority is only the Esteem of the People." Such esteem is "the natural Origin of all Power and Authority among a free People." The five nations, by their ferocity, have dominated all others, and this, along with their love of liberty, patriotism, and fortitude, makes them the equal of the "most renowned *Romans*." It is therefore erroneous to regard them as barbarians, since they're not merely fierce but "politick and judicious" in diplomatic dealings with each other as well as with the French and English (Colden 1747: 2–4).

Cruel they certainly are, Colden admits, but no more so than Achilles was to Hector, nor even than "the Christians burning one another alive, for God's Sake" (5–6). They record the results of their battles on tree trunks. Prisoners must run the gauntlet, and are then offered "to those that have lost any Relation in that or any former Enterprize" (9). If accepted, they are adopted and acquire a new identity; if rejected, they die in torment. The five nations practice lavish hospitality in food and women, and have no slavery nor "Bondage of Wedlock." Women plant and men hunt; the society is centered on military exercise, like Sparta (11–13). "Where no single Person has a Power to compel, the Arts of Persuasion alone must prevail." They consequently cultivate eloquence and love speech-making; the practitioners of this art have an *urbanitas* achieved by few, though all are sensitive to it. Their language is full of compound words and contains no "Labeals," which they therefore cannot pronounce: "they think it ridiculous that they must shut their Lips to speak" (14–15).

And so it is ridiculous—from the other point of view. Colden's evocation of this, even in his random and rudimentary sketch, genuinely acknowledges difference in the act of recording it. The difference is not located on a scale of our values, but is allowed to suggest the illogic in the closed-lip sounds of our own speech. It is pioneer ethnography, one of those rare moments when we can see ourselves as others, as but "a case among cases" (Geertz 1983: 16). It's the kind of moment that never occurs in the universalizing discourse of the period, and of course it doesn't last long. Yet it is there, like the black boy in *Pamela*, ready to be noticed even when ignored by the producers of the discourse. Colden indeed doesn't ignore it; it serves him as part of his primary argument, which is to gain more respect for the Iroquois as allies against the French. This is the aim of his ethnographic outline, and the reason that he insists throughout on the nobly Roman behavior of the five nations. Their pursuit of liberty, honor, and glory as superior to that of luxury and wealth constitutes the virtue of specifically republican Rome. Despite his strategic choice of this comparison to dignify the Iroquois and to deny that they're barbarians, Colden still refuses them full entitlement to civilization. They're subject to drunkenness and are very "superstitious about dreams." "Were they civilized," he concludes, they'd be even more "useful to us" (19).

Colden's notion of the military utility of these people, as possessing no mean sense of politics and government, as well as numerous talents and skills, requires them not to be classed as savages, who can by (legendary) definition possess none of these things. And precisely the old definition will prevail in the Scottish sociologists over all the observations to the contrary made in the very sources they are using. Not that the sources themselves by any means escape either the power of the definition or the current equation of the present savages with our ancient ancestors. For his purposes, Colden equates them not with the savages subdued by the Roman empire, but with the Romans of the nobler period that preceded it. The Jesuits, whose task is larger and more complex and whose sophistication is greater, also assume some variety of the equation while explicitly problematizing the definition in ways wholly ignored by the vastly more influential writers who mined their pages for anecdotal evidence.

Father Lafitau, who was a missionary among the Iroquois, announces his project of equation in his subtitle: to compare the manners of the American savages with those of pagan antiquity. The point of the comparison, for him, is religious: he will demonstrate, against the atheistic *philosophes*, that religion is not merely an artifice of those who wish to legislate fear. Hence he decries from the outset those who present the savage as without any sentiment of religion or divinity, any laws or form of government, who has nothing of man but the shape: "an idea of savages and barbarians which scarcely distinguishes them from beasts" (Lafitau 1724: 1.5–6). This notion is false, and he'll prove it by showing that the savages have just those religious notions that existed in the ancient world. The least interesting half of his thousand pages is taken up with this "proof," which is comparative mythography much in the manner of Vico.

But Lafitau is also a conscientious describer, and is aware of methodological difficulties. Though he knows the Iroquois best, he will report the manners of other nations, since they're all "rather similar." He acknowledges that commerce with Europeans has changed their customs, and will be reporting what these were before such alteration, as gathered from stories he has heard as well as earlier sources (1.25). He recognizes that the ways of life of different tribes can vary greatly: the Huron, for example, "cultivate fields, build cabins, and are rather settled in a single place," while the Algonquins "live a vagabond life at the mercy of chance" (1.91). Despite the breadth of Lafitau's curiosity and concerns, he too has his limits, imposed by the primary assumption that underlies his project, which he shares with the age: that since the savages are earlier versions of us, we already know their history. So Lafitau shows no interest at all in the stories the Iroquois themselves tell of their own history, one of which (the correct one) he blandly records and passes over: they were travelers from a far distant land in the west—i.e. eastern Asia (1.101–102). On the basis of their place-names, Lafitau will later conclude that they came from Thrace. Except for the myths that serve his religious polemic, Lafitau shares the contempt, typical of the age of print, for oral traditions as terribly feeble, untrustworthy, subject to constant loss.

But he nonetheless explicitly denies that the legendary definition of the savage applies to the society he's lived in. At first glance, he admits, savages seem deprived of everything: letters, sciences, laws, regulated worship—"as if they had just emerged from the clay of the earth, or from the forks of Dodonian oaks, according to the extravagant imagination of the pagans." They appear gross, stupid, ignorant, fierce, given to all vice that total liberty can naturally produce. But this view is inaccurate. They have in fact brains and good sense, admirable memories, traces of religion, and a form of government. They are proud and honorable, always self-controlled, courageous, heroic in torments, equable and civil in their fashion, respectful to elders, and show a deference to their equals that is surprising and hard to reconcile with their independence. Though undemonstrative, they are hospitable to a degree that would embarrass Europe. They have also the defects of their qualities—suspicion, treachery, cruelty, vengefulness—but none of our luxurious vices (1.105–106). Lafitau embellishes for a while this theme of the "noble" savage—that though they lack our attainments, they also lack our corruptions—a theme ever popular with missionaries. He excepts from his generalizing the former empires in Mexico and Peru, which were "polished" by comparison to the savages (1.108). The archaic verb he here employs—*policées*—makes a nice pun whose meaning is continually spelled out by the Scots: to be "polished" is to be "policed." Civilization is coercion.

Lafitau wrestles with this paradox on several occasions: that is, how these fiercely independent savages can have self-control, orderly political consultations, a "surprising" deference to others—without any agency of external compulsion, without a police force. This perplexes him. It won't perplex the Scots, who simply declare that the savages don't have any of these things at all. But Lafitau's whole procedure is to let his observations contradict the received idea of the savage as lacking all forms of manners and culture. To deny them government is as unjust, he says, as to deny them religion. Southern tribes have chiefs, while northern ones are oligarchies or aristocracies (1.456). Here and throughout, of course, Lafitau adduces constant parallels to their institutions drawn from classical sources. He also singles out for special praise the dignity and concision of their deliberation in councils and their oratory (1.485). He lauds their mutual respect of each other's autonomy, by which they avoid "an infinity of quarrels," and hardly ever get angry (1.486). Such respect, in the utter absence of coercive laws like ours, still secures both justice and public order, which is the end of any good government (1.501).

Having at length established the existence of religion and government among them, Lafitau continues with a virtual ethnographic survey of social practices and everyday behavior: marriage, education, war, amusement and games, medicine, commerce, and so forth. Agriculture and cooking, the province of women, are treated in some detail, which brings him to the received idea that savages have no sense of planning, storage, or management of food resources. We recall the Virgilian description of those folks born from tree trunks (to which Lafitau has earlier alluded), who "knew not how to yoke the ox, collect / Or store the yield" (*Aeneid* 8.316–17).

So indeed the Iroquois appear: they eat up whatever they have whenever they get it, stuffing themselves as if they never lacked and tolerating hunger without complaint when they have nothing. "I thought at first," Lafitau admits, "this was brutality and lack of foresight; but having examined the affair at length, I understand that they simply cannot conduct themselves in any other way without violating all their laws of civility and good behavior" (2.89). For the Indians are obliged to share all their food with elders, relatives, and friends; it's infamy not to. It's equally infamous not to provide one's share in the frequent communal feasts. Honor requires profusion, so it's no wonder they can't accumulate. A family with but a morsel between it and starvation will share that morsel with one who has nothing. "In Europe we find little disposition in similar cases to a liberality so noble and so magnificent" (2.90–91). Though Lafitau thus concludes, as he often does, with a moral example for us that simply inverts the place of the savage on our familiar scale of values, he has nonetheless succeeded in puncturing the received idea. He has invoked the legendary picture in order to explain it by grounding it in social values that are genuinely other than our own. It's not that they lack sense; they just have a different sense than we do of how to consume what they produce. What the legend takes as the absence of civility is actually a powerful form of civility—their form, not ours.

All of Lafitau's observations, of course, are made in furtherance of his thesis that the savages are comparable to, and temporally arrested in the condition of, the peoples of Mediterranean antiquity. So he offers Greek, Roman, and Old Testament analogues even for the practice that most impressed and horrified all European observers: the routine use and endurance of torture. Even here, though, he can observe the social grounding of the practice. Noting that children are trained to the endurance of pain from the age of five or six, he marvels that they can thus do by nature what the early Christian martyrs did by grace: to scorn life and lose it in the most frightful torments. Not only do they do this with equanimity, but with defiance, it being a point of honor for the victim to sing, boast, insult, and heap verbal abuse on his torturers (2.280–87). Gory details of this practice had constituted the sensational appeal of travelers' accounts (as they had of saints' lives) for centuries; Lafitau doesn't spare them, either, but is equally concerned with the social and ritual context in which they occur.

For his thesis is finally a larger matter than the discovery of ancient analogues for present savage practices. He wants to show that the natives have a society and constitute a culture, and is thus content to describe many practices without worrying about analogues. So he details the gentle treatment and gradual integration of slaves (prisoners of war) into Iroquois families as substitutes for those lost in battle (2.308–309). He describes the ceremonial feasts and dances that accompany their trading and diplomatic missions (2.332–34). In both these activities he has earlier observed their uses of seashell necklaces as ritual presents, a form of reckoning, of adornment, and a means of recalling events; he thus perceives the multiple functions of wampum as both words and money (1.502–503). He marvels at their medical skills and the healthfulness of their sauna baths, which do summon up the bathing habits of antiquity (2.368–72). But in spite of his thesis, he's too good an observer to succumb to the requisite and popular notion that their languages are some vestigial or debased form of Latin, Greek, or Hebrew. He finds their system of pronunciation too different: the Huron and Iroquois cannot produce *l*s—they make *r*s instead; and they have no labials (2.468). He finds the barbarian languages extremely difficult to learn even after years of study because they have such a different "economy" from ours (2.474). Their languages consist, he says, only of verbs, which they manipulate with such admirable artifice as to supply the other parts of speech. And he ends, alas, not wishing to bore the reader with any further details of their linguistic "economy" (2.489).

Doubtless Lafitau had a keen sense of how much (or how little) difference his audience could stand. Within his limits, which are large, he has at any rate paid serious attention to a wide range of differences, explaining them as social practices and continually refusing to see them as the mere absence of our own. His later, higher-ranking (in the Society of Jesus), and better-known colleague, Father Charlevoix, has both narrower limits and loftier literary ambitions, but will provide even fuller observations of the same kind. Charlevoix is a self-appointed historian of the whole newly discovered globe and the Jesuit missions to it; before embarking on his history of New France, he produced multivolumes on South America, Japan, and Santo Domingo. His treatment of Canada is mainly an institutional history (and defense) of Jesuit efforts to convert the savages and the difficulty these encountered—from both the intended beneficiaries and the crown. The treatment is enlivened in its final part by a journal (in the form of letters to a duchess) of his inspection tour of North America from 1720 to 1723, which took him from the Great Lakes all the way down the Mississippi and finally shipwrecked him on the coast of Florida. In his preface, Charlevoix makes elegant excuses for the meanness of his subject—not all history can "smell of majesty" (Charlevoix 1744: 1.ii)—and defends it as a success story to the greater glory of both the Church and France, the only nation, he says, "who had the secret of earning the affection of the Americans" (1.vii).

His limits are clear enough, and within them he is little disposed to acknowledge the differences he discovers. Particular severity, of course, is shown to those aspects of the natives' character and beliefs that make them recalcitrant to conversion. Of these, the most paradoxical is the ease with which they often assent to Christian teaching. Because "they hate nothing so much as dispute," it's very hard to know when they're truly converted (1.188). They may readily accept what they're told of Christianity out of pure agreeableness, or more often laziness. Or they may be deceitful, "duplicitous," and otherwise defective—this is Charlevoix's description of what he quotes a Huron as saying to a priest: "you tell us many fine things, and there is nothing in all you teach us that may not be true, and that's fine for you others who come from beyond the sea. But don't you see that since we live in a world so different from yours, there must also be another Paradise for us, and thus another way to get there" (1.189). No, of course, he literally cannot "see" this, and attributes such insistence on difference to ignorance, superstition, unconcern for what does not strike the senses, and excessive credulity (1.191). Charlevoix is baffled and irritated throughout the book by the Americans' strange (to him) mixture of materialism and spirituality. On the one hand, they're children who can't look beyond immediate sensual gratifications; on the other, they live in a world animated by spirits and omens, and receive divine commands in dreams. They're sunk in hopeless confusion and obscene ritual.

Fortunately, when he leaves the subject of the natives' convertibility, Charlevoix can reveal his own fascination with the innumerable oddities and differences of another way of life. Part of this interest stems from his wish to be interesting, according to the typical and urbane neoclassical conception of history as a form of rhetorical entertainment. He cultivates the high style that so much influenced the age of Pope, Gibbon, and the Scottish thinkers, producing prose of smoothly balanced elegance. Also, when not directly regarding the natives as raw material for Christianity, he has no overriding theory about them and is free to expatiate on whatever strikes him, or whatever he thinks will strike us. He does, however, at one point make his own tentative contribution to the vexed question of the Americans' origins. After an amusing review of the wildly various speculations on this subject, he suggests that the only means to decide the matter would be by linguistic comparison. This is because their own customs and traditions are much too fluid to be useful, not being preserved in writing. They are hence subject, over centuries, to endless effacements and reinventions (3.36–37). The utter untrustworthiness of oral tradition was the assumption of an age newly fixated (by print) on writing, and it doubled the denial of history to the savage: he can't have it because he doesn't write (whatever was inscribed on tree trunks or whatever symbolic recall was made possible by beads never counts as writing); and what he does have of it orally can't be right. Thus disqualifying the native as a witness to his own condition, Charlevoix goes on to a bit of linguistic comparison to establish at least the possibility of the hypothesis that he favors: the North Americans are the sons of Noah.

Father Charlevoix, however, is far more of a *raconteur* than a thesis-pusher, and he hits his ethnographic stride in the letters that constitute the journal of his trip. These are both chatty and reflective, full of concrete detail, anecdote, and judgments that confront difference (sometimes contradictorily) rather than erase it. He describes the government of the northern nations, frankly generalizing on the basis of the Huron of Detroit (3.266–68). They have both elected and hereditary (through the female line) chiefs of very little power. All decisions are made by a variety of councils: of clans (whose members are often picked by women), of elders, of warriors (who have no rank). There can thus be any leader of battle but no real "commander." The soldiers can desert if they like; yet the chief is virtually uncontradicted. "So true is it," Charlevoix remarks, "that among men who conduct themselves by reason, and who are guided by honor and patriotic zeal, independence does not at all destroy subordination, and that free and voluntary obedience is always that on which one may more surely rely" (3.269). He had earlier observed of these savages that "there are no men more attached . . . to their families and to their native country" (3.176). Charlevoix calls these attachments "honor" and "patriotism," and seizes on them to try to explain what for European observers is the central problem and paradox of savage society: the coexistence, in the absence of external compulsion, of independence and subordination, of freedom and discipline. This repeatedly perplexed Lafitau, and will become especially problematic for Charlevoix when he considers, in a moment, the upbringing of children.

But first he concludes his survey of their politics by praising their skills of deliberation and diplomacy. In their councils they "proceed with a wisdom, maturity, skill, and probity that would have done honor to the Aereopagus and the Senate" (3.269–70). Charlevoix deplores their equation of honor with vengeance, which they fanatically pursue, but is quick to point out that all the politeness of Christian Europe hasn't yet eliminated this either. In conducting foreign relations, the natives are appropriately dignified and deceitful, and the Iroquois are especially praised for their ability to play off French and English interests against each other (3.271).

However, there yet remain two great defects in savage society according to Charlevoix: first, they have no system of public criminal justice (revenge being a family affair); second, there is no punishment of children or of drunks (both being considered as not knowing what they do). Charlevoix dismisses the first as of no great consequence, since they lack the principal source of our civil disorders, "interest"—that is, the profit motive; they never dream of amassing wealth and care not for the morrow. But the second is a "great disorder," like the lack of subordination, and is even more obvious in domestic than in public life. Within the family, each member does as he pleases; father, mother, and children often live like persons assembled by chance whom no bond unites (3.272–73). What Charlevoix means by this is apparently the absence of a paternal hierarchy. Parents, he observes later, show great tenderness for their children, in a "purely animal" way, without caring to instruct them to be virtuous. So children show no respect at all for parents, especially for fathers (3.309). Later still, he is amazed at the perpetual and in-credible care that mothers take of infants: they carry them everywhere, are never without them, and nurse them until the age of six or seven (3.322). Children are, though, early inspired with "certain principles of honor" imparted indirectly by telling them stories of glorious ancestral deeds. Consequently, the children wish only "for occasions to imitate what one has made them admire." Children are never threatened, Charlevoix says, because no one is regarded as having the right to con-strain them. Instead, a man will tell a misbehaving child, "you dishonor me"; and this is rarely not effective. Children are extremely sensitive to reproaches because shame is their strongest passion. One would think, Charlevoix concludes, that a childhood so "badly disciplined" would produce turbulent and corrupt youth. But not at all: they're "naturally" calm; "reason" must guide them (3.325–26).

So the "great disorder" of the lack of punishment turns out to be no disorder at all. Charlevoix is struggling, and falling into contradictions, trying to understand a form of social conditioning that he is unable to conceptualize. He marshals all the categories he knows—honor, reason, nature, animality—in the effort to account for what is wholly unaccountable in his world: that disciplined and self-controlled adults are produced by letting them run wild as kids. But as his own evidence shows, they are not let run wild at all; it just looks that way to us (as, for example, the way Japanese infants are treated might look to us today). Occasionally he comes close to identifying the kind of control employed—something like "shame"—in traditional cultures where individual identity is overwhelmingly dependent on the social group, is established almost exclusively by belonging to a whole series of subgroups, where persons are virtually constituted by what the neighbors think. Other anec-dotes Charlevoix tells also provide glimpses of such a society. In one of them, a chief adjudicates a dispute between the owner and the finder of a lost necklace. He de-cides for the finder, but adds that if she doesn't want to be accused of avarice she will return it to the owner in consideration of a small present; they agree to this. It's "nice to observe," remarks Charlevoix, "that fear of being regarded avaricious has indeed as much power over the mind of savages as fear of punishment would, and that in general these peoples behave more by principles of honor than by any other motive" (3.276). "Honor" as social reputation, and how profoundly this is internal-ized by individuals, are indeed the issues. Charlevoix is familiar with the first, but doesn't quite grasp how the second makes external compulsion unnecessary, though he sees the results as identical.

He doesn't quite grasp it because to him, and to everyone who observed in this period, these savages incarnate individualism; they are seen as atoms, whose com-bination into social organisms is a source of constant wonder. They're atoms partly because that's what the legend describes them as, the enabling (for us; disabling for them) fiction that postulates their ignorance of any (our) form of social life. They do as they like and have no police force; how can they possibly constitute a soci-ety? The great distinction between the observers and the theorizers is that the for-mer allow this question to be genuinely posed and struggle to answer it; for the latter it is purely rhetorical. In the now familiar litany of praises for savage capacities—their keen senses, skill at navigation on water and in forests, excellent memories, eloquence, firmness of judgment, unimaginable endurance of torture—Charlevoix includes, as did Lafitau, their character and their social relations. They have an equanimity of spirit and self-control that we rarely attain from philosophy and religion (3.304–305). They deal with each other with a gentleness and respect not found among the more civilized. The young respect the old; they never quarrel with oaths or obscenities. Now Charlevoix attributes all this admirable behavior to their essential principle of individualism: "a man owes nothing to another." "From this bad maxim," he says, "they draw the good consequence of never wronging one who has done them no offense" (3.308). From an atomistic principle mysteriously springs a remarkable social cohesion; from a refusal to be obligated arises an incredible mutual obligingness; from an assertion of self-sufficiency is produced the very definition of justice.

This curious magic that somehow brings social order from the great disorder of their casual family life, their lack of subordination, and their refusals to punish has a very familiar ring. It's that old neoclassical harmony generated from discord, the blaring instruments of self-love uniting in the symphony of social concord conducted by the invisible hand. Charlevoix's language, the categories of his thinking, are describing *us*, not them. And this is the supreme irony in the European perception of the savage at the moment when modern empires are being formed: the untrammeled individualism seen in the savage world is not there at all, but here. It is we, not they, who require mysterious agencies to create public benefits from private profits, social cohesion from individual competition. The model of our society, whether we endorse covetousness, like Adam Smith, or deplore it, like the Jesuits, is projected onto that of the savages. They are seen as infernal and inverted doubles of what we both admire and fear in ourselves—at once opposite and identical to us.

Listen closely to this typical summation of Charlevoix: the savages who appear so "contemptible" at first sight are really the most "contemptuous" of mortals. They are fiercely proud, jealous, independent, suspicious, treacherous, deceitful, and vindictive. They do not value "the qualities of the heart": friendship, compassion, gratitude, emotional attachment. "They have something of all that," yes, but it isn't in their "hearts"; it is rather the result of "reflection." The care they take of the sick and abandoned as well as their admirable hospitality are "only the consequence of their persuasion that all should be common among men" (3.309).

Except for this final "persuasion," all the items in this criticism of self-assumed superiority and rational, calculated behavior in the absence of truly "felt" social and moral bonds apply to our society. They are its standard indictments in the many satires of the period, like Swift's in *Gulliver's Travels* (1726), where all "contemptuous" humanity is made to appear entirely "contemptible," or Gay's in *The Beggar's Opera* (1728), where calculation reigns supreme in the social world, wholly overpowering any emotional attachment at all. Only the motive is different: they calculate the common good and we the individual profit; otherwise Charlevoix's discourse joins what it divides—our world and theirs. It reflects, in other words, precisely our anxieties about our own society. Postulating of them what is true only of us, that individual independence and gratification are the mainsprings of society, results in the problematic paradoxes of freedom and discipline, equality and obedience, and the need to explain how any real society can possibly exist. It's we who need the explanation, and it was Hobbes who, first making the postulation, found it: we need a police force, a big one. That the need is consequent on the postulate is our problem, thrown into relief and intensified by the observed fact that the savages don't need one.

What they have in its place is not quite understood by Charlevoix, who yet sees that they have something, and that it works. He offers a final contrast of their character and ours that takes the appropriate form of a series of paradoxes: savages seem to lead a miserable life, but are perhaps the happiest folk on earth, being exempt from our cupidities. They have a mélange of manners: the fiercest and the gentlest, the defects of carnivorous beasts and the virtues of heart and mind that do honor to humanity. "One would think at first that they have no form of government, know neither laws nor subordination, and that living in entire independence, they are guided only by chance and unbridled caprice; however, they enjoy almost all the advantages that a well regulated authority can procure in the most polished/policed [policées] nations." They have "principles and usages . . . based on good sense" that take the place of law and supply authority. They may have less "delicacy" in their sentiments than we, but none of our hypocrisy or inequality in birth or rank (3.341–42). Here, "good sense" joins honor and patriotism as the categories Charlevoix has at his disposal to explain how a social organism with no police force can function. He cannot quite conceptualize the internalized mechanisms of social integration and control whose operation he has described throughout.

The most interesting of these, which he has mentioned before and now goes on to detail without much comment, is dreams. The savages regularly fast and take drugs in order to induce dreams propitious to a wide range of activities. Everyone, Charlevoix tells us, has a personal tutelary spirit, whose symbol is chosen after a week's fast in early adolescence according to what one dreams about most (3.346). In later life, dreams are accorded enormous importance as divine promptings and orders (3.353–55). Their functions are highly practical, determining strategies in war and informing hunters where to locate prey. Such enactment of dreams is also part of communal ritual. Charlevoix describes a Festival of Dreams held at the end of winter, two weeks of frenetic and amusing activity that looks like chaos to him. The people assume ridiculous disguises and run around smashing things, turning them upside down, and demanding that one guess their dreams, whereupon he must give them the dreamed object. Charlevoix sees in this an opportunity to get back at whomever has offended you, and several of his anecdotes indeed show the acting-out of hostility; for example, stabbing at a Frenchman's clothes seems a symbolic form of killing him. The Iroquois call this event "turning the brain upside down" (3.356–57).

Its obvious resemblance to European carnival is unremarked by Charlevoix, as is its obvious contrast to all the everyday behavior of dignified, disciplined, self-control he has previously described. Having defined the society as supremely individualistic and so been compelled to attribute its routine social orderliness to good sense, honor, and patriotism, he has no way at all to relate those categories to this strange interlude. It's just there, another weird curiosity. But it is there, observed and recorded, as the kind of practice characteristic of societies that are far from individualistic, in which the pressures of maintaining a socially prescribed and conferred identity (what Charlevoix would call "honor") require and receive this form of release. The dream festival, like so much else that is observed, reveals the extent to which the definition imposed on their society is but a projection of our own.

Like Lafitau, Charlevoix is also rich in all sorts of observations that acknowledge difference quite neutrally, or by relating it to social circumstances and social effects, even when these contravene our customary values. Thus he urbanely allows that the prostitution and concubinage practiced among the Huron differ from marriage only in the noncontraction of engagement. Children born of any union were all on the same footing, which "produced no inconvenience in a country where there are no inheritances to collect" (3.327). With respect to agriculture, Charlevoix is particularly interested (as a man of *bon goût*) in its results. Taking its practice for granted, he regards errant savages who do no cultivating at all as clearly exceptional. Women sow and tend the crops; everyone helps with the harvest. A delicate species of corn is grilled on the cob and is very tasty. Cornbread, to be properly appreciated, must be eaten hot (3.331–33). No such urbane connoisseurship is shown to the successful magic—accurate prophecies and cures—of those ecstatic charlatans, the medicine men; this is due simply to the devil (3.362–63). But Charlevoix goes on to observe that both they and many women have many effective, mostly herbal, remedies for all kinds of accidents and illnesses, including venereal and epileptic. Their sovereign specific is the sauna bath, which he precisely describes (3.365–67).

None of their remedies, alas, would avail them against the imported bacteria that did not exist on their continent. The saddest thing that Charlevoix observes is also symbolic of the fate of these savages in subsequent discourse. This is their decimation by disease. By the time he gets to them, the Huron are so depopulated that they can no longer fight the Iroquois. Like almost all European explorers and settlers before him, Charlevoix is baffled by the rapidity with which the natives die on contact with white men. The number of sick infants who died after receiving baptism was so great that it led the Huron to suspect that the priests were killing them. Charlevoix recounts and condemns as despair the logical conclusion drawn by the Indians a century before: "Each nation has its gods; our misfortune is to have those who are weaker than your god and cannot prevent him from destroying us." The then missionary offered them another explanation: since they had now heard the sacred Word, their unbelief in it was inexcusable, so God was punishing them with plagues; soon "He might take a rod of fire, which would exterminate them" (1.191–93). This attitude persists today among Protestants who preach to Amazonian tribes that their sufferings are deserved because they are slayers of Christ, both historically, as descendants of the lost tribes of Israel, and metaphorically, as unbelievers in the Gospel of the Prince of Peace (Lewis 1989). In 1721, Charlevoix, comparing what he sees to what he's read in Cartier, Champlain, and La Salle, guesses that the Indians around the Great Lakes are less than a twentieth of their number 150 years before (3.302). In Natchez, Charlevoix finds on the same basis an even greater and faster diminution of the savages; whole nations have disappeared in forty years (3.429). Baffled by the cause, but fully recognizing that their dying off is coincident with European contact, Charlevoix blames government policy for not gathering the savages into settlements far removed from those of European colonists and traders (the Jesuit method), and so preventing them from "diminishing astoundingly, disappearing inconceivably" (3.90–91).

The disappearance of the savages that Lafitau and Charlevoix so richly chronicle from the pages of the Scottish writers, who used both as sources, is no less astounding, though all too conceivable. For the sources are simply not allowed to interfere with the conception of the savage inherited from the founding legend and enshrined in their historiography. Not even the Jesuits' deliberate denials that these savages are like that—wholly without *mos* and *cultus*—can counter the determining power of the ancient myth. And all the evidence the Jesuits present that the savages are otherwise—that they possess manners, agriculture, government, diplomacy, eloquence, good sense, honor, and patriotism—is overlooked by the ideology of commercial and sentimental progress now identified with the myth's picture of civilization. The combination will prove as potent as our germs: the fiction determines what is seen and the ideology what is not. And the contemporary savage will vanish between them, erased by the discourse that defines him as our long-dead ancestor even as his actual death is brought about by our unwitting infection of his health and our willed destruction of his forests.

Chapter 20

༖

OVERLOOKING

William Robertson and America

At the summit of his career, William Robertson rushed his *History of America* into print in 1777, since, as he explains in the preface, the portion of it dealing with North America had just been overtaken by events of still uncertain outcome. Those events would change the meaning of "American" from the native inhabitants of the hemisphere (who were *amériquains* to the French Jesuits) to the ex-colonist citizens of its new northern republic. Robertson, renowned in his day for the sonority of his style, conceives his history of the whole hemisphere in the grand Augustan manner. He will record the march of civilization as the progressive peopling of the earth mainly by the agency of commerce. His discourse is the culmination of the neoclassical repudiation of difference and the clearest expression of the universalistic confidence that the "earth" has one history, and it's ours. So he needn't really have worried about the War of Independence changing much; his history of the European conquest of the western hemisphere remains just that—the history of that place begins with our invasion and is vindicated for as long as our domination of it continues. This is why his book was so popular and influential in the United States. Its whole design, which is but the legend rehistoricized in the manner of Ferguson and Smith, is the supposedly factual equivalent of Berkeley's poem and tells the new nation what it delighted to hear: "Time's noblest offspring is the last."

Robertson's general bias and tone is typified by his continual insistence that the decimation of the natives in the new world is due simply to their inferior nature. They have "a more feeble constitution than the inhabitants of the other hemisphere. They could neither perform the same work, nor endure the same fatigue, with men whose organs were of a more vigorous constitution." They're lazy, hate labor, and so are subject to disease (Robertson 1787: 1.243–44). He is aware, of course, that all travelers had marveled at the incredible acuteness of the Indians' senses (2.109), their splendid physiques, and the total absence among them of physical deformities. The latter he explains as the effect of hardship and abortion; their nature is still "feeble" (2.68–70). His odd insistence on this is, however, a logical consequence of precisely the legendary view of both the people and the landscape: being uncultivated, they are necessarily weak. Except for the monarchies of Peru and Mexico,

> the rest of this continent was possessed by small, independent tribes, destitute of arts and industry, and neither capable to correct the defects, or desirous to meliorate the condition of that part of the earth allotted to them for their habitation. Countries, occupied by such people, were almost in the same state as if they had been without inhabitants. Immense forests covered a great part of the uncultivated earth; and as the hand of industry had not taught the rivers to run in a proper channel, many of the most fertile plains were overflowed with inundations. (2.14–15)

Thus the "more noble animals," like the horse, were absent from America, while, owing to the lack of cultivation, "the active principle of life wastes its force in the productions of [the] inferior form"—that is, reptiles and insects. "Nature" itself is "less vigorous" there. Bears and wolves are smaller than Europe's. Birds, however, are anomalous; it is strange that America should produce the condor, "where the quadrupeds are so dwarfish and dastardly" (2.18–22).

This is the legend's psychobiology imposed with a vengeance on the whole un-suspecting taxonomy of the continent's fauna. Nor are the flora omitted; all, being unimproved, are in a childish state of weakness. And where even the quadrupeds are dastardly, we already know what to expect of the people. They furnish us, says Robertson, in the self-congratulatory voice of the modern who knows more of the world than classical antiquity, with wider views than the Greeks and Romans had. Man in America

> appears under the rudest form in which we can conceive him to subsist. We behold communities just beginning to unite, and may examine the sentiments and actions of human beings in the infancy of social life, while they feel but imperfectly the force of its ties, and have scarcely relinquished their native liberty. The state of primeval sim-plicity, which was known in our continent only by the fanciful description of poets, really existed in the other. The greater part of its inhabitants were strangers to indus-try and labour, ignorant of arts, and almost unacquainted with property, enjoying in common the blessings which flowed spontaneously from the bounty of nature.

Mexico and Peru always excepted, so closely do the inhabitants of the western hemisphere resemble each other, that any "diversity" in their "manners and insti-tutions" may be safely ignored. "The denomination of Savage may be applied to them all" (2.49–50).

Reality confirms the fanciful poet, whose legend is no longer past, but present history. As filtered through Hobbes, Vico, Vattel, Ferguson, and Millar (among many others), the legend, universalized in philosophy and law, now presents itself once again as fact. The voice of modernity can thus plume itself on its empirical objectivity. Nations that "remain uncivilized" are hard for us to know, Robertson avers, since we all are our own "standards of excellence." Men "affix the idea of perfection and happiness to those attainments which resemble their own," and where these are lacking, "confidently pronounce a people barbarous and miserable. Hence the mutual contempt with which the members of communities, unequal in their degrees of improvement, regard each other. Polished nations . . . are apt to view rude nations with peculiar scorn, and, in the pride of superiority, will hardly allow their occupations, their feelings, or their pleasures, to be worthy of men." Rude peoples seldom fall under "a candid and discerning eye" (2.51). One might hastily conclude that Robertson is here describing, with preternatural awareness, his own attitude. He is, of course, but quite unwittingly. The "peculiar scorn" that finds quadrupeds dastardly is not his, though; his eye is that more discerning one. For he goes on to distinguish his British and objective self from Spanish exploiters on the one hand (who denigrate the Indians because they want to enslave them: 2.52–53), and French system-builders on the other (who find them noble). Robertson himself will avoid conjecture, eschew system and study to avoid either admiration or contempt. He will also examine critically the "superficial accounts of vulgar travellers . . . and endeavour to discover what they wanted sagacity to observe" (2.56).

It's not really he, though; Robertson is using the editorial "we" at this point, associating his readers with this blithely assumed superiority, the arrogance of which is truly staggering, considering his blindness to what the non-superficial accounts did observe. But he is well aware of what these accounts assumed, and this furnishes his "method," which is to describe the individual. Robertson articulates this governing assumption, the projection of our (European) society, as a universal principle: "man existed as an individual before he became the member of a community." And this is especially evident in rude folk.

> Their political union is so incomplete, their civil institutions and regulations so few, so simple, and of such small authority, that men in this state ought to be viewed rather as independent agents, than as members of a regular society. The character of a savage results almost entirely from his sentiments or feelings as an individual, and is but little influenced by his imperfect subjection to government and order. (2.56–57)

What perplexed Lafitau and what Charlevoix labored to explain by paradoxes simply do not exist for Robertson. Where the observers found and wrestled with all kinds of evidence of communal bonds and social order that belied the assumption of individualism, Robertson finds none. Where the observers saw that the lack of our forms of regulation did not mean the absence of regulation, Robertson sees nothing. He never looks; he just overlooks. One wonders, indeed, how much he ever read of the works he cites. It is obvious, though, that he's read his colleagues Ferguson and Millar, whose views he reiterates at length.

Having defined the savage as the perfect hedonist, Robertson goes on to claim that the "feeble" constitutions of the Indians make their desires "languid." They

lack the "restraint and delicacy" of our sexual relations, and pay women no attention, except in the warmer climates, where the "animal passion" is "more ardent."
Since hardly any limit "is imposed on the gratification of desire, either by religion, laws, or decency, the dissolution of their manners is excessive" (2.66–68). The
limitless gratification of desire is part of the general improvidence of hunters, who
are gluttonous and abstinent by turns (2.82). The savage has no foresight, no thrift,
no computation; his behavior "differs . . . little from the thoughtless levity of children" (2.86–87). Although philosophers can argue whether "man has been improved by the progress of arts and civilization in society, . . . that women are
indebted to the refinements of polished manners for a happy change in their state,
is a point which can admit of no doubt. To despise and degrade the female sex is
the characteristic of the savage state in every part of the globe." Women may be
overworked in "unpolished societies," but in savage ones they're mere "beasts of
burden" (2.98–100). Children after infancy are left "at entire liberty"; hence the
absence of filial love and parental veneration; their families are like "persons assembled by accident" (2.104).

Though the last phrase is from Charlevoix, this whole description of their defective domestic and sentimental economy is largely Millar's. Ferguson's picture of
their political one will follow, after Robertson emphasizes the bestiality of hunters.
They at least are active, sagacious, and acute, unlike fishers—especially those (in
South America) who intoxicate the water—for whom Robertson reserves his most
peculiar scorn as the laziest of all, the most lacking in *mos* (2.108–109). He allows
that "we scarcely meet with any nation of hunters, which does not practice some
species of cultivation. Their agriculture, however, is neither extensive nor laborious" (2.111–12). It consists only of a few easily grown plants that merely fill gaps between kills, and often not even that. Because they have not domesticated the local
cattle ("knew not how to yoke the ox," we recall again) and cannot work metal, they
can't possibly depend on agriculture. These two skills are what give us our "empire
over nature," which civilized man changes and improves, cultivating the earth with
the aid of "animals whom he has tamed and employed in labour." By contrast to this
domination, "a savage, in that uncultivated state wherein the Americans were discovered, is the enemy of the other animals, not their superior. He wastes and destroys, but knows not how to multiply or to govern them" (2.117–21). With no
superior domination, no control and management of labor forces, even such agriculture as the hunters possess doesn't really count as agriculture; nor do they really
count as people. They're just "other animals." "A nation of hunters," Robertson
continues, resembles "beasts of prey," solitary and unsocial. "As long as hunting continues to be the chief employment of man to which he trusts for subsistence, he can
hardly be said to have occupied the earth" (2.122–23).

The worst thing about hunting, of course, is that it does not encourage "the
idea of property." The small results of chancy kills are shared, the "united efforts
of a tribe, or village . . . belonging equally to all." Hunting grounds are of the tribe;
"no individual arrogates a right to any district of these." "Even agriculture has not

introduced among them a complete idea of property. As the men hunt, the women labour together, and . . . they enjoy the harvest in common." Some tribes have public granaries; others,

> though they lay up separate stores, they do not acquire such an exclusive right of property, that they can enjoy superfluity, while those around them suffer want. Thus the distinctions arising from the inequality of possessions are unknown. . . . [B]eing strangers to property, they are unacquainted with what is the great object of laws and policy, as well as the chief motive which induced mankind to establish the various arrangements of regular government. (2.124–25)

But how, one might ask, can these folks possibly have such a practice of sharing things equally? They're pure individualists, solitary and unsocial like brutes, guided only by their private feelings and gratifications, childish hedonists, having no foresight at all, living only in the present. The total contradiction between the practices described and the legendary assessment of the savage character at least gave pause to the observers. Lafitau called their communal sharing "civility"; Charlevoix called it "honor." Robertson regards it as bestiality, and the contradiction gives him no pause at all. He is discerning and sagacious, cutting through the vulgar accounts to the principles that matter. He is empirically objective.

The utter vacuity of these claims should give us lots of pause; though empty as assertions, they are pregnant with excuses for erasure. It is the grimmest of paradoxes, first visible in the natural lawyers, that in the name of a covering law objectively discerned from an empirical survey of phenomena, we can do to the savage whatever the hell we please. And what pleases us came from the enacted legend that became that law that imposes our history and our story of it as progress on the rest of the globe. The science that will excuse our pleasure in the next century is nascent in the pages of Robertson, the science of racism, which is yet another, the most contemporarily authoritative, discursive empowerment of the categories of the founding legend. It allows us to deny that savages can have a society at all, demoting them from children to subhumans. The denial as well as the demotion are clear in Robertson, in defiance of the evidence available to him at the time. Our longest pause should be to reflect on the overwhelming power of fiction become ideology to determine what we see and what we don't, in both the world and the language we use to describe it.

To Robertson, the principles that matter are Ferguson's and Millar's. "Wherever the idea of property is not established, there can be no distinction among men, but what arises from personal qualities." Thus in times of war aged wisdom is consulted, and courage leads; but in peace "all pre-eminence ceases" and everyone lives "on a level." Savages are "independent" and disdain to be otherwise (2.125). "Where the right of separate and exclusive possessions is not introduced, the great object of law and jurisdiction does not exist"; hence, "no visible form of government is established" there. Where all things "are considered as belonging to the public stock, there can hardly be any such subject of difference . . . among the members of the same community, as will require the hand of authority to interpose in order to adjust it" (2.127). The absence of private property makes the state unnecessary; and the absence of its enforced obligations is the definition of their savagery. We recall that the culture-bringer in our founding legend was also and always a lawgiver; culture came with compulsion. "No statute," Robertson continues, "imposes any service as a duty, no compulsory laws oblige them to perform it" (2.127). Such duties as they may perform, like vengeance, are private matters. "Such was the form of political order" east of the Mississippi from the St. Lawrence to Paraguay for all those fishers and hunters who had some, however rudimentary, agriculture; those who had none were worse.

Robertson mentions a few exceptions (like the Seminole, who had hereditary chiefdoms) as those which prove the general rule (2.128–29). Also thus exceptional are the Natchez and some people in the Andes, who practiced a more settled tillage, and thus demonstrate the evolution that is the (only possible) history of the world. "Among people in this state, avarice and ambition have acquired objects . . . ; views of interest allure the selfish; the desire of preeminence excites the enterprising; dominion is contested by both; and passions unknown to man in his savage state prompt the interested and the ambitious to encroach on the rights of their fellow-citizens"—and this is "progress" (2.137). It's also Hobbesian individualism, tamed by the invisible hand into the best of all possible worlds, the one that requires the state to protect the property that it must leave individuals free to acquire. Thus law (as we know it) is born, the law that savages so lamentably lack. Their desire of vengeance comes up again, which, far from being related to anything we might think of as justice, "resembles the instinctive rage of an animal, rather than the passion of a man" (2.142). Similarly, their method of waging war is mere ferocity, ungoverned by rules of fair play. "They fight not to conquer, but to destroy," whereas "polished nations," by obtaining glory or "territory, may terminate a war with honour." They ambush, never engage in pitched battle, use camouflage, commit arson at night, and if opposed, retreat. "They regard it as extreme folly to meet an enemy who is on his guard, upon equal terms, or to give battle in an open field." They think it a disgrace to lose men in battle. Robertson, however, extends his indulgence to all this unsportsmanlike conduct so repugnant to civilization; it's not really due to their "dastardly spirit," but is simply "adapted to their condition" (2.146–48). Beasts will be beasts.

The grand finale to the theme of their bestiality is provided, of course, by examples of their competition to refine the lengthiest tortures of their prisoners, who are to display "undaunted fortitude." The latter is denigrated, as usual, as training not in "valour" but in "patience"; warriors are valued not for "their ability to offend, but . . . their capacity to suffer" (2.159). This neatly expresses one of the many diametric oppositions between our culture and theirs: we value injuring others; they value enduring injury themselves. To us, control over others' bodies is what the law grants—by exacting labor, awarding sexual possession, or imprisoning criminals; to them, lacking this notion of law, control over their own bodies is what counts. Robertson, naturally, is tempted into no such contrast, but only into sentimental and disingenuous revulsion: "a scene ensues, the bare description of which is enough to chill the heart with horror, wherever men have been accustomed, by milder institutions, to respect their species, and to melt into tenderness at the sight of human sufferings" (2.153). Disingenuous, given two of our "milder" institutions at the time: slavery (where it was sometimes cheaper to work slaves to death and buy new ones than to maintain them), and public executions (such popular spectacles that aristocrats had their servants occupy front-row places for them hours beforehand).

Still, the savages' endurance of torture and very ability to wage war confront Robertson with examples of communal solidarity and social bonding that even he can't quite ignore. So he allows them a virtue called "attachment to the community" (2.223). However they could acquire such a thing remains an uninterrogated mystery. He also mentions their love of dancing, emphasizing the lack of sexual interest in it, as both ceremony and pastime, and noting that the war dance appears to mime the coordinated actions of a group (2.199). But none of this is permitted to modify the general description, frequently reiterated, of the savage as the atomistic individual, incapable of "regular industry" in any form of labor (2.178), indolent, phlegmatic, easily distracted like a child, without government or history (2.214). Since human nature "is every where the same," says Robertson (echoing Hume), climate and society determine it in every stage of its "progress" (2.211). The stages are known in advance, extrapolated from the founding legend and become an historiography from which no one can escape. The savage stage is determined precisely by the absence of society; it is ground zero. There, man "stands as much detached from the rest of his species, as if he had formed no union with them"; there, "the pride of independence produces almost the same effects with interestedness in a more advanced state of society, it refers every thing to a man himself, and renders the gratification of his own wishes the measure and end of conduct." From this egotism spring their hard hearts, indifference to suffering, and emotional coldness (2.215).

With this comparison, Robertson unwittingly makes transparent the projection of our world onto theirs. It is indeed our profit motives that make our individual gratification the measure of our conduct; we are those lonely, self-referential, and unsocial creatures, cherishing our independence and being brutally indifferent to others. That's us, all right, as Robertson partly says; but it's certainly not them. Robertson and his colleagues have made it them, by postulating their mythical independence, imposed by the legendary definition of the savage as without culture and society. The paradox by which the savage is simultaneously seen as both our primitive selves (the childhood of the universal human nature that has progressed into us) and our present ones (projecting our individualism onto him) double-damns him. The poor devil can't win: barely emerged from bestiality in the first instance, and (as) vicious, ruthless, and self-seeking (as we are) in the second.

Whether as our ancient ancestor or our contemporary double, he is doomed. Time, in the form of our invading his territory, will outdate him; and justice, in the form of our own unadmitted self-hatred, will eradicate him. We have everything he hasn't (property, hierarchy, government), and he is everything we are (proud, fierce, treacherous, deceitful, etc.). Whatever he is that we aren't (ungallant to women) makes him our inferior; whatever he has that we haven't (control of his body, acute senses) makes him a beast.

All these damning paradoxes are made possible by the universalizing discourse of the Enlightenment in which there is literally no room for difference, no way for anyone to be genuinely other than ourselves. Turning the legend into historiography creates the savage as the "primitive." Thus seeing him as the earliest point on a single scale that leads up to us denies him a place in the now that we both in fact inhabit. He must develop (fast) or perish; coexistence is precluded. To call him "primitive" denies that he has a present, just as to scorn his oral traditions denies that he has a past. The only past he's allowed is our past, that is, our story of it, which has one time scale: from hunting and gathering through herding to agriculture and commerce. "The activity of commerce is coeval with the foundation of cities," announces Robertson (3.231), identifying the symbol and etymology of civilization with the global commerce of the modern world, which is what civilization now means. And along with it come the property, politics, and social organization that we have and the savage doesn't. The social organization he does have is overlooked, explained away, or erased; it is invisible. Without property, there can be no politics or government; without hierarchy, no social or even filial bonds. For us, a human community is not even imaginable in any other terms. Failing to imagine it, we can't see it.

The savage cultivates—but that's not agriculture; he trades in kind—but that's not commerce; he counts with wampum—but that's not computation; he builds granaries—but that's not foresight; he loves his children—but that's not affection; he tells stories—but that's not history; he speaks with eloquence—but that's not art; he is a sly diplomat—but that's not politics; he has deliberative councils—but that's not government; he has symbols on seashells and carvings on trees—but that's not writing; and above all, his behavior, without external compulsion, is consistently directed to maintain his dignity among and to secure the welfare of his social group, to the point of sacrificing his last morsel of food and his own life—but that's not sociable.

The legend as historiography overlooks the savages' present by locating it in our distant past. The Scottish theorists who made it historiography overlook the information actually supplied, however perplexedly, by their sources. What we think we know of the world never depends on the world; it depends on the stories we tell about the world, the structures of words that dream our own desires and anxieties. I have presented the case of the Scottish theorists and the Jesuit fathers in some detail, not only because it exemplifies this (Virgilian) process, but because it also typifies the process of ideological overlooking that made colonial exploitation and extermination possible throughout the eighteenth and nineteenth centuries.

The vanguard of this operation was in the place where the Scottish theorists had most influence, in the most successful and populous colonies of North America, which became, by manifest destiny, the continental United States. The overlooking that took place there has been demonstrated in the pioneering work of Roy Harvey Pearce (1953). Reviewing some of his, along with other, evidence will reveal how thoroughly our culture is defined for us by the legend in ways that palliate our destruction of others by producing endemic blindness to them.

Back in the formative days of modern colonial ideology, at least lip-service was paid, we recall, to some notion of coexistence. John Winthrop, one of the leaders of the New England plantation, asked in 1629 the same question that the early natural lawyers asked, and gave it the same answer. "What warrant have we to take that land, which is and hath been of long time possessed of others the sons of Adam?" This one:

> that which is common to all is proper to none. This savage people ruleth over many lands without title or property; for they enclose no ground, neither have they cattle to maintain it, but remove their dwellings as they have occasion. . . . And why may not Christians have liberty to go and dwell amongst them in their waste lands and woods, (leaving them such places as they have manured for their corn,) as lawfully as did Abraham amongst the Sodomites?

Besides, he concludes, there's plenty of land to go round (Winthrop 1629: 275–77). But sooner or later there wouldn't be.

Included in Colden's report on the Iroquois are the transcripts of various treaty councils held in the early 1740s with tribes in Pennsylvania. The issue in these documents is the sale and purchase of ever more territory (the morally approved way of negotiating colonial expansion); but they are moving testimony to the almost complete noncommunication between peoples who think that land is property, can be bought and sold, and those who relate to it differently. At one such meeting, the native spokesman apologizes that his gifts of deerskins are so few: "but your Horses and Cows have eat the Grass our Deer used to feed on," and he objects, as he receives payment for land sold, that the settlers are already encroaching onto unsold territory. "We know our Lands are now become more valuable: The white People think we do not know their Value; but we are sensible that the Land is everlasting, and the few Goods we receive for it are soon worn out and gone." The lieutenant-governor explains that the increase in the land's value is due to the "Cultivation and Improvement" of the whites, and that the measure of its value is just the same as that of the goods they receive for it: "the Value of Land is no more, than it is worth in Money" (Colden 1747: 64–67). But the native had another idea of its worth than its exchange value for money: he had contrasted the everlastingness of the land to the attrition of goods, and found that exchange inequitable and incommensurable. To him, the land is worth something more and something other than money.

The same point is made by other natives in a negotiation of payment for military services as well as land. To begin the bargaining, they receive from the colonial authorities a history lesson making the claim that the lands below the Poto-mac, in the colony of Maryland, belong to the Great King by right of conquest. They reply with their own history lesson: "tho' great things are well remembered among us, yet we don't remember that we were ever conquered by the Great King. . . . We do remember we were employed by *Maryland* to conquer the *Cone-stogoes*." And one of them evokes a far more philosophical difference: "the World at the first was made on the other Side of the Great Water different from what it is on this Side, as may be known from the different Colours of our Skin . . . , and that which you call Justice may not be so amongst us." They lose the negotiations, of course, and end by inspecting the goods they are to receive after making the despairing protest: "You know very well, when the white People came first here they were poor; but now they have got our lands, and are by them become rich, and we are now poor; what little we have had for the Land goes soon away, but the Land lasts for ever" (Colden 1747: part 2, 125–27).

And there would never be enough of it to share with people so uncivilized as to have no "love for exclusive property," as the Secretary of War for the new nation said in 1789. As its immigrant citizens spread inexorably westward, negotiation could be safely dropped and other directives followed. General Benjamin Lincoln described these in a letter of 1792: "Civilization directs us to remove as far as pos-sible that natural growth from the lands which is absolutely essential for the food and hiding-place of those beasts of the forests upon which the uncivilized princi-pally depend for support." Touring Michigan in 1793, Lincoln observes in his jour-nal that the land "is capable of giving support to an hundred times as many inhab-itants as now occupy it." Considering, he goes on, "that to people fully this earth was in the original plan of the benevolent Deity, I am confident . . . that no men will be suffered to live by hunting on lands capable of improvement, and which would support more people under a state of cultivation" (Pearce 1953: 68–69). The passive verb neatly displaces the agency of dispossessing the savages: God and civ-ilization have decreed it. Law and philosophy have justified and prescribed it. The enacted legend has produced it; and the rehistoricized legend has made it inevita-ble. Their dispossession is our progress.

Once inevitable, it's now possible to sympathize with it—up to a point. James Sullivan, in his history of Maine of 1795, writes that the savage "sighs . . . that the hills and vallies where he has enjoyed the chase, shall be covered with cities and cultivated fields of white men. His agonies, at first, seem to demand a tear . . . but when we reflect . . . that five hundred rational animals may enjoy life in plenty, and comfort, where only one Savage drags out a hungry existence, we shall be pleased with the perspective into futurity" (Pearce 1953: 66). The basis of our sym-pathy is precisely that delicacy of feeling and refinement of sentiment and com-passionate sociability that we have and he doesn't. Crèvecoeur, in 1801, makes these attainments a matter of our civilized diet: "It is therefore only at the period when man became granivorous that he was able to feel compassion and pity, that his fierce and savage customs were replaced by gentler affections, and that his neighbors became his friends" (Pearce 1953: 142).

It is ironic that the "pity" we cereal-eaters alone can feel had so often to be prevented from interfering with the march of progress. Sympathy gets evoked only to get discarded, as in Sullivan's picture of futurity, which was elaborately developed by President Andrew Jackson. Appropriately, too, since under Old Hickory, the new policy of forcibly marching the Indians westward to land nobody (yet) wanted got into full swing. The mortality rates and despair of these "removals," as they were called, were indeed such as to horrify us sweet and gentle consumers of grain. In his second annual message of 1830, the President acknowledges our feelings, and invokes the whole idea of civilization to nullify them:

> Humanity has often wept over the fate of the aborigines of this country, and Philanthropy has been long busily employed in devising means to avert it, but its progress has never for a moment been arrested, and one by one have many powerful tribes disappeared from the earth. To follow to the tomb the last of his race and to tread on the graves of extinct nations excite melancholy reflections. But true philanthropy reconciles the mind to these vicissitudes as it does to the extinction of one generation to make room for another. . . . Philanthropy could not wish to see this continent restored to the condition in which it was found by our forefathers. What good man would prefer a country covered with forests and ranged by a few thousand savages to our extensive Republic, studded with cities, towns, and prosperous farms, established with all the improvements which art can devise or industry execute, occupied by more than 12,000,000 happy people, and filled with the blessings of liberty, civilization, and religion? (Pearce 1953: 57)

No "good man" indeed could be expected to acknowledge a way of life different from his own. Our philanthropic grief finds its "natural" comfort in attributing the extinction of the savages to the natural, organic, order of things: it's just one generation giving way to another. The natural order is invoked, just as the law of nature had been formulated by the legal philosophers, to overlook all human agency, to occult all our responsibility, to excuse and legitimate all our desires. The force that is driving the southeastern tribes to Oklahoma, decimating them, is no natural force; it's the U.S. Army.

Coexistence in the same place between the savage way of life and ours had long ceased even to be hypothesized. Nature had ruled it out. Thomas Farnham, writing in 1839, finds the inevitable destruction of the savages merely "a melancholy fact. The Indians' bones must enrich the soil before the plough of civilized man can open it. . . . The sturdy plant of the wilderness droops under the enervating culture of the garden." They must give way, give place, rot and become fertilizer for us and our culture. It's just an organic process. Farnham recounts the brave and noble resistance of two nations led by Chief Blackhawk, who claimed never to have consented to the sale of their lands in Illinois, and dismisses it as just another melancholy and organic fact, since, "in the order of nature, the plough must bury the hunter" (Farnham 1843: 123–42). The synecdoche is concise, and neatly conceals the actual agent as usual; for it's not the plow that does the burying, but the sword. And yet, of course, the two have implied each other in our imperial civilization since Virgil: turning ploughshares into swords became proverbial for what in the *Aeneid* is the paradoxical destruction of the civilizer Saturn's peaceful agriculture by his own offspring, Saturnia. And now we are continuing in the new world to act out the story of the old, to advance, by the sword, the frontier cultivated by the plow.

Such progress entails also and obviously the destruction of the indigene's landscape, with which he is always identified and from which he must be displaced—which often suffices to destroy him. General Lincoln invoked this as a strategic policy—cutting down the forests to deprive the savage of subsistence—but now it too is just another natural fact. Francis Parkman, writing in 1851 the history of Chief Pontiac's rebellion, is categorical about the inevitable, necessary, and simultaneous demise of the childish savage and his environment: "both he and his forest must perish together" (Pearce 1953: 165). How simply organic this process was receives pompous emphasis in a novel of William Gilmore Simms (1859). The Indian hero's doom, if he fails (as he will) to accept progress, is thus explained: "then must he perish, even as the forests perish. . . . It is, perhaps, his destiny! . . . to prepare the wild for the superior race; and, this duty done, he departs: and, even as one growth of the forest, when hewn down, makes way for quite another growth of trees, so will he give place to another people. Verily, the mysteries of Providence are passing wonderful!" (Pearce 1953: 219). As wonderful, indeed, as the mysteries of the invisible hand, which brings as inevitably and organically, from selfish motives and private profits, the social cohesion and public good that constitute our civilization of property, hierarchy, and government.

It is remarkable how all the voices of our modernity, invoking the procedures of empirical objectivity and the concepts of natural process, so often wind up singing the same old mystical song. We've put the childish fiction of the Trojan legend far behind us, only to empower its plot by the irresistible mystified agencies of natural law, divine providence, and historical necessity. The operation of such magical, transcendent powers to disculpate our own agency in the transmission of our civilization is transparent. And they operate equally to disguise our need for disculpation by making our victims first negligible, and second invisible. Negligible, because they aren't really our victims; it's not we who are making them disappear, but those natural (or divine) forces that no one can resist. Invisible, because whatever they may actually be, the newly empowered legend systematically and by definition overlooks it. Pearce eloquently summarizes how this worked for the (in the new sense) Americans:

> The basis of their understanding had long been part of the grand rationale of westward-moving colonialism. This was the tradition of the natural and divine superiority of a farming to a hunting culture. Universally the Americans could see the Indian only as a hunter. That his culture, at least the culture of the eastern Indians whom they knew best until the second quarter of the nineteenth century, was as much agrarian as hunting, they simply could not see. They forgot, too, if they had ever known, that

many of their own farming methods had been taken over directly from the Indians whom they were pushing westward. One can say only that their intellectual and cultural traditions, their idea of order, so informed their thoughts and their actions that they could see and conceive of nothing but the Indian who hunted.

Biblical injunction framed their belief; and on the frontier practical conditions supported it. (1953: 66)

I have demonstrated that this belief predates the canonical scriptures of Christianity (some of which reflect it and were pressed into its service); that it was framed in Roman antiquity, disseminated and mediated in the west's central literary and historical traditions, and enacted throughout Europe so as to create frontiers, long anterior to the American one, whose conditions consequently supported it. We act out the story, and so produce in the world what it tells us to look for. Since the Renaissance, and the beginnings of our modern takeover of the globe, the story, diffused into other discourses, tells us increasingly what not to look for. And since the eighteenth century it does this by becoming the universal historiography of human development: they who lack what we have, from sentiments to technology and police forces, are simply primitive. What they do have is not seen, except as our past selves (before we got civilized) or our present ones (the projection of our individualism). Our narcissism (the less precise term is ethnocentrism) is double: deliberate and intellectualized, unconscious and pathological. And it denies to savages not merely their existence as a community, but the temporal continuum and the capacity to recall it in which all communities exist. They have no past of their own; incarnating our past, they have no present that is sharable with us; and so, inevitably, they can have no future.

Part V

THE LEGEND TRIUMPHANT—

AND PROTESTED

Chapter 21

OVERLOOKING IN OTHER DIRECTIONS

Humanitarians and Africa

While the Americans were making sure that the savages of North America would not have much of a future, the movement to abolish the slave trade, motivated largely by Evangelical Protestantism, was gathering strength in Britain. The link between these otherwise disparate enterprises—the one genocidal, the other humanitarian—is their mutual assumption of the rehistoricized form of our founding legend. The narcissism of our view of the savage could work both ways: to exterminate him (or just let nature do it) as unworthy of us or to try and make him worthy, to encourage him to grow up into agriculture and commerce. Either way, he is seen as the legend defines him, and is otherwise overlooked. Both the definition, being universal, and the ideological overlooking operated much the same way with respect to Africa as to the Americas. And soon they will operate across the globe, in Australia, southeast Asia, the islands of the Pacific: we know our story and can enact it anywhere. By the late nineteenth century, it will have been enacted so often, become so obvious—literally a kind of second "nature"—that its picture of the savage will be read back into and imposed upon the one colonial place that had always before been thought otherwise: India.

The pictures and the plot of our founding story had received, by the late eighteenth century, useful (hence rather suspect) confirmation from another founding story, that of the Inca empire in Peru. This story, which varies considerably in today's accounts, appears to exist in two main versions. In one, there are four brothers and four sisters, the youngest brother of whom outwits and eliminates the others and founds the city of Cuzco. In the other, this brother, Manco Capac, is a culture hero created by the sun, and gathers the tribes together to found the city (Mason 1957: 108–109). As William Robertson tells the latter version in his *History of America*, it simply replicates our founding story as filtered through the Bible, turning Manco into a *civilisateur* and gendering this role between him and his sister. The raw material that he civilizes is a perfect summary of everything we've heard from Virgil to Ferguson (and that Robertson has repeated) about indigenes: "strangers to every species of cultivation or regular industry, without any fixed residence, and unacquainted with those sentiments and obligations which form the first bonds of social union, they are said to have roamed about naked in the forests, with which the country was then covered, more like wild beasts than like men." They need and get the services of the culture-bringer: Manco Capac came down from the sun to instruct "the men in agriculture and other useful arts. Mama Ocollo taught the women to spin and to weave" (1787: 3.16–17).

This our ancient story of the culture-bringer who comes from elsewhere provides the rationale and inspiration for what the more "humanitarian" forms of nineteenth-century imperialism discovered as their civilizing mission. The first of these forms to organize itself was the late-eighteenth-century campaign in the British parliament, led by Thomas Clarkson and William Wilberforce, to abolish the slave trade. After a struggle of about twenty years, during which the revolutionary government of France had outlawed slavery in 1794 only to reinstate it in 1802, the slave trade in British territories was made illegal in 1807. Wilberforce, along with several key politicians who had supported the movement—Pitt, Canning, and J. B. S. Morritt—founded in the same year an organization, called the Committee of the African Institution, whose declared aims were "to diffuse useful knowledge" among and "to excite the industry of the natives" by introducing them to "agriculture, innocent commerce, and other means of civilisation" (*Report* 1807: 50). The "institution" in its title has the archaic meaning of "instruction," since that, of course, is what the natives most needed. That they were even capable of receiving it required argument, in the face of traditional claims that blacks were hopelessly stupid, lazy, and corrupt (20–26). The Committee, however, lays all the blame for their shortcomings on the slave trade to which they had been subjected for centuries, and maintains that its abolition provides the opportunity to remedy these. And the remedy envisioned is neither the acquisition of land nor the planting of a commodity-producing colony, but simply the encouragement of the natives' own "industry" (43). The Committee is a private and benevolent outfit, with moral objectives that are not those of either church or state.

Still, the remedy is conceived merely to fill up the legendary savage lack of *mos* and *cultus*. It should be stressed, perhaps, that this lack had long been regarded as even more grievous for blacks than for savages of other colors. Modern Europe's ignorance of sub-Saharan Africa was profound, and the long habit of treating its population as commodities was hardly conducive to regarding them as persons. The kind of opinion the Committee was up against was first expressed, so far as I know, in early modern Europe by a writer known as Leo Africanus. He was born a Berber Muslim, became a trader and diplomat, was captured by pirates and given to Pope Leo X, who admired his intelligence, educated and baptized him. In 1526 he wrote, translating his Arabic into Italian, a *Description of Africa* (not published until 1550), which is a lengthy geographical and historical survey of its northern portion from Egypt to Morocco, and was still, in 1800, a standard geographical text. He rarely mentions the sub-Saharan part of the continent except to condemn it categorically: "The people of the Land of the Blacks are brutes without reason, intelligence, or experience. They have absolutely no notion of anything at all. They also live like beasts, without rules and without laws" (Leo Africanus 1956: 1.65). Further bestial lacks are later listed: they are "without kings, without lords, without governments, without republics, without customs. They scarcely know how to sow seed." They have no proper wives, but copulate with whomever they please (2.461–62). In another such place, "one finds neither civilization nor knowledge of letters nor government. The inhabitants . . . are people without intelligence" (2.482). How much of these opinions is due to Leo's own culture (the Arabs traded in black slaves long before and somewhat after Europeans did) and how much to his education in Rome I don't know. But the opinions hadn't much changed in three centuries.

So the Committee draws heavily on the sense of the founding legend to provide a plausible rationale and precedent for its benevolent enterprise, claiming that transmission is the virtually inevitable way for civilization to occur. "If," writes the anonymous reporter,

> the polished nations of the earth, when they first emerged from barbarism, had possessed historians to record the causes of that change, we should probably discover, in some cases, that the talents or virtues of an individual . . . had suddenly imparted a new character to the institutions and manners of his country; and in others, that intelligent strangers from a more enlightened region of the earth had produced, by their information and their practical aid, the same benign effects. In the early traditions of Greece and Italy some traces of such sources of civilisation may be found: and the benefactors of nations, who were said to have descended from the skies, and were honoured as gods, are reasonably supposed to have been no other than intelligent foreigners, who first brought the useful arts of their own countries to a rude and ignorant people. A similar origin has been ascribed to the civilisation which was found in some kingdoms of South America. . . . If the nations of the old world had their Cadmus and Saturn, Peru had her Mango Capac, who instructed her once barbarous people in agriculture and the liberal arts, and whose accidental arrival from some unknown region probably gave rise to the fable of his descent from the sun.
>
> Conquest, it must be admitted, has been the harsh and more ordinary medium by which the blessings of civilisation have been conveyed from one part of the world to another; but this is because no other has often been attempted. Polished nations have commonly been too selfish to send the plow and the loom to any country, till they have first sent the sword and the sceptre. (*Report* 1807: 12–13)

Here is the euhemeristic mythography of Vico, harnessed to the universalized (legendary) history of ourselves: we and antiquity and the Peruvians got it from someplace and somebody else. Now, therefore, we can bestow it. The only question concerns the manner of the bestowal. And the humanitarian answer is the unselfish one: instead of conquest, instruction in agriculture and commerce.

The reporter's language makes the transmission of all civilization a powerful likelihood; Wilberforce himself, writing in the same year, makes it a dogma: "And we are well warranted, by the experience of all ages, in laying it down as an incontrovertible position—that the arts and sciences, knowledge, and civilization, have never yet been found to be a native growth of any country; but that they have ever been communicated from one nation to another, from the more to the less civilized" (quoted in Curtin 1964: 252). One can't be more definite than that. As dogma, it enjoins on us of course the white man's burden; it becomes our moral duty to bring civilization to them—otherwise it's simply impossible that they should ever have any. For they can't, and we couldn't, develop any unaided, without outside "irradiation." Civilization comes from elsewhere; it's never homegrown. The grand circularity of this is self-confirming for us and vicious for the poor savage. Because civilization comes from elsewhere, he can't have any unless we give it him; because he is savage, he doesn't have any. We become his only hope.

Self-flattering as it is, there's a kind of logic here, and it comes full circle in the course of the nineteenth century. That blacks lack (by legendary definition) what we have is never questioned; the reason why they lack it alters diametrically—but only makes us all the more their only hope. The humanitarian abolitionists found the reason in the slave trade; its degradation, enforced by us, accounted for savage ignorance. We kept them down, and are now to make amends. The Committee for the African Institution attempted this, by sending to West Africa seeds of various plants, cotton gins, and teachers. It couldn't do much of this, though, since most of its efforts for the next twenty years were taken up in waging further paper war against the still thriving slave trade. The abolitionist leader who succeeded Wilberforce, Thomas Fowell Buxton, wrote in 1839 that the British prohibition of the trade had only increased its profits, and that the only way to combat it effectively would be to develop commerce and agriculture in Africa that would be even more profitable—especially to the grossly ignorant and superstitious Africans who inhabit that "kingdom of darkness" (Buxton 1839: xi). What Buxton implies is spelled out by one of his associates, a geographer who was helping to make Leo Africanus obsolete. He simply reverses the diagnosis of the founders of the Committee, maintaining that the slave trade is the result, not the cause, of "African ignorance and barbarity" (McQueen 1840: xlv). The remedy for this is still to teach them cultivation and commerce, appealing now to their gain and interest (as well as ours, since we control the market they are to produce in and for) rather than to our sense of responsibility.

This latter had wholly disappeared by the end of the century for such staunch imperialists as James Anthony Froude. On his tour of the West Indies, he meditates on the cause of the blacks' inferiority (granting for the sake of argument what he elsewhere denies, that the races' capacities are identical). "We set it down to slavery. It would be far truer to set it down to freedom. The African blacks have been free enough for thousands . . . of years, and it has been the absence of restraint which has prevented them from becoming civilized" (Froude 1898: 125).

Froude argues throughout against the moral laxity that would grant independence to the islands, claiming that this will "drive them back into the condition of their ancestors, from which the slave trade was the beginning of their emancipation" (236).

A clever oxymoron, that slavery was emancipation—but logical precisely in the legendary sense: so deprived are they that to become our chattel is necessarily an improvement in their condition. Though this logic is purely and only legendary, it was something else for Froude and his contemporaries: it was science. He was able to cite "craniological" measurements proving that blacks were by nature inferior to whites. The history of this aberration—racism justified by the empirical objectivity of occidental science—is well known, and has been summarized by a contemporary historian as "perhaps . . . the most disastrous error scientists have ever made" (Curtin 1964: 29).

But the scientists did not invent the error; they merely confirmed it, lending it the sanctity and the authority of the presumed factual demonstrations of scientific discourse. The error was, and remains, inherent in the legend's picture of the savage. There, from Virgil through Spenser and until the late eighteenth century, the savage had always been situated at some ontological border between animality and humanity: "halfe beastly men." The enlightenment thinkers and the natural lawyers had made the border temporal as well and insisted on its universality: savages are now what we were long ago. It was a small step, partly taken by Robertson and his colleagues, to demote the savages from children to beasts. But they still appealed to the "conditions" of his life that made him so, as indeed did the humanitarians of the early nineteenth century. The large step is to declare that the conditions are either irrelevant or have operated so long as to produce an unbridgeable, qualitative, gap between the savage and us: he's inferior by nature. Burgeoning positivistic science took this step in the nineteenth century.

But it's the same old error from the same old story: the savage has no *mos* or *cultus*, does not know how to form a human community. And this conviction produced in European observers of Africa the same kind of systematic overlooking earlier perfected in America. The pattern is identical: early observations of what the savages possess (as Thomas Heriot found much to praise in their agriculture) are ignored or forgotten or explained away as the need to dispossess them becomes acute. The scholar who has traced this pattern in the areas of British domination, Philip Curtin, points out that initially the peoples of West Africa were seen to occupy the middle range of the eighteenth century's universal historical trajectory from savagery to barbarism to us. They were in part both settled and agricultural, and so were inserted in the "barbarous" middle of the scale (1964: 64). According to Vattel's criteria, they weren't idle hunters or rapacious nomads, so that even their political organization had to be legally recognized. "No one suggested at this point that shifting cultivation was a form of nomadism and thus an illicit use of land, though the idea would come with time" (280). And come it would, exactly as Robertson and whole generations of Americans were to deny that whatever and however the natives planted counted as agriculture. And if America had the Jesuits, West Africa had a pioneer ethnographer in Thomas Winterbottom, who wrote in 1803 a serious account of the natives of Sierra Leone, which also failed to modify in the least the legendary picture of them. Winterbottom observes incidentally that although the Africans themselves accuse each other of cannibalism, he's not found one authenticated instance of it, except for rare and ritual purposes. Curtin also cites a traveler who was perplexed trying to specify the stage on the path to civilization reached by Africans: "Since they practiced hunting, fishing, pastoralism, and agriculture all at the same time, the task was beyond him" (210).

The customarily paradoxical stereotype of the African was almost identical to that of the American savage: he was lazy, dumb, fierce, cunning, but also hospitable, careless, childish, hedonistic. Polygamy is especially reproached, along with labor, as keeping women in a terribly low status (404). The one slight difference concerns sex; it's slight because it merely attributes the same result to opposite attitudes. The European consensus about the native American's indifference to sex was still grounded in the legend: having no rules or customs to observe, he obtains it too easily. So does the African, except that he thinks of nothing else, is supremely lustful. He cares about it, and the Amerindian doesn't; but they both indulge in it and in forms of it that horrify our civilized restraint. The specification of sexual licence as the savage lack of *mos* only occurred in the sixteenth century, and appeared in the legend as the apparent result of the fantasies unleashed by the Europeans' first sight of darker-hued bodies wearing fewer and other clothes than they. (Leo Africanus, though, exhibits the identical reaction.) By now, this specification is typical, whether for interested or disinterested savages. Sexual licence, like cannibalism, is the excess that proves the ultimate lack of all law and order, which we are perforce obliged to supply. And even the humanitarian arguments for supplying it stressed the mutual profits to be gained. These have not changed since they were forecast by Sir George Peckham: the savage gets moral elevation and we get cash. Piety unites with commerce in the missionary reports cited by Curtin to make quite clear that "the equation was not merely, Christianity equals civilization. It was: Christianity equals civilization, which equals production for the world market" (421).

Curtin's conclusion about Africa is also the same as Pearce's about America: the savages are not seen, are even less seen as colonization proceeds. The "most striking feature" of the British image of Africans is "its variance from the African reality." It is impervious to ever-increasing data and is created by Europeans for European needs (479–80). It is thus impervious because it never came from "data"; it came from a story that has been told so often, enacted so widely, diffused into discourses of such greater scientific credibility than fiction, that it's untouchable. It's also generally European, not merely British. Curtin suggests this, and the work of a subsequent scholar on the French in Africa explicitly confirms it, which is unsurprising, since the legend that defines the savage also defines the civilization that all we Europeans share. Despite the traditional French boast that they, unlike the Anglo-Saxons, are tolerant and unprejudiced, their behavior shows them to be just as racist as anyone: "there were no significant national variations in European re-

actions to Africa" (Cohen 1980: 33). The French in Africa also had a pioneer ethnographer, Father Proyart, who (like Lafitau) disputed the received picture of the
savage in 1776; but nobody listened (68–69). The black remained lawless, lazy, and
lustful, vengeful, thieving, and mendacious—except when his better qualities could
be found noble (just as the native Americans' on occasion were) in order to criticize our own world. Cohen finds that the claims of racist science were especially
congenial to the French aristocracy, since they reinforced the notion of natural
superiority by blood that it had long asserted against the commons—thus transferring to race what was said of class (91, 216). In this connection, it is piquant to
learn that one of the foremost theorists of racism, Count Gobineau, actually held
no title at all; he just added it to his name himself (217).

Except for the revolutionary interlude, the cause of abolition never achieved
the power and popularity in France that it did in Britain. Following the terms laid
on them at the Congress of Vienna, the French outlawed the slave trade in 1817,
providing as a penalty for engaging in it a fine less than that for the theft of a loaf
of bread, and scarcely enforcing this. Full emancipation of slaves was summarily
enacted only at the next revolutionary period, in 1848. A contemporary remarked
that abolitionist appeals to reason and justice as made in France had not the force
of the Evangelical appeals made in England to a Bible-reading public (Cohen 1980:
201). Otherwise, the abolitionists in both countries were warm advocates of colonial expansion for the same set of reasons that unified the civilizing and/or Chris-
tianizing mission with the production and marketing of commodities. Both could
only be improvements, since the savage started at zero, and colonies would in addition be a splendid outlet for surplus or suspicious subjects—just as the sixteenth-
century projectors had foretold.

In Great Britain, the movement to free the slaves in its dominions succeeded in
1833. The Christian and moral humanitarianism which had brought this about was
obliged to continue the campaigns against both the trade and the practice as carried on elsewhere. But in British territories, the movement's energies could be otherwise directed. And they were directed mostly at continuing the aims that had
characterized the movement from its beginnings. They continued unquestioningly
to assume that the savage was as the legend pictured him, endeavored by the usual
means (encouraging agriculture and commerce) to raise him from this condition,
and rather desperately tried to stimulate public awareness of the almost unlimited
kinds of mistreatment he was undergoing. A more broadly based organization than
the old Committee was formed for these purposes in 1836, called, significantly, the
Aborigines' Protection Society. No doubt they needed protection, and no doubt
they could not protect themselves, so protecting them (from ourselves) is something that only we can do. The one campaign and line of argument developed by
this organization that violated the automatically assumed posture of paternalistic
superiority was its effort (of which more later) to secure land rights and titles for
indigenous peoples. This effort failed, of course, doubtless because it assumed,
against the legendary consensus, that indigenes both deserved such rights and were
capable of exercising them as they saw fit.

The organization's objectives and efforts are recorded in its publication, which began in 1847 and lasted until 1909, called *The Colonial Intelligencer: or, Aborigines' Friend*, known familiarly as "The Aborigines' Friend," which simplified title it eventually assumed. The first issue announces its aim "to promote the advancement of Uncivilized Tribes," and explains why this is necessary. With the small exceptions of providing some food to the starving and some Christianity to the heathen, "the intercourse of civilized man with the Aborigines has been a visitation of unmitigated evil, varying in its kind, but uniform in its tendency towards the annihilation of the feebler race" (*AF* 1847: 1.3). Much space is taken up in this and subsequent volumes merely to combat the often-deplored general apathy on the subject, with catalogues of atrocities committed against indigenes everywhere. The Society constantly exhorts the government to make the natives in the Empire full British subjects, and to endow them with a "civil organisation" that can deal with their local colonial authorities (1.14). The assumption, of course, is that they have no civil organization of their own. And, as before, the Society must argue (incessantly) that they're capable of recognizing one when it's given them. Occasionally, however, observation is allowed to contradict the assumption. In the course of a whole series of later examples designed to prove that natives are capable of getting civilized, the Hawaiians are praised for what they are seen already to possess: tools, settled agriculture, and above all, social hierarchy: "The arrangements of the Court were quite as ridiculous as those of this country; and as absurd a system of etiquette prevailed among their aristocracy as that by which our own is so inconveniently shackled" (*AF* 1848: 2.99).

The invidious iconoclasm of such comparisons was not best calculated to win wide public support, nor was it, by a long shot, the general tone of the Society's argumentation. But it's a refreshing reversal of the usual ironic moral criticism (as practiced by the Jesuits), which rebukes us with the native qualities (generosity, dignity, etc.) superior to ours—the whole idea of the "noble" (by our standards) savage. Such criticism (like Pope's picture of the Iroquois laughing at our dress and speech) always makes its point by assuming our untouchable overall superiority to the savage: we are shamed because even such a totally deprived creature can *still* excel us in this or that practice of (always) our own ethical values. Here, by rare contrast, the courtly protocol of the Hawaiians and the British is mordantly and equally silly.

But the dominant strategy of the humanitarian movement is merely to implement our legendary picture of the savage, to supply him (literally) with what it says he lacks. Thus the Society is supremely concerned to teach him settled agriculture. A small water mill and seeds are sent to a village of Maoris; carpenter's tools (to foster real home-building) are sent to the Kaffirs (*AF* 1850: 3.79, 83). And the dominant rhetorical tone of the Society is the earnest defense of this procedure, as exemplified in its Annual Report for 1850: "if the Aborigines are to be redeemed from their social degradation . . . it will be accomplished, not by the civilization of the cannon, the musket, and the sword, but by the civilization of the plough, the harrow, and the Book." They are acting out Virgil's myth, and not his poem; for the poem shows us that the sword and the plough, the cannon and the book, imply each other, that our civilization is not thus separable, that culture as we know it always comes with coercion. For the Scottish theorists, civilization was itself defined as the kind of coercion imposed by the state to maintain the system of private property. The Society's wish to separate the benevolent from the bellicose civilization may be admirable, but is certainly naive. And the Society's objective seems less than admirable by being predicated on the same old story, which postulates the degradation of the aborigine from which only we can redeem him.

Redemption by agriculture—of our massive commodity-producing sort, which also made it commerce—was the standard prescription and policy, not only of those who wanted to "redeem" the savage, but also of those who merely wanted to market the commodities. All the schemes to encourage or oblige the African to settle and grow grain merely reproduced the recommendation of Spenser in 1596 for civilizing the Irish. The shifting cultivation actually practiced by West Africans—some kind of which, it turns out, is the only agriculture possible in tropical rain forests—did not count, was overlooked and explained away as usual. The climate, with its sporadic but intense rainfalls, was even blamed for producing a "completely imaginary forest nomadism," which prevented permanent settlement and bred forms of roving warfare, which made the Africans themselves "natural slave-hunters" (Curtin 1964: 405). The climate along with the flora it produces gets more blame from Edward Phillips, an indefatigable colonial booster. The monsoons of central Africa, he claims, prevent settlement and make the people "roaming and predatory. . . . This very source of nature's profligacy in the vegetable world is destructive of civilised life in the moral" (*Colonial Magazine* 1847: 10.3). It is remarkable how the legendary identification of the savage and his landscape can be accomplished in any circumstances; wherever he is, he's autochthonous. In America (where our germs kill him), he's feeble, like those dastardly quadrupeds. In tropical Africa (where his germs kill us), he's profligate, like all that vegetation.

Despite, or because of, this vegetable fecundity, the African's lack of proper agriculture does not permit him the appropriately civilized diet. Another colonial enthusiast, John Crawfurd, a Fellow of the Royal Society, makes granivorousness a scientific principle: "No race of man, it might be safely asserted, ever acquired a respectable amount of civilization that had not some cereal for a portion of its food" ("Transactions" 1859: 149). There is a telling blend of cozy quantification and social convention in the phrase "respectable amount": civilization here becomes something that can be weighed out at the corner grocery. Crawfurd liked to fabricate quantified measures of civilization. He reported to a subsequent meeting of the British Association for the Advancement of Science that the number of species of birds that a society had domesticated was an infallible index to its placement on the scale of savagery-barbarism-civilization ("Transactions" 1861: 155).

To the redeemers and the marketeers are thus added the scientists, making their conscious contribution to the march of imperial progress. The connection between the last two was made clear by Sir Roderick Murchison, the president of the Royal Geographical Society who also presided over the newly created Geographical and Ethnological Section of the British Association. At its meeting in Leeds in 1858, Murchison praises the successful recent incorporation of ethnology into that section. This is, he says, "the natural result of the very constitution of the body politic of Britain and her extensive colonies," because "there is no branch of science which is more intimately connected with the best interests of commerce and manufactures than that which makes us acquainted with the products and inhabitants of distant lands" ("Transactions" 1859: 144). The *studium* goes along with the *imperium*, and will provide it with information to help it expand its markets. One form of possession follows another.

And all such forms are now, in the mid-nineteenth century, regarded as appropriate and necessary expressions of national destinies. Pious and commercial, benevolent and bellicose motives all converge to produce official policies that assume for the nation the legendary role of the bringer of omniculture. Hence the European scramble for the possession of Africa, culminating in its partition by the major powers at the Berlin Conference in 1884 (Hallett 1974: 432–34). However sincere may have been some humanitarian wishes to replace the sword and the sceptre with the plow and the book, the sword was never replaced by anything, except (after 1874) the machine gun (Wilson 1977: 90–91). Great Britain, enjoying imperial preeminence after the end of the Napoleonic Wars, gave the world the famous *pax britannica*. What this meant was that during the reign of Victoria (from 1837 to 1901), the armed forces of Great Britain fought only one war (the Crimean) even on the fringes of Europe. But in Asia and Africa during this period they fought, depending on who's counting, between thirty-three and forty-five wars (see Kohn 1987, Cook and Keith 1975). From Afghanistan to the Cape Colony to the North Island of New Zealand, Britain's wars against indigenous peoples are often called by (European) historians "small" wars. One historian, however, reminds us that what was small, in terms of manpower and investment, for the industrialized European powers, was total, in terms of commitment and, usually, defeat "for their African opponents" (Wilson 1977: 88).

Such wars were not only small by our material standards; they were also negligible in terms of the legendary self-image of the European powers. "Africa's new rulers considered themselves true heirs of Rome, bringing imperial peace to backward, warring peoples" (Wilson 1977: 178). We find chaos and establish order; we are the lawgivers, and we bring the peace that results from our wars of invasion. It's our peace on what is now our territory. The nationalistic scramble for territory, by warring against its aboriginal possessors, replaced in the nineteenth century the eighteenth-century scramble for trade of the European powers, by warring against each other. In this respect, the same historian finds that the old world learned a lesson from the new. Speaking of the mid-nineteenth century, he says, "it was still accepted by western opinion that one of the most obvious expressions of national prowess was to achieve control over the land and lives of other peoples as exemplified by the thrust across the continent and the subjugation of native Americans by the newly independent United States" (Wilson 1977: 294). Without, of course, citing the American example, the Committee on Colonisation of the British House of Lords declared that "to transplant our domestic habits, our commercial enterprise, our laws, our institutions, our language, our literature, and our sense of religious obligation to the most distant regions of the globe, is an enterprise worthy of the character of a great maritime nation" (*Colonial Magazine* 1847: 12.204).

How, in western opinion, could it be otherwise? Our civilization—and it's the only one, the one that progresses from hunting to omniculture—can only occur by transmission. As we have received, so shall we give: the imperial model of transmission has become our bounden duty. Were it not for our founding story, shaped by ancient Rome, reenacted and retold ever since in and by western Europe, the history of the globe would have been different. We could not have imagined, or justified, doing what we did. Soon enough, our naked and actual rule over the distant regions of the globe would appear unjustifiable; but that will not lessen the power of the legend either to define what is (and isn't) civilized or to prescribe its universal historiography. The legend was triumphant, and still is.

Chapter 22

EXPROPRIATING

Nineteenth-Century Colonial Discourse

In the nineteenth-century British Empire, the brutalities of expropriating the territories of indigenous peoples generated occasional protest, much less of course than that still aroused by slavery. Such protest was made invariably on familiar moral and humanitarian grounds, and never really called into question our assumption of the legendary civilizing role. It was almost exclusively a difference over methods, with hard-nosed settlers in the territories telling the government to exterminate the brutes, and soft-hearted liberals at home telling it to be kind to them and oblige them to progress. Two such episodes of protest are, however, worth looking at. One concerns the Hudson's Bay Company and reveals the contradictions in our assumed equation of commerce with civilization. The other concerns the Maori Wars, raises the (still) crucial question of aboriginal rights to land, and illustrates the difficulties of making expropriation legal even within the generous guidelines laid down by Vattel. Rather than isolate the discussion of these not very well known episodes of protest, thus giving a false impression of their prominence, I shall embed them in the context where they occurred, amid a mixed chorus of voices typical of the imperial discourse of the period. In this chorus, Aeneas will be invoked again, as the ultimate predecessor for the glorious actions of contemporary foundations. The Trojans are not yet (before Schliemann) readmitted to past history; but they reappear at the mid-Victorian apex of the enactment of their legend as present fact.

Most of the voices come from a mid-century publication that began in 1844 as *Simmonds's Colonial Magazine* and continued after 1849 as *The Colonial Magazine and East India Review* (hereafter *CM*). This journal contains a farrago of miscellaneous stuff, reflecting a wide spectrum of opinion, about the colonies: geography, botany, (genuinely "primitive") ethnography, trade statistics, politics, agricultural and manufacturing instructions, personal reminiscences and reports, travel narratives, book reviews, and poems—including some by Henry Wadsworth Longfellow and John Greenleaf Whittier. Insofar as it has an editorial policy, it is to encourage colonization (often deploring that the government does so too little) as emigration: defusing Chartism and political radicalism generally by making possible, and attractive, the removal of the starving masses at home to the vast territories overseas (*CM* 1847: 10.Preface). This policy makes it generally no friend of the aborigines, though its pages often express the usual sentimental humanitarianism as well as more stringent criticisms of colonial authorities. But its typical line is to advocate, as Simmonds, its originator, did, things like lowering the price of land in Australia to make it purchasable by laborers, thus creating permanent settlers in order to "introduce at the same time cultivation and civilization" (*CM* 1848: 14.v). Simmonds was succeeded as editor in 1849 by William Henry Kingston, a journalist of incredible fecundity, who specialized in colonial propaganda and boys' adventure fiction.

The dissemination of information about the colonies—one of the journal's declared aims—is not only designed to encourage their fuller possession; it is itself a form of possession. The strange and exotic becomes ours in both literal and discursive senses. As objects of knowledge and the subject matter of discourse, the colonies become yet another form of commodity. Words about them are not only marketed in such forms as this profit-making magazine; but the colonies themselves become a market for all other kinds of words. The point is graphically made, in a way exactly parallel to Simmonds' proposal to make Australia possessable by the lower classes, in an advertisement for John Murray's "Colonial and Home Library" that appears on the inside front cover of the first volume (1844). The house of Murray, publisher of Austen, Byron, Scott, Melville, and the annual reports of the British Association for the Advancement of Science, was one of the most successful such enterprises of the age. The aim of its Colonial and Home Library was "to furnish all classes of Readers in Great Britain and her Colonies with the highest literature of the day . . . at the lowest possible price." The latter would place "useful works, by approved authors . . . within reach of the means not only of the Colonists, but also of a large portion of the less wealthy classes at home, who will thus benefit by the widening of the market for our literature." Everybody gets more of everything (including John Murray, the real beneficiary of the widening market): let the masses colonize, and they can be sold things in a volume that will reduce the price of those things for the masses at home. The things are books, the first of which in Murray's series included one on the Bible, one on travels in India, and lives of Clive, Crabbe, and Pitt.

Enlarging possessions, and enlarging the number of those (of us) who can possess, work as well for literature as for land, since everything is marketable in our civilization. Enforcing our notion of private property with respect to printed words, however, in terms of the ownership of copyright, had long been problematic. The Colonial and Home Library was partly a response to recent legislation designed to protect British authors and publishers by prohibiting the sale of pirated reprints of English works in the Empire. Novelists like Scott and Dickens often bitterly complained of how much they were losing through unauthorized translations and reprints, especially in the United States. The Bern Convention, which bound all signatory nations to respect each other's copyrights (and which the United States did not effectively sign until 1955), did not exist until 1887. The ownership of reproducible objects, like printed words (and now films, sound and video recordings of all kinds, computer software), is notoriously difficult or even impossible to enforce. Although such media of communication are thus unlike real estate or pork bellies, they are all nonetheless commodities, objects for sale in that ever-widening market. And they are objects whose consumption (reading, hearing, seeing) can confer another kind of possession, which is knowledge. As the flora and fauna of the planet are being appropriated by our science and marketed by our commerce, its territories are being appropriated by our settlers and its ancient monuments (like the Elgin Marbles) by our museums; all these distant forms of appropriation are being made known, familiarized, by our mass journalism. And every form of appropriation by us is a form of expropriation for somewhere and someone else.

The expansion of markets is a constant theme in the pages of the *Colonial Magazine*. Edward Phillips, a frequent contributor, observes in 1848 that with all the interruptions of peace, which is the optimum condition for carrying on commerce, by the conflicts on the continent, now is the moment to develop colonial trade. He then goes on to a review of modern history that argues, paradoxically for the flourishing of commerce in peacetime, that the establishment of commerce should be a primary motive of making war, as indeed it had been. Phillips deplores all treaties made by Britain after 1763 for "supinely neglecting" to secure trade concessions as her national prerogative. He insists that "commerce (the steps by which she has chiefly risen to her present proud pre-eminence) is not always prized as it deserves" by the government. He reminds us that hegemonic power in the modern west comes from commercial supremacy, from the "maritime states of Italy" to the Hanse Towns and Antwerp in the sixteenth century to Amsterdam in the seventeenth to London now, as the "emporium of the world" (*CM* 1848: 15.131–32).

To maintain, by enlarging, this enviable position is the prescription of many anonymous contributors. One of them advocates the putting-down of piracy in the East Indian archipelago in order to create a market of thirty million people. This accomplishment is dithyrambically identified, as usual, with civilization. When these folks

> are brought within the circle of civilisation, they cannot fail to consume an immense amount of English manufactures, for the widening of the influence of European civilisation and the extension of European commerce progress very nearly in the same ratio. If, therefore, we can awaken these benighted millions from the sleep of barbarism, and create in them new ideas, new wants, and new habits and modes of life, shall we not, at the same time that we benefit mankind, derive a large addition to our own material prosperity? (*CM* 1849: 16.344)

We shall indeed, as the rhetorical question automatically affirms: everybody will get more of everything. This writer articulates a long operative principle of merchandising that will be codified by the advertising experts of this century: the creation of "new wants"—that is, both lacks or needs and desires. The newness here predicated on the awakening of barbarians to civilization will become purely psychological for us metropolitans; we will be taught by Madison Avenue to need and desire whatever it has to sell us. It is a pleasant reversal that puts us in the place of awakened barbarians as potential consumers all.

Not everybody, though, was always seen to get more of everything in the ever-expanding market. There were moments when the equation of commerce and civilization was threatened by a kind of commerce that palpably did not "benefit mankind" by encouraging the settled agriculture that was the basic precondition for civilization. This was the fur trade, as practiced by the Hudson's Bay Company (see Wolf 1982: ch. 6). The pelts of wild animals—mainly the beaver, whose layer of downy wool next the skin provided the felt for the hats fashionable in Europe from the late sixteenth to the early nineteenth centuries—are a uniquely anomalous commodity in the omniculture of our civilization. For only they require that the wilderness remain wilderness, that the forest not be cleared by the plow. Consequently, the native dwellers of the forest were easily recruited as a labor force to harvest the product. Victualing the trappers (whether native or European or, increasingly as the trade moved west, the combination of both called *métis*, or half-caste) became the livelihood of other native populations exploiting another native animal, the bison. Its meat, in the dried and cured form of pemmican, sustained the new commercial hunters on their long journeys as it had earlier generations of native hunters. From the seventeenth century, the growing demand rapidly decimated local populations of beaver, requiring the trade to push ever farther west, and supplying the motive for the Hudson's Bay Co. to secure title to the vast (and vague) expanse of land between that Bay and the Pacific.

A great many beaver pelts could be obtained for a single firearm or bottle of liquor. The overhead was therefore small—trading posts on a few of the many rivers that furnished good transport—and the profits enormous. Competition was inevitable, and crystallized into the rival North West Company in 1787, formed by merchants in Montreal who found the Hudson's Bay Co. too lethargic in exploiting its charter, given the opportunities to do so ever since the expulsion of the French in 1763. The North West moved rapidly west; the Hudson's Bay reacted strongly, and the rival trappers and traders in the field sought to suborn each other's native suppliers, and gradually fell to open warfare. They murdered each other with sufficient frequency to attract the attention of parliament just as another event occurred that escalated the violence in a different direction.

This was the foundation of the Red River Settlement (a tract in the basin of that river in what is now Manitoba, Minnesota, and North Dakota) by the Earl of Selkirk, a large enough shareholder in the Hudson's Bay Co. to obtain from it this grant of land. Selkirk, acting on the time-honored motive of relieving the impoverished at home, had a group of dispossessed Scots and Irish farmers brought there in 1812. The fur-trading interests of the Company were hostile to the project from the outset, and the North Westers actively cajoled and threatened the settlers to leave.

Some did; but more came in 1816, and open warfare was again the result. All the violence caused lengthy legal battles and scandals at home, which helped persuade parliament to decree the amalgamation of the rival companies in 1821.

The conflicts of interest in all this are apparent, and exhibit the mutual hostility between colonizers and traders in wilderness commodities. The latter preside over a system of production that is unjustifiable by the civilizing rationale of colonial ideology. This becomes clear when the histories of the Hudson's Bay Co. and the Red River Colony become issues for the *CM* in 1848. The occasion is a petition of the Hudson's Bay Co. (as the amalgamation is still called) to the Colonial Secretary for the grant of Vancouver Island, which the magazine passionately opposes. Pages of indignation are heaped on the Company's total neglect of its presumed obligations to provide missionaries and encourage settlement. Its income excites equal indignation: one of its governors, Sir John Pelly, is quoted as admitting in 1838 that for 110 years of the first century and a half of its existence (it was chartered in 1670), it made annual profits of 60–70 percent. Its murderous rivalry with the former North West Co. receives this mordant comment: "The Indian must have smiled to hear the white man call him Savage" (*CM* 1848: 14.428–29). To cede yet more territory to such an organization would be to defeat the whole imperial aim, which is to found "a Colony . . . that men of birth, intelligence, education, and enterprise shall be . . . glad to join . . . ; not a settlement for the convenience of a corporation of pedlars" (14.433).

The magazine continues the attack the following year in its review of a book on the Company, lambasting it for unmitigated greed and for deliberately keeping the Indians savage (*CM* 1849: 16.246–51). The same charges are made in a counterpetition to Earl Grey (the Colonial Secretary) by 977 residents of the Red River Settlement, who add a final allegation: "that from the systematic destruction of the game on which the Indians subsist, the natives . . . are being exterminated by famine, no precautions being taken by the Company to avert the calamity, by teaching the Indians to change the precarious livelihood obtained by the chase, for a certain subsistence derived from the cultivation of the soil" (16.475). The magazine ridicules Grey's decision, made by now, in favor of the Company. Though the *cause* was not really *célèbre*, it had been debated in the House of Commons, where the rising William Gladstone eloquently attacked the decision in a speech summarized in *The Aborigines' Friend*. Gladstone rehearses all the monopolistic abuses and excessive profits of the company, whose interests he castigates as expressly and necessarily anticolonizing, anticultivating, and, with respect to the natives, anticivilizing (*AF* 1848: 2.38–43).

So here is a form of commerce incompatible with, even antithetical to, (our notion of) civilization, just as Thomas Carte (see ch. 14) had imagined, a case in that profit-taking actually prevents culture-bringing. But it was, of course, an exceptional case which but confirmed the rule. Furs were the only major commodity that depended on the wilderness and that were acquired by the patently uncivilized means of hunting. The Jesuits in Canada had long observed and complained that the European trappers and traders who carried on this trade became as savage as the natives with whom they regularly dealt. The violence of the competition between the two companies validated this view for their British critics, whose indignation springs precisely from the violation of the rule that commerce equals civilization and the ancient assumption that hunting (though permissible as sport) as a livelihood is irremediably savage.

Their indignation about the profits of the enterprise, along with Gladstone's involvement, suggest an even larger contradiction in the ideology that had grown up around our founding legend. Gladstone began his reforming career while president of the Board of Trade, in 1843, by submitting some of the financial chicaneries of the railways to government regulation. That such regulation of corporate behavior should be necessary was an admission that the invisible hand wasn't doing its job, that private profits do not automatically and mystically secure the public good. The struggle to enact forms of public control over the monopolistic practices of great corporations occupies a considerable part of the political history of both Britain and the United States in the late nineteenth century. For social systems frankly based, to the extent of identifying the institution of private property with civilization itself, on the amassing of individual profits, it is anomalous to hear complaints that profits are excessive. Where is the measure of excess? How can there possibly be too much of such a good thing?

The measure of excess that became visible to nineteenth-century eyes was simply the widening gap between the rich and the poor, and the exponential multiplication of the latter: the starving urban masses and the rural dispossessed so often proposed as candidates for colonial emigration. It became undeniably obvious that the invisible hand was not recirculating individual profits as it was supposed to, that they did not "trickle down" (to use a later description of the same desideratum) in any form from those who amassed them to those who didn't. Instead, they stayed where they were, producing some plutocrats and a great many paupers.

The most famous and brilliant diagnosis of this problem was that of Karl Marx, who attributed it to the operation and organization of a relatively new mode of production that he called capitalist. Marx defined this as ownership of the means of production, which gave owners unprecedented power to confiscate for themselves as profits the surplus values produced by their laborers. Today, we call the phase of the system that Marx analyzed laissez-faire capitalism; and the gradual modification of its excesses, by government regulation (as pioneered by Gladstone), taxation, and the passage of laws to enfranchise workers and entitle them to a living wage and other forms of social security, practically constitutes the domestic history of the polished nations from then to now. The faith that the Scots theorists had in the invisible hand turned out to be misplaced; but their insistence on coercion, external compulsion, as the cornerstone of a property-based civilization was more profoundly accurate than they recognized. For it wasn't just the individual who needed policing; the newly formed capitalist industries needed it even more.

The enfranchisement and protection of workers did not happen overnight nor without protracted conflicts (nor is it yet complete). But it began while the British Empire was rising to its apogee and providing an escape hatch for the disaffected masses, from whose revolts throughout the rest of Europe in 1848 Britain was spared. The fear of such a prospect, however, as well as its logic, are manifest in the pages of the *CM*. The logic emerges from the association, by comparison and contrast, of the condition of workers with that of savages. This association, long obvious in the colonies themselves, now becomes apparent in the metropolis, and suggests the extent to which all "others" are, to our polished, liberal, bourgeois eyes, somehow alike: the victims of our system who inspire similar contempt, hostility, and fear. The association is psychological, but it springs from the perceived structural analogy of their victimization. Marx's analysis accounts nicely for this. Since for him capitalism itself was a gigantic expropriation from workers of the value of their labor, no wonder that they should be associated with and seen in the same ways as the more distantly expropriated.

So at any rate they were seen, for example, by one E. H., in the course of a not unsympathetic account of the Maoris. This writer urges (as did the Jesuits) that their sort of savagery, in the versatility of its skills and tasks, the generality of its knowledge, is not without either virtue or religion. Their life compares favorably to the deprived existence of the civilized working classes; the barbarian is both "better and happier" than they. "Without questioning the *necessity* of the savage man giving way before civilisation, may it not be doubted whether the first steps are not backwards?" Backwards indeed, E. H. admits, since the Maori is both better and better off in his present state than a worker in a Manchester cellar, a coal miner or a field laborer in England. But: this is no argument for letting the Maori alone to enjoy his savage and unexploited state, since "Man is progressive. Yesterday, he had savage vices; to-day, he has civilised vices. Yesterday, when his neighbor died, perchance he ate him; today, he does not eat him when dead, but, living, he starves him, hangs on him rags, binds him to a single spot an animal engine merely, or shuts him out from the cheerful light of day. But ever rolls towards us the unchallenged tomorrow" (*CM* 1848: 8.340).

Though the rhetoric, complete with the fantasy of people-eating, is perfervid and rambling, the contrast is succinct and specific. Civilization is a net loss: of freedom, knowledge, physical well-being, and mastery of varied skills. The latter contrast, between the versatility and acuity required of the savage hunter and the imbecile monotony imposed on the factory worker or rural laborer, had been made since the late eighteenth century, and was the sort of observation that prompted Marx to formulate the notion of the worker's alienation, under capitalism, from both the process and product of his work. For E. H., though, it's just a civilized vice, a necessary backward step in "Man's" inevitable progression; the savage must dwindle into a wage laborer, lose all he now has, give way to or be rolled over by the juggernaut of the future that civilization has sent hurtling his way. (I'm trying to make sense of the empty pomp in the last sentence above; your guess is as good as mine.) What savage in his right mind would not resist such a future; what worker not revolt from such a present? The contrast makes clear the logic of these reactions and the consequent fear of them. The expropriated can be danger-ous—more so at home, of course, than abroad.

There, what the savage is to be expropriated from is his land. So, as usual, the glories of the landscape are everywhere contrasted to the meanness of its inhabi-tants (who are still identified with it in other ways). E. H. writes lots of florid, styl-ized, and turgid descriptions of New Zealand's "sublimity," appropriating it by means of the clichés of European art. "Down in some deep glen, where the shaggy hills rose broken and confused around, the clear stream gliding over its rocky bed, the massive trunk fallen over the water, and the single beam of light pouring down at mid-day upon the silent pool, would remind you of the forest scenes of the Ital-ian painters" (*CM* 1846: 8.163). Admitting that the first effects of clearing the forests make such magnificence ugly, E. H. justifies it just as the Americans did: "But it is not . . . unpleasing to see the lovely in nature sacrificed to the excellent in use. There is a moral beauty in the reclaiming of the wilderness—the extension of the home of the civilised—the rooting-out of the lair of the savage" (8.161). The moral beauty in the reclaiming of this wilderness was somewhat tarnished by the series of wars fought from 1844 to 1872 to take it away from the Maori. The wars merely completed what intertribal rivalries, made lethal by firearms, and dis-ease had already begun: over half the Maori population perished (Pool 1977: 234–37; Sinclair 1980). During one of these wars, a pioneer settler, unconcerned with sublimity, wrote in 1863 of the territory he was acquiring: "Its splendid soil, its vast plains, its lofty ranges, its extensive lakes, are to be taken from the Maori rebels, and placed in the hands of those who will make use of them in a noble and useful manner" (Morgan 1963: 65).

The Maori were aggressive, agricultural, and considered not unattractive by Eu-ropean standards. The aborigines of Australia were none of these, and so the usual contrast becomes extreme in their case. William Westgarth exhorts us to

> Behold the aboriginal Australian, as he now appears, surrounded by civilised men. Behold him a wandering outcast, existing, apparently, without motives and without object; a burden to himself, an useless cumberer of the ground! Does not he seem pre-eminently a special mystery in the designs of Providence, an excrescence, as it were, upon the smooth face of nature, which is excused and abated only by the re-sistless haste with which he disappears from the land of his forefathers? Barbarous, unreflecting, and superstitious, how strangely contrasted is an object so obnoxious and so useless, with the brightness of a southern sky, and the pastoral beauty of an Australian landscape!
>
> Such are the reflections that will naturally occupy the mind of the passing observer, after a cursory glance at the wandering tribes of Australia. (*CM* 1847: 10.428)

"Naturally." An anonymous settler writes that the aborigines of New South Wales are the lowest of the low "in moral degradation and intellectual power." They've no chiefs, no laws, "few, if any" words for anything other than physical needs and kinship, and no shame at being "naked before white men" (*CM* 1847: 11.248). A reporter on South Australia finds the natives drifting, lazy, begging, and ineducable—a hasty conclusion for one who sees no need "to learn their gibberish." The women "are ugly and dirty." For their condition, ethnocide is the only remedy: "If they are to be at all improved it must be by an abnegation of their own language and manners, and an entire adoption of ours" (*CM* 1848: 14.85).

Such blots on the face of nature as these folks could hardly be supposed to have any title to the lands they thus encumber. Still, it was sometimes necessary to argue this case against "certain philanthropists" who think that aborigines have rights to their property by "previous possession." Edward Phillips rehearses all the commonplaces of the legend to show "Colonisation of New Countries No Injustice to the Aborigines of those Countries." To begin with, "when the command was given to 'replenish the earth,' it doubtlessly was never meant by our Creator that some of the finest districts of the globe were to be overrun by lawless savages." No, indeed; He meant rather that we should civilize the ignorant, brutal, and barbarous. So that while we "carry forward the process of cultivating districts on which the hand of culture was before unknown," we have "the high satisfaction of seeing new and flourishing communities arise where a miserable barrenness previously prevailed" (*CM* 1848: 13.19). Had the legend not already defined the *terre gastine* as simply uncultivated, it might seem contradictory that such fine districts are also miserably barren. But it's quite logical since we know the story, which Phillips continues with the examples of Alexander and the Romans as *civilisateurs*. Despite the carnage they caused, being "animated with the lust of universal dominion," they "may yet be said to have materially raised the condition of the countries conquered." Though conquest for mere profit (Cortez and Pizarro) is nasty, conquest for colonial possession is justified by "the glorious scheme of raising savage mankind to a condition more gentle and enlightened" (13.20–21). Phillips observes in passing that instead of being thus raised, most savages tend rather to disappear; but this does not deter him.

He vehemently denies (against Rousseau) that savage life might be better in any way than the civilized. As we need "laws and restraints" for our happiness, so we need to impose them on the savages for theirs, to "bestow . . . some sort of culture upon those tribes which exist in the destitution of savage life." He goes on to detail the destitution of the degenerate, vicious, and cowardly natives of Southeast Asia, proposing them as candidates for the "blessings" of Christianity and British colonization (13.24–27). He quotes another writer's version of the universal scale of civilized modes of life, in descending order: those of the cultivator, the pastor, the gatherer, the fisher, the hunter—his "the most savage" of all, says Phillips, "his instinct is ferocious, his manners horrid" (13.28–29). So God requires us "to raise his intellectual condition" in "arts and letters" as well as morality, "to bestow a higher culture." Hence England and France, who should cooperate instead of competing, can "colonise the world" with no injustice to the savages in its "waste places," in order to create "flourishing cities . . . where formerly the war-whoop . . . echoed through the trackless forests." He urges the rapid accomplishment of this cooperative project in the Indian and Pacific Oceans, to bring the savages there our "mental culture" and—not forgetting that we do well by doing good—to develop there a commerce that will pay our national debt (13.30–31).

Phillips has thus mobilized all the images and assumptions in the ceaselessly retold story, from George Peckham and John Winthrop to Vattel and Andrew Jackson, against the same objector invoked by the latter: the "philanthropist." One of the most cogent of these, against whom the *CM* will take up its cudgels shortly after the appearance of Phillips' article, was Louis Chamerovzow, the Assistant Secretary of the Aborigines' Protection Society. He published in 1848 *The New Zealand Question and the Rights of Aborigines*, arguing that savages have title to the land they occupy even if they don't cultivate it. What makes Chamerovzow cogent is that his arguments are less philanthropic than legal. They are addressed to both the specific case of the Maori and the general question of indigenous land rights. In a lengthy Appendix, two lawyers give their formal opinions on both matters; Chamerovzow expands all their points with detailed examples and additional arguments in the body of the book.

On the specific case, the lawyers are agreed. Both deny that Britain can claim any rights of discovery (the Dutchman Tasman first recorded the islands in 1642; Captain Cook visited them much later, but established no settlement) or conquest (their natives were never conquered) to New Zealand. Britain's claims must rest wholly on the Treaty of Waitangi, made with the Maori in 1840, according to which the natives accepted the sovereignty of Britain and were in turn guaranteed possession of the lands they occupied, granting to the Crown the right of preemption, that is, of the first opportunity to purchase such lands as they were willing to sell. This treaty (still a strongly contested issue, underscored by Queen Elizabeth's visit to New Zealand in February 1990 for the 150th anniversary of its signing) obviously recognized the Maoris' existence as a nation, their prior sovereignty over themselves, since one cannot cede what one doesn't have. Hence, Britain has only the right to buy what they wish to sell.

The lawyers then give identical, though differently arrived at, responses to the general question of aboriginal rights to land that is not cultivated. John Phillimore says: "the right of property is the same in all men. . . . [S]uch right can neither be modified nor altered by difference of customs and manners. . . . [T]he law of Nature . . . never conferred a right on Christian countries to wrest, forcibly, from their actual possessors . . . lands and districts effectually and permanently occupied by savage Nations" (Chamerovzow 1848: App.14). This, we recall, was precisely the opinion of the Spanish theologian Victoria in 1539 (see ch. 15). The unmodifiable universality of property rights established for him just what it does for this lawyer; it gives us no title to take away their land because they don't farm it. The other lawyer, Shirley Woolmer, summarizes Vattel making the contrary point—the obligation of all nations to cultivate their soil—and proceeds to qualify it. Before noncultivators can be displaced by Europeans fleeing overpopulation, proofs of such conditions must be submitted. He too emphasizes the Maoris' ownership of their territory and sovereignty over it, confirmed not only by the treaty, but also by subsequent directives of British governors, one of which he quotes: "the expenditure of labor on Land is not necessary to give a proprietary . . . right to the Land" (App.44). Assuming this is correct, Woolmer concludes that Britain can only buy the land it wants, perhaps by declaring a public necessity to force the purchase. And he reaffirms the principle that Phillimore, and Victoria long before him, had articulated: that savage tribes have "full possession . . . in the most extensive meaning . . . as understood by the natives themselves, and according to their usages, wants, and manner of life" (App.50).

Taking "their" usages seriously, making property rights genuinely universal, as the lawyers do, was to obliterate the ancient and legendary distinction between savage and civilized uses of land (and will for this reason never be allowed to prevail). And it indeed requires the modification of Vattel, treated throughout as the major authority on the matter. Chamerovzow returns more than once to this crucial task. Accepting Vattel's own criterion that de facto self-government in any form establishes both sovereignty and ownership, he points out that all European powers have violated this by claiming rights of discovery over lands "*already peopled*," to which "discovery" does not apply (37). It applies only to uninhabited territories and only in relation to competing colonial powers. He then quotes Vattel on the legitimacy of taking over for cultivation lands ranged by savage hunters, and comments: "To accord to such a principle as this an unqualified assent, would be giving deliberate sanction to all those encroachments, violations, abuses and atrocities which have proved so fatal not only to the tribes of North American Indians, but to many others inhabiting various remote parts of the globe" (39). To provide such sanction was of course the point of the principle. Chamerovzow later devotes an entire chapter to its qualification.

He cites Earl Grey (who had in 1846 ordered the governor and bishop of New Zealand effectively to ignore the Treaty of Waitangi) dissenting from the idea that savages have title to their hunting grounds. Grey quotes Dr. Arnold (the famous founder of Rugby, father of Matthew, and investor in the New Zealand Company) as an authority for the notion that "incult" land is not possessed. Chamerovzow identifies Vattel as the source of this idea, and quotes him at length on the obligation to cultivate (see ch. 17 for the passage). Chamerovzow accepts the principle, but claims that these views distort it, elaborating the point made by Woolmer. The obligation is for every nation to "wholly" cultivate its soil; only after this is done can a nation extend itself by colonization. Applying the principle at home would deprive aristocrats of their sporting grounds and landlords of what laborers are clamoring for. If natives can only own the land they till, then so can we (190–94).

This neat argument identifies the distortion of Vattel's principle as its selective application. Chamerovzow insists on its universal application, first to us and only then to the savages, in order to highlight the hypocrisy of our proceedings. For he concludes, as did the lawyers, by denying that the obligation to cultivate means that only cultivated land can be owned. Rights to land, he says, are not conferred by labor; savages possess their territory, so "civilized nations" must therefore purchase it and cannot simply "extinguish native title" to it. "This condition of acquiring new territory is imperative upon them, as long as they continue to violate, in their own case, the law by which they assert that their acquisitions are regulated" (199).

There remains the larger question of whether indeed any principle can be universally applied—that is, to civilized and savage nations alike. Chamerovzow attacks this matter by saying that we could deny the application only if we could draw a clear line that separates the two. His attempts to blur this line are as close as the discourse of his time ever comes (not very close) to putting the ancient dichotomy of our founding legend into question. He simply gives an extended catalogue of atrocities in European history to show that if sanguinary cruelty is the criterion, then we are more savage than they. And then, like the Jesuits and other observers, he praises the councils, deliberations, self-control, and wisdom of savage cultures from America to South Africa. Chamerovzow is capable of fervent indignation and some mordant description—as when he mentions "our heinous war in China [the first Opium War, 1839–42], undertaken to coerce the subjects of an independent monarch to buy poison of our merchants" (208). But he cannot finally see differences as merely different—that is, see our own notion of civilization as one among others. He too invokes the single, universal scale, on which difference is but quantitative and hierarchical. If civilization is measured by "laws and institutions," he says, "then does it, only in a lesser degree, exist amongst savages, who are regulated by their own rude laws and customs, which are as binding upon them as are ours upon us" (208–209). As binding, but inferior: on the only scale there is, we have more and they have less; we are polished and they are rude.

Chamerovzow illustrates once again how the savage is double-damned even by the universalism that asserts his property rights. This logic is impeccable; but it is canceled by the universalism that keeps the savage on the lower rungs of our legendary historiographical ladder. They've only got bits of the only civilization to be had; they remain beneath, subject, as usual, to our (however well-intentioned) efforts to improve them. The deepest irony of this position is that even the universalism that legitimizes their possession of land is a projection of our entire cultural system, a "right" that the Maori, who held most goods in common, like so many native Americans, could not comprehend. (Both have learned to comprehend it since, of course, as recent litigation for compensation in the United States and New Zealand testifies; we reap what we have sown.) The *Colonial Magazine*, on the other hand, comprehended it perfectly, and found its extension to indigenous peoples intolerable.

The *CM* prints a long (by its standards) review of Chamerovzow's book with the explicit aim "of refuting his arguments, that common justice, common humanity, and a proper sense of duty to our neighbours, would have been most consulted by leaving the Aborigines as we found them—a set of degraded, disgusting cannibals and heathen savages" (*CM* 1848: 15.215). As one would expect from this declaration, the refutation will be scarcely logical—some of it is impossible to follow—but its purport is unmistakably clear. In addition to its evocation of our militant Christian duty to extirpate heathenism, the review attacks, as it must, the legal claims made in the book, in both the particular and the general case. It simply dismisses the lawyers undiscussed—"too much the air of a brief"—and focuses on Chamerovzow's general contention that the *jus gentium* cannot justify the takeover of any independent nation by another. Had the European powers obeyed this law, in Chamerovzow's words, "the annals of their history had not then been polluted by the record of crimes committed under the influence of a thirst for power, nor would society have to deplore the consequent extermination of entire tribes, whom Christianity and civilisation were destined to redeem from barbarism, not more deeply to degrade and finally annihilate." "Our answer to this," replies the *CM*,

> is simply the question, were the inhabitants of New Zealand such an organised community as the law of nations would recognise as an equal party in any suit at issue? We think that the circumstances of life and of condition would outlaw them completely, and the idea of associating with enlightened States these savage barbarians, is almost the same thing as raising error to the dignity and value of truth. Cannibals are not Christians, nor New Zealanders European philosophers, and till Mr. Chamerovzow can prove them equal, and every way alike, on better grounds than merely because they happen to be both of the human species, he should cease contending that the principles of the law of nations apply to native tribes, to whom such an extensive term of organisation would be in direct contradiction to their habits, manners, and customs. (15.216)

There are two familiar and depressing paradoxes manifest in this reply. First is the vulnerability of Chamerovzow's efforts to blur the line between the savage and the civilized as a matter of degree. For the line remains; the categories are intact, ready to be reasserted, as they are here, in absolute terms. No matter how the line be drawn, if it exists, it permits the refusal to those below it of what is granted (property rights, equality of any sort) to those above it. And the refusal is the second paradox, the denial of one universal in the name of another: civilization is universal (not having ours, or even as much as we do, they haven't any), but humanity isn't (law applies to our species and not to theirs). The explicit rejection of "common humanity" shows not the degradation of the savage but that of civilized thinking in the age of scientific racism. The savage as legendary half-beast became formalized as a subspecies, a "primitive" form of us; one could prove it by measuring his skull, his nose, his lips, his and her sex organs and her buttocks (see Gilman 1985). Both the lawyers and the Scottish enlighteners were more consistent and intelligent than this; the former maintained the universal as such, and the latter at least historicized the category of "primitive" that has here become a fixed, ontological, and irremediable (because natural) condition.

Making savages a subspecies was a great convenience to settlers, who could rid their newly acquired land of such encumbrances with a clear conscience. A Cape Colonist, who signs his articles "Klip Springer," announces that he's fed up with sanctimonious objections to shooting the Kaffirs down. And with legal objections, too (though he needn't have worried; the British fought five wars to subdue the Xhosa between 1818 and 1898):

> As for the aboriginal rights, the settlers of 1820 received their land direct from the
> British Government, and from a desert made it a garden, and if they are now to be
> told that the natives are justified in cutting their throats to enjoy possession of it, I
> presume the same rule would apply to the descendants of Ancient Britons in Wales
> who determined to recover their aboriginal rights by cutting the throats of the farm-
> ers of Shropshire or Lancashire. (*CM* 1851: 22.340)

However morally embarrassing, the historical parallel is exact, and illustrates what
the legend has always told us, and what we have ever-obediently performed. The
transmission of our omniculture entails their dispossession in an endless chain from
epoch to epoch: the Trojans do it to the Rutulians and the Giants; the Romans to
the Britons; the Normans to the Saxons; the English, Spanish, and Portuguese to
the native Americans; the British, the French, the Dutch, the Belgians, and the
Germans to the rest of the world. It's what foundation means.

Our greatest poet of foundation springs to the mind of one W. Shaw while discussing the "Prospects of Australia"—by which are meant views of both its landscape and its commercial possibilities, the two being inextricably linked. "The
country is admirably adapted" to pasturage: "vast alluvial plains, covered with rich
verdure and succulent herbs, are spread over the interior to a boundless extent. The
traveller who crosses these magnificent pastures is forcibly reminded of Virgil's description of the Dardan plains—" (*CM* 1852: 23.243). He then quotes it (in poor
English couplets) from the *Georgics* (3.341–43).

And Virgil's epic appears yet more relevantly in an anonymous account of "A
Month in Western Australia." It occurs just when this writer is looking back
twenty-three years to the foundation of the Swan River Colony (now Perth) and
dramatizing the hardships of those who first made this desert bloom:

> when settlers began seriously to think of settling—when, except seaward, nothing
> but sand met the eyes, which became painfully tender from the frequency of such
> meetings, when each step . . . was . . . in the same yielding, dazzling, granitic dust—
> when, although they could not say with Eneas, "we are denied the hospitality of the
> strand," they discovered that it was the only hospitality they were likely to be treated
> with—when nothing good to eat but maggots was found on trees, and nothing fit to
> drink. . . . (*CM* 1852:23.414–15)

When finally this ornate and breathless period is over, these folks are mighty dis-
couraged. But those who persevere become founding heroes: "These families are
to Western Australia what the Normans were to England; they supply it with a
resident nobility and aristocracy, and proudly do the fair young damsels and their
active and speculative brothers tell you that their fathers were among the original
settlers" (23.414–15). Arch literariness reproduces in the writer's diction the feudal
flavor of the sentiment (proudly do the damsels tell). But the allusions are exact:
to the chain of foundations, the legend and its enactment in due course and order,
repeated, now recalled, in this place, which is appropriated, made to bloom, its first
European invaders becoming its resident aristocracy.

Evidence of the blooming is presented: from that sandy waste now spring vines, olives, figs, plantains, bananas, guavas, peaches—all unsurpassed; and from the forests come mahogany, gum, and sandalwood. Thus much for the culture that the bringers brought and its resultant commodities; now, to complete the last legendary detail, a description of the indigenes. Here, the writer's jocose condescension gets a real workout:

> What is that dark nebula on the road before us? A nearer approach resolves it into a cluster of men, women, and children; let us gaze at these our brethren as they pass beside us. They seem to be naturally coloured by iron rust, and artificially by red and yellow ochre. How bright their dark eyes! how black their long hair! how white their powerful teeth! (23.418–19)

This mixture of linguistic registers and perspectives is rich in contradictory implications. There is, first, the cloudy, undifferentiated mass seen from a distance; then people, who are given the archaic biblical appellation of "brethren." Then red and rusty bodies; then, perhaps suggested by the color, the enumeration of bodily parts in red-riding-hood talk. The simultaneous distancing and domestication performed by all of this is remarkable. The visual, linear movement of the zoom lens—from nebula to teeth—brings us spatially ever closer; and at the same time the connotations of the words take us temporally farther back, both in cultural (the Bible) and personal (our childhood) terms. Spatially, the human status of these creatures is elided as the brief middle stage in their transformation from a cloud into fragments. The listing of these in fairy-tale exclamations is the most complex register of all. "What sharp teeth you have, Grandma!" says little Red Riding Hood; only it's not grandma, but the Big Bad Wolf. This language acknowledges our fear and laughs at it; it arouses a response that it then dispenses us from taking seriously. And it evokes a story in which an ostensible human is really an animal that eats people.

The net effect of the entire passage is to deny what it asserts. As we seem to get closer to these rusty folk, we get farther away; they're not people, but frightening and funny animals in a humanoid disguise, who couldn't possibly be our brothers. They're just figments of our childhood terrors, to be dismissed, swept away, and nostalgically recalled by our adult lucidity. They are never seen, they are overlooked, appropriated by this rich mix of our cultural codes as a threat that is no longer threatening. They are Cacus, the Giants, the painted Britons, the cannibalistic natives of America and Africa—they are all the savage others that the founding legend has imagined and reproduced and destroyed around the world. The discourse makes them invisible as sentient human beings even as they're being gazed at. They are the black boy in *Pamela*. And whether they die of our smallpox or our bullets or our destruction of their environment, our legend, its discourse and ideology, has already erased them. That is its purpose, for they are to be expropriated.

The visitor to the Swan River Colony continues to describe the wandering life of the savage who does not cultivate: "He has no need of storehouse or barn; the hut in which a night has been passed had been constructed in a few minutes, and if not required for the following night, is employed as fuel to cook the rude repast." Their expropriation is then observed from the lofty pinnacle of our moral superiority: "We have taken from them their best hunting grounds, scared away their game, appropriated their wells, lessened all their means of subsistence; and are we to give nothing in return . . .?" No, it is our duty to give them "the law of the Creator," even though this will involve further impositions. "A loud cry is raised about the injustice of imposing our laws on a people whom we do not profess to have subdued, and who have never formally submitted to our sway; but can we look on quietly while they thus butcher each other under some mistaken idea of justice, and not interpose with our superior knowledge of good and evil?" (23:419–20) Obviously not. Their habits are atrocious and in desperate need of our discipline: they love freedom, hate work, abuse their women, and throw with lethal skill spears with barbs made of broken beer bottles. "To teach them to restrain these spears by our laws, which we have armed by our bottles, is only common humanity."

This neat compensation, this cute quid pro quo, is urged in the name of what this entire discourse has erased, has shown to be empty. For there isn't any common humanity. Or, as the *CM*'s reply to Chamerovzow made clear, what little is common is insufficient to require us to treat these people as human beings like ourselves, with the same rights and entitlements. For the viewer of Western Australia, the humanity of these savages has long vanished. In colonial ideology generally, it is null or vestigial, in spite of all the pious invocations of Christian brotherhood. The discourse cannot afford it, as it cannot finally accommodate difference. If common humanity were admitted, it would risk exposing all the systems of rationalization that comprise our high culture. So our discourse demonstrates that there's no such thing, nothing common across the line, spatial or temporal, that separates the savage from the civilized. And then the discourse appeals to the category it has emptied by dividing. Here, therefore, the phrase "common humanity" can mean only what the sentence describes: an (unequal) exchange, a prohibition, a coercion, something to compel them not to use what we have given them. We can expropriate the savage's land only because our language, like our founding legend, has already expropriated his humanity.

This separation of the inseparable is performed in words (savage from human) so that it may be performed in actuality (savage from land). But the performance requires effort, for the words mean and the discourse otherwise recognizes that they are inseparable—the savage, a member of our species, and his land. In the legend, he was autochthonous, so we now see him in the distant lands we have occupied as the very color of the soil: yellow or brown or black or red or "rust." He is, as always, paradoxically identified with the land that we will take from him. There is one particular image of this identification that the movies of our century will repeatedly enact. The image was recorded in earlier narratives of travel and exploration as a physical perception. A succinct form of it occurs in the earliest captivity narrative of North America (written in the 1660s but not printed until

1885). The young writer (who will be captured by the Iroquois), out hunting ducks near Three Rivers, Quebec, is warned by a cowherd to stay away from the surrounding foothills, "ffor, said he, I discovered oftentimes a multitude of people which rose up as it weare of a sudaine from of the Earth" (Radisson 1885: 26).

A more elaborated form of the image, a virtual scenario, occurs in an account of Captain Fremont's second expedition in 1843 from the Rockies to California. Here the landscape gradually, instead of suddenly, comes alive with savage forms that appear to be part of it:

> some dark-looking objects were discovered among the hills, supposed at first to be buffalo . . . but another glance showed them to be Indians approaching at speed. At first they did not appear to be more than fifteen or twenty . . . but group after group darted into view at the top of the hills, all the little eminences seemed in motion, and, in a few minutes . . . two or three hundred, nearly naked, were sweeping across the prairie. (CM 1846: 8.2)

Hollywood will film this scene over and over again, making visible the autochthony of the legend, showing us what this witness describes as "all the little eminences seemed in motion." Out of hills and rocks they come, as they came from Virgil's tree trunks, these naked, primordial creatures. They are not quite human, seen thus; they're uncanny, terrifying, mysterious. They are just what the legend tells us to see; the twentieth century gives us newly vivid ways literally to see it. But before they come sweeping at us on the screen, the same kind of scene will have been variously presented in some of the greatest fiction and some of the most ordinary prose of the rest of the nineteenth century.

Chapter 23

ॐ

THE LEGEND AS THE LANDSCAPE

Joseph Conrad

As the nineteenth century flows into the twentieth, a single fiction of one of Europe's greatest novelists presents a version of the autochthonous savage that will stereotype a continent. This is Conrad's *Heart of Darkness* (1899), whose symbolic potency is scarcely diminished even today. Though Conrad did not invent the stereotype of "darkest" Africa, he made a psychological/geographical symbol of it that almost no European reader, but more than one African writer, has felt obliged to contest (see, for example, Achebe 1977). The power of his text results in no small measure from its articulation of the legend in practically all of its eighteenth- and nineteenth-century forms. The novella not only recapitulates these, but gives them a new push into high-Modernist mysticism, translating, as it were, the old story into a contemporary form of art, thereby maintaining the elasticity of the myth and giving it the sanction of the newly fashionable opponent of the "scientific"—the "aesthetic."

Conrad was supremely well placed to perform this, having spent twenty years circling the globe in the British Merchant Marine, most of them in the coastal trade of southeast Asia. A servant of imperial commerce throughout his career, Conrad also of course made in 1890 in King Leopold's Belgian Congo the river journey that Marlow narrates in the book. Marlow, in several other tales and novels Conrad's narrative spokesman for his usual values of duty, integrity, camaraderie, efficiency, and restraint, seems more than usually identified with his author in *Heart of Darkness*. Marlow there describes himself as a child enthralled by exploration, putting his finger on the blank, unknown spaces of a world map and declaring he will go there when he grows up (Conrad 1973: 11). Conrad attributes the identical action—in some of the identical words—to himself on two much later occasions in his autobiographical writings (Conrad 1912: 13; 1926: 17). Since these are not exactly reliable, the identification gains added resonance from the uncertainty as to whether Conrad endowed Marlow with his childhood aspirations or appropriated those he invented for Marlow as his own. Also, of course, Marlow's condemnations of the "imbecile rapacity" (Conrad 1973: 33) of the European traders in the Congo echo Conrad's in the letters he wrote while there. Finally, both the character and his creator share the penchant for being often ironic about themselves. In the story, some of this irony is applied by the framing narrator, who, along with the grunts and somnolence of the other listeners, express mild impatience with Marlow's indirect and convoluted storytelling: "we knew we were fated . . . to hear about one of Marlow's inconclusive experiences" (10). Generally, though, the audience is respectful, and the framing narrator lends positively oracular authority to Marlow by describing his cross-legged posture and complexion on two occasions as those of a Buddha.

The audience—the four men in the text and all of us readers—is indeed "fated" to undergo an insistence on mystery, paradox, incongruity, and *bizarrerie* appropriate to that most arduous and obscure of Asian religions. Tinged with divinity, Marlow's inconclusive revelation is also, of course, designed to be universal. The absence of either definite or indefinite article in the very title of the story alerts us to what the text hammers home: the symbolic darkness at once geographical and psychological, "the horror" in the heart of man revealed at the end of the journey to the end of the world, a descent into hell. "Immense darkness" (the text's last words) everywhere—inconclusive merely because the text so relentlessly asserts its mystery. It pummels us throughout, as critics have occasionally observed, and with increasing frequency toward the end, with adjectives in the form of "unable." A few of these qualify forces: unextinguishable, implacable, interminable. A few more refer to morality: inexcusable, intolerable, unspeakable. But most have to do with cognition, and all deny, in varying degrees, its possibility. Objects, people, and events are constantly said to be: inappreciable, inexplicable, insoluble, improbable, impenetrable, inexpressible, incredible, inconceivable, indefinable, impossible, inscrutable, incomprehensible, innumerable, inaccessible, unfathomable.[1]

The primary object thus qualified as passing all understanding is nothing more nor less than the landscape itself, the "wilderness" and those who inhabit it. And this wilderness once included Europe, specifically the Thames estuary where on the anchored yawl Marlow tells the tale to his erstwhile shipmates. The imperial history of this place is reviewed at the outset by the framing narrator, who rhapsodizes on "the tranquil . . . waterway leading to the uttermost ends of the earth" (6; he repeats the same phrase in the final sentence, 111), its "great spirit of the past," Drake and "the great knights-errant of the sea," treasure, conquest, Lord Nelson, "the adventurers and the settlers . . . bearers of a spark from the sacred fire. What greatness had not floated on the ebb of that river into the mystery of an unknown earth! . . . The dreams of men, the seed of commonwealths, the germs of empires." To which Marlow replies after a while: "And this also . . . has been one of the dark places of the earth" (7). Marlow goes on to imagine the place "when the Romans first came here, nineteen hundred years ago—the other day," and the feelings of a cultivated commander of a trireme here "at the very end of the

---

1. I doubt that this list is exhaustive.

world. . . . Sand-banks, marshes, forests, savages,—precious little to eat fit for a civilized man. . . . Here and there a military camp lost in a wilderness . . . death skulking in the air, in the water, in the bush." Marlow admires their fortitude: "They were men enough to face that darkness." He then imagines a young Roman civil servant "coming out here . . . to mend his fortunes . . . and in some inland post feel the savagery, the utter savagery, had closed round him, —all that mysterious life of the wilderness that stirs in the forest, in the jungles, in the hearts of wild men." This fellow "has to live in the midst of the incomprehensible, which is also detestable," and has the "fascination of the abomination" (8–9).

The whole imagined scene is that of the new frontier in the old world, the transposition of present colonial experience of Africa into the beginning of Britain's past as it was regarded by the seventeenth- and eighteenth-century historians who discarded the Trojans but made their legend historiography. We too were savages once; but we're now the functional equivalent of the Romans: culture-bringers. Marlow, however, has none of the illusions about this role that predominate in the colonial discourse of his century. And yet the very crux of the text—the dissolution of Kurtz—depends precisely on his failure to enact the role. He sets out to bring the savages culture, but winds up becoming savage himself. Conrad's text revolves, inconclusively all right, around his deep ambivalence toward just this central meaning of our founding story: that civilization must be transmitted. His main anxiety is how dangerous this can be for the transmitter. He assumes the process while narrating how it doesn't work. He reinforces the categories of the legend while inverting its plot.

Marlow makes no distinction between the old conquest (Roman of Britain) and the new (Belgian of Africa); both are

> robbery with violence, aggravated murder on a great scale. . . . The conquest of the earth, which mostly means the taking it away from those who have a different complexion or slightly flatter noses than ourselves, is not a pretty thing when you look into it too much. What redeems it is the idea only . . . not a sentimental pretence but an idea; and an unselfish belief in the idea—something you can set up, and bow down before, and offer a sacrifice to. . . . (10)

Here, and throughout the text in his portrayal of those he ironically calls the "pilgrims"—the greedy and petty extractors of ivory and enslavers of the blacks—Marlow shows little but contempt for the commercial basis of colonialism. But he also never specifies the "idea" that redeems the activities of conquest and expropriation—except to distance himself from it. For the idea is simply the humanitarian rationale for colonialism, predicated on the legendary picture of the savage. This, presumably, is the sentimental pretense he encounters in his aunt's enthusiasm for the enterprise. She regards him "like an emissary of light . . . a lower sort of apostle." Marlow is benevolently scornful of her talk about "weaning those ignorant millions from their horrid ways," in response to which he "ventured to hint that the Company was run for profit" (18). Not for Marlow, nor his creator, the happy rationale that profit and piety go hand-in-hand. If not profit, and not conventional piety, nor even the kind of material instruction in the arts of cultivation (not mentioned in the text) that constituted the humanitarian program to raise the savages from darkness—what? The aunt's connections with the "gang of virtue," as the humanitarians are called by the pilgrims, form Marlow's first link with Kurtz, whose report on the "Suppression of Savage Customs" clearly indicates his initial and pious assumption of the white man's burden.

But it's not Marlow's burden. His next link with Kurtz is formed, also against his will, by the suspicious envy the manager and other Company officers display toward Kurtz: anyone they dislike must be interesting. It is his association with Kurtz, as opposed to them, that Marlow comes later to accept as "this unforeseen partnership, this choice of nightmares forced upon me in the tenebrous land invaded by these mean and greedy phantoms" (97–98). The redeeming idea to which Marlow makes his undefined appeal exists nowhere in the text, and is supplanted by Marlow's attraction to Kurtz's presumably "unselfish belief" in it—not a concept or an ideal but a person. For this is what, in the course of the story, Marlow sets up, bows down before, and offers a sacrifice to. This language denotes the adoration of an image; and Kurtz remains, notoriously, that: a god known, or inferred, only from the rites of his worshipers. These include the Russian, the savages, and Marlow himself. One of the two very brief quotations we are vouchsafed from Kurtz's supposedly eloquent prose claims that Europeans necessarily appear to savages "with the might as of a deity." The other quotation, of course, at the end of all the "altruistic sentiment," is the unsteady scrawl: "Exterminate all the brutes!" (72) Marlow's whole tale sets up the image of Kurtz, bows down to it by insisting on how remarkable a man he was, and sacrifices to it Marlow's visceral devotion to truth in the concluding lie to the Intended.

So if the idea is replaced by the image of Kurtz, what can be "redeeming" about this? Simply the "truth" that women can't bear, that Marlow praises Kurtz for recognizing at last: that in the heart of darkness he looked into his own heart and found them identical. "He had judged. 'The horror!'" This, claims Marlow, is "a moral victory, paid for by innumerable defeats, by abominable terrors, by abominable satisfactions" (101). And this is what claims Marlow's loyalty, a "truth" he honors by concealing it from both the Company and the pious folks back in Brussels, but which motivates his telling us the story. This mystified redemption is a form of self-discovery, and Marlow, brought close to it by attraction (and to death by sickness), shares it. Were it not for the routine discipline of work, the habitual restraint of duty, Marlow too might have succumbed.

To what? What is the positive agency in the text that breaks down Kurtz's restraint, that all Europeans need all their strength to resist? Nothing more nor less than the landscape, the ultimate mystery, the personified incomprehensible, something that woos our innate lusts with its own. The forest itself is the enemy.

Marlow begins to see it this way in contrast to the Central Station: "the silent wilderness surrounding this cleared speck on the earth struck me as something great and invincible, like evil or truth, waiting patiently for the passing away of this fantastic invasion" (33). And this wilderness behaves just as the legend prescribes, disgorging and reabsorbing its autochthonous inhabitants. A beaten Negro, taken sick, left the station and disappeared: "the wilderness without a sound took him into its bosom again" (34). In the moonlight "the silence of the land went home to one's very heart—its mystery, its greatness, the amazing reality of its concealed life" (37). At this moment, Marlow is painfully enduring the jabbering of the brickmaker; he wonders "whether the stillness on the face of the immensity looking at us two were meant as an appeal or as a menace. What were we who had strayed in here? Could we handle that dumb thing, or would it handle us?" (38) Even when celebrating the arrival of the rivets that will permit the repair of his steamboat, Marlow sees the landscape as having all the threatening power of an ocean: "The great wall of vegetation, an exuberant and entangled mass of trunks, branches, leaves, boughs, festoons, motionless in the moonlight, was like a rioting invasion of soundless life, a rolling wave of plants, piled up, crested, ready to topple over the creek, to sweep every little man of us out of his little existence. And it moved not" (43).

How Kurtz will "handle" this silent menace excites Marlow's curiosity, which is further stimulated by the gossip he overhears about Kurtz between the manager and his uncle. The former expresses contempt for what attracts Marlow—Kurtz's "moral ideas" (44) of using trading stations "for humanizing, improving, instructing." The uncle assures the nephew that the landscape will rid him of Kurtz: "my boy, trust to this," with a gesture that Marlow describes as taking in "the forest, the creek, the mud, the river" and summoning "a treacherous appeal to the lurking death, to the hidden evil, to the profound darkness of its heart. It was so startling" that Marlow leaps up, expecting the forest to answer (47). But its refusal to answer merely increases the threat, which Marlow feels more intensely once the journey is begun.

> Going up that river was like travelling back to the earliest beginnings of the world, when vegetation rioted on the earth and the big trees were kings. An empty stream, a great silence, an impenetrable forest. . . . And this stillness of life did not in the least resemble a peace. It was the stillness of an implacable force brooding over an inscrutable intention. It looked at you with a vengeful aspect. (48–49)

When the silence is broken, the threat merely assumes a different form: impenetrable silence becomes uninterpretable language. A "roll of drums" sometimes hovered in the air. "Whether it meant war, peace, or prayer we could not tell" (50). "We were wanderers on prehistoric earth, on an earth that wore the aspect of an unknown planet." Any fantasy that we were "the first of men" to take "possession" of such a place was rudely shattered by the sudden apparition

> of rush walls, of peaked grass-roofs, a burst of yells, a whirl of black limbs, a mass of hands clapping, of feet stamping, of bodies swaying, of eyes rolling, under the droop of heavy and motionless foliage. The steamer toiled along slowly on the edge of a

black and incomprehensible frenzy. The prehistoric man was cursing us, praying to us, welcoming us—who could tell? We were cut off from the comprehension of our surroundings. (51)

Meaninglessness is what this land and its people threaten us with, but even as Marlow asserts it, the language has already provided the ancient and familiar meaning of the legend. For the journey backward in time simply dramatizes the historiography that Marlow invoked at the outset, the darkness that was once us and is now them. Literally "pre"historic, prior to language, the primitive has no syntax, is shapeless and without differentiation, bodily fragments in a black frenzy. The forest holds, secretes, in its silent (but vengeful) stillness the furious motion of all this cacophonous life. "We could not understand because we were too far and could not remember, because we were travelling in the night of first ages, of those ages that are gone, leaving hardly a sign—and no memories." "We" are the post-enlightenment moderns, "too far" advanced beyond this world (assumed to be) without history, signless, to recall it. It, however, calls us—and that's the problem.

It's also the logical consequence of the legendary historiography that postulates us moderns as, way back then, just as primitive as present savages. Culture was brought to us; we developed out of this state—but once, indeed, we shared it. The possibility of sharing it, of knowing what it means, is precisely the final horror of Conrad's text, the threat worse even than that of meaninglessness. Marlow feels and articulates this threat at just this moment in the story, phrasing it exactly as the legend had postulated it in the neoclassical age: our "remote kinship" with the savage. "The earth seemed unearthly" in this now unknowable prehistoric state, like another planet,

> and the men were—No, they were not inhuman. . . . that was the worst of it—this suspicion of their not being inhuman. . . . They howled and leaped, and spun, and made horrid faces; but what thrilled you was just the thought of their humanity—like yours—the thought of your remote kinship with this wild and passionate uproar. Ugly . . . but if you were man enough you would admit to yourself that there was in you just the faintest trace of a response to the terrible frankness of that noise, a dim suspicion of there being a meaning in it which you—you so remote from the night of first ages—could comprehend.

We can comprehend it because "the mind of man is capable of anything—because everything is in it, all the past as well as all the future." Because the story of our civilization is thus universal, and confronts us with "truth—truth stripped of its cloak of time." Truth is atemporal, eternal, transcendental. Fools shudder, but a real man "must meet that truth with his own true stuff—with his own inborn strength. Principles won't do." So Marlow "didn't go ashore for a howl and a dance," not because of sentiments or principles, but simply because he was kept busy by the routine discipline of navigating the boat (51–52).

The lure, threat, and danger of the wilderness is predicated upon the chaotic violence, the raging energy—howling and dancing—of the life it harbors. It is the utter disorder of savage life, sans *mos* or *cultus*, that the legend assigns to forest-dwellers. These lacks appear in the text in their usual form as the enormities of cannibalism and human sacrifice.

The cannibals, engaged as the crew of the boat, occasion a long Marlovian disquisition of wonderment as to how they could possibly have the "restraint" not to eat the white men (58–60), whom they greatly outnumber. This, he concludes, is a "mystery greater" than the sound of grief in "the savage clamour" (60). It's a mystery precisely because it violates the legendary meaning of such enormities as the absence of all restraint, of all social conditioning. Though he notes that the cannibals regularly receive their salaries (59), it doesn't occur to Marlow to suggest that they may be so far socialized as to confess an obligation for a benefit received, and hence to refrain from eating their employers. No, the only motive Marlow allows them is that of hunger—hence the mystery that they do not act on it. The physical motive is, literally, the only one imaginable—the only one, in other words, that the legend will allow to creatures of whom Marlow opines: "I don't think a single one of them had any clear idea of time, as we at the end of countless ages have. They still belonged to the beginnings of time—had no inherited experience to teach them as it were" (58). Marlow insists: "No fear can stand up to hunger, no patience can wear it out, disgust simply does not exist where hunger is; and as to superstition, beliefs, and what you may call principles, they are less than chaff in a breeze." Anything, he goes on, is easier to face than hunger: "bereavement, dishonour, and the perdition of one's soul." Hence the mystery, since "these chaps had no earthly reason for any kind of scruple" (60). For they have no history, no community, no social tradition or inheritance from which a "scruple" might arise.

They are, exactly, savages as Robertson (see ch. 20) described them. And the utter mystery of their restrained behavior is produced by the attribution to them of one possible motive, which seems as much a projection of our present selves as was the individualism that Robertson and his colleagues saw as the essence of the savage. Marlow's very passion on the subject of hunger describes, of course, the impotence of *our* principles under the lash of lingering starvation—necessarily ours, since the savages are allowed none. Now, the psychological doubling of this modern view of the savage—as embodying both our ancient condition and our present fears—is a part of Conrad's conscious theme as it was not of Robertson's. But here Conrad seems scarcely aware that the cannibals have become a mirror of ourselves; their inexplicable restraint is merely (as savage dignity so often was for the Jesuits) an implied rebuke to our pretensions to rise, by civilized principles, above physical necessities. The issue here is the nature of the "remote kinship" that Marlow feels, and has predicated on the legendary historiography. But this issue is not raised with respect to the cannibals, whom the text presents as the ultimate other, whose restrained behavior is consequently "an unfathomable enigma."

Conrad, it should be clear by now, is mystifying the legend by psychodramatizing its universality. Unlike the *Colonial Magazine*, *Heart of Darkness* does not deny our "common humanity," but locates it at the lowest level of what human beings may be presumed to share, the level above which we restrained, civilized folks vainly fancy we've progressed. The whole vertical and temporal scale remains firmly in place; what is common is not our sociability, but their bestiality. Our atavistic longings to jettison restraint—to howl, dance, and receive the heads of our enemies in tribute as Kurtz does—are what make us kin. Savages are not like us (they have no past and no coherent society); but if we don't watch out, we will become like them. The darkness of external savage space equals that of our innermost emotional space, and is inherited (by *us*) from what we were when Caesar came to civilize us. The latter darkness has long since given way to the illuminated imperial metropolis; but the former still has a local habitation and a name: it is tropical Africa.

Those who venture into that terribly hostile space must see to it that their kinship with it remains "remote." The attack on the steamer immerses Marlow in a nearer kinship that he finds immediately intolerable. The attack comes, of course, from the organic identity of forest and inhabitants. Out of the silence stream, silently, arrows. Marlow "saw a face amongst the leaves on the level with my own, looking at me very fierce and steady and then suddenly, as though a veil had been removed from my eyes, I made out, deep in the tangled gloom, naked breasts, arms, legs, glaring eyes, —the bush was swarming with human limbs in movement, glistening, of bronze colour" (64). Then, "the bush began to howl" (65). The helmsman is killed by a spear, and his blood fills Marlow's shoes as Marlow must take over the wheel. He ends the attack by sounding the steam whistle, and summons a pilgrim to take the wheel: "To tell you the truth, I was morbidly anxious to change my shoes and socks" (67). While Marlow does this, he suspends the narrative for five pages, in which he gives us the fullest information about Kurtz that the story contains. As he flings one shoe overboard, Marlow realizes how much he had looked forward to a talk with Kurtz. At the end of this crucial digression, Marlow affirms that Kurtz is unforgettable, though perhaps "not exactly worth the life we lost in getting to him." This returns Marlow to the dead helmsman, who is also unforgettable: "the intimate profundity of that look he gave me when he received his hurt remains to this day in my memory—like a claim of distant kinship affirmed in a supreme moment." Marlow appreciates this relation: "He had steered. . . . It was a kind of partnership," and admits the oddness of "this regret for a savage who was no more account than a grain of sand in a black Sahara." He then laments the helmsman's imprudence in opening the shutter: "He had no restraint, no restraint—just like Kurtz" (73). Marlow puts on dry slippers, and heaves the helmsman's body overboard to prevent its consumption by the cannibals.

The claim of blood, the universal brotherhood of death, is both physically obnoxious and psychologically compelling to Marlow. Kinship is acknowledged as long as it's "distant." And the measure of the distance between Marlow and the double figure of his physical/psychic kin—the blood-triggered association of the helmsman and Kurtz—is their lack of civilized "restraint." The final emblem of this lack for Kurtz, the ultimate sign of his descent into savagery, is the other enormity of human sacrifice. When Marlow sees that the round objects impaled on poles around Kurtz's house are human heads, they but confirm the diagnosis: "They only showed that Mr Kurtz lacked restraint in the gratification of his various lusts, that there was something wanting in him." He had a "deficiency," a hollowness that no principle or sentiment could fill, of which Marlow thinks he only became aware "at the very last. But the wilderness had found him out early, and had taken on him a terrible vengeance . . ." (83).

And here, at last, the malevolent agency as imagined by Marlow throughout makes its fullest appearance, the legendary autochthony on its way to cinematic enactment. The steamer is anchored below Kurtz's house; the sun is setting:

> Not a living soul was seen on the shore. The bushes did not rustle.
>
> Suddenly round the corner of the house a group of men appeared, as though they had come up from the ground. They waded waist-deep in the grass, in a compact body, bearing an improvised stretcher in their midst. Instantly, in the emptiness of the landscape, a cry arose whose shrillness pierced the still air like a sharp arrow flying straight to the very heart of the land; and, as if by enchantment, streams of human beings—of naked human beings—with spears in their hands, with bows, with shields, with wild glances and savage movements, were poured into the clearing by the dark-faced and pensive forest. (85)

The magic wilderness thus emits both the indigenes, and, at their center, Kurtz himself on the stretcher. All the previously imagined menace now impends: "if he does not say the right thing to them we are all done for," says the Russian to Marlow. But apparently he does; the stretcher is borne to the boat as Marlow notices "that the crowd of savages was vanishing without any perceptible movement of retreat, as if the forest that had ejected these beings so suddenly had drawn them in again as the breath is drawn in a long aspiration" (86).

And there is more: the personified landscape is endowed with a soul to match its multiplicity of bodies. In the last rays of the sun along the shore

> moved a wild and gorgeous apparition of a woman.
>
> She moved with measured steps, draped in striped and fringed cloths, treading the earth proudly, with a slight jingle and flash of barbarous ornaments. She carried her head high; her hair was done in the shape of a helmet; she had brass leggings to the knees, brass wire gauntlets to the elbow, a crimson spot on her tawny cheek, innumerable necklaces of glass beads on her neck; bizarre things, charms, gifts of witchmen, that hung about her, glittered and trembled at every step. She must have had the value of several elephant tusks upon her. She was savage and superb, wild-eyed and magnificent; there was something ominous and stately in her deliberate progress. And in the hush that had fallen suddenly upon the whole sorrowful land, the immense wilderness, the colossal body of the fecund and mysterious life seemed to look at her, pensive, as though it had been looking at the image of its own tenebrous and passionate soul. (87)

The apparition is exotic, military, aristocratic, and erotic all at once; a "tawny" (not, one observes, black) amazon from the ancient Mediterranean imagination arrayed in contemporary colonial trash as a modern image of the feminized landscape who fills her conqueror with desire. Except that desire, here, is abomination. It no longer serves the founder, but thwarts and destroys him. Her fecund mystery is what we'd better not want to penetrate. And it's that of the land itself, sexualized mother earth since Gê, sublimated by this narrative into "soul." "She stood looking at us without a stir, and like the wilderness itself, with an air of brooding over an inscrutable purpose." All she does is to throw her arms up above her head, "as though in an uncontrollable desire to touch the sky, and at the same time the swift shadows darted out on the earth, swept around on the river, gathering the steamer into a shadowy embrace" (88). The tenebrous soul of the wilderness, gorgeous and magnificent, summons the darkness to embrace us. She repeats the gesture the next day as the boat leaves: "the barbarous and superb woman . . . stretched tragically her bare arms after us over the sombre and glittering river" (97). And this is the gesture Marlow remembers when a similar one, also "tragic," is made by the Intended at the end: "bare brown arms over the glitter of the infernal stream, the stream of darkness" (110).

In the literary versions of the legend from Geoffrey of Monmouth to Pope, the feminized sexuality of the landscape was either briefly assumed or explicitly developed. The desire it aroused was no mystery. Here it is both intensified and masked, a kinship the more attractive because distant, the more threatening because repressed (Marlow's memory recalls her naked arms, not those with wire gauntlets), and so turned into a mystery by the language, shrouded in satanic innuendo, enveloped in all the culturally prestigious registers of religion and metaphysics. Sexuality has become a (rather transparent) secret in Conrad's text, as it did in so much nineteenth-century discourse. The text, and Marlow, work very hard to assert mystery, no harder than at this moment, when Kurtz arrives on board and the tawny woman gestures and disappears. A conversation with the despicable manager pushes Marlow to his strongest identification with Kurtz, now his willed "choice of nightmares." But as Marlow directly says, it is less with the much diminished person, finally encountered, than with the mystified agent of his diminishment: "I had turned to the wilderness really, not to Mr Kurtz, who, I was ready to admit, was as good as buried. And for a moment it seemed to me as if I also were buried in a vast grave full of unspeakable secrets. I felt an intolerable weight oppressing my breast, the smell of the damp earth, the unseen presence of victorious corruption, the darkness of an impenetrable night . . . " (89). The volume of "un-ables" is raised as Marlow feels that *he* is buried in the earth; he and Kurtz at one with the savage land. Kurtz's identification with it is again explicit when Kurtz staggers off the boat and Marlow fetches him back, trying to break "the heavy, mute spell of the wilderness—that seemed to draw him to its pitiless breast by the awakening of forgotten and brutal instincts, by the memory of gratified and monstrous passions. This alone, I was convinced, had driven him out to the edge of the forest." Thus Marlow sees "the inconceivable mystery of a soul that knew no restraint" (95). And it is this, of course, that constitutes Kurtz's singularity, his attraction for and extortion of loyalty from Marlow.

There follows the last glimpse of the prehistoric autochthony that has destroyed Kurtz. When the boat leaves the next day, the crowd of savages "flowed out of the woods again, filled the clearing, covered the slope with a mass of naked, breathing, quivering, bronze bodies." They are led by "three men, plastered with bright red earth from head to foot," who "shouted periodically together strings of amazing words that resembled no sounds of human language; and the deep murmurs of the crowd, interrupted suddenly, were like the responses of some satanic litany" (96). Only the woman remains still as Marlow sounds the whistle so that the crowd will flee in terror, saving them from the pilgrims' rifles. Marlow's acts are humane; but his vision is that of his whole century and the legend of his whole culture. The forest and the people it pours forth are the inarticulate denizens of "the first ages"; they are the "powers of darkness" who claim Kurtz "for their own. . . . He had taken a high seat amongst the devils of the land—I mean literally. You can't understand," Marlow insists to his audience, we who live among butchers and policemen (70), so far from the dawn of these untrammeled brute instincts—which, however, will claim us if we lack "restraint."

But of course we can understand; we've been understanding perfectly since Virgil. For the Roman poet, civilization—the towers and institutions of a city-building agricultural order imposed from without—was inherently fragile, threatened by its own dynamic of transmission or repeated foundation, the furies of Saturnia wiping out the justice of Saturn. For Conrad, the fragility has become psychological: the slender hold that altruistic motives, humanitarian sentiments, and benevolent principles have on the individual. We think we're civilized—but just plunk us down in the wilderness and watch us disintegrate. This is what Conrad's text claims is incomprehensible. But it's logical; it follows from the universal time-scale and hierarchy of the founding legend since the Enlightenment; and the traffic on the scale is strictly one way. We can sink; but there's never even the possibility of their rising—by themselves. The "kinship" is on that one fixed scale of one kind of development; we can regress, but they can't accelerate (unless, of course, we suppress their savage customs). They have no language and no past, unless we give them ours; and that is the effort at which Kurtz, whom Marlow calls "childish" more than once, fails. That Kurtz has learned *their* language, with its inhuman sounds (how then can Marlow recognize them as "words"?), is but a further sign of his regressive degradation into gratified desires.

The ambivalence of Marlow, and of the text, is in the attitude toward this regression, given, of course, the disillusionment with the imperialist programs of missionary development and the brutalities of imperialist behavior. By contrast with these, Kurtz's "immersion in the destructive element" (a description of another of Conrad's doomed heroes, *Lord Jim*) becomes courageous and victorious. It is his total surrender, his utter lack of restraint, and his apparent awareness of it, that Marlow admires and hankers after himself. The abomination is fascinating; this is no mystery, either. But it is to Marlow and to Conrad, this moral collapse of whatever redeeming idea Kurtz is supposed to represent. "His mother was half-English, his father was half-French. All Europe contributed to the making of Kurtz" (70), as it certainly did to that of Conrad. He grew up among Polish nationalist revolutionaries to become a cosmopolitan and conservative aesthete; his second language (which he preferred to speak) was French, while he chose to settle in England after his seagoing career and to write all his fiction in English. All Europe (including, of course, the United States) produced, enacted, and reproduced the founding legend, too. And Conrad's tale advertises the mystery of its inversion: the unfounding of the would-be founder. No redemption, but personal damnation instead—and an attraction to this destiny which is a belated expression of Byronic romanticism.

Conrad's late-Victorian mystery play, however, sets the contest between good and evil (making the latter attractive in the Byronic way) at the last imperial frontier. Marlow goes there out of curiosity, Kurtz out of redemptive (which may include, as the word does, financial) longings. The place is regarded as all the colonial world was regarded in the adventure fiction of the day: as the testing ground for real manhood. It's where the European individual encounters the atemporal truth of his own being. Truth stripped of time meets the individual stripped of all his social, civilized accoutrements and supports. But the encounter happens in a particular place, here tropical Africa, which, as usual, is described but not seen. Whatever it may be is overlooked, here drowned in a sea of "un-ables," deliberately mystified, so that it can become merely the symbolic repository for everything that *we*, like Kurtz, "desire and hate" (101). Marlow, in contrast to his childhood avowal, is not very curious at all about what might be indigenously "there," in this place; he is rapidly disgusted by the pilgrims and obsessed by Kurtz. The indigenous life in most of Conrad's exotic fiction, from Borneo to Bombay, remains vaguely mysterious, a fragmented and shapeless mass, except for the few native individuals who must act upon the hero, providing him with the background or occasion for his moral crisis. It is the whole colonial world and its (darker-hued) people seen as the private moral gymnasium of a European male that generates the rhetoric of mystery in Conrad's fiction. The places themselves are overlooked in order to become the boxing ring of an occidental psychomachia, a screen on which we project ourselves.

The historiographical narcissism that postulated the single, universal scale of human development from savagery to civilization is complemented in Conrad by the fullest expression of its psychological corollary. The colonial landscape, the savage forest, is but our own interiorized space; we expropriate it by symbolizing it: it's that timeless, universal, ugly, throbbing, splendid, barbarous heart of darkness. The continent thus appropriated as the site where we discover our "true stuff" has exercised its fascination on generations of western literary critics up to the present day. They customarily accept not just the metaphor but also the supposed actuality of this place, about which there's no need to be more curious than Marlow is, since we already know what it's like, the forest of our founding legend. So the critics talk about the Africa of this text as if it were as Conrad mystified it: the "geo-

graphical heart of darkness"; the "rim of the universe"; the "descent into the primitive sources of being"; "the darkness of ignorance represented by the primeval environment and aboriginal inhabitants of the Congo."[2] Sophisticates of symbolism,
we know what we're going to find in Africa since Conrad, and do not hesitate to
find it in just about any subsequent novelist. Nadine Gordimer is praised by an
American reviewer: her "setting is Africa . . . but in her Africa, we find ourselves."
Thanks to Conrad, in fictional Africa we almost never find anything else.

The obliteration of difference was the project of natural law and eighteenth-
century social theory; these made the savage a child, a rudimentary form of us.
Making otherness absolute was the project of nineteenth-century colonial propaganda and racist science; these made the savage another species, ontologically
different from us. Conrad's novella does both of these things simultaneously, even
while explicitly dissenting from the latter sort of racist conclusions. For it thematizes the obliteration of difference as the great danger—the civilized can regress
into the savage—thereby making the maintenance of otherness a necessity for survival. And it thematizes otherness as all that unutterable mystery of the indigenes
in their jungle, so completely alien to anything we are, so totally baffling: their
drums, their frenzies, their words "that resembled no sounds of human language."
That mystery, that numbingly repeated refusal of cognition, must be maintained at
all costs—for if we *understand* it, we're lost; difference disappears, and we become
as all the versions of the legend have told us they are.

It is our legend of the savage that furnishes Conrad with the epistemological
and moral horror of "going native." What those natives are like, having no *mos* and
cultus, we already know, have always known, and so don't need to inquire, must
not find out. We must never know, to understand or experience, the people in the
real world whom we are expropriating, and whom we know from our founding
story to deserve this fate. Conrad finds expropriation repugnant in fact, but his text
performs it symbolically, making Africa the dark mirror of our (now very danger-
ously) common humanity. And his text masks the expropriation as a mystery, creates that mystery as a necessary (for us) otherness.

The exact location of this mysterious otherness constitutes the most interesting
twist that Conrad gives the legend: the displacement of hostility from the people
to the land itself. Marlow doesn't quite see the people, but he sympathizes with
their condition as victims. From the beaten and chained blacks at the Central Station to the autochthonous band of naked bronze folk at Kurtz's compound, Marlow attributes no malice to the indigenes. Even in their howling attack on the
steamer he hears sorrow and grief, and we learn even before it is narrated that the
attack was less aggression than it was a kind of desperate charm, intended more to
frighten than to injure (62). And of course Marlow finds the tenebrous soul of that
wilderness, the tawny lady, attractive indeed. No, it's the land itself that is filled

---

2. These phrases come from a popular casebook edition of the text (Conrad 1971). The subsequent
edition (1988) of the same text, however, has begun to include a few dissenting essays, including that
of Achebe.

with obscure and "un-able" intentions; the wilderness is vengeful; it handles, it threatens, it's full of darkness even on a sunny day; it knows us—why we must refuse knowledge of it—it finds Kurtz out and wreaks its vengeance on him. It is the personified agent, the incarnation of enmity to civilization. It is what inverts the plot of the founding story, for it, by ancient definition, can bring no culture; it can bring only death to the culture-bringer.

When our founding story functioned primarily to provide an entitlement to civilization, from the early Middle Ages to the Renaissance, it laid no stress on the woeful, cultureless condition of the indigenes in the place destined to become an empire. When, after the beginnings of the European conquest of the globe, the primary function of the legend became to justify the dispossession of the indigenes, their cultureless condition had to be demonstrated ad infinitum. It was the enabling fiction of the imperial enterprise. In literature, the change occurred with Spenser, who labored mightily to establish the criminal and incestuous nature of Britain's giants. And now, three centuries of colonial domination after Spenser's death in 1599, Conrad makes the wilderness the indigenes inhabit as nasty as Spenser made the giants. This displacement of hostility onto leaves and trees and bushes and water and weather came easily, no doubt, in this particular landscape, owing to the high mortality rate of Europeans in tropical Africa since the late eighteenth century. But it took a writer of genius to transform a bacteriological fact into a metaphor whose symbolic power stereotyped a continent. The transformation was easy, too, for its blueprint had always lain in the legend: the savage and his land are one.

Conrad's text actually *blames* the landscape, the tropical forest, for the destruction of Kurtz; it almost gets Marlow too. This is quite as illogical as Spenser's transferring the injustice of the giants' behavior to their land tenure. Blaming the landscape is the real mystery in *Heart of Darkness*, and all its asserted mysteries exist both to perform and conceal this operation. The mystery of Africa as the psychological testing of our "true stuff," where we confront our atavistic, savage longings, is based on the mystery of Africa as the dawn of time, locked into the unrecallable first ages of primeval humanity. And this place, the savage place, is the enemy.

Conrad was not the first so to construe it, but he was certainly the most influential. Nor was blaming the landscape for the fate of the white man who perishes in it confined to Africa. There are many American examples of this activity in the nineteenth century, one of which furnishes a large book on the subject with its title: *The Fatal Environment* (Slotkin 1985). The phrase was used by Walt Whitman in a poem praising the heroism of George Armstrong Custer, called "From Far Dakota's Cañons." That environment is called fatal because it contained the crafty "Indian ambuscade." There are, I shall argue, serious consequences to this ultimate variant of our founding story: making the wilderness itself—plain, hillside, canyon, desert, or jungle—an agent of savagery.

Blaming the landscape is the last refuge of humanitarian colonialism, the final effort to preserve the enabling fiction of the savages' lack of culture. It's not their fault; just look what their environment can do even to us more supposedly advanced creatures. It's also a convenient obfuscation of our desire to possess their landscape, to mine, harvest, and market its commodities. And it's the final mystification of their otherness, a splendid excuse for our inability and unwillingness to comprehend them. But it will become, this hostile place—in Conrad so ambivalently poised between demonic mother and avenging spirit—the object of our own hostility. And it will be transported from America and Africa to Asia, where, after it frustrates all our good intentions, we shall kill it.

Before Marlow arrives in the Congo and begins to weave the magic spell of this hostile wilderness, he reveals the lunacy of regarding it as hostile in a famous and striking image. Perhaps the image records something Conrad actually witnessed. At any rate, the action it describes will be performed a half-century later off the coast of Korea by the U.S.S. *Missouri* and will then be recorded as a humorous anecdote. Whether as fable or as fact, the action is the logical consequence that reveals the total absurdity of blaming the landscape—the last variant of the legend that Conrad's text itself invents, leaving it for the twentieth century to enact. This is the action:

> Once, I remember, we came upon a man-of-war anchored off the coast. There wasn't even a shed there, and she was shelling the bush. It appears the French had one of their wars going on thereabouts. Her ensign dropped limp like a rag; the muzzles of the long six-inch guns stuck out all over the low hull; the greasy, slimy swell swung her up lazily and let her down, swaying her thin masts. In the empty immensity of earth, sky, and water, there she was, incomprehensible, firing into a continent. Pop, would go one of the six-inch guns; a small flame would dart and vanish, a little white smoke would disappear, a tiny projectile would give a feeble screech—and nothing happened. Nothing could happen. There was a touch of insanity in the proceeding, a sense of lugubrious drollery in the sight; and it was not dissipated by somebody on board assuring me earnestly there was a camp of natives—he called them enemies!— hidden out of sight somewhere. (20)

Incomprehensible? Rationally, yes; but in terms of the myth that Conrad's text transmits and modifies, not at all. The nationalistic implication is amusing—it's the French who do such silly things—and recalls the fervor with which, so long ago, Brut was defended as true even as Francion was declared a fable. Fiction or fact? Both, as usual, in due course and in the mutual reproduction that constitutes the history and transmission of our civilization and its legend.

Chapter 24

᭡

THE MOVABLE FRONTIER

British Colonial Administrators

In the 1860s and '70s, Henry Sumner Maine, Oxford Professor of Jurisprudence, "introduced the idea that Europe's past could be studied in India's present" (Symonds 1986: 115). It was less an introduction, of course, than a transference. Maine was an historian of Roman law who spent a part of his career as a civil servant in Calcutta. For him, Roman institutions quite simply defined civilization, whose history was that of the gradual development of those institutions, and of their subsequent transmission, demise, and recovery in the modern west (Maine 1870: 168). Our society is thus unusually "progressive"; most others are "stationary." Hence, "the study of races in their primitive condition affords us some clue to the point at which the development of certain societies has stopped. We can see that Brahminical India has not passed beyond a stage which occurs in the history of all the families of mankind, the stage at which a rule of law is not yet discriminated from a rule of religion" (22–23). In the now very familiar laboratory of the colonialized present we can observe our own savage past, before we got Romanized. In the customary law of the Hindus "some of the most curious features of primitive society are stereotyped" (7). Here, therefore, in Indian or Oriental "political society . . . is a far more trustworthy clue to the former condition of the greatest part of the world than is the modern social organisation of Western Europe" (Maine 1875: 383). For we, of course, have "developed," while they are arrested at a far distant stage of the only history there is, the one Rome wrote for us.

The archaism Maine found in Indian religion and political society Hegel had already found in Indian religion and art. In his *Lectures on Aesthetics* (collected after his death in 1831), the philosopher applied to art the progressive dialectic of "spirit" becoming ever more conscious of itself that he had previously applied to history and philosophy. The first stage of art Hegel calls the "symbolic": it is characterized by a lack of appropriateness between form and content that sets them in continual strife and contradiction. And it belongs to "nations in their childhood" (Hegel 1970: 400–12). Of these, India represents the "fantastic" variety of the symbolic. In both narrative and visual arts, there is a grotesque mixture of forms, a riotous tumult of transformations and mixtures (animal and human, vegetable and divine, colossal and trivial), a "world of witches" (*Hexenwelt*) in which nothing is clearly defined or precisely graspable (431–35). Such a jumble, in which no "true beauty" is discoverable, is the initial inchoate stage that will give way to the "real" symbolism of the Egyptians and the "conscious" one of the Hebrews.

Both these varieties of nineteenth-century progressivism, Hegel's and Maine's, will supply the perspective that relegates India to the "primitive" condition long familiar in the legend. The theoretician of aesthetics and the historian of law thus accomplish in the realm of the *studium* what had been practiced in that of the *imperium*. This practice was that of the deliberate deindustrialization of the country, described in the 1840s by a spokesman for the East India Company: "this Company has, in various ways, encouraged and assisted by our great manufacturing energy and skill, succeeded in converting India from a manufacturing country into a country exporting raw produce" (quoted in Wallerstein 1989: 150.)[1] What was useful for the British economy—reducing India to the colonial function once fulfilled by America and now by Africa—thus became a principle of European scholarship: pushed into the (primitive for us) role of agricultural commodity production, India's whole culture could now be seen as primitive. What the universalized historiography of the legend had long prescribed about the indigenes of America and Africa came thus also to characterize those of the Indian subcontinent. They too were now drawn, by the irresistible confluence of material fact and learned fiction, into the established orbit of the legend triumphant. The rich and ancient history of the Hindu states and the Mogul conquests, all the evidence of competing civilizations that had prevented prior generations from regarding the peoples of India as savages, were now overlooked as all "native" subjects became belated members of that category, assimilated to centuries of European experience on frontiers of our own creation.

In the heyday of the Empire, from the crowning of Victoria as Empress of India in 1867 to the First World War, the frontiers of the British Raj in India were formally administered by district commissioners (later called collectors—what they collected was taxes). They presided over a staff of junior officers in the Indian Civil Service (mainly magistrates and tax collectors) as well as police officers, engineers, doctors, and educators. The DCs were responsible to the provincial governors, and so on up the line to the viceroy. The ICS recruited its members largely from the takers of pass—or nonhonors—degrees at universities, preferably Oxbridge. It was more concerned to find gentlemen than scholars, since, as one of them so recruited wrote in 1890, few holders of first-class degrees would come to India when their prospects of joining the ruling class at home were so good. The Colonial Office,

---

1. The destruction of India's arts and manufactures was also observed by Hobson (1905: 292.)

which provided the administrators of British Africa, recruited from the same pool, but more widely—from the redbrick universities—and with less rigorous standards. What, during this period, these young men took degrees in was overwhelmingly classics. Though Benjamin Jowett, the great translator of Plato, master of Balliol and vice-chancellor of Oxford, devised a postgraduate program to teach ICS candidates something about India itself, it was short-lived (Symonds 1986: 3–5). So the young men who sallied forth to rule the empress's subjects were qualified for the task by scraping through their exams in Latin and Greek, known at Oxford as "mods" (grammar and rhetoric) and "greats" (philosophy and history).

The young man, Donald Cowie, who understood the value of an Oxbridge first, was one among hundreds of colonial administrators who graduated from Oriel College in Oxford and subsequently described their overseas experiences in letters to their old tutor and friend, the Rev. Lancelot Ridley Phelps. A lecturer in political economy, Phelps spent the whole of his long life at Oriel, was provost of the College from 1915 to 1929, and kept an enormous collection of his correspondence (now in the College Library) from former pupils, dating from around 1880 to 1936, the year of his death. Amid the social bonding of old-boy gossip, requests for favors and polite chitchat, these letters reveal more directly than arguments intended for print the attitudes of their writers to what they are doing and to whom they are doing it.

What is most striking in the correspondents from India, even in a cursory survey like mine,[2] is the perhaps predictable absence of any serious comment on or analysis of the culture in which they find themselves, or interest in its history. One gets from these letters the impression that India had no history, save that of its relation to the Raj. One would at least expect some intellectual interests to be expressed to a former teacher, and some are. Various correspondents strive for apposite quotations in Greek or apologize that they've forgotten it in the effort to study local languages. Others discuss their reading, both serious and casual: Kipling, Froude, and Stevenson are great favorites; and one fellow likes Schopenhauer. Politics, both local and global, are often mentioned. But virtually none of the Oriel alumni who were governing the Indians evinces the least curiosity about their way of life, habits, customs, or society. Like all travelers to exotic places writing folks back home, they almost always describe the landscape, the climate, and their own amusements. But none (in my sample) ever so much as mentions what all such travelers usually notice, if only in passing: the local food, handicrafts or arts, dress, music, diversions—the sorts of things that the most casual sojourner in an alien world has always noticed, from Hakluyt's humbler voyagers to you or me writing postcards.

To be sure, imperial administrators were neither explorers nor tourists; they had routine tasks to perform, and they indeed sometimes describe those. But their odd

---

2. Of a few hundred among the 96,000 letters the collection is estimated to contain; it has never been catalogued.

incuriosity is not, I think, to be accounted for merely by the obvious insularity of the colonial bureaucrat and his general preoccupation with inter-service rivalries, hopes for promotion, and so forth. For the incuriosity is so pronounced as to amount to a kind of collective unconsciousness of these imperial subjects as people. Rather, they appear at best as objects, often refractory, of paternalistic concern; at worst they do not appear at all. Here is an extreme, but not untypical, example: one DC writes from "camp" somewhere in what he calls his "little empire of 2000 square miles" that the natives are incorrigible liars. He then remarks, "I much fear that I shall get no quail shooting this year, as the partial failure of the crops has left no cover" (A. R. Bonus, 10 Jan. 1889). Whatever other consequences than the destruction of a season's sport such a crop failure might have for those lying natives are simply not seen. The native as person is even more invisible to his lord and master than the aborigines of the Swan River Colony were to their Virgil-quoting observer: the latter at least looked at them, if only through the lenses of legend and fairytale; this DC doesn't even look.

And even when others look, what they see is seldom a person in a social world; instead, they see a savage in just that asocial state defined by the legend and solidified since the Enlightenment into an ideology that makes perception unnecessary. The very shapes and circumstances of the civil servant's physical world in India were contrived to create and maintain a qualitative distance between the ruler and the ruled that made concrete the ontological separation of the civilized from the savage. A recent arrival in Agra, who twenty-five years later will occupy a senior post in Lucknow, describes one such shape: "The roads are very good being so arranged as to have a middle part for driving [in carriages] called the pukka, made of kunkan a sort of limestone that binds like snow, and two side parts for riding and for natives to walk on, called the kutcha and composed principally of dust" (J. W. Hose, 10 May 1887). Horses and natives occupy the dust; civil servants do not walk. The next year, the same man describes his household in Agra, which consists of eight servants, three of whom are occupied full-time cutting fodder for his three ponies. He observes, with mathematical precision exaggerated as assertion, not as irony, that "with the exception of just one man in 5000 the native is a beast."

A young officer in Upper Assam classifies these beasts on a scale of increasingly negative value: the Assamese are worse than the Bengali babu. (This term, a respectful Hindi salutation, entered English as a pejorative designation for a native who had acquired a superficial or basic literacy in the language of the Raj, someone employable as a commercial or imperial clerk.) Worst of all are the hill tribes of Assam, whom the officer must propitiate in order, he says, to avoid raids. He does this by supplying them with opium, and appreciates the irony of the situation: "We have I am thankful to say improved on the old system of civilizing them: instead of sending up troops to burn their villages, we set up rum shops and mission schools and as they are beginning to put on coats and trousers and drink by the bottle one may fairly expect them to be civilized off the face of the earth before long." He is wryly uncomfortable that the government should be "mixed up" in the drinks traffic; "but drink the savages will and . . . government may as well profit as anyone else" (H. Le Mesurier, 24 Mar. 1887). Twenty-two years later this gentleman is DC in Dacca, fulminating against agitators for independence—a logical position for one who sees the natives as the mendacious children that savages naturally are: only adult persons, like us, can be independent.

The utter lack of independence in the administrators' judgments of their charges is numbingly repetitious, and lasts throughout the period. It is worth noting, therefore, that a few officers do indeed try to explain why the native appears, especially, as a congenital liar. One junior judge describes his work in Punjab: "The majority of cases brought before a youthful magistrate are for debts claimed by Hindu moneylenders against Muhammedan peasants, and I can't help taking advantage of any little hitch in the ordinarily plain-sailing course to the decree, to make a point in favour of the debtor. Imagine interest of 38 p.c. per annum—yet I had to decree that in a suit only yesterday" (A. J. Grant, 24 Aug. 1890). Another young magistrate in Punjab understands what this situation leads to, and writes, remarkably without indignation, of the Indians' habit of falsely accusing a neglectful debtor of assault, as a way of scaring him into paying up (P. W. O'Brien, 6 Apr. 1890). This writer, though, came from a family that had lived in India for thirty years, and so perhaps had both experience and equanimity that the others, fresh from the 'varsity, lacked. But one other, in Bombay, goes farthest in offering to exculpate the native from the general charge of untruthfulness on the grounds of differing cultural expectations: his courtesy, desire to please, and fatalistic philosophy are all invoked to suggest that his ways may not be ours (R. E. Brown, 1892).

This recognition, that the "native" indeed has (rather elaborate) social and cultural mores, is—like all the other recognitions, from Hakluyt to Charlevoix, that savage life is in fact not destitute either of *mos* or *cultus*—drowned in the chorus of legendary repetitions. A lawyer in Bangkok opines that "the Siamese are a contemptible race" (H. V. Page, 17 Sept. 1890); an officer in Allahabad finds the Bengalis "the most contemptible race I had yet struck in a country of mean men" (H. R. Nevile, 3 Dec. 1908). This favorite adjective is almost never illustrated by anecdote or description; it's a foregone conclusion. In the Northwest Frontier Province, an ICS officer finds welcome relief from the false accusations and petty thievery of the lowlanders, and formulates the principle of their treatment to which all his peers subscribe. It's foolish, he writes, to imagine equality between unequal races; as his father told him, "they are children," and are to be treated as such. This sage advice requires the confirmation of experience: "But till one has actually lived amid an inferior civilization (not in vice-regal lodge) one does not believe in its existence" (Arthur Scott, 5 Nov. 1905). The corollary of the principle is formulated by a writer in Campbellpore: "When you cease treating a native autocratically he ceases to be contented" (H. B. C. Arthur, 2 Aug. 1908). Like a child, he's happy to be arbitrarily disciplined; he wants domination. This postulated desire is the nineteenth-century equivalent of the desire imputed in the sixteenth century to the feminized landscape: she wanted to be penetrated, made fruitful, or even graciously raped, by the culture-bringing founding hero. The symmetry is transparent: she wanted, and they want, just what we want—us as possessors and dominators.

And it doesn't much matter where we dominate or what actual kind of native desires our discipline. The legend's historiography and ideology are universal, global: Assamese or Bengali, Siamese or Punjabi, Sudanese or Egyptian, Masai or Zulu—all are reduced in the eyes of those who ruled them as a matter of everyday routine to a status that varies only, as our definition of the savage always has, from the bestial to the infantile. This is why there is as much incuriosity about African life as there is about Indian on the part of the Orielenses who served on that continent, as they increasingly did after the First World War. One of them proudly quotes the Rev. Phelps to himself, from a speech he gave at a festive College dinner in 1925, in which he observed that Oriel "still holds a monopoly in the administration of the Sudan" (G. R. Bredin, 7 July 1927). The Sudanese, according to one of these monopolists, rival the worst Egyptians in "their aptitude for mendacity" (R. K. Winter, 17 Mar. 1909). As for the Egyptian, writes an alumnus in Cairo, he is "by nature an impulsive irresponsible and immoral infant" (Arthur Wiggin, 12 Nov. 1921). From Rhodesia we learn that the Zulu is "dirty" (T. F. Sandford, 14 Aug. 1910), and from Tanganyika that the Masai "are a very degraded type" (W. S. Baldock, 31 May 1923).

In Africa, too, there are very few exceptions to the rule of incurious contempt. The man who found the Zulu dirty also suggests, inadvertently, in the same letter, a reason why: "we teach him that he is dirt before the white man . . . wholesome as far as it goes. But we make no attempt . . . to teach him to rule himself speaking of the race as a whole." The writer goes on to express horror at the "behaviour of the white man, official and civil, when away from the restraints of civilization." Aside from such occasional moral qualms about the colonizers, the colonized remain largely invisible, as usual, except to an assistant commissioner, also in Rhodesia, who writes of learning Sesutu and finds the natives both "interesting" and "pleasant." He is, moreover, fascinated by their "extraordinary" customs, one of which he narrates in some detail, claiming that when a tribesman becomes too rich, the witch doctors have him ceremonially killed and redistribute his goods among the others, taking a percentage for themselves (E. W. Vellacott, 24 Feb. 1922). What is striking about such a report, whether accurate or not, is that it was made at all, given the rarity with which natives are ever seen to exist as members of their own (very different) social community.

The exceptions once again prove the rule, which is that of the legend. As applied to the landscape, the rule produces the now familiar paradoxical picture: it is both an object of desire and exploitation (of which the savage is incapable) and an object to blame for the degeneration of European settlers. A schoolmaster writes from Port St. John of Pondoland (on the east coast of South Africa) that it is "a quiet little spot and one of the most beautiful in Africa." Cecil Rhodes, he continues, "saw the immense natural advantages of the place and the possibilities of the Country behind us, at present in the hands of the Pondos, and totally neglected, while it is probably the most fertile and productive area in the Union." The heat of the climate, however, makes work difficult: "everything tends to laziness and slackness. Even our Parsons," he confides jocularly to the Rev. Phelps, put things off till the morrow, thus imitating the Kaffirs (F. E. Suckling, 5 Feb. 1914). A writer in Nairobi laments the degenerative effects of the climate on the whites and their children who remain there and do not have, as all the members of any colonial service do, regular periods of home leave. The provision of leave, of course, was the crucial safeguard against the awful likelihood of going native. Any settler, this writer maintains, who stays put for fifteen or twenty years becomes a "brute." He then offers an analysis of the brute's attitudes that perfectly summarizes all the kinds of overlooking and reducing practiced in colonial discourse, enacted by colonizers, and reinforced by the scientific racism of the period. The white man "knows that physically, mentally and morally he is the superior of the African. . . . Consequently he regards the African as something put into the world for his convenience, like his horse or cow. Usually he doesn't treat the African badly but then neither does he ill-treat his horse" (A. R. Wise, 22 Mar. 1924).

The point is wryly made; but only its tone distinguishes it from the claim to dominion over the earth and its creatures that Christians had, since the Middle Ages, read out of the Bible and used, since the Renaissance, to legitimize the colonial foundations mandated by the legend. That Adam was allowed by God to name the animals (Gen. 2.19–20) was accepted in the hermeneutic traditions of both Catholicism and Protestantism as signifying both man's knowledge of their natures and his consequent ability and natural right to dominate them, to use them for his purposes (Waswo 1987: 284–85). The epistemological and the political were fused in the act of naming—the use of language in which *studium* and *imperium* are inseparable. Now, at the apex of modern colonialism, those who in fact exercise the latter need only as much of the former as the legend supplies, and so can simply assimilate the natives—wherever they are and however various their own culture and history—to beasts of burden, creatures designed for our use. Centuries of commodifying and dominating the planet and its peoples have formed this attitude and trained its blindness; centuries of legal, economic, literary, theological, philosophical, historical, and scientific discourse have rationalized and justified it. And both behind it and within it lie almost two millennia of imperial storytelling, in which the ever-expanding frontier of city-building agriculturists brings the only civilization we can imagine to savages whose lack of it is all we need to know in order to domesticate, annihilate, or otherwise erase them.

But I have not exhumed these voices of Victorian and Edwardian imperial emissaries merely to provide further first-hand evidence of such erasures. I have done so rather to show how the legendary frontier is globally mobile, how the enactment of the legend makes it the same place, and its inhabitants reducible to the same status, wherever we plant that frontier. From the geographically European point of view, it moved first to the west—Troy, Rome, Troynovant, the Americas—then to the south and east—India, Africa, Asia. From the American point of view, it moves inexorably westward, across the continent, and, in 1898, across the Pacific with the official annexation of Hawaii and the Philippines. By the turn of this century, the only frontiers left are in the tropics (the polar regions being still frontiers only of exploration, since they as yet afford little in the way of marketable commodities). And it is the tropical landscape that gets blamed for the dissolution of the culture-bringer. It was this frontier in the Congo where Marlow and Kurtz tested their "true stuff." And it is the same frontier, relocated in India, where a generation later the moral fiber of the English characters in another great fiction is similarly tested.

Chapter 25

§➤

THE LEGEND AS MORE LANDSCAPES

E. M. Forster

The interchangeability of imperial frontiers indicates the great elasticity of the founding myth that tells us the difference between the civilized and the savage. The myth was given this tensile strength by becoming in the modern—that is, post-Enlightenment—west both a universal historiography and a scientific dogma. What was everybody's genealogy in the old days when the Trojan descent was history is everybody's destiny now that the sun never sets on the British Empire. So its administrators can deal equally with Africans or Indians as children or beasts; and so its novelists can find gymnasia for our moral exercise equally in both. The exercise in E. M. Forster's *A Passage to India* (1924) is rather different, of course, from that in the *Heart of Darkness*, but only as different as the individual temperaments, styles, and experience of their writers. The structure, strategy, and imagery of these texts share the Modernist symbolism of their age and perform a similar inversion of the founding story that at the same time assumes and deploys its categories. For both are stories of failed attempts at foundation; both dramatize the moral dangers of culture-bringing to the culture-bringers; and above all, both blame the failure not on the colonized (who are, in ambiguous ways, sympathized with), but squarely, if mysteriously, on the landscape.

Both stories motivate their plots by differentiating the European protagonist from his fellow colonizers, whom both humane, enlightened novelists depict with contempt as insensitive bigots. Marlow's self-estrangement from the "pilgrims" in the Congo is paralleled by Fielding's from the Club members in Chandrapore (the fictional location of the first two sections of the novel). Such estrangement is both cause and consequence of the heroes' willed attachment to what the bigots disapprove of: for Marlow, Kurtz; for Fielding, Aziz and his Muslim friends. Both Marlow and Fielding are characterized by their moral superiority, their truthfulness and liberalism, their compassion for the native imperial subject—all established precisely in contrast to the attitudes of the bigots. Forster's portrayal of the latter, in the "Turtons and Burtons" of the whole ICS apparatus in Chandrapore, is amply

confirmed by the epistolary voices of Rev. Phelps's correspondents. Not surprisingly, since Forster may well have met some of those very persons, and certainly
did meet many like them, during his two extended stays in India in 1912–13 and
1921. Their arrogance, isolation from and ignorance of the people they rule, as well
as the hysterical herd instinct of their behavior in crisis (the cruel rejection of Miss
Quested after her testimony in court)—all serve to distinguish the moral courage,
the individual integrity, of the hero who opposes them. The hero judges for himself, is lucidly self-aware, is not swayed by caste prejudice, greed, ambition, or necessity; he is dedicated to his profession, whether captain of a ship or principal of
a college, which embodies values of discipline, restraint, intelligence, and rationality to which he is unswervingly loyal.

This highest character-type of occidental civilization has been seen by a recent
critic as the defining aim of "major" modern literature, especially the novel: the
production of "autonomous ethical identity" (Lloyd 1987: 19). Marlow and Fielding are fine examples of the type, and are placed by their authors in the situation
that, both consciously and unconsciously, reveals its limits: the moral gymnasium
of the imperial frontier. The first limit is that neither is able to justify the existence
of that frontier or his own participation in it. Marlow cannot state or share the
idea that redeems the taking away of the earth from its darker-hued indigenous
possessors; he can only be loyal to the memory of the man who once had such an
idea. And Marlow is there in such a part of the earth only to fulfill a childhood
longing; he needed a job, and took this one for purely personal reasons. So, exactly, did Fielding. He tells Aziz and his friends, "I'm out here personally because
I needed a job. I cannot tell you why England is here or whether she ought to be
here. It's beyond me." Forster (the novel's omniscient narrator seems to me indistinguishable from its author) informs us biblically of Fielding that "the zeal for
honesty had eaten him up." So he is incapable of saying that "England holds India
for her good," or of judging the fairness of colonial dispossession. He just likes the
place, is "glad" and "delighted" to be there (ch. 9). No more rationalization or sentimental pretense for him than for Marlow. Fielding later articulates, in stating his
aim as an educator, the credo of the whole moral and literary tradition that produced his character-type: "I believe in teaching people to be individuals, and to
understand other individuals. It's the only thing I do believe in" (ch. 11).

The other, and more profound, limit of this admirable type appears in the effort
to achieve that understanding. This effort is central in all of Forster's novels, and
is almost always carried on in some variety of cross-cultural context, which is just
what complicates it and makes it difficult. Across the barriers of class at home and
those of national temperament abroad, Forster's well-intentioned individuals struggle, often vainly and with tragic consequences, to understand individuals whose
otherness lies in belonging to a different social and cultural world. From the encounter of the repressed, provincial English with the ebullient, impassioned Italians (*Where Angels Fear to Tread*, 1905) or merely with their art and atmosphere (*A
Room with a View*, 1908), through the collisions of social class, where the conflict
and attraction are between the cultivated cosmopolitan and the rural laborer (*The*

Longest Journey, 1907; *Maurice*, 1914) or the capitalist parvenu (*Howards End*, 1910)—all of them being opposed by the petty bourgeoisie—Forster's individuals strive, in his famous motto, only to "connect" with others. The connection is sought always in the privileged (since Richardson) sphere of personal relations: love (both hetero- and homosexual), marriage, and friendship. But it is seldom found there; only one of the novels (*Room with a View*) brings about the conventionally conclusive happy marriage. All the rest involve (sometimes violently) catastrophic consequences for the protagonists.

The conventional reading of these disasters, in part encouraged by the earlier books themselves, would be as a late Romantic pitting of the "individual"—sacred to liberal, bourgeois political ideology—against "society." The rational, humane, highly cultured, and compassionate individual is frustrated or destroyed by the insensitive, grasping brutalities of a social system too crude and stupid to appreciate him or her. But it is Forster's distinction, in his last novel, to suggest that the morally courageous individual's effort to understand and connect may be itself misguided, that the understanding striven for may not be obtainable in that way, on those terms. And Forster is led to the suggestion precisely by the limit situation, the moral gymnasium of the imperial frontier, by contriving a confrontation with the most radical form of otherness in all his fiction. *A Passage to India* is indeed a logical conclusion of his work (he wrote no other novel in the last forty-six years of his life). For it arrives at a blind alley in the central effort to "understand other individuals"; there's nowhere left to go, at least not, as we shall see, in language.

The limit of the character-type that Fielding articulates and that both he and Marlow embody was also suggested, differently of course, by Conrad. In the sea captain's fictional world, the focus is less exclusively on personal relations. His heroes, unlike Forster's, are not questing for "connection"; it is rather thrust upon them. Typically they encounter a kind of double, who mirrors some impulse crucially threatening to the moral professionalism of their own identity: Leggatt in "The Secret Sharer" (1910); *Lord Jim* (1900), whose status as "one of us" so obsesses Marlow; and of course Kurtz. The young captain has no trouble at all sharing and understanding the secret of his second self; the limit appears only in the older and more reflective Marlow, himself a virtual double of the author. Marlow recognizes the fascinating hold that Jim and Kurtz have on him; his verbal narrations are motivated by it, staged as his own effort to comprehend an "inconclusive" experience. The framing narrator of *Heart of Darkness* also describes what is peculiar about Marlow's storytelling: "to him the meaning of an episode was not inside like a kernel but outside, enveloping the tale which brought it out only as a glow brings out a haze"—like a misty halo made visible by the shining moon (Conrad 1973: 8). This splendid image, of meaning as mist, directs us to seek it not in what the story says—that is, the mystery that it so heavily asserts—but in the method, circumstances, process, and motivation of its telling. The point of a Marlovian story is not to figure out what its protagonist (Jim or Kurtz) really *is*, but to ask why and how Marlow gets involved with and obsessed by him. This is why his narratives are so carefully staged as oral recitations to a present audience; their meaning is not inside the tale, but outside it, in the act of telling.

Part of this hazy meaning of *Heart of Darkness* is the willed refusal to understand (the terror of even "remote" connection with) the savage other. And part of it, the part that suggests the limit, is the admitted inability of Marlow to understand, completely, the European other who is the double of the self, who has done something the self doesn't dare. Kurtz, casting away all restraint, goes where Marlow cannot follow, making "connection" impossible. And in so doing, he arrives at a final judgment, a victorious summing-up, that Marlow cannot make; when brought close to death, Kurtz had his word to say, but Marlow had none (Conrad 1973: 101). Similarly, Marlow does not finally know, toward the end of a long novel, just what to think about Lord Jim—whether he is ennobled by his lordship of Patusan, heroic in his self-imposed exile from the white imperial world, or still a childish egotist. Did he achieve there the grandeur of the idealism he had earlier violated? "For my part," Marlow answers his own elaborately posed question, "I cannot say what I believed—indeed I don't know to this day, and never shall probably" (ch. 34). And at the very end, even Jim's self-sacrificial death—what Marlow calls "his pitiless wedding with a shadowy ideal of conduct"—fails to resolve the question: "He is gone, inscrutable at heart" (ch. 45). Both would-be culture-bringers to the jungles of Africa and Southeast Asia wind up, for their fascinated narrator, as "inscrutable" as the landscapes they become identified with. But in addition to being a mystification of the legendary picture of those landscapes, the volume of "un-able" adjectives in Marlow's tales points steadily to a failure of cognition that is not a refusal to understand but a limit of the understander, something about his effort that dooms it. The doomed effort calls into question the terms in which it's been made, the whole perspective of the "autonomous ethical identity" that Marlow and Fielding exemplify.

Conrad never directly examines what these terms are; but Forster does. The reason he does is that his effort of understanding is directed in his last novel at the other, the "native" and his different culture, in ways that Conrad's almost never is. Marlow in the tropics becomes obsessed with other Europeans, who ought indeed to be understandable in his terms—but they escape, having somehow gone native. Fielding in India has transported there, as in their ways have Adela and Mrs. Moore, the Forsterian quest for personal connection. And when it fails, it leads to both quiet and cataclysmic interrogations of the terms on which it's been conducted.

The quiet, and the clearest, interrogation is made by Fielding himself at and as the very climax of his moral triumph in the book. He refuses to participate in the ICS Club members' massively racist reaction to the accusation of Aziz (for assaulting Adela in the caves of the Marabar Hills); the rest of the English comfort each other "by demanding holocausts of natives" (ch. 22). Always marginalized by his association with the Muslims, he now completes his self-ostracism by announcing his belief in Aziz's innocence to the Club and resigning from it. Fielding, though called a "swine" at one point, does this with cool self-control, dignity and tact, alone in keeping his temper when even the collector has lost his. He walks, and is shoved, out of the room and "to regain mental balance" goes directly out onto the upper veranda, where he looks at the landscape in a paragraph that concludes the chapter:

> It was the last moment of the light, and as he gazed at the Marabar Hills they seemed to move graciously towards him like a queen, and their charm became the sky's. At the moment they vanished they were everywhere, the cool benediction of the night descended, the stars sparkled, and the whole universe was a hill. Lovely, exquisite moment—but passing the Englishman with averted face and on swift wings. He experienced nothing himself; it was as if someone had told him there was such a moment, and he was obliged to believe. And he felt dubious and discontented suddenly, and wondered whether he was really and truly successful as a human being. After forty years' experience, he had learned to manage his life and make the best of it on advanced European lines, had developed his personality, explored his limitations, controlled his passions—and he had done it all without becoming either pedantic or worldly. A creditable achievement, but as the moment passed he felt he ought to have been working at something else the whole time—he didn't know at what, never would know, never could know, and that was why he felt sad. (ch. 20)

Forster does not allow Fielding to savor his triumph of autonomously ethical behavior; instead it evaporates like the light, overtaken by the dark mass of the hills, which leaves him unsatisfied with himself, regretfully incomplete, sensing that something is missing. In its quiet, understated way, this is an astonishing moment in modern fiction generally, and in Forster's particularly. For it makes somehow irrelevant just that exercise of moral courage which validates the character-type that so much of that literature aims to produce. Here the kind of character, self-consciously and painstakingly formed, who can exercise it and has just done so is made to feel his own emptiness.

The feeling arises, "suddenly," from the sight of the darkening Marabar Hills becoming one with the sky. "The sky settles everything" in India, we are told in the book's opening pages, "because it is so strong and so enormous" (ch. 1). And the sky has literally the last words in the novel, settling the final rupture of the friendship between Fielding and Aziz; it says, "'No, not there'" (ch. 37). It is the landscape-cum-skyscape that precipitated Fielding's moment of quiet interrogation; and it is that part of the landscape where the nonevent occurred that is the central issue of the novel's plot, Aziz's alleged assault on Adela. Something mysterious did indeed happen in the Marabar Caves, but not this; and it happened not to them, but to Mrs. Moore. And it is her role in the structure and design (what Forster called the "pattern and rhythm") of the whole novel that suggests what is missing in the exemplary Fielding. The way in which Mrs. Moore associates with Indians and experiences India, the way in which she is present (even after she dies) in all three sections—Mosque, Caves, Temple—as well as in the courtroom at the climax of the trial: all supply what the rational individualist lacks. And this turns out to be a pan-religious mysticism, an intuitive spirituality amounting to a kind of telepathic oneness with the rest of the universe that is similarly attuned. The pattern of the novel provides this somewhat coyly, and its language often makes it possible for us to dismiss it. But it's there, as the only alternative Forster can offer to the reasonable goodness of the right-minded. It's also there as a symbol of all India, which, in the formless chaos of its material existence, can be grasped or unified only in the mind of (a vaguely nonsectarian) God.

The land/skyscape makes Fielding feel inadequate; but India triggers off the innate intuitive capacities of the whole Moore family. What Fielding can never "know" he can come closer to by means of his wife, Stella, Mrs. Moore's daughter. He returns to India with her and her brother, Ralph, to see Aziz in the Hindu state of Mau in the last section of the book. Ralph intuits Aziz's malice and is praised by him as a true "Oriental" (ch. 36). Fielding finds in India a "link" that had been lacking between him and his wife, whom he passionately loves, but in whose presence he feels "half deaf and half blind." She is a spiritual seeker, like her brother, whose interest in Hinduism Fielding "can't explain, because it isn't in words at all" (ch. 37). The reconciliation of Fielding and Aziz before their final parting is presided over by the spirit of Mrs. Moore, of whom Professor Godbole has had a vision while dancing in the temple to celebrate the birth of Krishna (ch. 33). Fielding had earlier suggested to Aziz that "the Hindus have perhaps found" what religion has not yet been able to sing (ch. 31). Earlier still, resisting "the supernatural," Fielding and Adela decide, apropos of Mrs. Moore's belief in ghosts, that "the dead don't live again," whereupon Forster dryly comments: "There was a moment's silence, such as often follows the triumph of rationalism" (ch. 26). At the end of the chapter, "fatigued" by the momentous day of the trial and its aftermath, Fielding "lost his usual sane view of human intercourse, and felt that we exist not in ourselves, but in terms of each other's minds—a notion for which logic offers no support and which had attacked him only once before, the evening after the catastrophe, when from the veranda of the Club he saw the fists and fingers of the Marabar swell until they included the whole night sky" (ch. 26). This is not quite the "notion" that struck Fielding at that moment of quiet interrogation, but rather a specification of the vague dissatisfaction with himself that he then felt. It's Forster's dissatisfaction with the whole enterprise of fashioning an autonomous ethical identity, along logical, advanced, modern lines. And the novel is carefully designed to suggest, diffidently but insistently, that the dead do live again, precisely in other people's minds.

For this is just what happened at the trial, when the crowd, responding to the quarrel about the absence of Mrs. Moore, the Indians' friend, rhythmically chants her name, "Esmiss Esmoor," as the names of divine avatars are endlessly chanted, transforming her (to the disgust of Ronny, her son the magistrate) into "a Hindu goddess" (ch. 24). The chant calms Adela, causes her to lose the "echo," the buzzing in her ears that has been haunting her, whereupon she withdraws her accusation of Aziz. We later learn that this manifestation of Mrs. Moore's spirit occurred after her death at sea, shortly after leaving India (ch. 26). Well it might, for in life Mrs. Moore was supernaturally capable of intuiting other ghosts, like that of the drunken man, believed by the Nawab Babadur to have caused the accident to his car. Told the cause was an animal, Mrs. Moore blurts out, "a ghost!" and, asked by Adela to explain, disclaims it with, "I couldn't have been thinking of what I was saying." Indeed, it wasn't "thought," for the next paragraph informs us of the Nawab's conviction about the vengeful spirit of the man his car had killed nine years earlier. "None of the English people knew of this . . . ; it was a racial secret communicable more by blood than speech" (ch. 8). Mrs. Moore has got it, though, for she's a kind of innate Hindu, who, arguing with Ronny's opinion that the British Raj is not in India in order to behave pleasantly, says "The desire to behave pleasantly satisfies God. . . . The sincere if impotent desire wins His blessing" (ch. 5). It could be Godbole speaking, whose love for Mrs. Moore and the wasp that she loved (ch. 3) are products of his entranced vision during the Krishna festival in the final section. Hinduism as the religion that transcends speech, accepts good and evil as shared by all entities in the universe, and includes dirt, fun, practical jokes as part of its formless and mystical worship, is what the novel presents as a structural force, an agent in its plot, felt, though barely acknowledged, by the character-types to whose entire, rational, moral identities it is the intuitively benevolent alternative.

The accuracy of the presentation—of Hindus and Moslems alike, which has long been disputed—is not the issue. The issue is how the presentation functions in the novel as a critique of the rational individualism that all occidental civilization, and especially the fictional tradition in which Forster himself works, has produced. On one level, the critique can appear as but another late Romantic cliché, the privileging of feelings over reasoning, another version of embracing the irrational out of disillusion with what the (supposedly) rational has wrought. Again, Forster's earlier novels operated partly in this vein, staging crises in which the protagonists were driven to acknowledge their feelings and act upon them. But only partly, because even in those books Forster never presented feeling and thinking as mutually exclusive, but as equally necessary. And in *A Passage to India* the critique goes deeper because of both its context (the nonoccidental world) and its target (the rational *and* compassionate individual). Fielding cannot "know" what he should have been working at because it's not a matter of knowing in his conscious, controlled, self-perfecting way. Nor can he and Adela (or the reader) ever "know" exactly what happened to her in the cave. Neither they nor we can decide— Forster keeps it deliberately undecidable in the text and insisted on this during long subsequent years of critical argument and interview. A real attack by the guide? An hallucination? Produced by her asking Aziz about marriage? (It is popular and plausible to ascribe it, as David Lean's film did, to her terror of sexual desire.) A kind of vision, as terrifying in its way as Mrs. Moore's? We cannot, and Forster does not want us to, finally "know." We can instead interrogate, as Fielding does, the terms of our knowing. Our conventional rationalism is made irrelevant.

And what is also made irrelevant, by the same mystical medium of Mrs. Moore, is the other aspect of the admirable character-type: its individualism. As rationalism is found inadequate in Fielding's quiet questioning of his own character and its relation to the mystic Moores, individualism is what gets subjected to the cataclysmic interrogation of Mrs. Moore's experience in the cave.

This is the famous echo that "is entirely devoid of distinction," that reduces every sound to "boum." The cave is "crammed with villagers and servants." It is pitch-dark and stinks. Mrs. Moore "didn't know who touched her, couldn't breathe, and some vile naked thing struck her face and settled on her mouth like a pad." She panics and rushes out. She calms down, realizes "that the naked pad was a poor little baby, astride its mother's hip," but still declines to visit any more caves. She then sits alone and begins a letter to her other children in England. But the experience in the cave begins to obsess her: "She minded it much more now than at the time. . . . [T]he echo began in some indescribable way to undermine her hold on life." For it tells her that all things are identical, from piety to filth. She tries to continue her letter, but thinks then of "poor little talkative Christianity, and she knew that all its divine words" from Genesis to the passion of Christ "only amounted to 'boum'." Her vague discomfort from all the travel and anxiety of the last two months crystallizes: "she realized that she didn't want to write to her children, didn't want to communicate with anyone, not even with God. She sat motionless with horror." The "affectionate and sincere words" she had spoken to Aziz "seemed no longer hers." "She surrendered to the vision" and lost all interest in everything (ch. 14).

Indeed she does. From the sweet, outgoing, right-minded, sincere, honest, affectionate, pious old lady who won Aziz's heart at the chance meeting in the mosque with her remark that "God is here" (ch. 2), Mrs. Moore becomes withdrawn, bitter, irritable, indifferent, cynical, and uncommunicative. She drops out of the narrative entirely while the crisis of the plot occurs, and when she returns (for her last appearance in the flesh), it is to exhibit her transformation and quiet Adela's own "echo" by causing her (not by telling her) to think of Aziz's innocence. The scene begins with Mrs. Moore refusing to tell Adela about the echo: "Say, say, say. . . . As if anything can be said! I have spent my life in saying or in listening to sayings; I have listened too much. It is time I was left in peace." She refuses to attend the trial, claims that marriage is pointless, and concludes: "And all this rubbish about love, love in a church, love in a cave, as if there is the least difference" (ch. 22). This from the dutiful mother who brought Adela to India to be courted by her son the magistrate, and who worried early on (when distracted by thoughts of God) that she was not sufficiently keeping her mind on this "serious subject": "Would they, or would they not, succeed in becoming engaged to be married?" (ch. 5). Yet, all her transformation into indifference and ill-temper now subliminally persuades Adela that Aziz is innocent. Adela claims that Mrs. Moore said so; Ronny insists, correctly, that she didn't. When asked directly, she replies indifferently, "Of course he is innocent." But Ronny still convinces Adela that she's not well, is convinced that his mother is senile and determines to send her home. To the boat she goes in the next chapter, in which Forster comments at some deprecating length on the reductive shallowness of her vision and the pettiness of its effects. "Her constant thought was: 'Less attention should be paid to my future daughter-in-law and more to me, there is no sorrow like my sorrow,' although when the attention was paid she rejected it irritably" (ch. 23). But the power of her intuitive capacities to influence the plot is firmly established.

Mrs. Moore's revelation in the cave is the dissolution of all difference, and its effects on her are orchestrated around her relation to the social practice whose very operations—semantic and syntactic—depend on difference: language. The echo strikes the ear; the vile thing covers her mouth; the vision/echo takes her over only as she tries to write. Christianity, a religion of the book (like Islam in this respect; and Aziz, who writes poetry, is shown as wholly opaque to Hinduism), is "talkative." Mrs. Moore is weary of words, tired of explaining, finished with all effort to communicate, and she forthwith passes beyond them into death. In that state, however, communication will continue in other ways. She lives in others' minds, as in Godbole's trance, where, Forster tells us, "it made no difference whether she was a trick of his memory, or a telepathic appeal" (ch. 33).

The transformation of Mrs. Moore is a radical negation of the whole Forsterian quest for personal connection, for understanding other individuals. If there is understanding, it isn't rational; and if there is connection, it isn't with individuals. In the metaphysics of Mrs. Moore's "horror"—just as in Kurtz's—individuation, all basis for difference, disappears. That's what's horrifying: Kurtz, whom all Europe produced, is no different from the savages. Once supremely eloquent, Kurtz too has passed beyond explanation and communication; Marlow hears nothing from him except querulous childishness and his final word. And he lives on, too, in the memory of Marlow, which constructs his story. The horror is, precisely, what *The Colonial Magazine* avoided by denying: that humanity is "common," that at some (hideously regressive) level, as the echo says to Mrs. Moore, all human things from nobility to obscenity "would amount to the same" (ch. 14). She succumbs to a vision that denies the autonomy of the ethical identity that the modern novel has been dedicated to producing. For if humanity is common, then its "ethics"—in both the ancient sense of characterizing habits or customs and the modern sense of making moral judgments—cannot be autonomous, a self-given law by an individual. And identity is not personal, not individual; one is all and all is one—Mrs. Moore, wasps, stones, or Krishna. So it is logical that as Mrs. Moore subverts the whole literary enterprise she comes from, she at the same time negates its major concerns: love, courtship, and marriage. For dramatizing these, along with the threat to them constituted by adultery, *as* the most "serious" matters of moral choice that individuals can make (this is what distinguishes modern fiction from older comedy), is the central preoccupation of the bourgeois novel, from, say, Jane Austen to D. H. Lawrence. And in this negation, Forster's novel concurs: whether Adela will marry Ronny is not what it's about; and Fielding's courtship of Stella (who never appears) is ignored.

The novel, however, does not and cannot concur in Mrs. Moore's metaphysical negation. It both gives and takes away the mystic intuitiveness on which its plot, pattern, and rhythm is made to depend. What the mystic episodes accomplish in the structure of the story can be discounted by the language that narrates them. For, with the single exception of the "ghost" that the Nawab thinks wrecked his car, the text provides "rational" explanations for everything that happens. It colludes with Ronny himself, though with much greater intelligence and sympathy, in ascribing Mrs. Moore's transformation to "spiritual muddledom"—a twilit "double vision" of the world's simultaneous horror and smallness, "in which so many elderly people are involved" (ch. 23). She's a little crazy. So is Professor Godbole, from whose oracular utterances the reader is always distanced by humor, from his stories that end in cows (ch. 19) to the farcical disarray of his spectacles and grease-covered garments during the Krishna festival (ch. 33). Sinking all difference in moments of spiritual oneness is where this novel finds genuine "connection"— and if this is all that's available as the destination of the Forsterian quest, it's no wonder he wrote no more novels. For this place is beyond language; the unity there achieved, Forster makes clear, can't be articulated, or even thought, anywhere else; the experience of such unity is not expressible by anything other than itself. The spiritual adept, he writes of the festival in the temple, "may think, if he chooses, that he has been with God, but, as soon as he thinks it, it becomes history, and falls under the rules of time" (ch. 33). And under those rules, which are also those of language, all places and moments in the material world are full of the differences that make lasting connections impossible.

The supreme difference, the one that symbolizes the failure of the main connection in the book, the friendship between Fielding and Aziz, is that between the landscapes of India and Europe. Although this opposition is not quite between a settled city and a wilderness, the Indian landscape and its people appear, from the novel's first page to its last, as a variation (to borrow Forster's own musical metaphor to describe his fiction and its ambitions) on the theme of the legend. Such power has the fictional symphony of our civilization, that its melody is played even by texts explicitly composed to sing other tunes in quite another key. The melody is heard first in the opening description of Chandrapore's physically ascending social hierarchy: native residences along the river, Eurasian homes on the first rise, and the Civil Station of the Raj on the second. Here is the first level, where the bazaars are:

> The very wood seems made of mud, the inhabitants of mud moving. So abased, so monotonous is everything that meets the eye, that when the Ganges comes down it might be expected to wash the excrescence back into the soil. Houses do fall, people are drowned and left rotting, but the general outline of the town persists, swelling here, shrinking there, like some low but indestructible form of life. (ch. 1)

This is savage autochthony in its clearest form: the soil has excreted the whole neighborhood. The folks who live here are (literally) never seen in the book, which shows us only natives of the educated professional classes. These muddy people are protoplasmic, primeval, a "low" life form vaguely amphibian, stuck somewhere near the evolutionary beginning of the not-yet human. Their bazaars and dwellings are not visible from the Civil Station, being concealed by tropical trees that "burst out of stifling purlieus," being "endowed with more strength than man or his works." From this height the town "is no city, but a forest sparsely scattered with huts." It might as well be Africa. For as it looks to the elevated eyes of the Raj, so it will be treated.

Forster of course criticizes this perspective; but he also shares it. For it is the perspective of our whole civilization, which he tried so hard to make emotionally viable in all his fiction. And he had absorbed it first-hand, in early youth when he was just beginning to write, from the *Aeneid*, which he was hired in 1904 to edit for the Temple Classics (Furbank 1977: 1.110). In his introduction to the epic, Forster is uncomfortable with the straightforward imperialism of the poem, with what he calls its "patriotic," as opposed to its "human," appeal. He wonders how readers can still find it compelling, and decides that it's because in one central sense we are all still "patriots": "Our civilization comes from Rome, and it concerns us personally that she once became great. It is as important to us as to Virgil that she beat back the Gauls . . . and the Carthaginians" (Virgil 1906: xii). For all his ambivalence about empire, Forster was nonetheless persuaded that it constituted an order whose job was to "beat back" the barbarian forces of disorder.

In *A Passage to India*, these forces emanate, as usual, from the (colonized) earth itself. Forster's typical variation on the theme of the savage landscape is orchestrated around the opposition of form to formlessness. In his India, just as in Hegel's, nothing is distinct, everything merges into everything else: the land and the buildings on it (like shifting piles of mud) become each other and dissolve difference, without which no individual form can take shape, just as mystic spirituality does. The most extended performance of the theme is Fielding's perception of Venice as he sails homeward at the end of the novel's second part. "The buildings of Venice . . . stood in the right place, whereas in poor India everything was placed wrong. He had forgotten the beauty of form among idol temples and lumpy hills; indeed, without form, how can there be beauty?" He finds there "harmony between the works of man and the earth that upholds them, the civilization that has escaped muddle." He writes to his Indian friends, feeling "that all of them would miss the joys he experienced now, the joys of form, and that this constituted a serious barrier." For they would see the "sumptuousness" but not the "shape" of the whole "Mediterranean harmony. The Mediterranean is the human norm. When men leave that exquisite lake, whether through the Bosphorus or the Pillars of Hercules, they approach the monstrous and extraordinary; and the southern exit leads to the strangest experience of all" (ch. 32). It's our norm, all right, compared to which the rest of the globe (slyly including Britain) is deformed. But it's called the "human" norm, the universal standard. It's our source and ancestor, evoked by the name of one of our *civilisateurs* that was given by antiquity to the Straits of Gibraltar. Aesthetically, the beauty of our culture's individuated forms is not apprehensible by Indians.

They have no such form, or have so many in such mixtures that none is discernible. The classical harmony of Venice is shattered on the very next page by the initial description of Godbole's festival. There was music, "but from so many sources that the sum total was untrammelled. The braying banging crooning melted into a single mass which trailed round the palace before joining the thunder" (ch. 33). Like dwellings of mud, art blends back into nature. Everything is wrongly "placed." There is no distinction between inside and outside: "no Indian animal has any sense of an interior. Bats, rats, birds, insects will as soon nest inside a house as out; it is to them a normal growth of the eternal jungle, which alternately produces houses trees, houses trees" (ch. 3). The land and all its vegetable and animal life (including its human natives) are one undifferentiated "mass."

As such, the Indian landscape is ungraspable by the western mind: "India has few important towns. India is the country, fields, fields, then hills, jungle, hills, and more fields. The branch-line stops, the road is only practicable for cars to a point, the bullock-carts lumber down the side-tracks, paths fray out into the cultivation, and disappear near a splash of red paint. How can the mind take hold of such a country? (ch. 14)." It can't. The Club members are disquieted and afraid when "they realized that they were thousands of miles from any scenery that they understood" (ch. 20). The symbolic center of the incomprehensible landscape, and of the novel, is the hollow darkness of the caves in the Marabar Hills. Forster expounds the primeval geology of the hills at the edges of the Gangetic plain: "They are older than anything in the world." But they are sinking, encroached upon by the plain:

> Their main mass is untouched, but at the edge their outposts have been cut off and stand knee-deep, throat-deep, in the advancing soil. There is something unspeakable in these outposts. They are like nothing else in the world, and a glimpse of them makes the breath catch. They rise abruptly, insanely, without the proportion that is kept by the wildest hills elsewhere, they bear no relation to anything dreamt or seen. To call them "uncanny" suggests ghosts, and they are older than all spirit.

The caves they contain are monotonous, empty, featureless. The visitor "finds it difficult to discuss the caves, or to keep them apart in his mind"; their reputation "does not depend upon human speech" (ch. 12).

This scenery, alien to language and sanity and proportion, is the primeval dawn of time in the historiography of the legend, just like Conrad's jungle. Marlow travels back in time, and Forster, like Sir Henry Maine, finds Europe's past in India's present. The policeman McBryde sees political motives in the two tombs of Esmiss Esmoor that continue her cult in Chandrapore; but Forster rebukes him for "forgetting that a hundred years ago, when Europeans still made their home in the countryside and appealed to its imagination, they occasionally became local demons after death" (ch. 18). The place, whether jungle or dusty hills, is our past; what its present indigenes do is therefore primitive. And the symbolic center of the place is dark, older than anything, a regressive rendezvous of the western self with its own atavistic emptiness; it hollows Kurtz out, empties Mrs. Moore of her sweet manners and motherly concerns, uncivilizes them by eradicating difference, reducing each to states of childish (and savage) egotism. The Marabar Caves are the heart of India's formless darkness, the functional equivalent of Conrad's Congo. Both are uninterpretable, "unspeakable," and the source of terrible revelations to the Europeans who venture into them.

And above all, both are implacably hostile. Just walking on the ground, Forster observes, "fatigues everyone in India except the newcomer. There is something hostile in that soil. It either yields, and the foot sinks into a depression, or else it is unexpectedly rigid and sharp, pressing stones or crystals against the tread" (ch. 2). This perverse and nasty stuff is about as ludicrous as the "dastardly quadrupeds" Robertson imagined in America. Attributing malevolence to the surface of the colonized earth is, however, just as in Conrad, a consistent extension of the (il)logic of the legend, of a piece with Spenser's transferring the injustice of the savage giants' behavior to their land tenure. These are discursive moves, mere figures of speech; but what they record is the elasticity of our founding myth, stretching it to justify dispossession, and then bending it backwards to hold the dominated land responsible for the discomfort and collapse of the dominators.

The tropical climate has its usual large share in the process. The heat of the day "swelled like a monster" (ch. 22); advancing like an invincible warrior, it "stupefied . . . most of the Chandrapore combatants" (ch. 25). Aziz at one point makes a wry joke out of the colonial habit of blaming the weather. Informing Fielding of McBryde's having been caught in adultery with Miss Derek, Aziz comments: "That pure-minded fellow. However, he will blame the Indian climate. Everything is our fault really" (ch. 31). But the joke is like Marlow's astonished amusement at the French ship shelling the continent: it laughs at what the text itself also performs. Along with the torrential rains that blur all outline, the heat too melts everything into formlessness. This occurs, significantly, on the only occasion when we briefly visit the bazaars in the native quarter of Chandrapore, where Adela has wandered, alone and abandoned, after the break-up of the trial. Their smell, compounded of spices and sweat, "invaded her . . . as if the heat of the sun had boiled and fried all the glories of the earth into a single mess" (ch. 25). Difference obliterated, something fine spoiled. Marlow, in *Lord Jim*, produces a striking and functionally identical image of a similar scene, as he strolls through an Asian seaport toward the court where Jim is being tried. "There was, as I walked along, the clear sunshine, a brilliance too passionate to be consoling, the streets full of jumbled bits of colour like a damaged kaleidoscope: yellow, green, blue, dazzling white, the brown nudity of an undraped shoulder, a bullock-cart with a red canopy . . ." (ch. 14). The "damaged kaleidoscope" perfectly embodies the shattered symmetry of Forster's India: bright fragments that no prism can organize, no vision grasp as any kind of order. To the European nose, eye, and ear, the savage jungle and the native town are but chaos, kinds of aesthetic ruin reflecting and presaging the moral ruin of those who bring it our form of culture or seek with it our form of connection.

Fielding isn't ruined, of course, and gets glimpses of another form of connection, thanks to the abilities of Mrs. Moore, who is ruined, and her daughter. But the cross-cultural connection fails, in the final scene—defeated by the landscape. Fielding and Aziz are riding together on horseback, having an exuberant argument about English domination and India's independence. Aziz (presciently enough) predicts that when "'England is in difficulties . . . in the next European war . . . Then is our time.' He paused, and the scenery, though it smiled, fell like a gravestone on any human hope." What Forster, true to the novelistic tradition and character-type he has criticized, here means by "human" is personal friendship between individuals. That's what is doomed, and it is here implicitly opposed to the politics that the friends are discussing; it is a late-Romantic, high-Modernist antidote to politics. The "scenery" dooms it. On this note the book ends. Aziz repeats his prophetic wish to drive the English out of India, and says that only then can he and Fielding be friends. Their horses come together and they embrace. To Fielding's question, why can't we be friends now, as we both want it, the final paragraph gives the famous answer: "the horses didn't want it . . . the earth didn't want it . . . the temples, the tank, the jail, the palace, the birds, the carrion, the Guest House . . . they didn't want it, they said in their hundred voices, 'No, not yet,' and the sky said, 'No, not there'" (ch. 37).

This personified and speaking colonial landscape is the ultimate mystification of the force that separates these would-be friends. The landscape is blamed for what history has produced: there can be no meeting of individual equals between imperial rulers and subjects, where equality is denied and individuality an illusion. The structure and design of Forster's novel has undermined in advance the pathos of this conclusion. And Aziz's evocation of the actual historical situation undermines its strategy of blaming the landscape. The hostility isn't in the soil; it's in what power has built on it: the jail and the palace. By englobing these with that earth and that sky, by lumping them all in that formless mass that is India, the text does what it accuses India of doing. It is our language that obliterates difference, claims our aesthetics and our history as paradigmatic for all humanity, and then recoils in terror from the consequence that *we* may be somehow identical to *them*, rushing to reassert and maintain the differences that alone can constitute our identity as civilized. We tried, like Kurtz, full of the best culture-bringing intentions; but the land just wouldn't have it. The Congo took its vengeance; the earth of India defeated us. For Conrad, the mystified maintenance of otherness was obsessive, necessary, since its breakdown (understanding the other) meant total destruction—although just that destruction was profoundly attractive to Marlow. For Forster, this breakdown has been sought, and partly found, and has positive aspects that question the very terms (rational restraint and ethical autonomy) of our civilized identity—but finally we must remain other. The necessity of Conrad's text becomes in Forster's a sort of necessary evil. They—thank goodness, or alas—cannot be like us, nor we like them.

And so the barrier that maintains the separation—necessary no matter how we feel about it: whether bigotedly content or humanely wistful—becomes the mystified landscape. The very terrain occupied by the empire becomes in the language that makes it literature the agent of hostility and separation, the enemy. The literary discourse thus conceals the real enemies, the actual agents of separation, beginning with itself: our words, our stories and what they both prescribe and overlook. But in Forster's last novel, the design of the discourse also reveals what our stories have prescribed, questioning just that sacred individuality that the eighteenth-century version of the legend had projected onto the savage himself. Then, it was his untrammeled individuality that made him unsociable. Now, it is ours that makes us so.

The blind alley of the Forsterian quest—the suspicion that "personal relations" may be of little account, and the failure to establish them across imperial barriers—finally implies that we may be conceiving of our civilized selves as wrongly as we have of savage ones. Our legendary conception of the latter as asocial paradoxically turns out to define us. For by divorcing the "personal" from the social and the political, by imagining that our identities are autonomous, we misconceive ourselves and make it impossible to relate or connect to others. No human identity is "personal" in this atomistic sense, precisely the sense that the Scottish enlighteners imposed on the savage, refusing, as all subsequent discourse has refused, to see the social grounding and basis of his identity. Denying this to him, we have denied it to ourselves, refusing to see that whatever we personally are does not well up, self-legislated, from our individual bosoms, but is given (or taken away) by the social community in which we exist.

Forster sees this, but only as a necessary evil. All he depicts of the social conditioning of Fielding and Aziz is what keeps them apart: their sexual and conversational tastes, their way of expressing feelings, the feelings they express, and so forth. Never these twain shall meet. And Conrad saw it too, the essential social ground of individual identity—but only to deplore it as shameful weakness. In a famous passage from the story, "An Outpost of Progress" (1898), that was the blueprint for *Heart of Darkness*, he writes:

> Few men realize that their life, the very essence of their character, their capabilities and their audacities, are only the expression of their belief in the safety of their surroundings. The courage, the composure, the confidence; the emotions and principles; every great and every insignificant thought belongs not to the individual but to the crowd: to the crowd that believes blindly in the irresistible force of its institutions and of its morals, in the power of its police and of its opinion. But the contact with pure unmitigated savagery, with primitive nature and primitive man, brings sudden and profound trouble into the heart.

So Conrad creates characters, like Marlow, who are superior to the crowd, and gets them away from the crowd they know (us) to a crowd (all Asians and Africans) they must not know, where they can test whether they have, deep within their unique individualities, the true stuff. Alone, they may have it, whatever it is. But if they want not to be alone, if they desire, like Forster's exemplary protagonists, to connect with others, even the truest stuff (such as Fielding's moral courage) is not enough. Mysticism is the only way out of this dilemma that Forster can envision in his last and greatest novel. Conrad has contempt for the social basis of all human identity; Forster accepts it, but finds it can only be transcended in a state that cancels out both it and the language that defines it.

The refusal to acknowledge, or if acknowledged to appreciate, that the source of all human identity—one of the things that makes humanity common—is social: this is the late-Romantic and high imperialist consequence of the legend that had for two thousand years and more defined the savage as asocial. Now, for writers who feel alien to what their own society has wrought, asociality no longer serves to distinguish him from us. It can still damn him, of course, but it can no longer save us. And if we're all asocial, there's no material basis for humanity to be common on; there's literally no (physical) place where we and they could ever meet. And so the actual place where both we and they confront each other—the tropical imperial frontier—bears the blame for the nonmeeting. This freakish logic results from the legendary description of the savage (asocial through ignorance) remaining negative for him but becoming positive (asocial through ethical autonomy) for us. Yet Forster's fiction makes the freakishness transparent (as Virgil's made foundation morally dubious) by finding that positivity emotionally dubious. By this paradoxical transference, the loneliness of the savage has become ours.

Part VI

THE LEGEND IN OUR TIME

Chapter 26

ᔗ◓

THE LANDSCAPE IN THE MOVIES

The Western and John Ford

"You build a legend and it becomes a fact."

—John Ford

Film in the twentieth century, like printing in the sixteenth, offered our culture a newly reproducible and diffusible way to transmit itself. Though it took a couple of centuries for the new medium of print to impose its own system of order on the knowledge and narratives it was exponentially proliferating, it took only a couple of generations, at our accelerated pace, for film to do likewise. And film did so under the greatest pressure of commercial exigency and communal production. Made for exhibition to the largest possible ticket-buying public, and made by large teams of differently talented people—from writers and financiers through actors to technical experts of all sorts—films are the mass language, the fairytale and folk epic of our time. The seventh art remained the most popular and accessible of any until it was overtaken by television and video, which of course continue it by other technological means. The moving picture, equipped with sound after 1928 and color (gradually and optionally) after 1932, was unprecedented in its power both to reproduce and to contrive action and drama of all kinds, to record things happening and to make them happen before our astonished eyes and ears.

It would thus be logical to expect the most popular and powerful of art forms, corporately organized as an industry and early (1913) localized in southern California, to appropriate and remanufacture any and all of the mythologies current in the culture that gave it birth. And perhaps the most prominent among these was the story of the triumphant westward expansion of the American nation, formally complete only in 1912, when the last contiguous territories (Arizona and New Mexico) on the continent achieved statehood. At the time of its actual completion, this story was already producing in silent pictures a whole genre of movies—the Western—that would remain one of Hollywood's internationally beloved and

staple products for the next half-century. By this means, the American frontier acquired the iconic and spuriously unique status for moviegoers around the world
that the Republic's earlier writers, like James Fenimore Cooper and Frederick
Jackson Turner, had already given it. Hollywood inherited the frontier figure of
the woodsman, already a legendary composite of fiction and fact—Hawkeye, Dan-
iel Boone, Davy Crockett—and turned him cheaply and easily on the backlots of
Burbank and Culver City into the cowboy.

The mythical resonance of this square-shooting upholder of law and order,
who entertains the most ambiguous relation to the "settled" civilization (and the
women who represent it), whose order he partly enforces and partly escapes, owes
a great deal to both the physical locale and the visual demands of the new medium. Though Hollywood did not neglect the woodsman (and made four films of
the seminal text, *The Last of the Mohicans*, between 1911 and 1947: Daisne 1971),
he never became the subject of a genre and the object of worldwide adulation as
the cowboy did. For two reasons: the woodsman slogging through the forest on
foot or canoeing down the river is simply less dramatically visual, less *cinematic*, than
the man on horseback galloping across the wide open spaces. And the latter were
what were available, as forests and rivers were not, in the backyards of the studios.
(Location shooting came gradually, with increased expectations and resources.)
Second, the cinematic exhibition of the mounted rider connects him at a stroke
with the knights errant of medieval romance, whose quests for justice and tests of
physical and moral courage he will endlessly reperform.

Thus the physical circumstances of the filmed cowboy plugged him into the
mainstream of European popular fiction. He is, in a word, chivalric, *chevaleresque*,
most graceful in his mastery of the rituals and skills of violent combat. He is also
chivalrous, *galant*, and must be as careful as the medieval knight that his duty to
protect damsels doesn't get tangled up in any further relation with them. He is the
democratized aristocrat, tough and homespun but polite, shorn of eloquence and
elegance but retaining in the laconic awkwardness of his social manners a warm-
hearted sincerity and compassion. He is the ex-colonial Republic's variant of the
old metropolitan hero, whose virtues he repackages in a newly demotic and self-
made form. Cut loose from any constraints of birth or class, like the national ideology, he is the ultimate individual, the "historyless man."[1] Films almost never show
his parents or explain his background; he may have had, or come close to having,
a sweetheart, but he never marries or has children. (When he does marry, as in
High Noon, 1952, the genre is already self-consciously beginning to dissolve.) He
rides off into the sunset alone. This remarkable character has faded from the cinema of today; but merely his image continues to have astounding potency for merchandising. The cowboy, since his mobilization on the European front by Marlboro in 1970, still sells more cigarettes there than anyone else (Blair 1985). And
practically everybody in the world wears bluejeans—or would if they could get
them.

---

1. The phrase is from an unpublished poem by Nils Peterson, "Survey of American Literature."

The trouble with this remarkable character is that he has a severe identity problem—not surprising in one whose essence is to belong to nothing. Unlike his medieval predecessors, he has escaped all socially or politically hierarchical allegiance. His moral values and behavioral code are strict, but abstract, and quite beyond his ability to articulate. His loyalty to such a code, however, and his overwhelming technical competence—at tracking, riding, shooting, and so forth—are what define him. He is the ethically autonomous individual in its peculiarly American, and hence most popular and extreme form—cut loose from all social bonds except those with fellow-warriors, other autonomous males who are as likely to be enemies as friends. If he has a friend, it's a sidekick, a nonthreatening male who has his respect and loyalty and sometimes amused tolerance: a subordinate, signaled (not by class, as Sancho Panza to Don Quixote, but) by age or race (from Chingachgook, the last Mohican, to Tonto, the faithful Indian companion to the aptly named Lone Ranger)—a subordinate in a hierarchy of two, as hermetically isolated in the vast wastes of steppe and desert as Robinson Crusoe and Friday on the island. The movie cowboy is the existential hero both *avant* and *durant la lettre*: autonomous without an ethos or community, the loneliest man in the world, shaping his destiny with every sunrise, every decision an act of self-creation, dependent for his very survival on how fast he can ride today, how straight he can shoot tomorrow.

One of the main reasons for his loneliness is the historyless asociality that he shares with the (equally legendary) savage, whom he thus resembles and against whom he must often do battle. The paradoxical and unconscious projection of our individualistic European selves onto the founding story's picture of the savage was manifest in colonial ethnography and history of the eighteenth century. The paradoxical and conscious transformation of his negative into our positive loneliness was manifest in the Modernist fiction that criticized the colonial experience of the nineteenth century. And during the first half of this century Western movies were manifesting the paradox in its extreme form, recapitulating in the ontogenesis of the American cowboy hero the phylogenesis of our ever-elastic founding myth.

The cowboy and his immediate American ancestor, the woodsman, are obliged in order to survive to share the skills of the savages they fight. They're all great hunters. The specifically literary history of the American woodsman as an ambiguous blend of husbandman and hunter has been recounted by Richard Slotkin (1973). Hunting, we recall from Pope's *Windsor-Forest*, and observe in the leisure activities of today's Americans, is legitimate as civilized sport in a commodity-producing landscape, but illegitimate as savage sustenance in a forest "waste." The myth reincorporates, and the society enacts, in one context what it rules out in another. And both myth and society do more: by such reincorporation they project figures of heroism (role models) and forms of education that assimilate the savage and civilized identities whose opposition is otherwise insisted on.

Lord Baden-Powell founded the Boy Scouts at the height of the British Empire (1907) as a way of stiffening urban youth for the rigors of outdoor imperial service in savage landscapes. The specific service, and the name, derived from

Baden-Powell's experience at gathering military intelligence in South Africa during the Boer War, in which he became the hero of the siege of Mafeking.[2] The Boy Scouts of America were founded in 1909, shortly followed by foundations in twenty other European and South American countries, and Japan, before the First World War. After it, the movement continued its expansion worldwide and increasingly stressed its educative purposes in civic morality, based on (nonsectarian) religion and patriotism, but tinged with the idealism of international cooperation and brotherhood. Today there are about sixteen million Scouts in over 120 countries.

But in the first half-century of its existence, the Scouting movement became most popular in the United States, where it grew contemporaneously with the vogue for Western movies. By the end of the Second World War, more than half the world's Scouts were in the United States (Nagy 1984: 125). For American youth didn't have to travel overseas to find either the wilderness that would test its survival skills or the remnants of the savages who had devised them. In practice, American Scouting made a fetish of the Indian, incorporating (heaven knows what) versions of tribal ritual and regalia into its own European paramilitary hierarchy: named and numbered ranks earned by demonstration of skills, signaled by uniforms, and respected by salutes. For older Scouts there was a "secret" society called the Order of the Arrow: a neat appropriation of the savage by a cult of honorific feudalism (like the Order of the Garter), complete with a decorative sash worn with the uniform. (The World Scout Bureau devised in 1935 a similarly feudal decoration, the Bronze Wolf, to honor the loyal service of its administrators.) Membership in the Order of the Arrow was confined to somehow outstanding or well-liked Scouts and was conferred by consensus of the group; individuals thus honored were singled out at a ceremony around a campfire and subjected to sundry ordeals of initiation. The sole purpose of the group was to dress and paint as Indians and perform rain and war dances at Jamborees and lesser festivals. Kid stuff, indeed, but organized by grown-ups into a social institution of considerable influence and prestige. Boys who make the highest rank of Eagle Scout are generally bright as well as diligent; their local communities honor them, and they stand good later chances for such things as admission to the best universities and Rhodes Scholarships.

Scouting is a striking recent example of how our culture at large has institutionalized and reexported its own legend: born in the present of the most powerful modern empire as both moral and physical therapy for the masses of boys in industrial towns, it was rapidly adapted to similar conditions around the globe. Like other social institutions (schools, churches, sports teams, armed forces), it is a mechanism for transmitting the culture of transmission, appealing explicitly to the future (training leaders, encouraging both individual initiative and teamwork), and nostalgically preserving the past. It would have been strange indeed if Scouting had

2. The latest hagiography of B-P and the Scouting movement is Nagy 1984; a good analysis of its origins is Rosenthal 1986.

not achieved its predominant development in the United States at precisely the period in mid-century (from after the First World War until just yesterday) when hegemony over the capitalist world was passing from Britain to America, from the old style of imperialism, which included political domination, to the new style, which is mainly economic. In particular, the American style of Scouting preserves the bifurcated past of occidental imperialism, mimicking its ancient hierarchies and codes (Scouts are supposed to be quite as chivalrous as knights and cowboys) while subsuming within these the rituals and skills of the savage other.

Such subsumption and containment of the difference on which civilized identity depends risks, as it has since the legend moved from history to historiography, a kind of amalgamation that blurs the distinct identity the culture must elsewhere assert. The blurring becomes acute in the cinematic cowboy, whose loneliness makes him a mysterious ally, sometimes (just as in earlier social theory and fiction) a double, of the savage enemy. The cowboy serves civilization—helps to reclaim a "waste" wilderness or there performs a commodity-producing task—but is not really part of it himself. To some parts of it, symbolized in films by greedy landowners, corrupt politicians, or effete intellectuals, he is actively hostile. He advances the frontier and goes with it; he makes settlements possible, but never settles down. As hunter or pastoral nomad, he's neither here nor there, but constantly on the move, inhabiting by preference the borderland between the legendary opposition that he uneasily incarnates: law and lawlessness, sociability and aloneness, kindness and cruelty.

As scholars have long observed (see Cawelti n.d.), the whole career and character of the movie cowboy, all his blurred ambivalence between the savage and the civilized, descends from Cooper's woodsman, Hawkeye, born Natty Bumppo, also known as Leatherstocking (the appellation of all the tales Cooper wrote about him between 1823 and 1841), Deerslayer, Pathfinder, and (to his Huron enemies) The Long Rifle. He is in several tales employed as a scout (a function he shares in the fiction and in fact with many Indians) by one army or another; both Boy and Girl Scouts in German-speaking countries are known as "Pathfinders." The multiplication of his names indicates not only the nature of his skills but also the protean precariousness of his identity, defined exclusively by what he, as individual, can perform. That's all that counts on the frontier, that supreme democracy where status is achievable, and must be continually reachieved, only by individual acts of prowess and sagacity—where no one asks a man about his past and the fastest gun is but a target for all aspirants to the title. Except for movies based on actual families, like the James boys or the Earps, the Western, like Cooper, delights in devising monikers, *sobriquets* or *noms de guerre*, for its rootless heroes. The practice was of course current in the journalism and merchandising of real life (Billy the Kid, Buffalo Bill) and echoes the heraldic masking of identities in medieval chivalric romance: The Black Knight, The Ill-Made Knight, The Knight of the Woebegone Countenance. The movies offer a long array of "Kids" (The Cisco Kid, The Ringo Kid), monikers derived from place (Laredo, the Virginian), and a few heroes who right wrongs only in masks (Zorro, the Lone Ranger). Their masks, however, are almost never as motivated by particular circumstances or character as the knights' were. Zorro, for example, is a (Mexican) nobleman in good standing who masks himself to fight corruption in his own society just like Robin Hood; he has not, like that worthy, been himself dispossessed by that corruption. And the Lone Ranger is never seen without his mask; he *is* a mask; we never find out who he is, for he isn't anybody; his identity isn't human, it's a role.

Aside from its appeal (and its merchandising tie-in) to the childish delight in masquerade—white urban kids painting up as injuns, sending off cereal boxtops for Tom Mix gear—the masking and monikering of the movie cowboy graphically presents his divided selves and allegiances. His divisions and ambivalence are the twentieth-century embodiment of the story the founding legend tells about the triumph of progress, the inevitable domination of the savage by the civilized. Only now the dominator is ambivalent, riding in to clean up the town or settle the range war or defeat the Indians and riding off at the end; clearing the space for civilization but not joining it. He is thus a very attenuated *civilisateur*, his role has changed since the days of the legendary Trojans, unambiguous givers of laws and founders of dynasties, bearers of one name that also becomes that of the founded place and people and language. Brut and Francus were also not much more than their role, which, as founders, was to give some group an identity, a name. The cowboy founds nothing, has no identity or name to give. He has nothing to leave behind and nowhere to go, except on. "Shucks, ma'am, 'twarn't nothin','" he says, and rides away, slowly or briskly, but never looking back, getting smaller and smaller, disappearing into a backlit mass of cloud, desert, and jagged horizon, being engulfed by a stupendous and barren landscape. The music swells, and "The End" appears on the screen.

With this final shot, the camera is showing us that the pathos it is extracting on behalf of our lonely hero is just his link to the savage, his willing absorption into that vast, unreclaimed, inhuman landscape from which the savage springs, into which he too disappears, with which both he and the cowboy are now, on the screen before our eyes, identified. The pathos of the victor thus becomes a kind of unacknowledged guilt for the vanquished. It is the price exacted, after long centuries, for our cultural narcissism: since we have portrayed the savage as the mirror of our past, depriving him of his own and foreclosing his future, he now reflects *us* (our hero, the cinematic cowboy) as without past or future, existing alone in an impossible present, impossible just because it comes from and goes nowhere, is isolated from the temporal relations in which all life takes place. In the moving (in both senses) picture of the cowboy, we have become our own legendary picture of the savage, locked into an eternal time warp, reverting back to primal autochthony, swallowed up by that immense wilderness, that fatal and beautiful environment. Conrad's Kurtz succumbed to it, went native all the way, and died. The cowboy learns its ways without succumbing, goes native halfway, and survives, but only by becoming nobody, by forfeiting all belonging.

This Western wilderness found its major filmic poet in John Ford, for the simple reason that he took as his recurrent subject the whole history and legend of its civilizing. And his films show toward the subject just the kind of ambivalence that the hero and the legend had been acquiring since Cooper. There has been much critical disagreement about Ford's Westerns, how chauvinistic they are or how humane, how racist or how sympathetic to the Indian, whether they're sentimental copouts or ironic fables. But they are, of course, all these things in turn, depending (but not only) on the attitude of the viewer, because, like the fictions of Conrad and Forster, they are part of the legend they both perpetuate and criticize. Ford knew well how to build a legend in cinematic terms, and spent a large part of his career wrestling with the problems of the one he inherited. He also knew that if it was well enough built, it would become a fact. He applied this principle, uttered as a description of his own filmmaking in a taped interview (Stowell 1986: xiii), in an odd and suggestive way to his own life. For he seems to have been an interviewer's nightmare, always joking, concealing, and outright falsifying such things as his real name and date of birth—to the extent that his most serious biographer has some ado to set the record straight (see Gallagher 1986). It seems more than coincidence that this poet of our precariously ambivalent civilized identity should have taken somewhat successful pains to disguise his own.

The one thing he never tried to disguise was his Irishness. Whether he was born Sean O'Fearna (et alia) or John Martin Feeney (according to Gallagher), he was a son of Irish immigrants who centered many of his films throughout his career on Irish material, from his versions of modern Irish literature (O'Flaherty's novel *The Informer*, 1935; O'Casey's play *The Plough and the Stars*, 1936) to stories of Irish characters or settings (*The Quiet Man*, 1952; *The Last Hurrah*, 1958; *Donovan's Reef*, 1963).[3] His Westerns almost all contain some scenes of specifically Irish buffoonery. Ford also brought to the screen other popular novels and plays, among them: *Arrowsmith*, 1931; *The Grapes of Wrath*, 1940; *How Green Was My Valley*, 1941; *Mister Roberts* (as co-director), 1955. Ford had no college education but was highly literate, an omnivorous reader with an excellent memory according to those who knew him—though he often tried to conceal this beneath a bluff macho-Irish/homespun-cowboy manner. The things he did well at in high school were football, English, and Latin. An American of the first generation, Ford brings to the nation's legend of itself a perspective that is at once impassioned and detached, committed as citizen and Naval officer, but retaining a keen sense of and attachment to his own European origins. And yet we know him not as Feeney, but as one of the most famous and infamous names in American history—a name he was content to borrow from his brother Francis, who selected it when he preceded John to Hollywood to seek his fortune as an actor; a name already in process of becoming a legend, synonymous with the populist energy and innovative industrial power of the nation, a household word (and vehicle) for the common man.

3. Dates of movies are rather slippery, there being no consensus in the many available dictionaries and encyclopedias of film on whether to give the year of completed shooting, first showing, or general release. Nor, for earlier films, are all of these knowable. Nor is the date of the same film always consistently given within a single source. Informed readers will therefore expect variations, which, in the recent case of Ford, are slight enough not to matter.

John Ford recognized a legend when he saw one, fabricating himself as he fabricated in films the American variant of the founding story. A couple of the films will dramatize the process of such fabrication.

Ford dealt more directly and consciously than any Western moviemaker with the issues and images of our founding legend, bringing to the surface its definition of what civilization is. The favorite adjective of all his critics to describe the scope of his ambition and photography is "epic," which is literally correct in the Virgilian sense, beyond the mere promotional meaning of "big" (à la Cecil B. De Mille). Ford's Westerns are a twentieth-century version in its (then) farthest-reaching medium of what the Renaissance regarded as the noblest literary genre: a story based on fact, containing many episodes of war, love, and politics, of central importance to the people in whose language it is composed in a highly embellished style, which explains their historical destiny as part of a divinely ordained order. Hollywood was Ford's Maecenas, and the embattled experience of World-War-Two America his inspiring Augustus. His high style is the huge and dynamic sweep of his camera over and across all kinds of exterior space, plus its manner of enlarging the stature of its heroes by seeing them from below, against nothing but the sky. Although he thus tinges them with demidivinity, like the epic heroes of old, Ford trades the divine order they serve for a social and secular one. Religion appears in his films as an emblem of civilization but not as its guarantor. The people who read Ford's epic were international moviegoers. Made in America about America when America was at the apogee of its power, exporting itself around the globe, Ford's films were globally popular. And they were first taken seriously by French film critics, well before the British and American critics followed suit. The European founding epic had of course produced the American one, which in the now international language of cinema was readable throughout the known world, as was Virgil's Latin in his time. Ford's profoundest resemblance to Virgil is his awareness that legends become facts, that stories told can produce histories enacted.

Ford began concentrating on his epic theme at the height of his powers, in three films all made, as war impended and began in Europe, in 1939: *Young Mr. Lincoln* (said to have been the favorite movie of Sergei Eisenstein), *Stagecoach*, and *Drums Along the Mohawk*. All concern frontier life, the experience of pioneers, in different places and periods. The first dramatizes Lincoln (Henry Fonda) as populist hero caring for the common people, finally deciding to abandon farming for politics. The latter two, however, are pure fictions, and exchange the narrower focus on embryonic individual greatness for a wider view of a social community. The difference between the communities in these two films establishes the poles between which Ford's vision of our civilization sometimes uneasily vacillates.

In the Western, the little community is a group of travelers assembled by chance on a stagecoach that is attacked by Indians; the party is saved mainly by the exertions of the cowboy passenger (John Wayne). Though the film ends with the cowboy's ritual gunfight against the murderers of his family, its main interest is in the relationships and antagonisms among the characters as the journey proceeds. The protagonists are the marginals, the outcasts: the young outlaw, called The Ringo

Kid (Wayne), the whore with a heart of gold (Claire Trevor), the boozy doctor (Thomas Mitchell), the declassed aristocrat become gambler (John Carradine). These are opposed to the hypocritical and crooked banker, the proper army officer's wife, and the weak but sympathetic liquor salesman. Mediating among them all is the upstanding Marshal (George Bancroft) and the buffoonish driver (Andy Devine).[4] The social antagonisms are made clear at the outset, when a ladies' "Law and Order League" (led by the wife of the embezzling banker) expels the disreputable whore and doctor from the town of Tonto.

This is Ford's "classic" Western, in which exposure to the dangers of the wilderness brings out the best in the outcasts and the worst in the other conventional types. The doctor, aiding a birth and tending the wounded salesman, recovers his self-respect; the cowboy and the whore acquire some by falling in love. The journey through the wilderness is regenerative self-discovery; the challenges of its violence are liberating. And the liberation of the selves leads to the formation of a genuine community, which, even if but temporary, comes to be mutually tolerant and respectful—the antithesis of the town they left behind. The cinematic energy, the rendering of the physical effort of the journey, is exhilarating and spectacular for the viewer. The sheer labor of the driver, along with Wayne's leaping astride the stage horses to recover the dropped reins, are the most heroically photographed actions in the picture, along with the stagecoach itself. It is shot from many angles at all ranges, streaking along in front of its plume of dust when pursued by Geronimo's Apaches through Monument Valley, Utah, the landscape that Ford first used in this film and would use in all his subsequent Westerns. In *Stagecoach* that landscape, like all frontiers, is the physical and moral gymnasium of all the characters, the testing ground of their true stuff. But the characters who pass the test are not the culture-bringers—except the good-hearted Marshal—they're the rejects of such culture as here exists. Mitchell sums it up when, at the very end, the Marshal lets Wayne escape with Trevor: "They're saved from the blessings of civilization."

In diametric contrast, the community of farmers in *Drums Along the Mohawk* is entirely composed of culture-bringers. The film is set in northern New York during the War of Independence. A young farmer (Fonda) fetches a bride (Claudette Colbert) from an elegant family in Albany. She is terrified by the long and hard journey through the forest, deeply depressed by the crude rusticity of the frontier outpost, and has shrieking hysterics when a friendly local Indian wanders into her log cabin. Both she and the audience will learn what makes enduring all this inconvenience worthwhile: for her, love and motherhood; for us, civilization itself. The film is virtually a schematic diagram of the idea of civilization in the entire Virgilian *oeuvre*: the pastoral community, the georgic labor, the epic combat and foundation. It especially celebrates the labor of clearing the forest and planting the crops. All the neighbors pitch in to help Fonda clear more land for his farm; "great

4. In Ford's films I name the stars rather than the characters, because it is they and their aura to which we respond, which we remember, and which Ford helped to create and maintain, using several of the same actors, both major and minor, in film after film.

soil for wheat," says one of them (Ward Bond). No sooner are the crops grown, and Colbert pregnant, than war breaks out. Hostile Indians led by a Tory spy (John Carradine) descend on the new farmhouse and the fertile fields, their conically linear little haystacks richly gleaming in the autumn sunshine (in Technicolor), and burn them. Colbert has a miscarriage from all the stress; she and Fonda are obliged to hire themselves out to work the land of a widow neighbor. The war continues; Fonda and Bond join the local militia and go off to battle. The widow and Colbert gamely carry on, working the land. Fonda returns wounded, and in delirium confesses his horror of killing and his amazement at the pleasure it gives Bond. The crops grow, and at harvest time Colbert gives birth to a son, celebrated, along with the wedding of a younger couple, at a joyous dance. The baby boy toddles amid the ripening corn. The spy leads the Indians in a final attack on the settlement. All gather in the local fort and are sorely besieged. Fonda breaks out and runs for reinforcements, pursued by three Indians. The Indians storm the fort, brutalizing the children, and are about to carry off the women when the reinforcements arrive. The war is over and the American flag is raised over the fort in the final scene, with glowing close-ups, one by one in a continuous pan, of everybody's radiant faces—all the protagonists plus the friendly Indian and the widow's black servant.

The mythic message is unmistakable: racially united America at the moment of its foundation; simultaneous public/communal and private/individual victories (Colbert mastering hardship; she and Fonda inheriting the farm of the conveniently killed widow); the fertility of the soil is that of the family. National patriotism takes over, as it did in the Renaissance, the imperial epic; the historical event is, as one critic says, "the triumph of white civilization in the wilderness" (Place 1974: 57). And the film dramatizes in detail what that civilization has always meant, with a contemporary (1930s) emphasis on and glorification of the labor required: forest-clearing, cereal-producing agriculture. The film also dramatizes the displacement—of the nonwhite—that foundation entails. The savage and his forest are one, as usual; the hostiles favor night attacks and emerge as black shadows from the shadows of trees (a nice visual rendering of "men from tree trunks born"). Their savagery is established, as usual, by their violence to women and kids. But not quite all are hostile, and those that are have been misled by the nasty spy. The film maintains the possibility of savage assimilation to the new order—but only in a subordinate capacity signaled (as in Pope's *Windsor-Forest*) by humor. The friendly Indian is comic; and in one scene even the hostiles are comically baffled by the defiance of the widow when they attack her in her home. Whenever in this movie they enter a domestic, "civilized," interior space they are funny. So they can be thus literally accommodated there, as amusement, within the dwellings we build on our cleared land. But if they oppose that activity, they must die, as they do, copiously and graphically in the climactic battle for the fort. It's a melancholy necessity, this killing, as Fonda's revulsion makes clear. We're not supposed to enjoy it (though some do), but to accept it as the price of foundation. The other racial accommodation is perfunctory and crystal clear: the black is a servant, period.

Here, then, in these two films of 1939 are the poles of Ford's vision, which are those of the entire historico-literary development, variation, and revision of the legend between Virgil and Forster:

> The culture-bringers are the noble and hard-working bearers of civilization to the wilderness who unambiguously conquer it; the savage possessors of that place are justly annihilated if they resist, but are welcome to accept the tutelage of the new order and join the only possible march of progress.
>
> The culture-bringers are ambiguously motivated bearers of a high-minded but often corrupt civilization who are likely to be destroyed by the wilderness they invade; only exceptional or marginal members of our culture can avoid both its corruption and destruction by the wilderness, which they accomplish by entering into some relation with its savage possessors but at the same time remaining distinct enough from them to annihilate them when necessary.

The old hero (Aeneas, Brut, Francus) swept the savages away, planted fields, walls, and towers, administered justice, and left his dynasty to expand. After two millennia of this, the new hero (Marlow, Fielding, the cowboy) admires or becomes partly like the savage, assists the planting or administration, and leaves, founding no dynasty. Even in Ford's schematic presentation of the first pole there is one crucial feature of the second. Fonda's community-saving act is beautifully and lengthily photographed, with him silhouetted at one point in a single distant shot speeding alone across a flaming red horizon, then followed by his pursuers. The sequence shows him accomplishing the act by a skill he shares with the Indians: he doesn't (and doesn't like to) blast them with superior technology (The Long Rifle); he outruns them—they are shown dropping from exhaustion. Even in this most archaic of modern retellings of the legend, the culture-bringing founder survives and prevails by virtue of his likeness to the savage: the feature of the cowboy that alienates him from the civilization he serves is here projected back onto the unalienated hero.

Ford will return to this alienation, its circumstances and degrees, in his next half-dozen Westerns, and will discover a particular locus where there is a form of community halfway between the chance collection of outcasts and the dedicated band of culture-bringers, combining elements of both. Ford's interest in community, in the sociality that our civilization claims, is what makes his Westerns grade A and distinguishes them from grade B shoot-em-ups. In his sound movies he never made (so far as I know) a stock cowboy picture in which the hero is a blithely isolated, historyless paragon like the Lone Ranger. The one film that focuses on such an isolated figure (*The Searchers*, 1956) is an extraordinary study of his pathology, a man whose history has turned him into a tragic psychic cripple. He's tragic just because he's ruled himself out of sexual and family life. The family is a vital image for Ford, and though it is presented in many films with cloying sentimentality, its importance as the basic social unit is apparent.

Even more important is the landscape, the spectacular and barren desert, where, in all Ford's subsequent Westerns, whatever community there is must struggle to survive. The landscape Ford chose for the large exterior shots in these films (no matter if it's called Texas, Arizona, or Dakota) offered the broadest and strangest vistas he could find. It was Monument Valley, Utah, that enormous flat expanse of sand and sagebrush out of which rise with geometric abruptness the thick, square masses of butte and mesa, the thin and twisted fingers and obelisks of rock, which produce the impression that gives the place its name, as if sculpted by a giant or a god—monumental, but of no human commemoration. This is the impression from a distance. Up close, when the films' protagonists are herding cattle, pursuing and being pursued, the monuments are toweringly unapproachable, resting on steep, unscalable inclines of jagged shale or piled boulders; and the distant flatness resolves itself into an unending series of rolling fissures, gorges, and narrow defiles. It frustrates access and bars passage. Ford filmed all (most entirely, a few only in part) his Westerns here between 1939 and 1964; he made its image famous, synonymous with the American West (it appears occasionally in Marlboro ads).[5]

It is an image of the utterly inhuman, the absolute other. It is as remote as possible from any earthly picture of cultivation or use: no trees, no grass, no water, no houses, no roads. It appears uninhabitable. Its magnificent forms are bizarre, uncanny, mysterious—the result of ageless forces beyond our comprehension. The physical anomaly of its abrupt and massive excrescences closely resembles Forster's description of the Marabar Hills at the edge of the Gangetic plain (the buttes and mesas also have caves, where savages and outlaws may lurk). Both are emblems of what lies on the other side of the frontier and is other to our civilization, or even our planet. Ford's desert vastness is lunar, weird, literally unearthly, its remoteness enhanced by being photographed in black-and-white (until 1956), unlike anything we've seen or can see, even itself, unmollified by everyday yellowness of sand or blueness of sky. It's like the famous night desertscapes in Edward Weston's photographs: supernatural grayness, frozen in moonlight.

And Ford's way of putting human figures and habitations into this forbidding landscape, as some critics have suggested, recalls the typical procedures of American painting, in which outdoor space overwhelms the people in it, remains unmasterable, uncomposed, unbounded, never "complete," always extending, melting away imperceptibly into haze and sky. Whether river or sea, forest, mountain or plain, and whether offered as a Romantic rendering of deific Nature or a realistic depiction of nature's indifference to humanity, the space is always inaccessible and remote, its distances intimidating. This description of American painting is that of John McCoubrey (1963); one critic invokes it as characteristic of the Western movie in general (French 1974: 105–107). Another comments that Ford uses Monument Valley "as [Winslow] Homer used the sea"—to portray a grand and untamable element in which the most one can do is survive (Place 1974: 171). Ford indeed does all of this and more, since his ever-receding spaces are the inanimate

---

5. Ford made more than mythic history in Monument Valley, which was and is a part of the Navaho Reservation. He used the local Navaho as extras in most of his films, and was the first director to pay them union wages. He was proud of providing them employment and of being made a blood brother of their nation (Gallagher 1986: 341).

void (not a background, but a surround) within which the fragility of any sort of civilized community is terribly exposed. How can a community form or survive here? What merely human power can create and perpetuate it among these monuments to far greater, far slower, far more implacable powers?

The way Ford films his Westerns in the place he chose poses these fundamental questions, which find various answers in the scripts that address them. The place is not personified, any more than it is in painting; for it cannot within the visual conventions of (so-called) "realistic" cinema be endowed with a will, in the way that Conrad and Forster can attribute malice to leaves and stones. So Ford's desert waste is not itself hostile in this sense, and the less because of its strange beauty; the camera lingers on it, famously, makes it attractive. And yet it is nonetheless a kind of enemy, just by its overpowering presence. Its ungraspable space is the (opposite) American equivalent of the suffocating enclosedness of Conrad's African jungle; they play the same role in the same legend, exercising the same power and fascination on the exceptional hero and the reader/viewer. Marlow saw the soul of savage darkness in the tawny lady and felt its beauty; in Ford's Westerns *we* see the beauty of the inhuman landscape, and thus feel how the hero is drawn to it, akin to it, however remotely.

Such a feeling—the ambivalence of the attenuated *civilisateur*, the ethically autonomous individual as sea captain or woodsman or movie cowboy—is now inherent in the legend, and Ford will evoke it throughout his career in Westerns that continue the saga of our founding story. The indomitable landscape is the site, the hostile condition, of the two forms of frontier community that Ford will now explore: the one that needs policing, and the one that provides it—the town and the army.

Chapter 27

THE EPIC AS HISTORY

John Ford's Westerns

Ford's commercial, but not his filmmaking, career was interrupted by naval service from 1941 to 1945, during which he made numerous movies of all sorts about the war: educational, documentary, propaganda. Resuming his usual energetic rate of production in Hollywood, he returned to Monument Valley in 1946 to make *My Darling Clementine*. The sentimental song title alludes to the subplot of the picture, which helps it to stage the famous gunfight between the Earps and the Clantons at the O.K. corral in Tombstone, Arizona, as another triumph of civilization. The actual incident, which occurred in 1881, permits no such reading, no clear identification of cops and crooks. But it was already a legend (and an earlier movie), endowed with moral clarity, which Ford had no trouble adapting into his ongoing epic of our founding story. The hero's relation to the landscape in this film both explains and enriches its stereotypical ending (the occasion of some critical disappointment).

For in Ford's version, the Earp brothers are cowboys, shown in the opening sequence worn, unshaven, and exhausted from driving their cattle. The camera privileges Wyatt (Henry Fonda) in a heroic shot from below, on horseback against the desert monuments and the sky. The youngest brother is left to mind the cows while the three others ride into Tombstone to relax and clean up. Fonda's barbershop shave is interrupted by some drunken villain shooting up the town, whose citizens, including the barber, scurry for cover, leaving Fonda—irritated at the interruption—to go out, still lathered, and subdue the villain. The citizens try to persuade him to become their peace officer, which they desperately need; he refuses, saying he's just passing through. Meanwhile, the Clanton brothers, led by their Pa (Walter Brennan), have stolen the Earps' herd and killed the youngest brother. Fonda becomes Marshal and promises the brother's grave that kids will one day be able to grow up safe in Tombstone. Fonda's performance, costume, and treatment by the camera throughout make this another "classic" Western and him the mythic, incorruptible hero. He is sober (even when he drinks), cool, modest, quiet, tautly calm, controlling obviously great passions (for justice and revenge), decisive (everyone depends on and respects him), invincible. His public authority is the socially willed and sanctioned emanation of his enormous personal force.

This enforcer, this bringer of law (he acquires a warrant to arrest the Clantons), is also linked to the rest of our culture that comes with it. First, and unusually, to the talismanic icon of high culture in the American west, Shakespeare. Since Twain (in *Huckleberry Finn*) so memorably ridiculed the itinerant actors who recited garbled fragments of the Bard to frontier audiences, those figures remained generally comic chiselers in the movies, which abused them as an easy sport. Not so here. Fonda has met and befriended Doc Holliday (Victor Mature), who runs a local saloon. The Doc, by title, education, and Eastern upbringing is a civilized Byronic figure, touchy, self-despising, and proud, fallen from his background to live as an alcoholic gambler with a Mexican mistress (Linda Darnell); he's dying of tuberculosis. A popular and drunken actor (Alan Mowbray) comes to town, and the Clantons hale him into the saloon for a mock-command performance. Tensely controlled, Fonda watches with Mature while the Clantons torment the actor into speaking a few lines, which they recognize and scorn as "pomes." Mowbray attempts his big number—"To be or not to be," of course—but breaks down in the middle of it and asks for help. Whereupon Mature smoothly takes it up and finishes it, quietly, inwardly, as the camera focuses on him (to make clear that it's his own life he's thinking of ending), and Fonda looks on sympathetically. Mature leaves with the actor, and the scene ends with a face-off in which Fonda gets the drop on the Clantons, permitting him to exit. Pa (Brennan) then clubs two of his sons to the floor with a whip, to reinforce the advice he then gives them: "when ya pull a gun, kill a man." Brennan plays with superb snarling brutality throughout.

The second link of our hero to the sociality of civilization is shown at one of Ford's favorite such scenes, a dance and a festive meal. This takes place as a part of what now becomes the subplot of the picture: Mature's avoidance and rejection of his fiancée, Clementine (Cathy Downs), who's come from Boston to reclaim him. But he, sunk in shame and self-hatred, is beyond reclamation. So Fonda, smitten himself, must escort the lady to the big affair the citizens are holding to promote the building of a church. It's held on the church floor, which doesn't yet have walls; only the frame of its steeple is in place, flanked by two American flags. It's seen first from a distance in a long tracking shot as the couple approach it; as it and they (and the viewer) thus draw nearer, the hymn the citizens are singing gets louder. One critic well describes the effect of the shot: the "skeletal bell-tower rises at once sturdy and precarious, from the prairie wilderness, the distant peaks of Monument Valley simultaneously dignifying the scene with natural grandeur and suggesting the context of the non-human within which man must establish himself" (Wood 1980: 375). The dance follows and is interrupted when Fonda, as the town's undisputed leader, arrives with Downs and is given the honor of a solo turn. They whirl alone on the large floor, surrounded by the admiring citizenry.

They personify civilization, this policeman and the lady from Boston: he's the power to transplant it, and she's its product, who will transmit it in her turn (she remains as Tombstone's schoolmarm at the end); they are the *imperium* and the *studium*. Fonda dances beautifully, of course, but he's not quite at ease here (not as he is at the poker table or on horseback). He's graceful but rigid; his expression is stern and uncomfortable until, warmed by the dance, he finally breaks into a smile. The subplot partly motivates the discomfort—he's making a very public couple with the betrothed of his best friend—but only partly. For he doesn't, quite, belong here, as a member, even the supreme one, of this community; it's not, emotionally, his element. That element is the landscape he rode out of at the beginning, rides back into later in pursuit of Mature, and will ride back into at the very end.

To this end the film now hastens in a series of swift, suspenseful actions. A jewel belonging to the dead Earp brother is found on Mature's mistress, allowing him to be briefly suspected of the murder. The Clanton boy who gave it to her shoots her to keep her quiet. Fonda commands Mature to try his long disused surgical skills by operating to save her life. He does so, and Fonda toasts this last effort to regain his self-respect. A deputized brother Earp, named Virgil, has pursued the fatally wounded assassin to the Clantons' place, where Brennan shoots him in the back. The warrant arrives and the climactic gunfight is prepared for by a distant shot of the shabby town, adrift in a sea of sand, dwarfed by a huge, dramatically streaked wash of sky, lingered on by the motionless camera in total silence. (Almost the only music this film has is performed onscreen at the saloon and the dance; gone are the ubiquitous Alfred E. Newman strings of *Drums Along the Mohawk*.) How can there be a community here? Only by the power of the incorruptible gun. Darnell has not survived the operation, so Mature is eager to join Fonda in the gunfight, in which he dies. At the outset of it, Fonda asks the Clantons to surrender to his warrant; they sneer, forfeiting law. At the end of it, all the Clanton boys are dead, and Fonda tells Brennan to "start wanderin'" in misery and grief. As Brennan starts to ride away, Morgan Earp (Ward Bond) sees him pulling a gun and shoots him dead. In the last scene, beside a split-rail fence along an empty road, Downs informs Fonda she's staying on to teach school. He takes politely awkward leave, saying he'll visit his father, buy some more cows, and maybe pass this way again. He then canters off alone, the camera watching her watching him disappear into the enormous wilderness.

The complaint of the critics is based on the just observation that his departure is "not at all necessitated by the narrative" (Wood 1980). The death of Doc has after all made possible the marriage, symbolizing the achievement of civilization here, which would merely ratify what was earlier shown at the dance. Or if dramatizing the wedding seems inappropriate, Fonda could just stay, maybe put his arm around her, or otherwise suggest the off-screen nuptial (in the way that Wayne and Trevor ride off together in *Stagecoach*). Or they could, standing together, perhaps contemplate the now advanced stage of construction of the church, symbolizing the same achievement. The narrative of the movie would indeed permit (for the complainants, it requires) some such unambiguous conclusion. But instead we have the ambiguous conclusion. It is "necessitated" not by this narrative, but by the legend of which it is a part (for the complainants, a succumbing to cliché).

This larger necessity is compelling and meaningful in both individual and social terms. The cowboy hero who can't settle down (especially when he so easily might), who must keep going nowhere alone, back into that inhuman landscape, embodies not merely his own ambivalent position between the civilization he brings and the savage landscape he brings it to, his own blurred identity. He also suggests something about that civilization that might make the wilderness a preferable alternative: the simple fact that he—all his invincible power of destruction—has been required to establish it. This ambiguity is not moral; Fonda here is always right, just, legal. The Clantons are literally beasts, the antithesis of all fair play or compassion; they despise Shakespeare and can only be exterminated. But Fonda is a reluctant exterminator (again unlike Bond), never eager to use his invincible power. He has no choice. He triumphs and leaves, perhaps not wanting to be a policeman for the rest of his days.

Our founding legend has always been mobilized and modified for use at historical moments to which its relevance is usually transparent. *My Darling Clementine* is no exception, being virtually an allegory of how America saw its participation in the Second World War: the victim of a treacherous attack coming to the aid of European civilization against its barbarians within, and triumphing by the (somewhat) reluctant use of the new and supreme power of the atom. In this allegory, the Earps and the town are the nation, the Clantons do duty for both the Japanese and the Nazis, and Fonda becomes the citizen-soldier, a contemporary Cincinnatus, drafted into heroic service only under extreme provocation, to save his country and return to civil life. But the life Fonda returns to isn't civil, and what Ford's use of the legend thus suggests about civilization has broader and deeper resonance than its contemporary application.

For it suggests just what Virgil suggested: that the ploughshare implies the sword, that our forms of culture require organized force to transplant and preserve them, that if someone owns cows there will be cattle thieves (like Cacus), that our form of community will always require protection from an enemy within, can never be fully achieved and so must continually be reachieved, founded over and over again, in different places or in the same one, Rome itself. The cowboy hero opts out of the successive reachievement, embracing solitude. Or does he? Does he rather ride off to reachieve it again somewhere else? Is he a compulsive founder, like Aeneas, or is he weary of founding, wishing to escape, willing to give up the pleasures of civility, sociality, politeness in order to be free of the burden of policing necessary to maintain them? We don't exactly know: and that's the richness of Ford's ambiguous ending, which functions much as the abrupt ending of the *Aeneid* does, to suggest that in addition to the price we make others pay for our foundation, there's a price we must pay ourselves. We are invited to ask if it's worth it.

In the genre of countless Westerns, the cowboy hero is indeed a compulsive reachiever and ambivalent upholder of our civilization. But John Ford never again portrays him in quite that role. Only two of his subsequent Westerns have a cowboy hero—John Wayne in both *The Searchers* (1956) and *The Man Who Shot Liberty Valance* (1962). In the former he is a vengeance-mad double of the Indian he hunts, in the latter a partial antagonist of the law-bringer. *Two Rode Together* (1961) is about two law officers, one corrupt, rescuing from a band of Indians two white people no one wants; *Wagonmaster* (1950, which spawned a long-running TV series) dramatizes the relatively uncomplicated trek of culture-bringing settlers. The rest of Ford's Westerns deal with the army. He doesn't abandon the legend, but only the cowboy as its individual agent. He focuses now on its collective agent, the national and professional police force, by making three films all from stories by James Warner Bellah, and all about the Seventh Cavalry: *Fort Apache* (1948), *She Wore a Yellow Ribbon* (1949), *Rio Grande* (1950). In the frontier army outpost Ford finds a form of community that brings together the dedicated civilizers and the exceptional, ambivalent outcasts. It unites them in two forms of temporal continuity, those of the family and the institution, the regiment. And it pits them against the savage other, the enemy from without.

All the films are frank celebrations of the army and the common soldier, glorifying their hardships and humanizing them with domestic problems, courtships, and episodes of comic farce. They're war movies, especially the last two, designed more to elicit sympathy for our fighting men and their families than to examine what they're fighting for, or how. The point is made in all of them that facing the common enemy requires a unity that overrides and incorporates both ethnic (Irish) and historical (Confederate) differences. The latter two films are articulated around the pathos of the hero (John Wayne): in the first, his impending retirement, a problem because his wife is dead, so he has no family to retire to—his soldiers are surrogate sons; in the second, his estrangement from his wife, who arrives at the fort Wayne commands to talk their son, who's just enlisted there, out of entering his dad's profession. Between the introduction of these emotional problems and their happy resolution at the end, the army goes about its routine, which includes defending itself, in *She Wore a Yellow Ribbon*, against the Indian tribes that are massing for a great assault after the defeat of Custer, and in *Rio Grande*, against the sneak attacks of Indians who then take refuge in Mexico, where the army can't pursue them. The savages here are merely the menacing enemy, behaving nastily as usual: burning the man who sells them rifles, kidnapping a wagonload of children. The army is beleaguered, defensive, hampered by governmental policy. But it will prevail: by a ruse in the first film, and by ignoring, with the connivance of General Sheridan, the political interdiction of invading Mexico in the second.

The two films thus precisely reflect the self-perceived situation of the American military during the years of their making, which were the formative years of the Cold War and the onset of the war in Korea. They are fairly subtle propaganda (as was the *Aeneid*) for the necessity of America playing the world's policeman, maintaining global garrisons against the godless and ubiquitous communist menace. Wiping out the Indians (shooting them from inside a church) in *Rio Grande* by invading Mexico is eerily prophetic of General Douglas MacArthur's advocated invasion of China (Chinese troops aiding the North Koreans had produced a stale-mate with the South Koreans and their UN and American allies)—for which he was removed from command in April 1951. The subtlety of the films is to shroud their strategic advocacies in lots of domestic sentiment, laid on particularly heav-ily in *Rio Grande* by a group of crooners who serenade at the slightest provocation (though their rendition of "I'll Take You Home Again, Kathleen"—the name of Wayne's estranged wife [Maureen O'Hara]—is both affecting and relevant to the happy end). But both the advocacy and the sentiment make these films much less interesting than the first of the trilogy, which explores the tensions within the community of police, making explicit both what it fights for and how it does so.

The credits of *Fort Apache* unroll in front of long shots of the cavalry, then more briefly of the Indians, riding across Monument Valley under enormous skies, which remain in the opening shots of the action: a stagecoach arriving at an iso-lated post-house in the desert and a small detachment of soldiers arriving to meet it. Here is the wilderness and those contending for its possession, with the focus on our side of the contention, which consists of two social orders: the civil and the military. The ensuing encounter clearly opposes the ordinary humanity of the former (stage drivers) to the disciplined protocol of the latter (the officers), with the common soldiers caught uneasily between the two. The detachment is there to escort Lt. O'Rourke, a new graduate of West Point, back home to the fort where his father (Ward Bond) is Sergeant-Major. It's a triumphant, affectionate meeting between the young man and the soldiers among whom he grew up (led by Victor McLaglen). But the stagecoach also contains the new commander of the fort (Henry Fonda) and his daughter Philadelphia (Shirley Temple), arriving ahead of schedule and unannounced because the Apache have lately cut the telegraph. Hierarchical embarrassment mars the homecoming, in spite of the Lieutenant's cession of the escort to his commanding officer, intensified by Fonda's finding fault with the soldiers' dress and behavior. Their arrival at the fort interrupts a dance, and again Fonda's attitude casts a pall on all festivity.

For Fonda (wearing a moustache, as in *My Darling Clementine*) is a martinet, a rigid, by-the-book disciplinarian, appalled by the laxity of frontier military habits. In early conversations with his daughter and his second-in-command, he makes clear his vexation with this assignment to the back of beyond, far from any pos-sibility of either career advancement (and elegant social life for Temple) in Wash-ington or glory in the big campaigns against the Sioux in the northern plains, stuck here defending nothing against a scruffy rabble of renegade Apache. He is an un-happily exiled metropolitan, whose attachment to social hierarchy is as rigid as that to the military one. Temple and the Lieutenant fall in love (we know they will from the first scene), and father absolutely forbids her to marry the son of an en-listed man. He can't figure out how anyone not born a gentleman could have got an appointment to West Point in the first place, even though he knows that the sole exception is for the sons of soldiers who have been awarded the Medal of Honor. In an ironic exchange, Bond admits to possessing one. In meetings with his staff Fonda gives brusque orders, which conclude with his rising and saying "Any questions?" It's a dismissal, not an invitation, and he is not pleased when a subordinate has anything to ask. In conversation his language is ornate, stiff, and pompous. He never unbends—not even at another dance in his honor. He's frigidly unsympathetic throughout (the only such role he ever played for Ford); and he's good at it.

To it the principal contrast (aside from the good-hearted fellowship of the men and their wives) is clean-shaven Capt. York (John Wayne), whose first extended speech is a humorously ironic explanation of army protocol to Temple on the occasion of the Lieutenant's leaving his card. He knows the etiquette, but doesn't take it too seriously; he's easygoing and casual about the regulation forms of spit-and-polish demanded by Fonda, enforcing them when he has to with a wink of sympathy to the men. Fonda wears a fully buttoned tunic on all occasions, and a billed army cap with a cloth covering the neck attached to the back of it, like a French Legionnaire's cap. His example is not lost on any of his officers except Wayne, who was buttoned up for the formal dance but goes about his daily business in the frontier fatigues of open-necked shirt, bandana, and sombrero. The costume links him to the landscape, foreshadowing his role as negotiator with Cochise, the Apache chief. Wayne knows the ways of the savage wilderness, as does Bond's son, who was raised in it. Fonda is contemptuous of such knowledge and sees his local experts as tainted by it. Preparing to rebuke the young man for taking his daughter riding without asking his permission, Fonda commends his knowledge of the "savage Indian" only to accuse him of behaving like one, instead of like an "officer and gentleman," repeating that the Lieutenant is no better than an "uncivilized Indian."

Unbending and unpleasant as he is, utterly arrogant in his presumption that he and his rigid codes alone are civilized, Fonda's adherence to them is absolute, and in two early instances is shown to be admirable. In the first instance, he and Wayne lead a small troop to investigate the premises of the local Indian agent, whom Wayne suspects of corruption. They find concealed stores of rifles and liquor that he illegally sells to the Apache. The agent himself arrives, a squirming hypocrite, and Fonda eloquently denounces him, ordering the soldiers to destroy the guns and booze. When the rulebook is violated his wrath is righteous and his justice swift. And he makes no exceptions for himself, as the second instance shows. Irritated at what he imagines to be the lower-class parents' complicity in their son's courtship of his daughter, Fonda bursts into their quarters at the fort. Bond reminds him that this invasion of privacy is a breach of army etiquette. Fonda offers a formal apology, if not gracious at least graceful, and withdraws. This costs his pride a lot; but it is the justice prescribed by the rulebook for his violation, so he must render it. Doing everything, large or trivial, by the book is what makes him a self-appointed representative of civilization. He lives and will die by it.

With the character contrast and the class conflict within the police community complete, the plot moves toward the final confrontation with the savage enemy. Wayne and a Spanish-speaking ex-Confederate Sergeant ride out to seek Cochise, to persuade him to give up his sporadic raiding and return to the reservation. They ascend a long canyon of monuments and emerge on a rocky summit, from which they see ridges of barren mountains receding before them. Their lonely journey is intercut with scenes of the social life back at the fort: Fonda's apology, the shy lovers, the preparations for the big dance, the dance itself. As part of the official routine, Fonda has learned that Cochise is not as negligible an enemy as he thought, that his capture or pacification may well be a path to glory. Wayne and the Sergeant ride into the mountains, empty as far as the eye can see. They've no specific idea where to find Cochise, of course; they figure he'll find them. So he does: high up on one side there's a sudden flash, a mirror signal, answered by another on the other side. The camera then confirms their knowledge that this emptiness isn't empty: from one crest of the rocky defile we watch from behind a scattered group of Indians watching them as they ride slowly through it, far below. They arrive; the Sergeant presents Wayne, in Spanish, to Cochise, and the parley begins.

Back at the fort, everyone but Fonda is fully enjoying the formal dance, which Wayne's return interrupts. He reports that he has persuaded Cochise to return to U.S. territory to discuss his grievances with the commanding officer. Fonda directly halts the festivities and orders the whole regiment out at dawn in full battle gear. Wayne protests that this manifestation will make a liar of him, violating his word of honor. Fonda refuses to consider this, saying that no word can be given to a "breechclouted savage" (most of those seen so far were wearing loose Mexican peasants' trousers and shirts) or "an illiterate, uncivilized murderer . . . there's no question of honor between an American officer and Cochise."

Dawn: Temple, Bond's wife, and the wife of the second-in-command are shot from below against clouds, watching the regiment mount and depart, company by company, to the tune of "The Girl I Left Behind Me." Outside the fort, in a medium shot at eye-level, the mounted troops, now singing "She Wore A Yellow Ribbon," file in line past the camera; the upper three-quarters of the screen is sky. The sequence concludes with the three women, shown as at the outset, watching the file disappear; one comments that all she can see is the flags. Then the column of troops is shown in a slightly elevated medium shot, all in order two-by-two, riding through the sagebrush toward a clear monument on the right, while their trailing haze of dust covers the view on the left. Then longer shots of the line of troops, now unformed and struggling in a still larger expanse of desert landscape. As Fonda gives Wayne orders, they're seen from below on horseback, against the dramatic clouds. Wayne tells him the Apache aren't where he thinks, but where the dust cloud is. He points, and the camera shows us a huge sky, with one monument to the left and the horizon the empty brow of a hill over which the Indians now ride, all at once, not in a line but abreast, casually, as if (as usual) they emerged from the earth. The parley takes place. Cochise complains, in Spanish, of the corrupt agent and refuses to return. Fonda takes this as a threat, and, in high dudgeon, insults him. The Indians gallop off, vanishing into a dust cloud at the dark base of a mesa. Our troops, all aligned, watch; they're panned one by one at eye level, against the clouds. We then see Cochise and four braves standing on a crest, also from eye level against clouds; they watch the line of troops file across

the distant horizon; three-quarters of the screen is sky. Cochise picks up a hand-
ful of dust and tosses it contemptuously away; the music makes this gesture omi-
nous.

The regiment pursues the Indian dust cloud to the entrance of a narrow, rocky
defile. Wayne now tells Fonda that this dust cloud is fake; he replies sarcastically
that one would think Cochise were Alexander or Napoleon, and orders a charge
into the narrow gap. Wayne says this is "suicide," and Fonda relieves him of his
command, calling him a coward. Wayne throws down his gauntlet in a challenge
that Fonda accepts but postpones, ordering Wayne to dig in the wagons and remain with them. Fonda leads the charge across the flat; Indians ride out of the
defile and pick off the bugler; they turn around and dash back into it with the
charge in hot pursuit. The camera does quick cuts from among the boulders high
above the defile; behind each boulder is an armed Indian, waiting, most wearing
the light, loose clothing that is the same color as the rocks. The charging troops,
their line now broken and slowed by the terrain, enter the defile and are shot like
fish in a barrel; Fonda falls first. Wayne, hearing the disaster and watching the dust
rise from the entrance to the defile, rides into it and brings the wounded Fonda
out. He insists on rejoining his command; Wayne tells him it's wiped out. Fonda
mounts groggily and rides back into the dust; Wayne looks admiringly after him.
Fonda finds the tiny remnant of the regiment, including Bond, pinned down near
the entrance. The camera pulls back and shows a horde of galloping Apache
emerge from the defile and ride over the remnant, leaving only dust. The horde,
led by Cochise carrying the regiment's flag, approaches Wayne and the dug-in
wagons, and stops, becoming obscured in its own dust cloud. Wayne disarms, and
walks alone into the dust as Cochise rides up to him and plants the flag in the
ground. Wayne brings it back through the dust from the receding hoofbeats of the
departing horde.

The movie isn't over yet; it has a surprise for us in its next and final scene. To
appreciate this, let us pause to review the scope and meaning of what the film has
shown so far about the contenders for and in this landscape. I've described it in
some detail partly because its visual contrasts between the contenders are typical
of the genre, as several critics have observed. One writes (apropos of *Cheyenne Autumn*, 1964):

> The Indians seem to be a part of the landscape; they spread out over it without cut-
> ting into it the way a line of horse soldiers does. This difference between the cavalry
> and the Indians is characteristic not only of Ford, but of almost all Westerns. It rep-
> resents the white view of the difference between whites and the Indians, and it pro-
> vides a visual rationalization for the conquest of the West. Whites have an organized
> approach to life, taking over and regimenting the land itself; the Indians simply live
> on it. . . . The whites are orderers of the environment, whereas the Indians are sim-
> ply a part of it. (Place 1974: 233)

Another, defending the correctness of Ford's portrayal of Indians (as both noble
and brutal), says he "presented them as the true children of the landscape, with

the . . . Cavalry lumbering in blue and out of place in the red and sandstone bluffs of Monument Valley" (Sinclair 1979: 149). The cavalry doesn't of course lumber along in color in the black-and-white films of the forties; but the contrast is even starker, the savage identification with the land more obvious, in the dark vs. light clothing of *Fort Apache*. Another critic summarizes this aspect of the film:

> The Indians are outside the system; they are the Other, the enemy . . . they are like the land, something to be controlled. And dust is their constant ally: dust thrown by Cochise as sign he will engage the cavalry . . . dustclouds warning York the Apache are near; dustclouds squaws create to fool Thursday [Fonda]; dust engulfing the trapped regiment; dust into which the Apache disappear . . . and which then rolls over York's men. (Gallagher 1986: 249)

This "white" view of the landscape's "children" is the cinematic realization, the now literally moving picture, of the savage autochthony in our founding legend. And this, from its beginnings, was a fictional response to historical experience, which would help to reproduce that experience in the world. So is the ambush in *Fort Apache* (and in many other Westerns). It reproduces legend and history at once, by pitting the indigenes who know their home terrain against its invaders who don't know it. Every American schoolchild used to learn about the English General Braddock's march in the French and Indian War. He insisted on marching his ordered files of redcoats through the forest seeking the Indian enemy, in order to engage it in the European way, on some open terrain. He ignored the advice of his local junior officer, George Washington, who told him that this was folly, that his troops could not move, dress, or fight in the European way in this place against this enemy. So, lumbering through the forest, they were massacred by the invisible enemy, who filled them with arrows shot from the treetops. A more immediate historical precedent for the ambush was the famous last stand of Custer, suggested in the film by Fonda's wish to be up there where the action was. The action in that "Indian ambuscade," as Whitman called it, was the same kind of folly as Braddock's, only it became a legend of heroism (as will Fonda's). The folly is the failure to adapt one's strategy to the conditions and nature of colonial warfare, the failure to understand both the landscape and the psychology of the indigenes. And the failure proceeds from the legendary classification of those indigenes as savages: there's nothing worth understanding about them. So their military behavior is castigated as unfair and treacherous—as Virgil portrayed the Rutulians, Geoffrey the giants, Spenser the Irish, and countless movies the Indians.

In *Fort Apache*, the failure and its cause are equally emphasized. For Fonda adamantly holds the legendary view: the savage as "illiterate" and "uncivilized" is not us but a subspecies, worth no words—neither of honor nor of negotiation—but insults. Fonda could easily have told Cochise that his main grievance, the corrupt agent, was being dealt with. But he doesn't, because his attitude is that of British colonial administrators in India and Africa: one must be firm with savages, who, like children, are confused by explanation and need only be required to obey. The penalty for this attitude is swift and catastrophic. Cochise, it turns out, is more like Alexander than Fonda. And the stupidity of the attitude in the circumstances is made clear by the systematic contrast between Fonda and Wayne becoming extreme opposition during the battle. Wayne is right (and Fonda wrong) on every point, precisely because he knows the place and the indigenes (like George Washington) and is even willing to respect them. Wayne is the cowboy figure (unmarried), the ambivalent partial savage, who can negotiate across the frontier, riding into that forbidding landscape and out of it again, just as he both rides and walks into and out of the dust. The latter scene is a powerful visual endorsement of his position in the film as opposed to Fonda's. For Cochise renders respect for respect, not only sparing Wayne and his small contingent (which includes Bond's son, so he can marry Temple), but understanding quite enough of "honor" to pay him the compliment of returning the regimental flag. In the community of the army, Ford has staged the sharpest of conflicts between the dedicated culture-bringer and the ambivalent, attenuated *civilisateur*. What most crucially divides them are their assumptions about, treatment of, and relationship with the savage. The newer form of the legend has prevailed over the older: survival demands accommodation with and respect for the savage; the old definition has become dangerous to our health.

But in the final scene of the picture, the contest evaporates, and both forms of the legend are reunited as Wayne visually and verbally becomes Fonda. Now the commanding officer, he stands in a buttoned tunic (though still wearing his bandana) in front of Fonda's portrait, telling a group of reporters about Fonda's heroic charge, which has become part of the glorious history and the esprit de corps of the regiment. As Wayne waxes eloquent about the service and sacrifices of the common soldier, he goes to stand at the window. From outside it, the camera shows a ghostly procession of the dead soldiers riding across the clouds reflected in the window pane against Wayne's chest. "They've not died," he says. The shot gives them both celestial and memorial life—they're in his heart—and the reporters write it all down. The regiment is forever. "Any questions?" says Wayne dismissively. Then he introduces them to Fonda's baby grandson (product of the marriage Fonda forbade), puts on a foreign-legion cap, and goes out to lead his troops. They mount and file out to "The Girl I Left Behind Me," watched by Bond's widow and Temple with the baby, shown against the sky. The final shot is middle-distance, from lower than eye-level against the sky, of the column as it leaves the fort, led by Wayne. All conflict is resolved here into the passage of generations; the enmities of one become the alliances of the next. The community absorbs the differences between its members. Wayne becomes what he opposed, nourishing Fonda's glory for the good of that community he now leads, whose self-transmission seems its greatest glory.

It's easy to see why there should be considerable disagreement and discomfort about the ending of *Fort Apache*. Is it a sentimental evasion of the conflict it has so carefully constructed? Or does it mean to suggest that the cowboy really ought to become the martinet, and if so how much of him? Just enough to impose the discipline necessary to maintain a police force? Just enough to admire his willing-

ness to die for the code he lives by without sharing his snobbish, arrogant, and sui-
cidal racism? Or does the movie finally endorse these attitudes? Or, on the contrary, does the final scene discredit them ironically? Though neither its characters
nor its photography seem ironic, the situation is: an act that the audience has seen
to be futile and destructive is being (literally) rewritten as a triumph. We know it's
hollow. We also know it's not, that it's just what Whitman (and the press) did for
Custer, that the glory sought has, in an even greater (and posthumous) irony, been
found. And it's found in the story of what happened, not in the happening.

All of these possible contradictions in Ford's ending—which are those inherent
in the legend itself—are evoked by its staging of the history-making moment. Not,
to be sure, the moment of acting it, but the moment of telling it and writing it
down. Ford concludes this version of the founding story with a dramatization of
its manufacture. It's a Virgilian moment, this awareness of how the fiction shown
becomes a different fiction in the telling. The telling is for public consumption:
the journalists and the audience; for the camera realizes for us what Wayne is telling them about the eternity of the regiment. And the camera continues, as it has
throughout the film, to present as epically heroic this police community that brings
our culture to the wilderness. The narrative opposition between the martinet and
the cowboy complicates, as literature had already complicated, this heroism, but
doesn't fundamentally alter it. The narrative (and the camera in a shot or two) also
even allows the Indians to share some of it. They are (in part) worthy adversaries:
just by being (legendarily) autochthonous, they are here victorious. But it's not
their victory that becomes part of the legend at the end: it's Fonda's defeat. Our
actual loss (those dead soldiers) becomes our moral, community-building gain (the
memory of their personal courage). So even though we lose, we win; for we are
telling the story to ourselves. There is no contradiction that a live myth can't me-
diate, incorporate, and keep at the ready for future enactment. Wayne's troops ride
out in the last shot to go on enacting it—and not only in subsequent films. Ford's
audacity is to have shown the myth in the making and to have revealed the agency
of film as the maker: his camera rebuilds the legend it inherited and photographs
itself in the process.

The last Western Ford made that dramatizes the process of culture-bringing also
dramatizes as its narrative frame the power of a legend to become a fact. *The Man
Who Shot Liberty Valance* (1962) combines the situation of *My Darling Clementine*
with the structure of *Fort Apache* into as schematic a version of our founding story
as *Drums Along the Mohawk*, only set this time in the western frontier town of Shinbone. The town needs law, like Tombstone, as protection from the brutal enemy
within; the story of its bringing is articulated, as in *Fort Apache*, around a character contrast. Only now the contrast concerns neither the police nor the savages (no
army, no Indians—but a Mexican cantina in the town and a black servant for the
hero—and no sweeping landscapes), but the two functions of the legendary hero
split into two characters: the lawgiver and the general; the just ruler and the warrior. The former is Senator Stoddard (James Stewart), who arrives years before, as
a tenderfoot lawyer from the East, with his books (which are ripped up by the vil-

lain). The latter is Tom Doniphon (John Wayne), who raises horses: a cowboy figure by virtue of likeness not to the Indians, but to the villain; he's the better gunman, whom the villain fears. The Senator and his wife (Vera Miles) chug into Shinbone on the new railroad in the film's opening shot, in order to attend Wayne's funeral (he's died a pauper). They chug out of it the same way in the final shot. The story is told (the whole film is a flashback) by Stewart to the editor of the local paper, who insists on an interview even in the midst of mourning. The point of the story is to demonstrate that these two antagonists and rivals in love are both essential parts of the same process—with some pathetic and ironic weight tilting toward the warrior as the more essential.

The situation is simple: the town is terrorized by the vicious robber and murderer, Liberty Valance (Lee Marvin), who brutalizes widows and beats people to death with a whip. Stewart is brutalized by Marvin in a stage robbery, is found and brought to town by Wayne. Stewart believes in the law and thinks he can have Marvin arrested; Wayne tells him it's different out here, where "every man settles his own problems." The town Marshal (Andy Devine) is a cowardly, amusing glutton; he counts for nothing. Wayne is the town's toughest citizen, the only one who can personally defy Marvin. He says that if Stewart can't shoot, he'd better leave. Stewart, recuperating, washes dishes and serves in the eating house of Miles's parents. He is mocked for wearing an apron. He is befriended by the then editor of the newspaper, a Shakespeare-quoting drunk (Edmund O'Brien), and hangs out his shingle on the newspaper office. Stewart is determined to civilize the place, and starts by teaching young and old alike to read and write (beginning with Miles, who is tearfully embarrassed about her deficiency in this department).

The big cattlemen in the territory want to keep it open range, and oppose statehood; the citizens and the small farmers want statehood. Stewart and O'Brien become the leaders of the latter group (which includes Wayne), and the cattlemen hire Marvin to do some terrorizing. Stewart has reluctantly been learning to shoot; he and O'Brien are elected (over Marvin) as the town's delegates to the statehood convention in the territorial capital. O'Brien prints news about Marvin's crimes; Marvin beats him nearly to death and destroys the newspaper office and press. He challenges Stewart to a gunfight. Stewart gamely faces him (still wearing the apron), is shot in the right arm (Marvin tickled by his incompetence), picks up his gun with the left and fires. Marvin falls dead. At the statehood convention, the crippled O'Brien nominates Stewart as the territory's delegate to Washington, saying he's a true defender of the farmers and shopkeepers, who are the "builders of cities" and of "law and order." The cattlemen's spokesman disputes this, saying that Stewart (famous as the man who shot Liberty Valance), having taken the law into his own hands, has forfeited any legislative trust. Stewart feels the same way, as if he's betrayed his trust in law, and is ready to give up and go back East. Wayne appears to tell Stewart that he can be elected with a clear conscience, since it was Wayne (acting throughout as Stewart's guardian angel) who killed Marvin. The scene is played again from a different angle to show us how. Stewart is acclaimed as the delegate.

Back to the narrative frame: the present editor of Shinbone's paper, at the end of Stewart's story, rips up the notes of the reporter who's been writing it all down. Asked by Stewart why he's not going to print it, he replies with a résumé of Stewart's distinguished political career: first governor, then senator, then ambassador to the Court of St. James, and now, if he wants, Vice-President of the United States. He ends by telling Stewart a local journalistic rule: "when the legend becomes fact, print the legend." Stewart wants, though, to leave Washington and move back to Shinbone, as he hints to his delighted wife in the train as they leave. Nothing she'd like better than to come back to her roots in a place that, thanks to her husband, she says, was "once a wilderness, now a garden." Both the beginning and end of the film are heavy with nostalgia for the real hero, the enforcer who made possible the glorious political career that brought this culture, and who died alone and poor, mourned only by his faithful black servant (Woody Strode). Miles brought a cactus rose to his coffin, replicating his gift to her earlier in the film.

The coalescence of the lawyer and the gunslinger here is a good deal clearer and less problematic than that of the martinet and the cowboy at the end of *Fort Apache*. It roundly affirms what the ambiguous ending of *My Darling Clementine* left questions about: that civilization—democratic government for citizen-tillers of the soil—requires force, that law is nothing without it, that firepower must precede lawgiving. But it's in the past, this force; since it is indeed indistinguishable from the force it defeats, it is unnecessary in the new order that the railroad has brought to Shinbone. The film mourns the fact that the day of the Hawkeye hero and his racial subordinate is over. Only, of course, it's not over, not in the public mind. The editor is not going to disturb the coalescence of law and force in the legend of the man who shot Liberty Valance; he's not going to reveal that these things were and may be separable, even opposed. The political career is fact; the legend, here simply the lie, that launched it will continue to be printed. The film prints it, too, in spite of showing Stewart's discomfiture with it. The whole film is structured ironically to reveal the lie and to secure the audience's admiration for the self-sacrificing (he gives up the girl) hero who knows how to use force without scruple (as he says at one point). He uses it, even if illegally, in the good cause and suffers in silence; he's still the essential incorruptible gun, only now condemned to unhappiness and obsolescence.

The Western movie itself in the fifties and sixties is reaching both the final efflorescence of its own mythology (*Shane*, 1953) and its dissolution (*Broken Arrow*, 1950; *High Noon*, 1952; Ford's own *The Searchers*, 1956; *The Scalphunters*, 1967). But its legend, in all senses, continues to be fact. The cowboy as reluctant exterminator and ambivalent *civilisateur* fades from the screen in gusts of admiring nostalgia. In *Liberty Valance* Ford splits the idealized unity of Fonda's Wyatt Earp (both force and law) into conflicting principles, anticipating in fiction the actual subsequent usage of the word "cowboy." In the late fifties (attested by the *OED*), it is slang for law officers, policemen. In the mid-eighties, the word is used for persons hired by the CIA to use the kinds of force in the kinds of ways that are explicitly prohibited by law. As Oliver North's secretary explained on television in 1987 to a

Congressional Committee and a worldwide audience, there are times when the law must simply be ignored in order to defend the good cause by force.[1] On the screen, this position, arrived at in cowboy movies, becomes that of the enormously popular spy thriller. The James Bonds are but sexually loosened-up cowboys, legally employed to do all sorts of spectacularly illegal things—licensed, indeed, to kill. The myth of the cowboy is dead; long live the spy.

In the world, the cinematic cowboy's position becomes that of the CIA cowboys (and their counterparts in the west, all of whom competed with the Soviet KGB) who fomented rebellions, planned assassinations, suborned elections, and armed both guerrillas and dictators from South America across the Middle East to Southeast Asia. It was Virgil who presented history as the acting out of stories in his retelling of the founding legend that we have never stopped either printing as legend or enacting as fact. And John Ford dramatized the process, even as he made the legend visible in the new medium that offered to the world the epic of its current hegemonic power. As a military officer, Ford shared this power; as a filmmaker he rationalized it historically, justified it morally, and attempted to influence its policies. In the exercise of both professions, his was a truly Virgilian career, serving by his art the empire of his time. The service was well rewarded, not only by the worldwide public, but by the American government, which gave him the rank of full Admiral and the Presidential Medal of Freedom in 1973 (Gallagher 1986: 454). The legend he (re)built in cinema became fact in more ways than one.

An incident from Ford's wartime filmmaking, and a similar one from his last Western, show the process at work yet again. He had taken up his commission in the U.S. Navy in order to do during the Korean War what he had done in the previous one. In the course of making a documentary film of this war, he contrived to replay as fact the bizarre fiction of shelling a continent from Conrad's *Heart of Darkness*. Ford did this as a kind of jokey experiment in order to obtain a spectacular shot for his film. Aboard the U.S.S. *Missouri*, he convinced the vice-admiral in command of the need for something spectacular, and asked him whether the battleship "had ever fired all of her sixteen-inch guns in one broadside and in one direction. The vice-admiral replied that no American battleship had ever done that, for fear that the recoil would make the ship turn turtle." Ford piqued his curiosity and persuaded him to try it, since he was only six months away from retirement. "The next day a target was selected somewhere on the mainland of Asia, and all the huge guns of the 'Mighty Mo' were trained on it." Ford and his cameraman, Armistead, hovered above the ship in a helicopter.

The *Missouri* fired her thundering broadside into Korea. The battleship rocked sideways on the recoil, heeling nearly halfway over, until her starboard decks were awash. Then she righted herself, shaking off the water like the leviathan she was. Armistead

1. She and North were staff members of the National Security Council, which is attached to the White House. As part of their oath of office, Presidents of the United States swear to uphold the laws made by its legislative body.

got the shot, Ford had a climax for his film, the vice-admiral settled a navy puzzle, and somewhere in Asia there was a series of vast explosions. (Sinclair 1979: 163)[2]

The (presumably) actual incident shares with its fictional antecedent the function of unconscious revelation. Whether as lunacy or experiment, the absurdity in each case proceeds from the gap between the motive, the putative purpose, and the result. In Conrad, a supposed enemy is aimed at, and nothing happens; in Korea, something wholly unspecified is aimed at, and a great deal is made to happen to the vessel. In both cases the target is invisible and the result of the "explosions" unknowable—with respect to the event. With respect to its telling, the absurdity of the event in Conrad reveals that of a major operation in the text itself: blaming the landscape. In Korea, however, the absurdity of the event is subsumed in the perfectly rational process of its staging: Ford wants an impressive shot and gets it. Yet the telling highlights the absurdity that in order to get it, "somewhere" in Asia (twice repeated) is in fact blown up by all those sixteen-inch shells (almost treble the size of those a half-century earlier). This telling thus suggests an ironic answer to the question that Conrad's scene poses: what can we imagine we're accomplishing by "firing into a continent"? We're doing it in order to watch ourselves doing it; let the shells fall where they may. And we are able to do it for the simple reason that it's not *our* continent; it's the other one, the generalized abode of a savage enemy, Africa or Asia—"Indian country" in the parlance of the American military (lately used of southern Iraq) for any hostile territory.

In Ford's last Western (*Cheyenne Autumn*, 1964), there is a scene of an Indian ambush that depicts the shelling of the landscape. The film attempts to recount (along with much else) the heroic sufferings of the Cheyenne in 1878 on their trek to escape confinement in Oklahoma (Monument Valley) and go home to their northern plains. But it was too late for most of them, and it's too late for Ford, who, when he can't find some form of our occidental community to celebrate, can give no focus or coherence to the narrative. Early in the film, the Cheyenne make their escape, knowing the army will pursue, and directly prepare an ambush in a little canyon. They dig trenches for the women and children, and the armed men wait behind rocks. The army column arrives, led by Capt. Archer (Richard Widmark), who wears a buckskin jacket. Both his name and his garb signal the ambivalent cowboy figure; but neither the script nor the situation can give him any heroic action to perform. He wholly sympathizes with the Cheyenne, so the most heroic thing he later does is take leave from the army to go to Washington (risking his career) and persuade the Secretary of the Interior (Edward G. Robinson) to try to settle the Cheyenne in the north. At this point the Cheyenne have surrendered and are being starved in Kansas by an alcoholic, authoritarian German officer (Karl Malden).

As Widmark's column enters the canyon, the camera pans its rocky emptiness, and he, true to his role, senses the ambush. He halts the column and sends two men

2. Sinclair, himself a novelist, tells the story well and attributes it to conversation with Armistead.

ahead to reconnoiter. They are gleefully shot at by an intemperate young brave (Sal Mineo), giving the game away, much to the disgust of the chief in command. Widmark makes camp, content merely to block the canyon's entrance. A blustering Major arrives with some large cannon, which he immediately orders to start blasting the Indians out of there. The cannons boom away into the rocks, at no visible target. A few women and children are hurt, but while the bombardment proceeds some braves sneak down and drive off the soldiers' horses. The Major is killed in the skirmish, and the Cheyenne continue on their way.

The film makes no legend of this embarrassing episode in which our sympathy, directed by the hero who is also the film's narrator, is with the Indians. The distance between this action and the ambush in *Fort Apache* has been plausibly seen as Ford's reflection of the decline in American self-assurance between the nation's postwar dominance in 1948 and the multiply competitive world of 1964. But the episode, again, has both a longer and a more precise range of meanings. First, it dramatizes an historical condition for the subjugation of the savage that is usually omitted from Westerns: our crushing technological superiority in weaponry. Heavy artillery does not typically appear on the filmic frontier—never before in Ford, if only because the battles, to be cinematically suspenseful, must be between more or less equally equipped sides. The artillery appears here ironically, of course, just as it did in Conrad and in Sinclair's account of Ford in Korea. It is counterproductive. The Indians escape it with ease and are finally obliged to surrender by sickness and starvation.

Second, this very irony is both retrospective and prophetic. As it looks back to a long history of superior firepower being frustrated by autochthonous savages, it looks forward, in the year before American infantry troops were sent to fight in Vietnam, to a war that massively superior firepower could not win. In that war, what was ironic farce in fiction will become a kind of tragedy in fact. In the jungles of Indochina the metaphor implicit in the transferred epithet of "hostile territory" will be literally enacted. The land itself becomes the target of a massive attack that is made possible materially by our technological superiority. But only long, long after it has been possible symbolically, after a couple of millennia of identifying the indigenous enemy with the land from which he springs, after a few centuries of enactment from New England to New Zealand by making him and his forest perish together, and after a century or so of resentment at the resistance offered by desert and tropical landscapes to the efforts and well-being of the culture-bringer and his police force. The modern fictional forms of our founding legend in prose and film project as incidents of grotesque pointlessness—shelling the bush and the rocks—what will be performed as military strategy in Indochina.

Chapter 28

§✥

DEFOLIATING THE LANDSCAPE

The War in Indochina

In three ways, the usual name of "the Vietnam War" (or the War in Vietnam) is somewhat misleading. It implies that there was a single, separable period of combat in a single country that qualifies as a "war." The last point is a technicality, but is not without importance. For the war, just like the War in Korea, was never declared by the U.S. Congress. It is therefore officially called (by the Library of Congress) the "Vietnam Conflict, 1961–1975." It clearly ended in 1975, with the withdrawal of all the American forces, the surrender of the South Vietnamese, and the unification of the country under those of the victorious North Vietnamese and Vietcong. But it's much harder to say when it began. The official date of 1961 is when the American military advisers to and trainers of the South Vietnamese Army were authorized to accompany their units into combat. These advisers, however, had been advising since 1956, when the Vietcong began armed rebellion against the government of South Vietnam, then headed by Ngo Dinh Diem, which had been installed with the assistance of the United States. The occasion was his refusal to hold an election on unification promised for that year. Some standard sources (e.g. Kohn 1987) therefore give 1956 as the beginning of the conflict. But the regime of Ngo Dinh Diem had also been engaged the previous year, which was also that of its installation, by an armed rebellion of three religious sects. This initiated what has been called the "Vietnamese Civil War of 1955–65." Its terminal date means only the overthrow of this regime by a military coup, and the installation, with American support, of Generals Nguyen Cao Ky and Nguyen Van Thieu as the heads of state.

This civil war was the direct consequence of the "French-Indochina War of 1946–54." At the end of the Japanese occupation, Ho Chi Minh (a veteran of an uprising against the French in 1930) organized a political party, the Vietminh, to proclaim the independence of Vietnam from France, whose colony it had been (in the north, technically a "protectorate") since 1883. France had similarly held Cambodia since 1867; in 1893 Laos was formally incorporated into the whole, called

325

French Indochina. To acquire all this France had fought four wars in the second half of the nineteenth century against all these peoples plus the Chinese (Kohn 1987: 170–71). In the late 1940s the Vietminh began guerrilla attacks in the countryside and on French garrisons. The French established a provisional government, under an emperor, which was recognized by the United States in 1950. The Vietminh, inspired and aided by Mao Zedong, refused all accommodation with the French, were joined by rebel groups in Laos and Cambodia, and finally defeated French forces at the famous siege of Dienbienphu. A truce agreement negotiated in 1954 the withdrawal of the French and divided Vietnam at the 17th parallel into two nations, the Vietminh-ruled North, and the noncommunist South, with the incumbent emperor at the head of a state backed by the French and the Americans. In a referendum of the following year, South Vietnam became a nominal republic, and Ngo Dinh Diem its premier. The election he refused to hold on unification had been mandated by the truce agreement. The Vietcong were natives of the south, mostly returned veterans from the Vietminh campaigns that had expelled the French. Together with North Vietnamese forces, they formed what they called the "National Liberation Front," which after nineteen years of war also managed to expel the Americans.

For the victors, therefore, the war was a protracted struggle against two western powers and their local allies that lasted twenty-nine years. For the French, its dates are unambiguous. For the Americans, its beginnings are uncertain. The official date is the participation of American officers in combat. A more plausible date is the participation of those officers in organizing and training the South Vietnamese Army. But neither of these would correspond to the popular awareness of the war in the United States, which, though it was fully reported, scarcely entered the public consciousness until early in 1963 (a photo story in *Life*), and became an issue of public debate in 1964. The difficulty of dating, though, shows clearly enough that the war cannot be understood as a neatly bounded period of straightforward hostilities, initiated by some event like those at Fort Sumter, Sarajevo, or Pearl Harbor.

Nor was it ever confined to Vietnam. The French had created Indochina (just as the British did Nigeria) out of a geographically contiguous and culturally disparate collection of peoples, mainly the Annamese, Cham, Laotian, and Khmer. These groups had been sporadically contending against each other as well as against the Thais and the Chinese since the fifth century B.C. The "nation" of Vietnam was constructed only as a result of the Vietminh revolt against the French in the late forties. It was composed of three regions that had been variously independent since the sixteenth century: Tonkin (the north), Annam (the narrow middle), and Cochinchina (the south). The latter had been directly governed by France as a colony since 1867; the other two were governed through native rulers as "protectorates." In 1949, France allowed them all to federate; this was the provisional government recognized by the major western powers in 1950. The federation hardly existed until it was split in half by the truce of 1954, creating two countries out of none. Nor was the subsequent war confined to these two countries. The other two, Laos and Cambodia, created at the same time, were undergoing similar rebellions of Vietminh forces together with local communists against the regimes left in place by the departing French. The topography of the region also insured their involvement in the escalating warfare in Vietnam. Both land and river routes by which North Vietnam furnished troops and supplies to the Vietcong in the South ran through one or the other of the neighboring countries, which were increasingly bombed as the war went on.

So: variously extended in time, according to the various participants and kinds of participation; confined to no single country in a situation where just the creation of a "country" was the point of the fighting; and where this fighting was at once internal (a civil war of classes and ideologies) and external (a response to invasion from without)—on all counts it's really too multifarious to be called "the" Vietnam War. Because it was many wars in many places, but was indeed confined to a single region founded by a colonial power, some international organizations refer to it as the "Second Indochina War." This label has the advantage of both spatial and temporal accuracy. And thus to denominate this conflict the successor of the First (that is, the French-Indochina War) identifies it as a war of decolonization. The great extent to which it was precisely a colonial war, that of an indigenous Asian population seeking to rid itself of occidental domination, was never understood by American policymakers, not even by those who came to oppose it for other reasons (see Clifford 1991). The irony of this, for a nation that created itself by a war of independence from a colonial power, has often been noted both then and since.

And there are greater ironies. A former assistant secretary of defense (who edited a multivolume *Systems Analysis of the Vietnam War* published by the Department of Defense but not available to the lay public) has argued that no one responsible for waging the war understood it strategically (Thayer 1985). The title of his book, *War Without Fronts*, suggests why. It was seldom a matter of visibly massed armies attacking and defending particular places or positions. It was largely guerrilla warfare: constant ambush, hit-and-run—the sort of war that indigenes fighting on and for their home terrain have always waged against invaders with superior equipment. This much was obvious, and caused some professional soldiers to become dubious about the prospects. General Maxwell Taylor, who in 1961 had advised President Kennedy to send American troops to Vietnam, changed his mind by 1965, when he was the American ambassador to South Vietnam. He then advocated sending no more combat troops, since he had found the American soldier was "not a suitable guerrilla fighter for Asian forests and jungles" (Clifford 1991: 409). The physical nature of the war was clear; what no one understood, according to Thayer's semiofficial account, was what to do about it.

The early strategy was that of winning the "hearts and minds" of the rural population, in order to create "pacified" villages loyal to the South Vietnamese government. But this appeared to work only when troops were present. It yielded to the more aggressive policy of "search and destroy," which presented the great problem of finding the guerrilla enemy, or more precisely, of recognizing him when found. The final strategy was to rely on our immense technological superiority and engage in a war of attrition, in the belief that our firepower would simply outlast the enemy's tenacity. Hence the massive bombings: the leveling of villages in areas of high guerrilla activity; the continuous attacks on the supply routes from North Vietnam, its harbors, and its industrial capacity. All the stages in this escalation required more of everything, men and materiel. By 1968 there were 536,000 American troops in Vietnam (Thayer 1985: 37). By 1970, the total area of Indochina cratered by bombs was about 5,000 square miles—larger than the state of Connecticut (Weisberg 1970: 69–70). And nothing worked. If a trail was obliterated, tunnels were dug; if a bridge was blown today, there would be rafts or pontoons tomorrow.

Though the massive destruction of the attrition policy had none of its designed strategic effects on the will and ability of the enemy to continue fighting, it had other and profound effects on the nation supposedly being defended, which were soon theorized into a strategy. The effects were these: in 1955 85 percent of South Vietnam's population lived in rural areas; in 1970 60 percent of it lived in cities. The population of Saigon increased tenfold. In 1964 South Vietnam exported 48.5 billion metric tons of rice; in 1965 it imported 240 billion (Weisberg 1970: 24, 27). Contemplating such effects, a Harvard professor of government, then an official in the State Department, figured that they offered the strategic answer to guerrilla warfare. The answer, specifically, to the well-known theory of such warfare as practiced and promulgated by Mao Zedong. Revolutionary guerrillas could, Mao found, operate indefinitely in the rural countryside just by being part of it, by blending into the local peasantry whose cooperation they secured ideally by persuasion, practically by helping with chores and supplying an occasional luxury like medicine, but if necessary by coercion. The guerrilla in Mao's famous metaphor was a fish in the sea, living on and in his element, the rural peasantry. The political scientist saw in the enormous effects of the bombing the obvious answer: if you can't catch the fish, drain the sea.

He argues that political control of the population is the real issue of the war, and observes that the central government cannot achieve this in countless rural villages where small local groups traditionally do the job; here is the strength of the Vietcong. Just for this reason, he welcomes the social revolution of massive urbanization, thanks to the intensification of the war since 1965. The urban slums to which the refugees from the ravaged rural areas flock are, he says, "for the poor peasant the gateway to a new and better life" (Huntington 1968: 649). On the average, their incomes double. He sees the recent Tet offensive—attacks for the first time on virtually all the major cities and over a hundred towns in South Vietnam—as an attempt to discourage this urban migration and divert military attention from the rural areas. He thus deduces that the United States "in an absent minded way . . . may well have stumbled upon the answer to 'wars of national liberation.'" The effective response is neither conventional military action nor "gimmicks of counter-insurgency warfare. It is instead forced-draft urbanization and modernization which rapidly brings the country in question out of the phase in which a rural revolutionary movement can hope to generate sufficient strength" (652). He concludes by advocating "formal decentralization" of political and military efforts in order to arrive at "accommodation" with the real, local, and varied sources of power.

This article in the prestigious pages of *Foreign Affairs* acquired an immediate notoriety, pro and con, and was sometimes cited, erroneously, as the blueprint for a deliberate policy of "forced urbanization."[1] In fact, the policy of generating refugees went back to State Department memos of 1966 (Gibson 1986: 228–30). Huntington's article theorized a supposedly inadvertent effect into a possible strategy, but didn't really, indeed couldn't, suggest pursuing it. For its conscious pursuit would have repeated on a far grander scale just the kind of absurdity already evident in the practice of "pacification." Americans had long been seeing on television what this meant: someone would say that such-and-such a village had been pacified, and the camera would pan a blackened, empty space, where it had been burned to the ground. To make it peaceful was to make it cease to exist. The use of the term "pacification" to mean wiping out goes back, one scholar notes, to 1573, when Philip II of Spain decreed that it replace "conquest" (Drinnon 1980: 440). To urge that rural areas simply be destroyed in order to deprive the fish of sea would have made nonsense of our avowed purpose of defending the country, transposing "pacification" to the national scale: we defend it by killing it. This could hardly be *said*; but of course, as Huntington observed, a considerable amount of it had already been done.

The difference between saying and doing in the whole conduct of the war at every level—from the falsification of reports in the field through their systematization by analysts in the Pentagon to the resultant self-deception of the policymakers who thus misinformed the public—amply deserves the analysis it has received as a kind of Orwellian "doublethink" (Gibson 1986: 177–80). But in Huntington's article, matters are not quite that convoluted: his way of describing and conceiving of what was done merely overlooks, as usual, the people it's done to; he literally doesn't see them. He dismisses the refugees to a "better" life in the city because their incomes double. (Even an economist might suggest that so do their expenses.) Others, who both saw and studied the peasants' way of life, were not convinced that urbanization would improve it. For these peasants identified themselves so completely with the place they lived in and cultivated that the worst human fate they could imagine was to wander, to be displaced. To destroy their rice paddies, forests, and villages was to explode the entire "physical and spiritual foundation" of their lives (Weisberg 1970: 25). This cultural and psychological devastation seems so utterly obvious as to make Huntington's casual assertion that their lives are better ridiculous, if not disgusting. The assertion, moreover, is gratuitous, not at all required by the argument. People are habitually erased in the abstractions of discourse about strategy; they're just units to be politically controlled; their ac-

1. See, for example, Ronk and Chomsky in Weisberg (1970).

tual condition as refugees or how they might feel about it are irrelevant. So where does it come from, this bizarre assertion that their lives are improved by displacement?

It comes from the whole conception of history latent in the "modernization" that bombardment has so happily accelerated. It resides in the postulation of "the phase" out of which the country is thus forcibly to be brought. Phase of what? Development, of course: just a stage through which all (people or nations) must pass—as we say of a fractious adolescent, "She's just going through a phase." The assertion is made possible (logically, emotionally, morally), is imaginable, only by assuming the universal historiography that our founding legend became in the eighteenth century. The phase the peasants of Indochina (or all of Asia according to Hegel) are in is simply primitive: those thousands of tiny villages, cultivation by hand and buffalo, no technology, no cities. We invented the primitive (it was what we were) and found it everywhere: Ireland, America, Africa, Asia. On the only possible historical trajectory there is, the primitive is intolerably anachronistic; it has no sharable present with us because to us it is by definition not a present but a past. So here in Vietnam twenty-odd years ago we can find improvement in the condition of the very people whose primitive, un- or under-"developed," way of life is destroyed, just as we found it a century ago in that of the Maori, or four centuries ago in that of the native Americans and the Irish. Since they all, by legendary definition, start from nowhere, *anything* would be an improvement.

Only the (il)logic of the legend can make this assertion comprehensible, providing its ground and having as its consequence the commission and justification of ethnocide. For the *ethnos* in question is zero (or worse); it is negligible, empty (or an obstacle to "progress"), not requiring to be understood except as degradation or regression, a throwback to a phase that should have been gone through, a case (like India) of "arrested" development. It must go. By destroying a savage, or barbarian, or primitive way of life, we thus "save" the people who lead it, get them back on the right track, the only one there is. So Spenser recommended the extirpation of Irish kinship structure, dress, and language (see ch. 11). So a nineteenth-century observer wrote of the Australian aborigines: "If they are to be at all improved it must be by an abnegation of their own language and manners, and an entire adoption of ours" (see ch. 22). So an American diplomat said of Vietnam: "To make progress in this country, it is necessary to level everything. The inhabitants must go back to zero, lose their traditional culture, for it blocks everything" (Weisberg 1970: 95).

Everything? Well, everything that counts as progress in that universalized totality that the legend tells us is world history, for no better reason than that it is our history, the Roman story of the *translatio imperii et studii* from Troy to Rome to Troynovants throughout Europe to the twenty Troys in North America. The logic of this story, in all its diffused and accreted forms, is acted out once again in Indochina: its historiography mandates the ethnocide of indigenes who are assimilated to its category of savage and whose landscape itself becomes the object of unprecedented attacks.

The (patho)logical operation of the legend to justify dispossessing someone else has been signaled since the sixteenth century by particular figures of speech and general uses of language that obscure, and therefore draw attention to, just who is doing what to whom. The transferred epithet has been a recurring figure, from the "unjust" repulsion (of imperial invaders) and the "unjust" possession (of aboriginal natives) to the "hostile" territory (to those who want to transform it, not to those who live in it). Locutions that obfuscate agency have been legion; the grandest of them is probably the nineteenth-century attribution to Nature of the demise of the savage. The diplomat's declaration makes an odd and telling use of a verb for much the same purpose. The Vietnamese are said to be under an obligation or compulsion ("must") to "lose" their culture. The sense of "culture" here is clearly not that of some elevated attainment—as one might lose, through disuse, an ability to speak a foreign language or play Bach, or forget one's manners—the sense is that of a whole way of life. How can you lose this? You can't mislay it, or leave it lying around somewhere. The verb is used transitively, with a direct object that makes no sense in that use. Only the intransitive use makes sense, but with a different class of object: we lost (suffered the loss of) our land; we lost (were defeated in) the championship. The meaning of the declaration is the latter—an action of which the subject is not the agent—but its form is the former—as if the subject were the agent. Then there's the compulsion, of unspecified source, attributed to the same subject: *they* must lose. The locution says something like: they oblige themselves to mislay their way of life. And it means: they shall be compelled to suffer the loss of their culture. The locution says they're doing what is being done to them, that *they* ought to lose what *we* are destroying.

The inhabitants whose culture must be lost and land leveled are, without qualification, the peasant farmers of Indochina, the great majority of its population. No distinction is made here between fish and sea, guerrilla enemy and peaceable citizen. They're all primitive others, so regarded by the diplomat, and so treated by many American soldiers. Telling the fish from the sea was the supreme problem of the war for those who had to fight it. In the countryside, the enemy was unidentifiable to occidental eyes, and so everyone became the enemy. In areas of high guerrilla activity, notably those surrounding Saigon, this was officially decreed: "everything that moves is considered Charlie [Vietcong]" (Whiteside 1970: 11). The American military was under great pressure to show results in the form of enemy casualties—the famous "body counts." In the field, this pressure was translated into a rule-of-thumb expressed by one soldier as: "anything that's dead and isn't white is a VC" (Drinnon 1980: 451).

Racism, of course—the automatic assumption of the inferiority of any nonwhite people—had been a part of the discourse and enactment of modern western imperialism since the discovery of the new world. As science, it was read back into the old worlds of Africa and Asia in the nineteenth century. Skin color was the easiest way to tell the difference between savagery and civilization, them and us. Both the discourse and the enactment reached extreme forms in the United States, and have been extensively analyzed, since the pioneering book of Roy Harvey Pearce (1953), in the work of Richard Slotkin (1973; 1985). The ways in which the American enactment and mythology of imperialism (itself an heir of the European) were reproduced in Indochina have been most fully described by Frances FitzGerald (1973) and Richard Drinnon (1980).

The latter points out (ch. 21) the direct transference, in the Spanish-American War of 1898 (America's first overseas imperial venture), to the Philippines of the vocabulary, attitudes, and personnel that had been employed against the Indians. The peasant population of the islands, whose rebellions 70,000 U.S. troops were still putting down in 1900, were called "goo-goos" (Drinnon 1980: 313). The U.S. Marines, doing the same thing in Haiti in 1920, called the natives there "gooks" (549). This became the standard derogatory term for both Koreans (only then noticed by the *OED*) and Vietnamese. The language and behavior of American Generals and G.I.s in Vietnam often descended directly from the history and cinema of Indian-fighting. Maxwell Taylor made the same paradoxical observations about the Vietnamese that Philip Sheridan did about the Sioux: they wholly lack any sense of organization or team spirit, and are yet remarkably effective in rebuilding forces and maintaining morale (369–70). This is exactly the kind of paradox—the co-presence of anarchy and order as we envision them—that exercised the Jesuits in Canada long before (see ch. 19). Some soldiers were reported to have taken scalps for the fun of it. One commented: "Some people were on an Indian trip out here." Another paraphrased General Sheridan's most famous remark as "the Indian idea . . . the only good gook is a dead gook." Another summed up these attitudes with conclusive precision: "they're all fucking savages" (Drinnon 1980: 457).

The diplomat could never have said it so directly, but that conviction is the precondition, the enabling fiction that the legend has long provided, for his advocacy of ethnocide. Whatever we do to savages, whatever they lose, is necessarily an improvement in their condition. That condition, postulated as a mythic past in the founding legend of ancient Rome, discovered in the global present of the market-expanding Renaissance, rationalized by the Enlightenment as the initial stage of all human history, has always been defined as the lack of whatever we (the definers) have. Whatever they have is overlooked or ignored or explained away or seen as requiring total destruction. And this is what it got, in a massive new form, from the most recent enactment of our founding legend in Indochina.

Foundation has always entailed destruction; it's what justifies it. Although American policymakers claimed to be founding a new and just political order in South Vietnam, for the South Vietnamese, the way in which those people were in fact viewed and treated made the claim as empty as that of the conversion of the heathen was for the European conquests of the last five centuries. To say this does not impugn the sincerity of any individual, then or now, who made such a claim; it is to insist that history is not made by the motives of individuals, that what happens in the world is not thus explicable. What happened in Indochina is comprehensible, I submit, as another consequence of the story we have so long and in so many forms told ourselves about our civilization—a story that is both fiction and fact, each becoming the other.

The massive new form of destruction justified by our foundational efforts in Indochina was the immediate consequence of a colonial attitude that arose in the nineteenth century: that of blaming the landscape, especially the tropical landscape. This attitude was powerfully reinforced by the problems and circumstances of guerrilla warfare. It was so difficult to find and recognize the enemy, to tell the fish from the sea, that the entire rural population came in some areas to be regarded as the enemy. And from here it was only a small step, not only to the draining of the sea (by the bombardments that made urban refugees of the peasants), but to its destruction by defoliation. The sea in another sense than Mao's—not only the rural populace but the land itself, the tropical jungle—became the enemy.

In an ordinary tactical sense, it had been recognized as the enemy early in America's participation in the war. Defoliation began in 1961–62 with two fairly limited and traditional objectives: to inhibit or prevent ambushes by destroying the cover of trees and bush along roadsides and canal banks; to destroy certain food crops (yams and manioc) in the highlands, whence the guerrillas were supplied (Whiteside 1970: 1). A special unit of the U.S. Air Force (the 12th Air Commando Squadron of the 315th Wing) was formed in 1962 for these purposes; its history has been written by the officer who trained the spray pilots (Cecil 1986). The official name of the project was "Operation Hades" (Whiteside 1970: 8); but it was generally called "Ranch Hand." The destruction of vegetation—for example, firing fields to deprive an enemy of cover or food—had been a military tactic at least since biblical and Roman times. What was new about its practice in Indochina were its means and its scale: it became itself a kind of strategy. It expanded rapidly beyond ambush-prevention, which it had abandoned by 1969, when a half million acres of crops had been destroyed and about five million acres sprayed, some up to three times, with herbicide. This is 12 percent of the total area of South Vietnam, an area a little larger than Massachusetts (Whiteside 1970: 3).[2] By this time, defoliation was no longer used on roadsides because bulldozers, equipped with blades called "Rome Plows" that shaved off all vegetation (including smallish trees) at ground level, had been found to be more efficient.[3] The objective now was generally to prevent infiltration from the north (89). Massive defoliation was regarded, said an Admiral to a Congressional Committee, as a "small investment of military effort" that solved the problem of "the inability to observe the enemy in the dense forest and jungle" (86). Both vertical (from the air) and horizontal (from the ground) visibility was greatly improved by spraying herbicides.

The Admiral did not explain, nor can I, how a tactic became a strategy, how a technique for protecting lines of communication became an easy way to deal with one of the crucial problems of the war. But it did; and almost nothing is known, even by the official historian of the operation, about "the upper-level political and military decisions that guided RANCH HAND because most of that material remains

2. This excellent reporter does not exaggerate the statistics; they appear in a U.S. government report: *Technology Assessment* 1969.

3. For one soldier's persuasive testimony that defoliating roadsides, by any means, did not at all prevent ambushes but rather made them more difficult to escape, see Gibson (1986: 123–24).

classified" (Cecil 1986: x).[4] Maybe it was never really decided; maybe it just grew, even more inadvertently than the forced modernization produced by bombing. Defoliation was much in request by field commanders, for the obvious reason stated by the Admiral. If the enemy disappeared into the greenery, he could be made visible by removing it. So a great deal of it was removed, between 1962 and the cessation of the operation in 1971. The statistics that are knowable come largely from the Ranch Hand operation conducted by aircraft. But "the full story of environmental warfare in Southeast Asia has yet to be told," since a hundred spray-fitted helicopters were also employed, along with trucks, boats, and backpacks for ground spraying. This was a war of high technology against a place and society wholly lacking it: "The attack on the Asian landscape was only one facet of this application of modern science and industry to the solution of social and political problems" (Cecil 1986: 177). The radio call sign of the Ranch Hand pilots was "cowboy" (79).

The scale of the attack on the landscape was made possible by its chemical means. These were primarily the famous compounds 2,4-D and 2,4,5-T, a mixture of which composed the main defoliant, called Agent Orange (Whiteside 1970: 6–8). They are not poisons. They operate by mimicking the growth hormones of the plant, compelling it to grow regardless of the food supply; so it feeds on itself, literally eating itself to death. These compounds were developed and employed by the British in the 1950s in Malaya as weapons in the same kind of guerrilla warfare as in Indochina (Westing 1984: 4). The chemicals had such biological effectiveness that they were soon widely marketed as the main ingredients in commercial weed killers, as 2,4-D still is. Almost no homeowner in the occident was or is without them. They work best against broad-leafed plants, and were supplemented or replaced by other chemicals of even greater destructiveness when other vegetation was targeted—Agent White against forests, Agent Blue against rice—the use of which was not commercially routine but generally forbidden (Whiteside 1970: 7). The routine chemicals in Agent Orange, however, were applied at thirteen times their concentration in domestic use. Overall, about 91 million kilograms[5] of herbicides were sprayed on Indochina (Westing 1984: xiii).

The portion of them spent to destroy the half million acres of croplands of all kinds (rice paddies in the south as well as fields in the highlands) constituted the "food-denial" program. This "appears to have been counterproductive . . . as predicted by many officials from the beginning," not only because it horrified world opinion, but because it hit those least able to bear it, in no way diminishing the enemy's ability to fight (Cecil 1986: 78). The nutritionist Jean Mayer pointed out in an often-cited article (reprinted in Weisberg 1970) that food shortages in any wartime society typically most damage the old, women, and children—not the

---

4. Defoliation is mentioned only twice, quite incidentally, in the massive collection of documents that constitutes the *Pentagon Papers* (1972).

5. According to U.S. government figures, about 19 million gallons (Summers 1985: 67).

fighters, who are treated as the highest priority. But much the greater part of the biochemical war against the land of Indochina was devoted to defoliation and deforestation. Although aerial spraying is a skillful, high-tech operation, it remains subject to the vagaries of the atmosphere. All the statistics are derived from areas targeted, and cannot possibly include all those affected. Even light wind drift can result in damage up to fifteen miles from the point of spraying, much of which occurred to "friendly" crops in the area of Saigon (Whiteside 1970: 11). By 1970, whether deliberately or by drift, a third of Cambodia's rubber trees had been damaged and its latex production, the highest in the world, was diminished by 35–40 percent (15–16). The loss from herbicidal spraying of commercial timber in South Vietnam has since been estimated at 20 million cubic meters (Westing 1984: 11). The apologist for Ranch Hand (Cecil 1986) often insists that it was a war against plants, not people—as if destruction on this scale had nothing to do with any human economy, material or psychological.

The long-term effects of this biochemical assault on the landscape are certainly difficult to measure, if not to see. The short-term effects were deemed militarily useful. But the use of biochemicals in Indochina was brought to a halt in 1971 by a series of reports concerning their potential effects on people. What was reported were birth defects and miscarriages. Experiments with rats demonstrated the considerable teratogenic effects of 2,4,5-T; the U.S. Department of Defense announced a policy, often violated, not to use it against "populated areas" (Whiteside 1970: 17–33). Public argument and protest from ecologists and scientists was considerable, so defoliation ceased as the number of American troops in Vietnam gradually diminished and the peace talks in Paris dragged on. It was reported in 1974 that the Air Force, stuck with a great deal of Agent Orange, was trying to sell it in South America, especially to Brazil (Drinnon 1980: 551).

Not until after the war had been over for a few years did some of those who handled the chemicals, as well as troops who had been in sprayed areas shortly after spraying, begin to develop a wide range of disturbing symptoms. Agent Orange came back into the headlines for a brief while and then headed for the law courts, where it never arrived; its manufacturers made a $180 million settlement of the veterans' case (Gibson 1985: 7). The dangers Agent Orange presents to human and animal life do not come directly from the ingredients of the compounds, but as a by-product of their use, which produces potent poisons called dioxins that have a half-life in the soil and the food chain of roughly five years (Westing 1984: 175). Their effects are various, and none has been conclusively demonstrated according to the one international scientific conference to investigate the effects of herbicidal warfare, held in Vietnam in 1983, partly under the auspices of the United Nations Environmental Program (Westing 1984 is the record of its proceedings). Although a large variety of problems—from headaches to hepatitis—seems plausibly traceable to dioxins, the evidence does not confirm that monstrous births are among them. It does suggest, however, that other adverse outcomes of pregnancy may result even from the union of males exposed to the chemicals with unexposed females (Westing 1984: 20–22).

Long-term damage to the land is more obvious, but dependent on so many variables that it is difficult to assess. A forest sprayed only once or twice should be well on the way to regeneration in thirty or forty years; a forest sprayed three times is severely depleted and regenerates only feeble trees, if any. Freshwater fish are greatly reduced in numbers and species; birds and mammals are depleted by a factor of seven. The worst damage was sustained by the mangrove swamps (a rich and fragile ecology) in the Mekong River delta, of which 40 percent were sprayed. Only 1 percent of these are returning; the rest is a wasteland (Westing 1984: 18–19). This is about all that has been documented so far; documenting it is not high on our (the First World's) list of research priorities. The consequences of our biochemical warfare in Indochina are, and may well remain, incalculable. And yet it was an historic event, as a member of Vietnam's Health Ministry pointed out: "the first such massive employment in the history of war" (201).

But it's something that we'd just as soon forget (not to mention the reluctance of the U.S. Department of Defense to make public any information about it). Those it was done to cannot soon forget it. At the height of the war, in 1968, even the South Vietnamese Minister of Information, a member of the government that we were ostensibly defending, said: "Our peasants will remember their cratered rice fields and defoliated forests, devastated by an alien air force that seems at war with the very land of Vietnam" (Weisberg 1970: 53). To be at war with the land itself is to enact the fiction of savage autochthony, making the indigenes and their forest perish together. It was enacted by Indian-hunters on the ground and pilots in the air who called themselves "cowboys." It goes back from centuries of assuming that the only trajectory of "progress" is the one that our civilization supposedly followed, through centuries of clearing the transalpine European landscape for our kind of city-supporting agriculture, to the empire based on that agriculture, which gave it to us as the Trojan legend.

It is thus historically exact that the generic name of the blade that can shave the surface of the earth (it weighs about 3,000 kilos), and that replaced Agent Orange as a roadside defoliator, is the Rome Plow. For what it does, powered by a bulldozer, is just what ancient Rome defined for us as civilization. Ironically, though, the blade is not a "plow" at all, and is highly prized for clearing land in tropical regions just because it does so without breaking their fragile soil, by avoiding tillage (see Land Clearing 1986). It is a contemporary Saturnia, a perfect material embodiment of Virgil's metaphorical insight that ploughshares and swords, cultivation (of all kinds) and force, imply and become each other in the culture the Trojans brought to Rome. The blade that is a weapon of war against savage guerrillas and their landscape is also what prepares that landscape for our form of peaceable, large-scale, surplus-producing agriculture. It gets its name from that of its manufacturer, the Rome Plow Co., so called from being founded in 1932 in Rome, Georgia. Its lineage is direct, and suggests that Virgil's Jupiter was in one sense right when he predicted for the Romans an "empire without end." In name and in deed it lives on, transported from old Rome to the ten Romes in the United States, and thence around the world. This empire is no longer one of proprietary colonialism;

it doesn't need to be now that it's economic and (as it always was) cultural. Its ideas and laws and language (English: used globally in science, technology, tourism, banking, air travel, and popular music) and market hegemony, above all its history and its legend, are the engine of the bulldozer that shaves the tropical earth, leveling it to receive our kind of foundation. The Rome Plow is the Cybele of our time, a more than symbolic goddess of western civilization.

Chapter 29

୨☙

CURRENT EVENTS

Development

In 1914, H. G. Wells published perhaps his most remarkably prophetic tract, thinly disguised as a novel, called *The World Set Free*. In it he imagines a Europe destroyed by atomic warfare in 1956. London, Paris, and Berlin go up in nuclear explosion and radiation along with most of the capital cities of the world. A Frenchman, supported by the American president, spends three years persuading what's left of the world's leaders to meet at a conference to end the holocausts and establish a new world order under a single government. The only obstacle to the conference's breathtaking reorganization of the world is one Balkan king, called the Slavic Fox, who refuses to give up his atomic bombs, and so must be killed. The moral shock of the massive destruction and ensuing chaos makes possible the dissolution of all present forms of political economy, especially those of capitalism and nationalism, and the creation of a global republic governed by a council of the intelligentsia. Here, poverty and wage labor no longer exist, disease is minimized, private property and religion are irrelevant, and all of humanity can liberate its creative, as opposed to destructive, impulses. "The majority of our population consists of artists," says the narrator about the World Republic at some unspecified time after 1975 (Wells 1976: 155). The book ends with a sage urging women to become full equals with men in the scientific adventure of controlling the evolution of an ever more perfect human species.

Wells's brilliant projection is a Platonic utopia (he looks forward, as did his friend George Bernard Shaw in *Back to Methuselah*, to the day when humans will evolve right out of their bodies and become pure mind) empowered by positivist empirical science. "The history of mankind," Wells explains at some length, "is the history of the attainment of external power. Man is the tool-using, fire-making animal" (7). Harnessing the power of the atom is thus the final stage of human development, and its misuse paves the way for its proper use. Wells's vision is a kind of apotheosis of the Enlightenment faith in universal rationality implemented by the evolutionary thinking, the technological accomplishments, and the reforming

338

passions of the nineteenth century. As such, the vision both contains and is contained by the story of our civilization. Though Wells happily projects the demise of its imperial politics, he assumes its categories and consciously applies its historiography.

As visionaries go, Wells was famously hard-headed and well-informed. In *The World Set Free* he devotes more space to describing both the destruction of the old order and the planning of the new than to extolling the delights of the latter. After dramatizing the meeting of the conference in a meadow near the Swiss town of Brissago, he places it in the universal historical perspective that our legend had long become. His point is that new social arrangements must accompany the mastery of new forms of energy; the atomic blow-up merely made more dramatic the "clash between the new and the customary" (131) that existed from the dawn of time. Man was then a "hunter and wanderer and wonderer," who

> was never quite subdued to the soil nor quite tamed to the home. Everywhere it needed teaching and the priest to keep him within the bounds of the plough-life and the beast-tending. Slowly a vast system of traditional imperatives superimposed itself upon his instincts, imperatives that were admirably fitted to make him that cultivator, that cattle-minder, who was for twice ten thousand years the normal man.
>
> And, unpremeditated, undesired, out of the accumulations of his tilling came civilization. Civilization was the agricultural surplus. It appeared as trade and tracks and roads, it pushed boats out upon the rivers and presently invaded the seas, and within . . . seaport towns rose speculation and philosophy and science and the beginning of the new order that has at last established itself as human life. (132)

We recognize this story as ours, all right: savages at length coercively subdued to the sociality of settled agriculture, then gaining wealth and venturing forth into commerce and literate thinking. But it's assumed, as usual, to be everybody's story: it's "human life."

And it continues:

> Already before the release of atomic energy the tensions between the old way of living and the new were intense. They were far intenser than they had been even at the collapse of the Roman imperial system. On the one hand was the ancient life of the family and the small community and the petty industry, on the other was a new life on a larger scale with remoter horizons and a strange sense of purpose. Already it was growing clear that men must live on one side or the other. One could not have little tradespeople and syndicated business in the same market, sleeping carters and motor trolleys on the same road, bows and arrows and aeroplane sharpshooters in the same army, or illiterate peasant industries and power-driven factories in the same world. (132–33)

Why not? Wells doesn't say, but merely goes on to insist that the "ambitions and greed and jealousy of peasants" must not be equipped with modern weapons. Why can't the simple possibility of coexistence (of the modern and the traditional) occur to this most acute of reforming imaginations? Because there's only one path of "progress," only one imaginable scale of human development, and one imaginable *telos*: the mastery of more powerful tools, the technological domination and control of more and more, up to and including human genetics. There's no space (market, road, army, or world) or time (the primitive, here the "peasant," is our past, which must be grown out of) that our form of civilization can share with any other. There isn't any other but ours: that progress from venereal savagery through nomadic barbarism to settled agriculture, commerce, literacy, industry, and the supreme power of the atom.

The governing council imagined by Wells enforces all these assumptions of the universal historiography of the founding legend:

> "There can be no real social stability or any general human happiness while large areas of the world and large classes of people are in a phase of civilization different from the prevailing mass. It is impossible now to have great blocks of population misunderstanding the generally accepted social purpose or at an economic disadvantage to the rest." So the council expressed its conception of the problem it had to solve. The peasant, the field-worker and all barbaric cultivators were at an "economic disadvantage" to the more mobile and educated classes, and the logic of the situation compelled the council to take up systematically the supersession of this stratum by a more efficient organization of production. It developed a scheme for the progressive establishment throughout the world of the "modern system" in agriculture, a system that should give the full advantages of a civilized life to every agricultural worker, and this replacement has been going on right up to the present day. (146)

The "scheme" is a kind of kibbutz, collective farming by "guilds" made productive and mobile by machines, so that farmers can live in towns and cities and thus get civilized. Wells's disdain for what is to be superseded is another apotheosis of modernist arrogance:

> Already this system has abolished a distinctively "rustic" population throughout vast areas of the old world where it has prevailed immemorially. That shy, unstimulated life of the lonely hovel, the narrow scandals and petty spites and persecutions of the small village, that hoarding, half inanimate existence away from books, thought or social participation and in constant contact with cattle, pigs, poultry and their excrement is passing away out of human experience. In a little while it will be gone altogether. (147)

This primitive "phase" of civilization disappears: the cottage and village life of "barbaric cultivators," sunk in manure, illiteracy, and asocial viciousness, is fit only for elimination. Without cities and writing, made possible by our form of surplus-producing agriculture, there is no civilization. The elimination Wells fantasized in 1914 became the elimination that the Americans found necessary and practiced in the 1960s in Indochina: that of the peasant culture the Vietnamese "must lose." It's the elimination that the legend has always entailed on those who either resist our foundation or merely occupy in our present a "phase" of development that we think we've gone through.

The elimination has been and continues to be brutal and direct—in the form of deliberate killing—as well as benevolent and indirect—in the form of bringing culture to the savage and vice-versa. The motivation for Wells's version of the latter is humanitarian in a quite postcolonial and contemporary sense: to eliminate "economic disadvantage." Peasants and nomads cannot compete (with us, on our terms) and so they are to be made competitive and literate, endowed with commodity-producing agriculture, industrialized, and aestheticized. In his utopian fantasy, Wells can eliminate economic disparity, along with the capitalist competitiveness that maintains it, at a stroke—the World Council distributes the world's goods equally to the world's population (the details of this are not gone into). For the noblest of motives, much like the early humanitarians who sent cotton gins and mission schools to Africa, Wells consigns to oblivion all forms of human life that our legendary categories exclude from civilization. We tool-users and energy-masterers *are* "human life." They are a primitive phase, an arrested development that is to be "systematically" superseded. Bye-bye to the barbarians, with no more qualms than Brut had in exterminating the giants. They are evoked, as usual, only to be erased; there is nothing worth preserving about their way of life, which is literally (in Wells's imagery) shit. All of occidental culture went into the making of Wells, whose benevolent fantasy is yet limited by that culture's legend of itself. For even his dream of economic equality and human liberation cannot include the uncivilized. There is, again literally, no place for them in the world we control.

Wells thus realizes both senses of the Greek pun that Thomas More bequeathed to our vernaculars: the world shocked into social justice by nuclear holocaust becomes the "good place" (*eu-topos*) for us, but "no place" (*ou-topos*) at all for the savage or the barbarian, the indigene or the tribal. So the places they in fact inhabited and inhabit have become, are becoming, our places; and they have disappeared, are disappearing, from our earth as they disappear in our discourse, whether of fantasy or fact.

The agency of their disappearance is precisely our notion of "development": the legend become the single scale of a universal historiography. The notion that limited Wells's fantasy early in this century has now, toward the end of it, become formalized in the most factual discourse we know, that of statistics. The current equivalent of Wells's World Council—minus, of course, the power that his scenario gave it—is the United Nations Organization, one of whose branches is wholly devoted to measuring, monitoring, and encouraging the progress of "development" in the world. This is the United Nations Development Programme (UNDP), which has published various kinds of reports on the subject since 1970. The concept of "development" in these reports has itself undergone development—from one based mainly on the income per capita of each nation (its Gross National Product divided by its population), to one that includes two additional factors that allow it to be called "human development." This innovation appeared in the 1990 Report (since when the reports have been issued annually), which ranked 130 countries according to the resultant Human Development Indicator (HDI). The interesting thing about this confected quantification is that it shows only a somewhat parallel, by no means identical, relationship to income per capita. More than money is required to rank highly on the "human" development scale.

The UNDP Reports are sophisticated, humane, and diligent documents, produced by international teams of social scientists. They acknowledge that the idea of human development cannot be reduced to their own measure of it; they provide technical explanations of how (most of) the statistics are constructed; they are primarily concerned to encourage rich countries to provide more aid to poor ones, and to encourage poor ones to use it more effectively. They are crammed with all sorts of collateral information. The 1991 Report, for example, showed by different statistical measures how during the 1980s the rich got richer and the poor poorer (PNUD 1991: 23–24, 91)—a gap that continues to widen (PNUD 1995: 15–16). They calculate subtle modifications of the numbers they collect (when available) to provide more reliable and just comparisons. Thus they correct the income per capita to a fairer comparative index by using the Gross Domestic Product and converting it to units of Purchasing Power Parity expressed in Eurodollars. Thus they correct the final ranking of nations on the HDI scale by measuring the difference between a nation's HDI for men and for women. They also attempt to correct the ranking by adjusting it for the unequal distribution of income within a given country.

It is clear that the reports do an honest job, fully aware that any statistical exercise has only a comparative value. And the job is, precisely, comparison: getting (almost) everyone in the world on the same scale so that this may be logically and mathematically performed. The units of comparison are of course nation-states. There are 174 of them in the 1995 Report, divided into 47 "industrialized countries" (all in Europe—including the former Soviet Republics—and North America except Japan, Israel, Australia, and New Zealand) and 127 "developing countries" (PNUD 1995: 249). Of the latter, 44 are classified as "least developed countries" (28 in Africa; all the rest, except Haiti and Yemen, in Asia and the South Pacific). What is to be compared in these units is the HDI, the innovative measure that makes development human. To the formerly exclusive yardstick of income per capita are added (1) life expectancy and (2) the rate of adult literacy. By a complex series of logarithmic calculations, the three yardsticks are made to yield a single decimal figure between zero and one, which is the HDI; and all the nations are ranked in descending order on this scale (the higher the figure, the more human the development), with Canada at the top and Niger at the bottom.

The point of the added criteria is clear: money, though indispensable, isn't enough by itself to count as development in a human sense, so health and education are factored in. The 1991 Report regretted at some length not being able to factor in "liberty," too, reviewing some efforts to confect a Human Liberty Indicator (HLI), but finding insuperable obstacles at every level: selection and weighting of criteria, lack of both data and a method for quantifying them (19–22). No further news is given of the HLI in subsequent reports, each of which has a different thematic focus, that of 1995 being the global socioeconomic inequalities between men and women. The HDI remains, however, as the consistently recalculated index to a nation's relative success (with Canada and Japan vying for the top position and Niger and Sierra Leone for the bottom) at securing the well-being of its citizens.

From the manner of measuring this well-being, one can readily perceive the conditions that define it, that underlie the UNDP's concept of human development. It depends, first, on citizenship in a nation-state, on participation in the national economic, political, and social system whose statistics are being recorded. And then it depends on what gets recorded: income, longevity, literacy. To be "developed" (to any degree) on this scale presupposes that the human individual is integrated, however marginally, into the systems of our modernity that Wells wished to see replace rustic and barbarian life.

It is apparent that none of these conditions is that of thousands of indigenous groups or tribal peoples around the globe. Most of their cultures are oral, their languages unwritten; they seldom die in hospitals or get counted in censuses; in some countries they are not even nominal citizens (as native Americans were not granted citizenship in the United States until 1924). Above all, only a few of them have even marginal incomes, and then only when engaged at the lowest, most exploitative levels of the world economy—participation in which is precisely what measures "human development." From this measurement they disappear, invisible to the UN indices, slipping through the statistical net that defines well-being by the standards of the only "development" we recognize. People who at this moment continue to lead traditional lives on and with the earth—in the Arctic, in Amazonia, in Africa, in pockets throughout Asia—simply do not count. For they do not dominate the earth as we do, mastering ever larger "external powers" over it, building walls and cities (or airports and chemical refineries) on it. They're still, it is frequently repeated, in the stone age, locked in the time warp where our invention of the "primitive" placed them long ago.

In this discursive time warp of our own creation, they exist only to be necessarily, in Wells's smooth abstraction, "superseded." In our discourse and statistics of "development," they don't exist at all. They are denied both time and space by all the discourses that have exfoliated from our founding legend and by all its enactments that have expropriated their space and ended their time. And yet, of course, some survive, here and now, still an actual presence that our discourses count as absence. How many of these people are there, living with and on the land as their ancestors did, hunters and gatherers and nomads, shifting cultivators, utterly undeveloped, existing within but virtually unintegrated into the life of the modern nation? How many "savages" are left in the world? About 250 million, according to the most recent estimate, which is deliberately restricted to distinct linguistic/cultural groups having some territorial base and practically no influence in the nations where they live. This is roughly 4 percent of the world's population and comprises about 5,000 groups or tribes (Burger 1990: 18, 180).

These human beings are not only overlooked by our way of measuring "development"; their very existence, physical and cultural, is as threatened by our practice of development as it was by our practice of colonialism. For they are much the same practice, with the old direct political control now replaced by economic incentives and penalties that make it indirect, but scarcely less coercive. No better example could be found than the policy of the World Bank with respect to the agriculture of the Third World in general and the "least developed countries" in particular. The World Bank is, of course, the major international institution for financing development projects of all sorts, and is just what its name means: a stock-issuing corporation whose business is to make money by lending it at interest. The stockholders are nations, which are also required to be members of the International Monetary Fund. The Bank spun off a subsidiary organization, the International Development Association, in 1960, in order to extend loans at reduced rates of interest to the poorest countries, thus enlarging its general purpose of doing well by doing good. Though most interested in projects to stimulate certain forms of industrialization in the Third World, the Bank has paid increasing attention to agriculture since the 1970s, for the simple reason that most of the world's poverty is rural. Here, its announced aim is "to bring the rural population 'from traditional isolation to integration with the national economy,' and therefore the international economy" (Hayter and Watson 1985: 159).

What this means is the supersession (just as Wells imagined it) of self-sufficient cultivation. For the Bank, the point of agriculture is the production of exportable commodities. Its own statements show a clear aversion to subsistence farming, which merely insures local survival and contributes nothing to the world market. In Papua New Guinea, the Bank finds that

> nature's bounty produces enough to eat with relatively little expenditure of effort. The root crops that dominate subsistence farming are 'plant and wait' crops, requiring little disciplined cultivation. . . . Until enough subsistence farmers have their traditional life styles changed by the growth of new consumption wants, this labor constraint may make it difficult to introduce new crops.

In Africa, according to another Bank report, "the dominance of subsistence production presented special obstacles to agricultural development. Farmers had to be induced to produce for the market, adopt new crops, and undertake new risks" (quoted in Hayter and Watson 1985: 158). The Bank's aversion to agricultural self-sufficiency amounts, as one critic described it, to an "attack on self-provisioning peasantries" (158). It is motivated (just as Wells's fantasy was) by the benevolent aim of ameliorating economic disadvantage, boosting the output of a national economy. So the Bank refuses to accept purely domestic food production as the aim of a lending project. According to a former employee, "the Bank firmly maintains that growth must be export-led and that it is money earned from exports and not local food production that makes food available" (275).

This is as precise a statement of neocolonialism as could be found: to gauge it, we have only to ask if it could be made about any occidental nation. In the United States or France or Switzerland, is it the case that money (however earned) and not food production makes food available? By "food," we're talking about what a whole population can live on, not about all of the delicacies, everyday (coffee) or exotic (passion fruit), that our money can buy. The "growth" that the Bank is defining is exclusively that of a commodity-supplying economy—formerly colonial and now national. It's the kind of economy that we, since the sixteenth century, have created worldwide in order to serve us. And the World Bank wishes it to continue serving us: this is what "integration" into both national and international economies means. It means production for export (to us, and in a market we control) and not for local needs. It means self-sufficiency (in most food staples) for us and dependency (on our tastes and technologies) for them. So that when we don't need so much copper anymore, or when the price of coffee crashes, many citizens of Chile or of Kenya find that they have no money to buy food with. Not that they had much more before, those that labor to produce those commodities, for the profits in an export economy go mainly to the exporting agents (often including the government) rather than the laborers. The world today is in some ways postcolonial; but its economy is still what it has been since we started making it global five hundred years ago.

Self-sufficient agriculture (the sine qua non of the massive surpluses that created, maintain, and define our civilization) is, on the small scale practiced by tribal peoples, vaguely offensive to the World Bank. Centuries of colonial condescension echo in the judgment that tropical climates too easily produce a crop that satisfies local needs, without enough "effort" and "discipline." Such satisfied farmers must "have their traditional life styles changed" by becoming consumers (of our goods in our economy); they must "be induced to produce for the market." So the Bank will induce them to do so by financing only agricultural projects that will produce exports, not those that will merely feed the local people. This method of inducement is more delicate than the brute force formerly applied; but the goal is identical. How this goal appeared to one on whom it was imposed earlier in this century reveals in a poignant way just whose interests are served by what has since become the Bank's dogma of export-led growth: that money, not food production, makes food available.

The testimony comes from Matungi, a chief in the eastern province of the Belgian Congo, and was published by the anthropologist Colin Turnbull in 1963. Matungi's grandfather had been killed by one of the expeditions of Sir Henry Stanley, his father by later white colonists. Becoming chief in his turn, Matungi supplied the colonists with food until their demands grew too great. When the colonists started using guns and whips to force his people to labor for them, Matungi escaped with his village into the forest. Eventually, black soldiers found the group and removed them to a road-building site, where they were told to provide laborers.

> I remembered my father, and I said I would not let my people work for them. Because of the guns . . . I said that we would supply whatever food we could spare, and for a time the white men accepted that. . . . Then they . . . told us we had to plant cotton and other things we did not want to plant. . . . I explained that if we planted cotton we would have to grow less food. They said we could buy food with the money we got for the cotton and I told them this was like the play of children, because we could easily grow our own food without money, and have enough left over to give them.
>
> It was then that they told me that I was not a man, that I was evil. (Quoted in Wilson 1977: 195)

The transaction that appeared, for obvious material reasons, to Matungi as "the play of children" is now the World Bank's policy of "development" for the tropical nations that the former colonies have become. Whatever or whoever is being thus developed, it is certainly not the producers themselves. They're simply being destroyed in one way or the other: they starve, or they become the most marginal of our economy's consumers at the cost to them of their "traditional life style." Physical or cultural death (as the Americans inflicted on and prescribed for the Vietnamese peasantry) is their destiny under our policies. It has been the destiny of savages in our founding legend since Virgil: they join civilization or it rolls over them. In the world today joining civilization still means what it has meant since Columbus: producing for our money economy. Feeding oneself without money—mere self-sufficiency—is inadmissible: "evil," as Matungi's rulers called it; archaically "rustic" to H. G. Wells; simply unproductive by the standards of the World Bankers. So if "traditional life styles" can do without money, we can easily do without (and away with) them. They have no place in our world, literally cannot be counted in its official indices of development, do nothing but block what we count as progress. They disappear, are made to disappear, from our discourse and from our earth.

Invisibility

Today, even subsistence farming is regarded in our culture just as hunting is in all the varieties of our founding legend: as evidence of a (savage) "life style" that is therefore negligible, not worth preserving. Both activities have become, for us, avocations, sports (as in gardening contests to grow the fattest pumpkin), things to beguile the leisure of the civilized. Pursued as ways of life and livelihood, they are things of our past, "primitive," and their supersession is thus inevitable. That supersession can and does mean extinction—of persons, languages, and cultures—is not something that we wish to examine very closely. So we tell a story, in myriad forms, about our own civilization that allows us to regard its destruction of those who do not share it as something automatic, built into the nature of things. The present versions of the story (like some of its past versions), whether fantasy or fact, bring us this comfort by making the savage or traditional or tribal or indigenous person invisible. He and she are not only absent, made absent, in our discourses. Invisibility, overlooking, erasure, as I have been describing them in this book are not just tropes, figures of speech. They are also ways of thinking about and acting in the world—and they are the more powerful precisely because our legend has diffused them throughout the discourses of our culture.

In recent years, spurred largely by the growing awareness in the occident of the ecological crises of the planet and the role of tropical rain forests in regulating its climate, increasing attention has been paid to indigenous peoples throughout the world. At the same time, some of these peoples have become more vocal in their own defense, notably by initiating lawsuits on the basis of nineteenth-century treaties to obtain title to their lands in the United States, Canada, and New Zealand. Since 1970, an independent charity, Survival International (SI), has been the most active of several such nongovernmental organizations in seeking to protect the rights and the lives of what its president and founder calls "the largest minority in the world" (Hanbury-Tenison 1984: 210)—the 4 percent of its population that our legend qualifies as savage. SI has achieved occasional successes in persuading governments, mainly in South America, to halt the wholesale destruction of tribal peoples and their lands. It has influenced the World Bank and some donor nations to withhold funds from a few projects that would do the same. And it has tirelessly publicized its efforts, to the extent that London journalists can make jokes about the trendiness of yet another demonstration or cocktail party in favor of the Yanomami.

Yet neither SI nor the Yanomami are exactly household words in the west today. The organization cannot compare in funding or in recognition with, say, Amnesty International or the World Wildlife Fund. And the reason it cannot is that it is swimming against the current of our founding legend, asking us to care about people whose ways of life the legend defines as semibestial, negligible, archaic. Political prisoners are by definition sympathetic; baby seals and pandas are cute. So, of course, are children, and SI makes moderate use of this appeal in the photographs of its publications. But support for the objectives of SI cannot readily be thus mobilized, not in the way that we might write a check to UNICEF after seeing a picture of a starving Ethiopian child in the newspaper. We respond with a wish to alleviate the suffering of an individual. But SI is trying to enlist our sympathies for whole communities composed of people whom our culture and its legend have for millennia assured us could not have community. We may know this to be false; we may have read enough anthropology to know it in some detail. Or we may have seen a few documentaries on television about such communities, and marveled not merely at their exotic strangeness, but been impressed by their social cohesion and the skillful ways they live on and in their environment without destroying it. And we may even, depending on the style and tone of the book or the documentary, have romanticized all this a bit, feeling nostalgic melancholy for a bygone way of life admittedly superior in ways to our own.

But we also know, don't we, that it is bygone? We're convinced, aren't we, that it's doomed (justly or not) by the sheer momentum of modern history? How could we not know the story we've heard and seen in so many forms for so long?

And so we know that we can't do anything about it. Writing a check may actually bring food to a starving person, but it can't possibly turn back the clock of historical time to the period in which indigenous people exist—the immemorial past. This is the ultimate invisibility, this (dis)placement of the actual, present indigene into a "primitive" time remote from ours. It has always been thus remote. This is where he was in Virgil; this is the zero point on the time scale formalized during the Enlightenment, when it became the measurable assurance of our advancement from it to civilization; this is the heart of darkness into which we may ourselves relapse if we lack discipline; and this is that huge shadowy forest we've seen on television, home to naked brown or black bodies that are at ease performing tasks but awkward and bemused when meeting the gaze of the camera. They relate to each other, but not to the medium that places them before us, here and now. We do not see these people as inhabiting our time, sharing our present. We do not feel that they are part of our world. This, I believe, is the profoundest and cruelest consequence of all the forms of our culture's legend of itself that I have been chronicling in this book. That legend has trained us not to see, in this sense, what it shows. Its savages are the black boy in *Pamela*: a presence purely textual, wholly unregistered by, absent from, our emotions. The indigenes are there in the story, in the picture or on the screen, but they are not here, where we are, because where we are is now; but they are then.

Our story of civilization as that which comes from elsewhere has, I suggested in the introduction, a stranglehold over the western imagination, as evidenced by the (now discredited) archeological theory of cultural diffusion from a single source, and by the (still popular) speculation that the planet's culture derives from interstellar intervention. This stranglehold comes from the legend's portrayal of cultural space, its emplotment as a journey, its creation of frontiers, its necessity of transmission. The other stranglehold is more over our feeling than our imagining, and it comes from the legend's portrayal of cultural time, its relegation of the uncivilized to a phase, a stage, an infancy or a primeval dawn, long past and irretrievable. It is as gone, for us, as the time and space of our cultural origin: the always already destroyed city of Troy. Those who live *there, now*, are hopelessly "anachronistic"— literally outside of time. We (speakers of SAE languages) feel this, even though we may know better. We feel that tribal indigenes are doomed, and that this is inevitable, and that we can't help it. For if we felt otherwise, then surely Survival International would be as well endowed as the WWF. SI's founder has remarked that his greatest disappointment is his failure to enlist big-time philanthropy in so good a cause: for "while it is pleasing and admirable to donate a new wing to a museum, save the tiger or endow a school, to save whole cultures of mankind from extinction must represent the greatest charity of all" (Hanbury-Tenison 1984: 221). One might think it "must"; but it doesn't—not by a long shot.[1]

---

1. The income of Survival International in 1990 was $980,000 (SI *Review* 1991: 16); that of Amnesty International in 1986 was $11.5 million (AI *Financial Supplement* 1987: 7). In 1990 WWF Inter-

For the cultures threatened with extinction do not count as cultures in our stories about what culture is. It's not merely a matter of the practical and official obstacles to the preservation of indigenous groups. The effort to secure inviolable possession of their lands for tribal peoples goes against the political and economic policies of virtually all governments, whether in the First, (now formerly) Second, or Third Worlds. And so, of course, do the efforts to preserve the "human rights" of all citizens who may dissent from their governments, and to preserve the existence of animal or vegetable species decimated by commerce or industry. But we're used to opposing official policies in the latter two cases for the sake of some higher or longer-term value or principle; if we weren't, we'd never give a penny to either Amnesty or the WWF. We do not, however, oppose government policies on the same scale when it comes to saving the world's largest human minority. For we do not, emotionally, see them as part of our space and time. We have thus internalized the legend—all those documents and monuments of civilization and barbarism that have never ceased telling us that we and the savage cannot possibly share, coexist in, the same space and time.

The refusal of such coexistence has also been seen to characterize much of even the professional discourse that brings us news of others—that of anthropology. Johannes Fabian points out that even after the evolutionary paradigm (the version of the legend's universal historiography that fueled Wells's fantasy) has long been discarded, the temporality it assumes remains unchanged. The other as object of ethnographic description still inhabits another time (not merely another place) than that of the describer (1983: 147–48). Anthropologists have lately subjected their discipline to various searching criticisms designed to overcome the relegation of their objects to the static past of primitivism, and to acknowledge the mutual temporal presence of both observer and observed (Marcus and Fischer 1986). The very concept of the "primitive," especially as appropriated by twentieth-century Modernist art and popular literature, has been analyzed as (what it always was) our own invention, masking our desires, projecting our anxieties, consolidating our powers (Hiller 1991; Torgovnick 1990). All such analyses constitute our better knowledge, against which we yet feel that the supersession of archaic people is irresistible.

For the legend that so characterizes them has not ceased to make the feeling fact in all its enactments: the rise of the west, the centuries of imperial and commercial and technological success that have formed the political and economic interests of our present governments and linked them to those of governments in the formerly colonized world. Here the legend is more triumphant than ever, and provides the contemptuous dismissal of tribal peoples' protests against destruction. One such ongoing protest was begun in 1991 by the Bhils and Tadavis, tribal peoples of west central India, 60,000 of whom are to be displaced by an enormous

---

national *spent* $38 million (WWF *Annual Report* 1991: 20): this does not include figures for the national WWF affiliates in 28 countries, who disbursed about $20 million in 1986/87 (WWF *Yearbook* 1989), nor does it include the endowment income of WWF International, which covers all its administrative costs (*Annual Report* 1991: 22).

system of dams on the Narmada River, which will flood all the territory they occupy. There is no sufficient land available on which to resettle them. The Bhils live by keeping cattle, fishing, and gathering food in the forests; they regard the river as sacred. They have marched on Delhi and mounted other peaceful demonstrations of protest in which they were beaten by the police. An Indian official responded to their efforts to preserve their way of life by saying, "What is this great culture people are talking about? These tribals live in nakedness, in illiteracy and hunger!" And the Chief Minister of Gujarat declared, "I do believe that tribal culture should be preserved, but in the museum, not in real life." Precisely: it's not "culture," it's not "real," this life, except as archaic misery that we have escaped. It's fit only for elimination followed by exhibition in the papier-maché models and dusty dioramas of, say, *le Musée de l'homme*, in Paris. And the people who lead such a life, now, and wish to continue leading it, are not seen. The Innu of Canada, protesting the damage to their environment by a NATO airbase, are simply ignored. An Innu woman remarked, "We are treated as if we are invisible, as if we did not exist."[2]

In Venezuela, the founding legend has been evoked in more detail as a reaction against a local decision to grant some Indians in the southern Federal territory title to their lands. A campaign of newspaper advertisements expressed horror that "the previous Governor of the Territory gave away 50,000 hectares of land to the Piaroa Indians just so they could go on living in barbarism." The ads went on to ask a series of rhetorical questions that (in the 1980s) could have come straight from the pages of Vattel or the orations of Andrew Jackson: "Who owns the land in this territory where there is land in excess but a lack of audacious men to work it? It is said that the land belongs to those who work it. Is that right? Is it right to give 50,000 hectares to some nomadic Indians so they can wander about and deny possession to colonists who are risking all in the difficult task of bringing civilisation to the territory?" The ads concluded by making it (needlessly) clear that civilization means simply "the capitalist system" (quoted in Colchester 1984: 101). And so it does, now; so it has done since the formation of the global market during the sixteenth century. But our legendary picture of civilization, that rules nomads and savages out, is far older than this, and is not necessarily tied to any particular economic system. It is an elastic myth, as internalized by and as serviceable to ruthless profit-hunters as to socialist reformers like Wells. The myth is about the culture within which our various political ideologies have arisen. It is common to us (whatever our own political positions), and it imposes the displacements in its own real and fictional history on the uncivilized, who thus become invisible.

For the first millennium and a half of its existence, the myth, like most of its kind, was crucially concerned with names. It began as the etiology of ancient Rome, deriving, from both the Trojan victors and the assimilated Latin van-

---

2. This information and quotations are from a special issue of Survival International's *Review* to commemorate its twenty-one years of existence. At this writing (1995), the Narmada River project is suspended, awaiting a decision by the Indian Supreme Court.

quished, the names of places and ruling families in the achieved Empire. And it continued as a history that did the same for virtually all the peoples and dynasties of western Europe. To tell a story about a name is to provide a history; to have a name is to have an identity; to know a name is to recognize something or some-one, to single it out, make it visible for further possibilities of recognition. (The black boy in *Pamela* has no name.) No one, it seems fair to say, knows the names of the estimated five thousand indigenous peoples in the world today; just as no one will ever know the names of all the tribes or groups of such people whom our culture has made extinct. To hear a name, or to see it in writing, is a prereq-uisite for making visible to consciousness. Our founding legend takes our names very seriously; they're a window into both real and imagined history—the occa-sion for the mythological fantasizing of Renaissance scholars and the more re-strained argumentation of today's etymologists. Much may be learned from names—but only if we have them, only if they've been recorded.

The only published attempt I know to record at least some of the names of ex-tant indigenous groups is *The Gaia Atlas of First Peoples*, by Julian Burger. I should like to record here the names of other groups *not* found in that book, names that I have never happened to see in any book, newspaper, magazine, or ever heard pronounced. I've compiled the list from miscellaneous Newsletters and Bulletins issued by Survival International over the last decade or so. I offer the list, thus ran-dom and haphazard, as evidence of what I am aware is invisible to me. I don't know what history lies in these names; but each is the name of a human culture which no doubt tells stories about itself that might be the subject of a book like this one. The names themselves may be quite inauthentic, that is, not what that people call themselves, but what they get called by others, for whatever reason, accident, or mistake. However the Piaroa got that name, for example, they call themselves the Dearuwan, which means "forest people" (Colchester 1984: 95). Nonetheless, to record such names as exist is to provide a cast of characters for sto-ries yet unknown; to begin to do for the others of our story what that story did for us in the "dark" and "middle" ages—simply to insist that they (we) are (were) here (there) now (then):

in South America there are the Wayapi, the Palikur, the Akawaio, the Pemon, the Waiwai, the Chimanes, the Mojeno, the Siriono, the Yuracare, the Paez, the Guambiano, the Pehuenche, the Wichi, the Chorote, the Mbya, the Chachi, the Tsachila, the Urueu-wau-wau, the Chulupi, the Krenak, the Awa;

in Africa there are the Anuak, the Barabaig;

in India there are the Pardhan, the Naikpod, the Konda Reddi, the Kolam;

in Southeast Asia (including Australia) there are the Hupla, the Berawan, the Oenpelli, the Mapoon, the Weipa, the Aurukun, the Warlpiri, the Warumungu, the Alywara, the Kaytej, the Higaonon, the Atta, the Isneg, the Aroman Manobo, the Lumad, the Yao.

All these people are here (on our planet) now (in our time). But some of them probably won't be much longer. The Awa and the Krenak have been reduced in this century from populations of several thousand to a few hundred. And still others are not here any more, having been made extinct in my adult lifetime: in 1966 the last Selk'nam died; in 1976 the last Ona. Both of these peoples were native to Tierra del Fuego; their names can be recorded only as a memorial. No headlines lamented their departure; it was not news. Even the fact of their becoming invisible was invisible.

Stories

To produce such invisibility is one of the primary functions of our founding legend, the stories we tell ourselves about the places we take over, whose inhabitants are timeless, cultureless, and therefore hopeless. That they may acquire hope—hope to survive, hope to negotiate their own relationship to the dominant economy and technology of our world—requires the acknowledgment of their presence and of their community. And since refusing such acknowledgment is one aim of our culture's stories of itself, providing it would require both hearing those stories differently and telling other stories. Fully to acknowledge other presences and other communities would require us to tell a different story of ourselves.

The history I have offered in this book of our founding stories—tracing the continuity of their power in the variety of their forms and enactments—is one way of hearing them differently. And to hear them differently is about all that I, as a member and a professional student of occidental culture, can do. I am able to do it partly because I have heard other stories, told by members of other cultures, and partly because our culture has generated its own forms of self-criticism, its own ways of interrogating, while transmitting, itself. But I cannot tell another story— say, a story in which civilization is not something transmissible that arises from one way of dominating the earth, but something that may or may not arise in any human community, to be shared with and modified by contact with other communities. And I'd like to invent such a story, to manufacture a countermyth to our founding legend that would dispense with the very idea that civilization comes from our kind of "foundation." But even if I could invent such a story (as some novelists, like Achebe and Le Guin, already have), it would not, by itself, offer any countervailing force to the power of real legends and real myths. For these are not manufactured by individuals; they are like languages: collective products of long accretion. A language may have its usages extended or a legend receive definitive form by the exertions of an individual talent; but neither can be imagined or brought into being by an individual alone.

So, though I'd like to tell another story, I know that it could never have the power of the founding legend. I have sought to demonstrate that power in this book by the kind of argument called "counterfactual": if the occident had not told this story of its foundation, the planet would be a different sort of place—physically, emotionally, politically. I believe that this kind of argument would be true of all cultures: that the language and legends of any society determine (not in the sense of fix in a single direction, but in the root sense of establish the limits of) the perceptions and actions of its members. So I attribute to stories the crucial importance that Virgil did: since we do what we are told, we might change the doing by changing the telling. Hence my desire to tell another, a counter, story about our own civilization—one that would make others present and visible.

Where could I find such a story, which, to have countervailing power, should come from the western stock of myths and legends? Let me, to conclude, indulge a last counterfactual effort to find a replacement for Saturn, Hercules, Noah, Aeneas and all the sons of Priam, Brutus, Francion, the merchant gentry, the yeoman farmer, the missionaries, the ethical individualists, and the army of cowboys who form the line of culture-bringing heroes. Who is available, and in what different story from that of journey, conquest, and foundation?

How about the most obvious ancient alternative, the one that Rome might have chosen, but didn't—the great wanderer Odysseus? The man of many talents, devious, brilliant, eloquent, as skilled at improvisation as at planning—who needs all these abilities simply to outlast the persecution of the gods and finally arrive, alone, at his home and family, which he must do battle in order to repossess. A journey homeward, a story of resistance against great odds and of final recovery—the opposite of displacement: Odysseus literally regains the place (property and power) that was his and that others wished to take from him. He is the supreme survivor; unconcerned either to transform the landscape or dominate the world, he expends all his ingenuity in coping with it. So do most of us; so certainly does Leopold Bloom in James Joyce's modern, semiparodic version of the story. What Poldy regains is his place at the foot of Molly's bed (and in her erotic memory)—an only somewhat diminished equivalent of the ancient Greek's repossession of his faithful Penelope.

This is an attractive story, more of a domestic comedy than an epic, continuously retold and associated with enough high cultural attainments (mainly wit and eloquence—whether the hero's or the author's) to suggest distinctly "civilized" values. What these might be today would follow from Joyce's confinement of Ulysses' wanderings to a day in Dublin and thus making them, with respect to the hero, psychological. With respect to the text, the wanderings constitute a kind of cultural encyclopedia, a vast medley of recondite allusions and linguistic styles. Both literal and psychological homecomings end in the reunion of a family, mainly a man and a woman; and this reachievement of something (necessarily or inevitably) interrupted—a marriage—is the story told by another genre of Hollywood films, identified by Stanley Cavell (1981) as "the comedy of remarriage." Cavell's text, too, is a kind of cultural encyclopedia, finding in the films concerns that echo from Plato through Shakespeare and Emerson to Wittgenstein. I am suggesting merely that the story of Odysseus is quite as elastic as the founding myth, and has received similarly extensive stretching in both the elite and popular culture of this century.[3]

The themes that Cavell teases out of such movies as *The Philadelphia Story*—the need for and acceptance of adventures, sexuality, reprieve, and forgiveness amid the

3. Ulysses' peregrinations through much of western literature and history are elegantly surveyed by Boitani (1994). One complex variation on his theme, in the specific context of subsequent western imperialism, is Derek Walcott's *Omeros* (1990).

ordinary pressures of daily life, which are celebrated; the ongoing maintenance and negotiation of a social contract at once private and public—could pretty easily be read out of Homer, too. Joyce found something like them there, in his ironic transposition of the heroic fable into the unheroic, workaday present. In these psychological odysseys of modern life, what seems to make it civilized—as indeed in Homer—is, as in the founding legend, its sociality. Only here this is portrayed not as a coerced achievement that separates some human populations from others, but as a person's capacity to respect other persons (Homer called this honoring the gods), to form commitments, and to adapt the self as these and need may require (thus internalizing Odysseus's craft and skill at role-playing). Altogether, and in most of its extensions, an arguably more "civilized" story than the one of successive foundations.

Yet even here, in the tale of wandering and self-adaptation, the mutual respect that might serve as a model for civilization in a broader sense seems payable only among members of the same culture. From Homeric strangers (*xenoi*) to the Jew in Ireland, the characters in this story can acknowledge each other because they honor (at least some of) the same gods. The story is exclusively about us and our community of (at least nominally) shared values. Its sociality can be uncompelled and nondiscriminatory because its plot does not confront us with a radically other community. Women as temptresses are its main antagonists and agents of otherness. Its Homeric version, moreover, has a famous encounter with an otherness whose monstrosity furnished an image of savagery that Virgil incorporated into the founding story. This is Polyphemos, the cave-dwelling, man-eating giant, one of the Cyclops (one-eyed), who were sons of Poseidon. In Virgil he becomes Cacus (*kakos* is Greek for evil, foul), the cave-dwelling, fire-breathing, cattle-thieving giant, a son of Vulcan whose doorway is decorated (as Kurtz's was) with human heads (*Aeneid* 8.196–97). Hercules destroys him by terrific force (219–67). Odysseus, of course, blinds Polyphemos and escapes with his undevoured companions by ingenuity and ruse (*Odyssey* 9.307–479).

The episode of Polyphemos has occasionally been alleged as the paradigm for subsequent colonial encounters between the west and the rest of the world. So it may be—but only indirectly, and after incorporation into the Virgilian story that became our history, after localization at the site of the imperial metropolis. In the Homeric story of Odysseus, there is no historical destiny to be accomplished at the site of the giant's cave; there is no political purpose to the hero's presence there. For he is no founder; he has not come to find allies, or take over the territory and build walls. Odysseus has no colonial designs at all; he doesn't even particularly need the provisions (cheeses and animals) that his men try to persuade him to make off with from the giant's cave. He just wants to get a look at the giant—a curiosity, he ruefully admits, of fatal consequence to several of his fellows (228–30). And for himself, the consequence of thus offending Poseidon is another decade of exile from home. But if the narrative motivation of this encounter removes it from the colonial context, the characterization of the "abominable" (*schetlios*: 478) man-eater is an image of the other that will indeed constitute the savage in that context.

The encounter, in short, is not paradigmatic; but the character is. Polyphemos is the supreme example in the poem of what isn't "us"—that is, humanity. He is just what Odysseus fears to meet on the various shores he visits. In the Homeric formula (9.175–76; 5.120–21; 13.201–202), he wonders if these unknown coasts have inhabitants who are excessively violent (*hubristai*), wild and fierce (*agrioi*), or, on the contrary, are righteous (*dikaioi*), hospitable to strangers (*philoxeinoi*), and god-fearing (*theoudês*). Polyphemos exemplifies the former, tends his flocks alone, remote from his siblings, lives on meat and cheese, and seems not to belong to "bread-eating men" (*andri ge sitophagô*: 9.191). The other epithet that describes him is "lawless" (*athemistia*: 189), in the sense of disregarding all rights. All these negative epithets (which are often rendered by "savage" in English translation) go into the Virgilian summary of the indigenes as wholly without agri- or socio-culture. But since the Homeric avatar of the savage does not occupy the site of the imperial city, he does not need to be displaced—in time or space. Odysseus maims him, in self-defense, and sails away, unable to resist revealing his own name to the giant in a parting taunt (9.504–505), thus identifying himself as the target for Poseidon's wrath.

Polyphemos remains present and visible; his malevolence will determine the hero's future. Only when the giant becomes a figure in the founding story must he be erased: present only in an already mythic past, and there only to be made extinct. It is only in that story that he becomes "primitive," a former presence, an earlier phase, long superseded, now invisible.

So perhaps the story of the wanderer might do, after all, as an alternative story of what civilization might be. But, like all the documents and monuments of our civilization, it too has its barbarism. This consists in the postulation of that very category: others who (in the original meaning of the word do not speak our language) are not quite people, are not entitled to the mutual respect owing among those who honor the same gods. By his own behavior (people-eating) in the fiction Polyphemos forfeits this respect, and lives on as a troublesome individual. But the category he will come to represent is defined in advance by such behavior, and so always subject to erasure. Empires of our agricultural sort must manufacture barbarians as they create frontiers—a process brilliantly described in a novel of J. M. Coetzee (1980). Generating the categories of barbarian (as nomadic meat-eating other) and savage (as hunter, fisher, gatherer) is what "civilization" means and does. It requires others who, in order to be justly destroyed or superseded, must be seen as not wholly other, as arrested, "primitive" versions of ourselves. Hence our universal historiography of progress, which denies the universality of humanity as language-using, community-forming animals. "What is denied," writes Todorov (1984: 42) of Columbus's perceptions of the indigenes, "is the existence of a human substance truly other, something capable of being not merely an imperfect state of oneself."

And what does the denying is our story of ourselves. To tell another story, that casts us in another role than that of *civilisateur*, would allow us to enact that role. The role of curious Odysseus is one possibility. Playing ourselves as survivors, as in need of survival, might give us an interest in the survival of the world's largest minority, those human species who remain endangered by our founding role. That they not go the way of the Aztecs, the Inca, the Tasmanians, the Selk'nam, and the Ona, that their presence be acknowledged and their communities respected, would be, and would require, another story. For "there is no story that is not true."

References

Aborigines' Friend. 1847–1851, vols. 1–3; 1855–1866, vols. 1–2.

Achebe, Chinua. 1959. *Things Fall Apart*. Greenwich, Conn.

———. 1977. "An Image of Africa." *Massachusetts Review* 18: 782–94.

Agnew, Jean-Christophe. 1986. *Worlds Apart: The Market and the Theatre in Anglo-American Thought, 1550–1750*. Cambridge.

Alföldi, A. 1964. *Early Rome and the Latins*. Ann Arbor, Mich.

Amnesty International *Financial Supplement*. 1987. London.

Annius of Viterbo. 1512. *Antiquitatum variarum volumina XVII*. Paris.

Ariosto, Ludovico. n.d. *Orlando Furioso*. 2 vols. Milan.

Bailey, Cyril. 1932. *Phases in the Religion of Ancient Rome*. London.

Bartlett, Robert. 1982. *Gerald of Wales 1146–1223*.

Bascom, William. 1965. "The Forms of Folklore: Prose Narratives." *Journal of American Folklore* 78: 3–20.

Beaune, Collette. 1985. "L'Utilisation politique du mythe des origines Troyennes en France à la fin du Moyen Age." In *Lectures médiévales de Virgile*. Rome.

Belleforest, François de. 1573. *Les Chroniques et annales de France*. Paris.

Benjamin, Walter. 1973. *Illuminations*. Tr. Harry Zohn. [London.]

Bergeron, David M. 1971. *English Civic Pageantry 1558–1642*. Columbia, S.C.

Blair, John G. 1985. "Cowboys, Europe and Smoke: Marlboro in the Saddle." *Revue française d'études americaines* 10:195–212.

Blegen, Carl W. 1963. *Troy and the Trojans*. London.

Boiardo, Matteo Maria. 1951. *Orlando Innamorato*. 2 vols. Ed. Aldo Scaglione. Turin.

Boitani, Pietro. 1994. *The Shadow of Ulysses: Figures of a Myth*. Tr. Anita Weston. Oxford.

Bömer, Franz. 1951. *Rom und Troia*. Baden-Baden.

Bonwick, James. 1870. *The Last of the Tasmanians*. London.

Brady, Robert. 1685. *A Complete History of England from the Romans . . . .* Vol. 1. London.

Braudel, Fernand. 1985. *The Perspective of the World* (vol. 3 of *Civilization and Capitalism, 15th–18th Century*). Tr. Siân Reynolds. London.

Bridges, Barry. 1971. "George Augustus Robinson." *Tasmanian Historical Research Association: Papers and Proceedings* 18:100.

Brotherston, Gordon. 1986. "Towards a Grammatology of America: Lévi-Strauss, Derrida, and the Native New World Text." In *Literature, Politics and Theory*, ed. Francis Barker et al. London. Pp.180–209.

Brown, Paula, and Donald Tuzin, eds. 1983. *The Ethnography of Cannibalism*. Washington, D.C.

Bucher, Bernadette. 1981. *Icon and Conquest: A Structural Analysis of the Illustrations of De Bry's Great Voyages*. Tr. Basia Miller Gulati. Chicago.

Buck, August. 1963. "Zur Geschichte des italienischen Selbstverständis im Mittelalter." In *Medium Aevum Romanicum*, ed. Heinrich Bihler and Alfred Noyer-Weidner. Munich.

Burger, Julian. 1990. *The Gaia Atlas of First Peoples: A Future for the Indigenous World*. London.

Buxton, Thomas Fowell. 1839. *The African Slave Trade*. London.

Camoens, Luis de. 1880. *The Lusiads*. Tr. Richard Francis Burton. 2 vols. London.

Canny, Nicholas F. 1973. "The Ideology of English Colonization: From Ireland to America." *William and Mary Quarterly* 30: 575–98.

Canny, Nicholas, and Ciaran Brady. 1988. "Spenser's Irish Crisis." *Past and Present* 120: 201–15.

Carile, Antonio. 1976. "Le Origini di Venezia nella tradizione storiografica." In *Storia della cultura veneta*, vol. 1. Vicenza.

Carte, Thomas. 1747. *A General History of England*. Vol. 1. London.

Castagnoli, F., et al., 1975. *Lavinium II: Le tredici are*. Rome.

Cavell, Stanley. 1981. *Pursuits of Happiness: The Hollywood Comedy of Remarriage*. Cambridge, Mass.

Cawelti, John. n.d. *The Six-Gun Mystique*. Bowling Green, Ohio.

Cecil, Paul Frederick. 1986. *Herbicidal Warfare: The RANCH HAND Project in Vietnam*. New York.

Chamerovzow, Louis Alexis. 1848. *The New Zealand Question and the Rights of Aborgines*. London.

Charlevoix, François-Xavier de. 1744. *Histoire et Description Générale de la Nouvelle France*. 3 vols. Paris.

Charron, Jacques de. 1629. *Histoire généalogique des roys de France depuis la création jusques à présent*. Paris.

Cheyfitz, Eric. 1991. *The Poetics of Imperialism: Translation and Colonization from The Tempest to Tarzan*. New York.

Clements, John. 1989. *California Facts*. Dallas.

Clifford, Clark, with Richard Holbrooke. 1991. *Counsel to the President*. New York.

Coetzee, J. M. 1980. *Waiting for the Barbarians*. London.

Cohen, Mark N. 1977. "Population Pressure and the Origins of Agriculture: An Archeological Example from the Coast of Peru." In *Origins of Agriculture*, ed. Charles A. Reed. The Hague.

Cohen, William B. 1980. *The French Encounter with Africans: White Responses to Blacks, 1530–1880*. Bloomington, Ind.

Colchester, Marcus. 1984. "Piaronoia: Venezuelan Indigenism in Crisis," *Survival International Annual Review*, no. 44: 94–104.

Colden, Cadwallader. 1747. *The History of the Five Indian Nations*. London.

Coleman, Christopher B., tr. 1922. *The Treatise of Lorenzo Valla on the Donation of Constantine*. New Haven, Conn.

Colonial Magazine. 1844–1852. Vols. 1–23.

Conington, John, and Henry Nettleship. 1883. *The Works of Virgil*, vol. 3. London.

Conrad, Joseph. 1912. *A Personal Record*. London.

———. 1926. *Last Essays*. Ed. Richard Curle. London.

———. 1931. *Lord Jim*. New York.

———. 1947. *Almayer's Folly and Tales of Unrest*. London.

———. 1971. *Heart of Darkness: A Critical Edition*. 2d ed. Ed. Robert Kimbrough. New York.

———. 1973. *Heart of Darkness*. Harmondsworth.

———. 1988. *Heart of Darkness: A Critical Edition*. 3d ed. Ed. Robert Kimbrough. New York.

Cook, Chris, and Brendan Keith. 1975. *British Historical Facts 1830–1900*. London.

Cornell, T. J. 1975. "Aeneas and the Twins: The Development of the Roman Foundation Legend." *Proceedings of the Cambridge Philological Society*, n.s. 21:1–32.

————. 1977. "Aeneas' Arrival in Italy." *Liverpool Classical Monthly* 2:77–83.

Curtin, Philip D. 1964. *The Image of Africa: British Ideas and Action, 1780–1850*. Madison, Wisc.

Daisne, Johan. 1971. *Filmographic Dictionary of World Literature*. Ghent.

Danielsson, O. A. 1932. "Annius von Viterbo über die Grundungsgeschichte Roms." *Skrifter utgivna av Svenska Institutet i Rom* 2:1–16.

Davis, R. H. C. 1978. "The Carmen de Hastingae Proelio." *English Historical Review* 93: 241–61.

Dekker, Thomas. 1612. *Troia-Nova Triumphans*. In *The Dramatic Works*, vol. 3, ed. Fredson Bowers. Cambridge, 1958.

Deonna, Waldemar. 1929. "La fiction dans l'histoire ancienne de Genève et du pays de Vaud."*Mémoires et documents publiés par la société d'histoire et d'archéologie de Genève* 35: 1–177.

Donne, John. 1622. "A Sermon Preached to the Honourable Company of the Virginian Plantation." In *The Sermons of J. D.*, vol. 4, ed. G. R. Potter and E. M. Simpson. Berkeley, 1959.

Dougherty, Carol. 1993. *The Poetics of Colonization: From City to Text in Archaic Greece*. New York.

Drinnon, Richard. 1980. *Facing West: The Metaphysics of Indian-Hating and Empire-Building*. Minneapolis.

Dubois, Claude-Gilbert. 1972. *Celtes et Gaulois au XVIe siècle: le développement littéraire d'un mythe nationaliste*. Paris.

Duby, Georges. 1973. *Hommes et structures du moyen âge*. Paris.

Dumville, David N. 1975. "'Nennius' and the *Historia Brittonum*." *Studia Celtica* 10: 78–93.

Dury-Moyaers, Geneviève. 1981. *Enée et Lavinium: A propos du découvertes archéologiques récentes*. Brussels.

Eckhardt, Alexandre. 1943. *De Sicambria à Sans-Souci: histoires et légendes franco-hongroises*. Paris.

Eden, P. T. 1975. *A Commentary on Virgil: Aeneid VIII*. Leiden.

Fabian, Johannes. 1983. *Time and the Other: How Anthopology Makes Its Objects*. New York.

Faral, Edmond. 1929. *La Legende arthurienne*. 3 vols. Paris.

Farnham, Thomas J. 1843. *Travels in the Great Western Prairies*. In *Early Western Travels*. ed. R. G. Thwaites. Vol. 28. Cleveland, 1906.

Ferguson, Adam. 1767. *An Essay In the History of Civil Society*. Edinburgh.

Ferguson, Arthur B. 1979. *Clio Unbound: Perception of the Social and Cultural Past in Renaissance England*. Durham, N.C.

Ferguson, R. Brian. 1992. "Tribal Warfare." *Scientific American*. January.

Fielding, Henry. 1980. *Joseph Andrews and Shamela*. Oxford.

FitzGerald, Frances. 1973. *Fire in the Lake*. New York.

Fordyce, C. J. 1977. *Aeneidos libri VII–VIII*. Ed. John D. Christie. Glasgow.

Foreville, Raymonde, ed. and tr. 1952. Guillaume de Poitiers, *Histoire de Guillaume le Conquérant*. Paris.

Forster, E. M. 1979. *A Passage to India*. Ed. Oliver Stallybrass. Harmondsworth.

Foucault, Michel. 1970. *The Order of Things*. New York.

————. 1972. *The Archeology of Knowledge*. Tr. A. M. Sheridan-Smith. New York.

French, Philip. 1974. *Westerns: Aspects of a Movie Genre*. New York.

Froude, James Anthony. 1898. *The English in the West Indies*. London.

Furbank, P. N. 1977. *E. M. Forster: A Life*. Vol. 1. London.

Galinsky, G. Karl. 1969. *Aeneas, Sicily, and Rome*. Princeton, N. J.

Gallagher, Tag. 1986. *John Ford: The Man and His Films*. Berkeley.

Geertz, Clifford. 1973. *The Interpretation of Cultures*. New York.

———. 1983. *Local Knowledge*. New York.

Gentili, Alberico. 1933. *De jure belli*. Tr. John C. Rolfe. Oxford.

Geoffrey of Monmouth. 1966. *The History of the Kings of Britain*. Tr. Lewis Thorpe. Harmondsworth.

Gibson, James William. 1986. *The Perfect War: Technowar in Vietnam*. Boston.

Gilman, Sander L. 1985. "Black Bodies, White Bodies: Toward an Iconography of Female Sexuality in Late Nineteenth-Century Art, Medicine, and Literature." *Critical Inquiry* 12: 204–42.

Gimpel, Jean. 1975. *La Révolution industrielle du Moyen Age*. Paris: Seuil.

Goez, Werner. 1958. *Translatio Imperii: Ein Beitrag zur Geschichte des Geschichtsdenkens und der politischen Theorien im Mittelalter und in der früher Neuzeit*. Tübingen.

Gould, Stephen Jay. 1978. Review of Lewis Thomas, *The Medusa and the Snail*. In *Dialogue* 12.

Graf, Arturo. 1882. *Roma nella memoria e nelle immaginazioni del medio evo*. 2 vols. Turin.

Grafton, Anthony. 1990. *Forgers and Critics*. Princeton, N. J.

Graham, Victor E., and W. McAllister Johnson. 1974. *The Paris Entries of Charles IX and Elisabeth of Austria 1571*. Toronto.

Gransden, Antonia. 1974. *Historical Writing in England 550–1307*. London.

Gransden, K. W. 1976. *Aeneid Book VIII*. Cambridge.

Graus, Frantiack. 1975. *Lebendige Vergangenheit: Uberlieferung im Mittelallter und in den Vorstellungen vom Mittelalter*. Cologne.

Greenblatt, Stephen. 1991. *Marvelous Possessions: The Wonder of the New World*. Oxford.

Greene, Thomas M. 1982. *The Light in Troy: Imitation and Discovery in Renaissance Poetry*. New Haven.

Grimal, Pierre. 1985. "Conclusions." In *Lectures médiévales de Virgile*. Rome.

Grotius, Hugo. 1655. *The Law of War and Peace*. Tr. C[lement] B[arksdale]. London.

———. 1682. *The Rights of War and Peace*. Tr. William Evats. London.

———. 1853. *De jure belli et pacis*. Tr. William Whewell. 3 vols. Cambridge.

Guenée, Bernard. 1980. *Histoire et culture historique dans l'occident médiéval*. Paris.

Gundersheimer, Werner L. 1973. *Ferrara: The Style of a Renaissance Despotism*. Princeton, N.J.

Gurr, Andrew. 1980. *The Shakespearean Stage 1574–1642*. 2d ed. Cambridge.

Habermas, Jürgen. 1971. *Knowledge and Human Interests*. Boston.

Haggenmacher, Peter. 1988. "La Place de Francisco de Vitoria parmi les fondateurs du droit international." In *Actualité de la pensée juridique de Francisco de Vitoria*. Brussels.

Hakluyt, Richard. 1589. *The Principall Navigations, Voyages and Discoveries of the English Nation*. 2 vols. London (facsimile repr. Cambridge, 1965).

Hale, J. R. 1977. *Renaissance Europe: Individual and Society, 1480–1520*. Berkeley.

Hallett, Robin. 1974. *Africa Since 1875*. Ann Arbor, Mich.

Halphen, Louis, ed. and tr. 1967. Eginhard, *Vie de Charlemagne*, 4th ed. Paris.

Hanbury-Tenison, Robin. 1984. *Worlds Apart: An Explorer's Life*. London.

Hanell, Krister. 1956. "Zur Problematik der älteren Römischen Geschichtschreibung." In *Histoire et historiens dans l'antiquité* (Fondation Hardt, Tome 4). Geneva.

Harris, David R. 1977. "Alternative Pathways Toward Agriculture." In *Origins of Agriculture*, ed. Charles A. Reed. The Hague.

Harrison, G. B. 1933. *Shakespeare at Work*. London.

Hay, Denys. 1967. *Europe: The Emergence of an Idea.* Rev. ed. Edinburgh.

Hayter, Teresa, and Catherine Watson. 1985. *Aid: Rhetoric and Reality.* London.

Hegel, G. W. F. 1970. *Vorlesungen über die Ästhetik.* In *Werke,* ed. Moldenhauer and Michel, vol. 13. Frankfurt.

Hemming, John. 1978. *Red Gold: The Conquest of the Brazilian Indians.* London.

Higounet, Charles. 1966. "Les Forêts de l'Europe occidentale du Ve au XIe siècles." In *Agricoltura e mondo rurale in occidente nell'alto medioevo.* Spoleto.

Hiller, Susan, ed. 1991. *The Myth of Primitivism: Perspectives on Art.* London.

Hobbes, Thomas. 1651. *Leviathan.* Ed. C.B. Macpherson. Harmondsworth, 1968.

Hobson, J. A. 1905. *Imperialism.* 2d ed. London.

Holtz, Louis. 1985. "La Redécouverte de Virgile aux VIIIe et IXe siècles." In *Lectures médiévales de Virgile.* Rome.

Homer. 1878. *Odyssey.* 2 vols. Ed. W. W. Merry. Oxford.

Hooker, Richard. 1593. *Of the Laws of Ecclesiastical Polity.* In *Prose of the English Renaissance,* ed. J. William Hebel, Hoyt H. Hudson et al. New York, 1952.

Hughes, Merritt Y., ed. 1957. *John Milton: Complete Poems and Major Prose.* New York.

Hulme, Peter. 1986. *Colonial Encounters: Europe and the Native Caribbean, 1492–1797.* London.

Hume, David. 1807. *The History of England from the Invasion of Julius Caesar. . . .* Vol 1. London.

Huntington, Samuel P. 1968. "The Bases of Accommodation." *Foreign Affairs* 46: 642–56.

Huppert, George. 1970. *The Idea of Perfect History: Historical Erudition and Historical Philosophy in Renaissance France.* Urbana, Ill.

Hutton, Ronald. 1987. *The Restoration.* Oxford.

Joly, A. 1870. *Benoît de Sainte-More et le roman de Troie.* Paris.

Judson, Alexander C. 1945. *The Life of Edmund Spenser.* Baltimore.

Jung, Marc-René. 1966. *Hercule dans la littérature française du XVIe siècle.* Geneva.

Keller, Werner. 1975. *The Etruscans.* Tr. Alexander and Elizabeth Henderson. London.

Kelley, Donald R. 1970. *The Foundations of Historical Scholarship.* New York.

Kelly, Amy. 1952. *Eleanor of Aquitaine and the Four Kings.* London.

Kendrick, T. D. 1950. *British Antiquity.* London.

Kermode, Frank. 1975. *The Classic.* London.

Kingsbury, Susan M., ed. 1906. *The Records of the Virginia Company of London.* Vols. 1–2. Washington, D. C.

Klaits, Joseph. 1976. *Printed Propaganda under Louis XIV.* Princeton, N.J.

Kohn, George C. 1987. *Dictionary of Wars.* Garden City, N.Y.

Krusch, Bruno, ed. 1888. *Fredegarii et aliorum chronica* (Monumenta Germanicae Historica, Scriptores rerum merovingicarum II). Hannover.

Kupperman, Karen Ordahl. 1980. *Settling with the Indians.* Totowa, N.J.

Lafitau, Joseph-François. 1724. *Moeurs des sauvages ameriquains, comparées aux moeurs des premiers temps.* 2 vols. Paris.

Land Clearing and Development in the Tropics. 1986. Ed. R. Lal, P. A. Sanchez, R. W. Cummings, Jr. Rotterdam.

Laslett, Peter, ed. 1970. John Locke, *Two Treatises of Government.* Cambridge.

Layamon. 1847. *Brut or Chronicle of Britain.* Ed. J. Madden. 3 vols. London.

Leckie, R. William, Jr. 1981. *The Passage of Dominion: Geoffrey of Monmouth and the Periodization of Insular History in the Twelfth Century.* Toronto.

Le Goff, Jacques. 1966. "Les Paysans et le monde rural dans la littérature du haut moyenâge (Ve-VIe siècles)." In *Agricoltura e mondo rurale in occidente nell'alto medioevo.* Spoleto.

―――. 1988. *The Medieval Imagination.* Tr. Arthur Goldhammer. Chicago.

Le Guin, Ursula K. 1972. *The Word for World is Forest.* New York.

Lemaire de Belges, Jean. 1882. *Les Illustrations de Gaule et singularitez de Troye.* Ed. J. Stecher. Vols. 1 and 2. Louvain.

[Leo Africanus] Jean-Léon l'Africain. 1956. *Déscription de l'Afrique.* Tr. A. Epaulard. 2 vols. Paris.

Lewis, C. S. 1954. *English Literature in the Sixteenth Century.* New York.

Lewis, Norman. 1989. "A Harvest of Souls." *The Independent Magazine.* 1 April, 20–28.

Life Magazine. 1963. 25 February.

LIMC (*Lexicon Iconographicum Mythologiae Classicae*). 1981–94. 7 vols. Zürich.

Livy. 1961. *Ab Urbe Condita* (Loeb Classical Library). Vol. 1. London.

Lloyd, David. 1987. *Nationalism and Minor Literature.* Berkeley.

Lloyd, T. O. 1984. *The British Empire 1558–1983.* Oxford.

Lot, Ferdinand, ed. 1934. *Nennius et l'Historia Brittonum.* Paris.

Lovejoy, Arthur O., and George Boas. 1935. *Primitivism and Related Ideas in Antiquity.* Baltimore.

Lynche, Richard. 1601. *An Historical Treatise of the Travels of Noah into Europe.* London

Mack, Maynard. 1985. *Alexander Pope: A Life.* New Haven and London.

Maine, Henry Sumner. 1870. *Ancient Law: Its Connection with the Early History of Society, and its Relation to Modern Ideas.* 4th ed. [1st ed. 1861] London.

―――. 1875. *Lectures on the Early History of Institutions.* London.

Mandrou, Robert. 1973. *Louis XIV en son temps.* Paris.

Marchello-Nizia, Christiane. 1985. "De l'*Enéide* à l'*Eneas*: Les attributs du fondateur." In *Lectures médiévales de Virgile.* Rome.

Marcus, George E., and Michael M. J. Fischer. 1986. *Anthropology as Cultural Critique.* Chicago.

Marx, Karl. 1934. *The Eighteenth Brumaire of Louis Bonaparte.* Tr. from 2d ed., 1869. Moscow.

Mason, J. Alden. 1957. *The Ancient Civilizations of Peru.* Harmondsworth.

Mattingly, H. B. 1976. "Q. Fabius Pictor, Father of Roman History." *Liverpool Classical Monthly* 1:3–7.

McCoubrey, John W. 1963. *American Tradition in Painting.* New York.

McNeill, William H. 1963. *The Rise of the West.* Chicago.

―――. 1974. *The Shape of European History.* New York.

―――. 1976. *Plagues and Peoples.* Garden City, N.Y.

McQueen, James. 1840. *A Geographical Survey of Africa.* London.

Mézeray, François de. 1688. *Histoire de France avant Clovis.* Amsterdam.

Millar, John. 1771. *Observations Concerning the Distinction of Ranks in Society.* London.

Milligan, Joseph. 1859. "On the Dialects . . . of the Aboriginal Tribes of Tasmania." *Papers and Proceedings of the Royal Society of Tasmania* 3:275–78.

Milton, John. 1671. *The History of Britain.* In *Complete Prose Works*, vol. 5.1, ed. French Fogle. New Haven, 1971.

Monod, Gabriel. 1885. *Etudes critiques sur les sources de l'histoire Mérovingienne: La Compilation dite de "Frédégaire."* Paris.

Morgan, William. 1963. *The Journal of W. M.* Ed. Nona Morris. Auckland.

Moufrin, Jacques. 1985. "Les *Translations* vernaculaires de Virgile au Moyen Age." In *Lectures médiévales de Virgile.* Rome.

Munday, Anthony. 1605. *The Triumphes of Re-United Britannia*. In *Pageants and Entertainments of A.M.*, ed. David M. Bergeron. New York, 1985.

———. 1611. *A Briefe Chronicle, of the Successe of Times, from the Creation of the World, to this instant*. London.

Murray, Alexander. 1978. *Reason and Society in the Middle Ages*. Oxford.

Nagy, Gregory 1979. *The Best of the Achaeans: Concepts of the Hero in Archaic Greek Poetry*. Baltimore.

Nagy, Laszlo. 1984. *250 Millions de Scouts*. Lausanne.

Nicholson, Ranald. 1974. *Scotland: The Later Middle Ages*. Edinburgh.

Nussbaum, Arthur. 1962. *A Concise History of the Law of Nations*. Rev. ed. New York.

Partner, Nancy. 1977. *Serious Entertainments: The Writing of History in Twelfth-Century England*. Chicago.

Pearce, Roy Harvey. 1953. *The Savages of America: A Study of the Indian and the Idea of Civilization*. Baltimore.

Pentagon Papers: The Defense Department History of United States Decisionmaking on Vietnam. 1972. Senator Gravel Edition. 5 vols. Boston.

Pezron, Paul. 1706. *The Antiquities of Nations*. Tr. D. Jones. London.

Phelps, Lancelot Ridley. Correspondence, Oriel College Library, Oxford. Divided into bundles by region of origin by P. C. Lyon. 1939.

Place, J. A. 1974. *The Western Films of John Ford*. Seacaucus, N.J.

PNUD (Programme des Nations Unies pour le Devéloppement). 1990. *Rapport mondial sur le développement humain*. Paris.

———. 1991. *Rapport mondial sur le développement humain*. Paris.

———. 1995. *Rapport mondial sur le développement humain*. Paris.

Pool, D. Ian. 1977. *The Maori Population of New Zealand 1769–1971*. Auckland.

Pope, Alexander. 1961. *Pastoral Poetry and An Essay on Criticism*. Twickenham Edition, Vol. I. Ed. Audra and Williams. London and New Haven.

———. 1962. *The Poems*. Ed. John Butt. New Haven.

Postlethwayt, Malachy. 1758. *The Importance of the African Expedition*. London.

Pufendorf, [Samuel]. 1703. *Of the Law of Nature and Nations*. Oxford.

———. 1934. *De Jure Naturae et Gentium Libri Octo*. Vol. 2. Tr. C. H. and W. A. Oldfather. Oxford.

Quint, David. 1993. *Epic and Empire: Politics and Generic Form from Virgil to Milton*. Princeton, N.J.

Rabb, Theodore K. 1967. *Enterprise and Empire: Merchant and Gentry Investment in the Expansion of England, 1575–1630*. Cambridge, Mass.

Radisson, P. E. 1885. *Voyages*. Ed. G. D. Scull. Boston.

Rawley, James A. 1981. *The Transatlantic Slave Trade: A History*. New York.

Renfrew, Colin. 1973. *Before Civilization: The Radiocarbon Revolution and Prehistoric Europe*. London.

Report of the Committee of the African Institution. 1807. Vol. 1. London.

Richardson, Samuel. 1962. *Clarissa*. Ed. George Sherburn. Boston.

———. 1980. *Pamela; or, Virtue Rewarded*. Ed. Peter Sabor. Harmondsworth.

Robertson, William. 1787. *The History of America*. 3 vols. Vienna.

Robinson, George Augustus. 1966. *Friendly Mission: The Tasmanian Journals and Papers of G. A. R*. Ed. N. J. B. Plomley. Kingston, N.S.W.

Ronsard, Pierre de. 1950. *La Franciade. Oeuvres complètes*, vol. 16. Ed. Paul Laumonier. Paris.

Rosenthal, Michael. 1986. *The Character Factory: Baden-Powell and the Origins of the Boy Scout Movement*. London.

Rossi, Paolo. 1984. *The Dark Abyss of Time: The History of the Earth and the History of Nations from Hooke to Vico*. Chicago.

Ruffhead, Owen. 1769. *The Life of Alexander Pope, Esq*. London.

Ryan, Lyndall. 1972. "The Extinction of the Tasmanian Aborigines: Myth and Reality." *Tasmanian Historical Research Association: Papers and Proceedings* 19:61–77.

Sahlins, Marshall. 1985. *Islands of History*. Chicago.

Schauenburg, Konrad. 1960. "Aeneas und Rom." *Gymnasium* 67: 176–91.

Schelling, Felix E. 1908. *Elizabethan Drama 1558–1642*. 2 vols. Boston.

Schilling, Robert. 1954. *La Religion romaine de Vénus*. Paris.

Schleiner, Louise. 1990. "Spenser's 'E.K.' as Edmund Kent (Kenned / of Kent): Kyth (Couth), Kissed, and Kunning-Conning." *English Literary Renaissance* 20: 374–407.

Scullard, H. H. 1967. *The Etruscan Cities and Rome*. London.

Serres, Michel. 1983. *Rome: Le livre des fondations*. Paris.

Sheridan, Richard B. 1974. *Sugar and Slavery: An Economic History of the British West Indies 1623–1775*. Aylesbury.

Simon, Reneé. 1961. "Nicolas Fréret, académicien." *Studies on Voltaire and the Eighteenth Century* 17. Geneva.

Sinclair, Andrew. 1979. *John Ford*. New York.

Sinclair, Keith. 1980. *The Pelican History of New Zealand*. Harmondsworth.

Slotkin, Richard. 1973. *Regeneration Through Violence: The Mythology of the American Frontier, 1600–1860*. Middletown, Conn.

———. 1985. *The Fatal Environment: The Myth of the Frontier in the Age of Industrialization 1800–1890*. New York.

Smith, Adam. 1976. *An Inquiry into the Nature and Causes of the Wealth of Nations*. Ed. Campbell, Skinner, and Todd. Oxford.

Sommella, Paolo. 1974. "Das Heroon des Aeneas und die Topographie des antiken Lavinium." *Gymnasium* 81: 273–97.

Spenser, Edmund. 1934. *A View of the Present State of Ireland*. Ed. W. L. Renwick. London.

———. 1912. *The Poetical Works*. Ed. J. C. Smith and E. de Selincourt. London.

Stones, E. L. G. ed. and tr. 1965. *Anglo-Scottish Relations 1174–1328*. London.

Stowell, Peter. 1986. *John Ford*. Boston.

Summers, Harry G., Jr. 1985. *Vietnam War Almanac*. New York.

Survival International *Review*. 1991. London.

Symonds, Richard. 1986. *Oxford and Empire: The Last Lost Cause?* London.

Tanner, Marie. 1993. *The Last Descendant of Aeneas: The Hapsburgs and the Mythic Image of the Emperor*. New Haven.

Tatlock, J. S. P. 1950. *The Legendary History of Britain*. Berkeley.

Technology Assessment of the Vietnam Defoliant Matter. 1969. Report to the Subcommittee on Science, Research, and Development of the Committee on Science and Astronautics, House of Representatives. Washington.

Thayer, Thomas C. 1985. *War Without Fronts: The American Experience in Vietnam*. Boulder, Colo.

Tigerstedt, E. N. 1964. "Ioannes Annius and *Graecia Mendax*." In *Classical, Medieval and Renaissance Studies in honor of B. L. Ullman*, ed. Charles Henderson, Jr., vol. 2: 293–310. Rome.

Tilliette, Jean-Yves. 1985. "L'Influence de l'*Enéide* sur l'épopée latine du XIIe siècle." In *Lectures médiévales de Virgile*. Rome.

Todorov, Tzvetan. 1984. *The Conquest of America*. Tr. Richard Howard. New York.

Torgovnick, Marianna. 1990. *Gone Primitive: Savage Intellects, Modern Lives*. Chicago.

"Transactions of the Sections." 1859. In *Report of the Twenty-Eighth Meeting of the British Association for the Advancement of Science*. London.

"Transactions of the Sections." 1861. In *Report of the Thirtieth Meeting of the British Association for the Advancement of Science*. London.

Trithemius, Joannes. 1601. *Compendium sive breviarium . . . chronicorum . . . de origine gentis et Regum Francorum*. In *Opera Historica*. Frankfurt.

Tyrrell, James. 1698. *The General History of England*. Vol. 1. London.

Vargas Llosa, Mario. 1990. *The Storyteller*. Tr. Helen Lane. London.

Vattel, Emer de. 1760. *The Law of Nations; or, principles of the Law of Nature applied to the conduct and affairs of nations and sovereigns*. 2 vols. London.

Vermaseren, M. J. 1977–87. *Corpus Cultus Cybelae Attidisque*. 7 vols. Leiden.

Vico, Giambattista. 1970. *The New Science*. Tr. Bergin and Fisch. Ithaca, N.Y.

Victoria, Francisco de. 1917. *De indis et de jure belli relectiones*. Tr. John Pawley Bate. Washington, D.C.

Virgil. 1906. *The Aeneid*. Tr. E. Fairfax Taylor. Intro. and notes by E. M. Forster. 2 vols. London.

———. 1955. *Aeneid*. 2 vols. (Loeb Classical Library). Cambridge, Mass.

Von Daniken, Erich. 1969. *Chariots of the Gods?* Tr. Michael Heron. London.

Vorilhon, Claude. 1978. *Space Aliens Took Me to Their Planet*. Vaduz.

Wallace-Hadrill, J. M., tr. 1960. *The Fourth Book of the Chronicle of Fredegar*. London.

Wallerstein, Immanuel. 1974. *The Modern World System I: Capitalist Agriculture and the Origins of the European World-Economy in the Sixteenth Century*. New York.

———. 1980. *The Modern World-System II: Mercantilism and the Consolidation of the European World-Economy, 1600–1750*. New York.

———. 1989. *The Modern World-System III: The Second Era of Great Expansion of the Capitalist World-Economy, 1730–1840*. San Diego.

Warren, W. L. 1973. *Henry II*. London.

Waswo, Richard. 1987. *Language and Meaning in the Renaissance*. Princeton, N. J.

Weisberg, Barry, ed. 1970. *Ecocide in Indochina*. San Francisco.

Wells, H. G. 1976. *The World Set Free*. London.

Westing, Arthur H., ed. 1984. *Herbicides in War: The Long-Term Ecological and Human Consequences*. London.

White, K. D. 1970. *Roman Farming*. London.

Whiteside, Thomas. 1970. *Defoliation*. New York.

Whorf, Benjamin Lee. 1956. *Language, Thought, and Reality*. Ed. John B. Carroll. Cambridge, Mass.

Wilkinson, Alec. 1989. *Big Sugar: Seasons in the Cane Fields of Florida*. New York.

Williams, Gordon. 1983. *Technique and Ideas in the* Aeneid. New Haven.

Williams, Raymond. 1976. *Keywords*. [London].

———. 1977. *Marxism and Literature*. Oxford.

Wilson, Henry S. 1977. *The Imperial Experience in Sub-Saharan Africa since 1870*. Minneapolis.

Wolf, Eric R. 1982. *Europe and the People Without History*. Berkeley.

Wood, Robin. 1980. "John Ford." In *Cinema: A Critical Dictionary*, ed. Richard Roud. London.

World Wildlife Fund *Annual Report*. 1991. Gland, Switzerland.

World Wildlife Fund *Yearbook 87/88*. 1989. Sion, Switzerland.

Woudhuizen, Fred. 1992. *The Language of the Sea Peoples*. Amsterdam.

Wright, Neil, ed. 1984. *The Historia Regum Britannie of Geoffrey of Monmouth*. vol. 1. Cambridge.

Wroth, Warwick. 1894. *Catalogue of the Greek Coins of Troas*. London.

Yates, Frances. 1975. *Astrea: The Imperial Theme in the Sixteenth Century*. London.

Young, Jean I., tr. 1964. *The Prose Edda of Snorri Sturluson*. Berkeley.

Zimmermann, Ernest, ed. 1822. Eusebius, *Constantini Oratio ad Sanctos*. Frankfurt.

Index

UNIVERSITY PRESS OF NEW ENGLAND publishes books under its own imprint and is the publisher for Brandeis University Press, Dartmouth College, Middlebury College Press, University of New Hampshire, Tufts University, Wesleyan University Press, and Salzburg Seminar.

ABOUT THE AUTHOR

Richard Waswo is Professor of English at the University of Geneva and the author of *The Fatal Mirror: Themes and Techniques in the Poetry of Fulke Greville* (1972) and *Language and Meaning in the Renaissance* (1987).

LIBRARY OF CONGRESS CATALOGING-IN-PUBLICATION DATA

Waswo, Richard.
    The founding legend of western civilization : from Virgil to
Vietnam / Richard Waswo.
        p.   cm.
    Includes bibliographical references (p.) and index.
    ISBN 0–8195–5296–8 (cloth : alk. paper). — ISBN 0–8195–6304–8
(pbk. : alk. paper)
        1. Civilization, Western—History.   2. Legends—History and
criticism.   3. European literature—History and criticism.
4. English literature—History and criticism.   5. Historiography—
Europe—History.   6. Social sciences—Europe—Philosophy.
7. Europe—Territorial expansion.   8. Landscape in literature.
9. Landscape in motion pictures.   I. Title.
CB245.W28   1997
909'.09812—dc20   96—32079

DATE DUE

			Printed in USA

HIGHSMITH #45230